D0914403

HANOVER COUNTY CHANCERY WILLS AND NOTES

HANOVER COUNTY CHANCERY WILLS AND NOTES

A Compendium of Genealogical, Biographical and Historical Material
as Contained in Cases of the Chancery Suits
of Hanover County, Virginia

Compiled by

WILLIAM RONALD COCKE, III

This volume was reproduced from
an 1940 edition located in the
publishers private library
Greenville, South Carolina

Please Direct all Correspondence & Orders to:

Southern Historical Press, Inc.
P.O. Box 1267
375 West Broad Street
Greenville, S.C. 29602-1267

Originally published: Ann Arbor, 1940
Reprinted by,
Southern Historical Press, Inc.
Greenville, S.C., 1998
ISBN # 0-89308-287-2
Printed in the United States of America

TO MY BELOVED
WIFE

GRACE   THOMAS   COCKE

WHO NEVER
DOUBTED

INTRODUCTION

THE most ancient of all the American commonwealths is Virginia. Her history stretches from 1607 to the present day. Through all these years she has remained a land of invincible loyalties. From George Washington, Thomas Jefferson, Patrick Henry and Henry Clay down to Woodrow Wilson her sons have adorned and enriched the life of this nation. Twice in her story devastating wars have swept across her territory; and of both tragedies the heroes were her sons - George Washington and Robert Edward Lee. She has tasted life in its fullness, prosperity and disaster, strength and weakness, political oppression and unflinching resistance, and today emerges wealthy, powerful and free.

It was here in Hanover Courthouse the eloquent Samuel Davies, founder of the Presbyterian Church in Virginia, and subsequently President of Princeton College, on May 8, 1758, recruited Captain Samuel Meredith's Company and sent them forward to the old French War. Within the walls of this historic building, Patrick Henry, on December 1, 1763, made his great speech for the people in the "Parsons' Case" taking the bold ground that when the King had violated his duty the compact between the people and the King could be dissolved. The torch of the American Revolution was lighted on that memorable day.

Near this spot, on April 12, 1777, was born Henry Clay, "the Mill Boy of the Slashes," three times the candidate of his party for the Presidency of the United States, "The Great Pacificator" who "had rather be right than President."

In the old Tavern across the road from the Courthouse, Lord Cornwallis had his headquarters in May 1781, and from this spot dispatched Lt.-Colonel Tarleton to Charlottesville in the attempted capture of Thomas Jefferson and the Virginia Legislature.

Here on May 27, 1862, was fought the Battle of Hanover Courthouse between General Porter's Corps of McClellan's Army and Confederate Forces under General Branch. Here on the Court-green the Confederate Cavalry General J. E. B. Stuart had his headquarters during the month of July, 1862, after his famous ride around Richmond. Here he received his commission as Major-General and here he organized the Cavalry Corps of General Lee's Army.

Upon the velvet carpet of the Court-green arises the Confederate Monument inscribed: "Hanover - To her Confederate Soldiers and to her noble Women who loved them - 1861-1865," with the names of 1464 of her heroic men of the great War between the States.

On the walls of the court room hang portraits and memorial tablets of many of her citizens distinguished in war and in peace, among them, Judge R. H. Cardwell, Henry Rose Carter, Hill Carter, Henry Clay, Rev. Samuel Davies, George P. Haw, Patrick Henry, Admiral Hilary Pollard Jones, Judge John E. Mason, Colonel Wm. B. Newton, Thomas Nelson Page, Judge Samuel C. Redd, Thomas W. Sydnor, John R. Taylor, Captain David Algernon Timberlake, John H. Timberlake, Henry Taylor Wickham, General Wm. C. Wickham, Philip Bickerton Winston, and William Overton Winston.

HANOVER COUNTY was named for the Duke of Hanover, afterwards George I of England, or from the Prussian province and city belonging to him. It was created from New Kent in 1721, which in turn had been taken out of York in 1654. Between 1642/3 and 1634, this section was called Charles River, one of the original shires or counties formed in the latter year. In 1742 Hanover lost that portion now embraced in Louisa.

Saint Paul's Parish embraced the entire county from its formation until 1726 when Saint Martin's Parish was established from its western portion, and included:

"That part of the Parish of St. Paul . . . which lieth in the neck between the North & South branches of the Pamunkey River and also that part of the parish that lieth above Stonehorse creek . . ."

This line commenced at the junction of the Pamunkey and what is now the South Anna River, and continued up the latter to what is now called Stone Creek, thence to its southernmost source to the tri-county lines of Hanover, Henrico and Goochland. This line appears to have been one of the bounds of battalion, confining military districts, which were also revenue districts.

Soon after the Revolution there was a movement on the part of some persons of Saint Martin's Parish for the creation of a distinct county out of the western portion of Hanover, with its seat of government at Negrofoot. The line to run "nearly by bounds of battalion." A little later advocates came forward for the annexation of the southwestern portion of Hanover to Goochland. The distance from the Courthouse was the reason for these proposals, which were rejected by the General Assembly.

In 1781, when the British Troops were on the march in the upper part of the county, the records of the Superior Courts, which were at the time in Hanover, were ordered removed to some place of safety. Matt Pollock was employed by one of the State Quarter-Masters for this purpose, who supplied wagons and conducted them as far as Ground Squirrel Bridge, where he encountered a party of Tarleton's Legion. To make his escape, he dismounted and concealed himself in the woods, but his horse and accoutrements fell into the hands of the Enemy. He appealed to the General Assembly for relief, stating:

" . . . that as he was engaged in securing the Records and Papers of so much importance to the Community when he sustained this loss that Compensation may be made to him by the Publick."

His prayer was rejected. Evidently the records were preserved, but their present whereabouts are unknown. Doubtless they were lost in the destruction of the General Court Building during the evacuation of Richmond.

The following letter, published by Morgan P. Robinson, State Archivist, in his invaluable "Virginia Counties," 1916, which incidently has been the source of some other references herein, throws light upon the destruction of most of the records of Hanover, which occured on April 3, 1865:

Richmond, Va.,
Dec. 24th, 1915

"Mr. Morgan P. Robinson,
  State Library Bldg.,
  CITY.

Dear Sir:-
    Your letter of December 23rd, just received. I note that you ask me to give my recollection or knowledge of the destruction of our Court records during the War between the States.
    Responding to your inquiry, I have to say that I was raised in Hanover County, about eight miles east of Hanover C. H., but was rarely at Hanover C. H. until after the close of the war. The lower part of Hanover, reaching within a few miles of Hanover C. H. was occupied by the armies of McClellan and Grant, and was the subject of frequent cavalry raids, which took in Hanover C. H., and the Clerk of the County Court of Hanover County as a precaution against the destruction of the records of that Court removed them to Richmond and they were deposited in the Court Bldg., which then stood on the Capitol Square just in front of the Franklin Street entrance from the east, just about where the fountain now stands, which building was destroyed, and so far as I know no papers of value were taken or [saved, in conse]quence all of the records of the County Court of Hanover County were burned. The records of the Circuit Court (which Court then had its own clerk in the same building with

the County Court Clerk) were allowed to remain in the Clerk's Office at Hanover C. H. and though that section was several times raided and the Clerk's Office opened, and some few papers probably lost, I do not think any of the record books were destroyed, and, so far as I know, no papers of value were taken or destroyed. Among the records thus preserved two old books bound in raw hide dated about 1730, remained in the office and were not hurt.
    I do not know if this answers fully your inquiry, but if you desire any further information and I can obtain it for you will be very glad to answer any inquiry you may make.
                      Yours very truly,
                      GEO. P. HAW."

THIS old county is still rich in memorials of her past. The devastations of war, the conflagrations of ancient buildings and homes, the besom of the tidy housewife, and the backyard bonfires have destroyed much, but much still remains. In the garrets and cellars and closets of old houses, in ancient mills and storerooms and barns, on dusty shelves and in discarded trunks are precious relics of the lives lived by her people. Their letters, their writings, their daybooks and ledgers, old deeds, old bonds, old Bibles, old books, old newspapers and the epitaphs of old tombs, all that will enlighten men as to the details of their lives are of lasting and inestimable worth. These are the things that tell faithfully the forces radiating from church and school, from legislatures and law courts, from court-greens and hustings, which moulded our forefathers and recorded their very existence.
    The papers of the Chancery Causes are among the few documents remaining in this office after the War, and are by far the most important relating to the ante bellum period. Because of the nature of these thousands of miscellaneous papers the genealogical and historical facts contained therein have been practically inaccessible, and their contents little known.
    Mr. Cocke is to be commended for his interest in these historical records in general, and in the Chancery Causes in particular. His digests of the Supreme Court Reports, which are published serially by William & Mary College in its Historical Quarterly, have long been an authentic and important source of information. His work in the chancery suits of Hanover lasted for many months and was a most tedious and painstaking undertaking. He has brought to light a wealth of information concerning our forebears which will increase in importance with the passing of the years. The facts have been admirably treated and clearly presented.

Samuel W. Taylor

Hanover Courthouse, Mar. 20, 1940.

PREFACE

HANOVER COURTHOUSE - BUILT 1735

SINCE the destruction of most of the Hanover County Records near the close of the War between the States, there has been a very definite need for a knowledge of the extant Hanoveriana comprising especially the vital facts relating to the ante bellum period.

Believing that by diligent search much source material of this character should be assembled from the miscellaneous records and documents which remained in the Clerk's Office of Hanover through the war, from public archives and libraries, and from church and private sources, the writer became interested in pursuing the idea with the view of compiling such information found for wide dissemination.

Because of the extent of memorabilia found in the Chancery Causes, and the time and expense of compilation, this volume, of necessity, is confined to the Chancery Wills and Notes, and a few digests from two old volumes.

Some of these cases were continued over a span of more than three score and ten years - long after the original parties had passed from the scene. The papers of these suits consist of the bills or petitions, answers of defendants, powers of attorney, subpenas, copies of wills, deeds, accounts of Executors or/and Administrators, depositions, receipts, letters and other exhibits - all contributing the information. Sometimes, as in the Burnley suits, the papers were written by many persons of several generations.

The chirography and orthography of these numerous papers are so variable that conciliation in many instances was difficult or impossible. The difference, if any, in the initials "I" and "J" and "L" and "S" was rarely legible. Proper nouns enjoyed special license when, for example, Totopotomoy was rendered Totopomoy and Totopotomoi. Sometimes considerable changes occurred in the names of the same individual, for instance, when Josiah became Joseph, Mary and Martha became Polly or Polley, Susan became Susanna or Susannah, Octavia became Sally, and Sally and Margaret became Peggy, Arianna became Elizabeth , and often Elizabeth became the diminutive Eliza, Betty, or both. Some of these apparent changes may have been because such persons may have been known by more than one of their baptismal names. An acknowledged change occurred when Freeborn adopted Richard. Even family names were spelled by their owners two ways when Bird was sometime Byrd, and Kennon was rendered Cannon.

In the treatment and presentation of these Notes, the object has been to extract every detail of genealogical, biographical and historical import, and to arrange when convenient alphabetically in relation to families, and chronologically as regards genealogy. Reference is made to the title or style of the suit, year of institution, and the ended file number. When more than one suit was found involving the same families or litigants, to eliminate duplication, they were broken down, and a composite digest made. It is believed that every case pertinent to the period falling within the scope of this compilation, has been included. Suits which were continued too late were noted briefly or disregarded.

In the handling of the Wills, the aim has been to provide either a comprehensive abridgment or an authentic verbatim copy, without attempt toward formal facsimile style. In some instances were questionable portions or flagrant misuses appear, underlines have been added.

It should be borne in mind that all the members of a family may not have been concerned in some of these suits, therefore those not involved may not have been named. The terms "issue" and "survived by" or similar expressions used herein may not be conclusive, and are used for the want of better words.

In making possible this volume, which would run approximately 500 pages in the size of the average historical quarterly, the most economical format and method of production was necessarily utilized.

The writer wishes to acknowledge the very efficient helpfulness of Mr. Clarence W. Taylor, Clerk of Hanover County Court, and his capable deputies and assistants, Mr. Francis A. Taylor, Miss Gertrude Paynes, and Miss Sarah W. Taylor; the intelligent co-operation of the lithoprinters, Messrs. Edwards Brothers, Inc; and to express his appreciation for the many kindnesses of Mr. and Mrs. J. B. Ferguson and family, especially Miss Virginia Ferguson, of the old Hanover Tavern; Miss Fanny Saunders, Mr. and Mrs. J. C. Coleman, and Mr. Jourdan Woolfolk, for their many kindnesses during the progress of this work.

Columbia
Fluvanna County
Virginia

MEREDITH VS. ANDERSON'S ADMR. & OTHERS, 1835 (25)

Alexander Anderson's Will (Abstract)

ANDERSON, ALEXANDER, of Hanover County. Will dated 11 December 1821. "I, Alexander Anderson of Hanover County being in my perfect senses do make this my last will and testament in manner and form following, that is to say, 1st I give to my illegitimate son Nelson Tyler the tract of land whereon his mother Elizabeth Tyler now resides but she is to have the privilege of living on the same during her natural life and to have the rents or profits thereof. It is the land I bought of Snead Browning and wife containing thirty-one and one-half acres, also the following negroes to wit: George, a man, Milley, a young woman, and her two children Isaac and Harriet, with their future increase to him and his heirs forever. He is not tho to have possession or any control over the aforesaid property until he arrives to the age of twenty-three years." Devises to his daughter Polly, wife of Robert Meredith, two large looking glasses, one corner cupboard and its contents consisting of "Plate, chine &c." Desires that the residue of his Estate both real and personal to be sold by his Executor and proceeds invested in bank stock or public securities, and divided amongst the children of his daughter Polly Meredith and his grandson Reuben Anderson Meredith, son of Elizabeth, dec'd, and Dr. Reuben Meredith. Slave boy Reuben to be bound out to a barber, or apprenticed to some good trade, after which service, he is to be emancipated. His two slaves Mosen and Rose to be clothed and supported for their lives. Appoints his son-in-law Dr. Reuben Meredith sole Executor.   Alex Anderson
Witnesses: Thomas Tinsley, Edmund B. Crenshaw, Robert Meredith.
Will was proved in Hanover County 27 February 1822.
     Teste, William Pollard, C.H.C. A Copy, Teste, Benja Pollard, D.C.H.C.

ALEXANDER ANDERSON. Will dated 11 Dec. 1821; probated 27 Feb. 1822. Survived by two daughters, and an illegitimate son, Nelson Tyler, son of Elizabeth Tyler.
1. POLLY, wife of Robert Meredith in 1821. He qualified as Executor of the Estate of Alexander Anderson, and in 1835 is dec'd, and Thomas Gardner, his Executor. Issue:
   1. JOHN A. MEREDITH.
   2. EDMUND P. MEREDITH
   3. ROBERT A. MEREDITH.
   The last two are infant in 1835. Edwin Shelton, Guardian.
2. ELIZABETH, survived by her husband Dr. Reuben Meredith prior to 1821, and an infant son, of whom, in 1835 Edwin Shelton is Guardian:
   1. REUBEN ANDERSON MEREDITH.

ALEXANDER VS. ALEXANDER, 1855 (32)

ALEXANDER, CHURCHILL, of Hanover, died intestate in 1852. Possessed 150 acres of land. Survived by his widow, Nancy Alexander and the following issue:

1. HENRY ALEXANDER.
2. JAMES ALEXANDER.
3. EDMUND ALEXANDER.
4. JANE, wife of Robert Foe.
5. MARTHA ALEXANDER.
6. FANNY ALEXANDER.
7. THOMAS ALEXANDER.
8. CHURCHILL ALEXANDER.
9. NANCY ALEXANDER.
10. JUDY ALEXANDER.

ANDERSON'S ADMR. VS. CURTIS, 1840 (1)

ANDERSON, BARTLETT, of Hanover County, died in 1823. John H. Saunders, Admr. He was survived by a sister, Maria A. Anderson, now dec'd, of whom Dr. Henry Curtis is Executor. It is stated that Dr. Curtis married on 22 June 1836, Miss Amelia Anderson, aparently another sister.

Others mentioned: Deposition of Chastain Cocke at home of William A. Cocke in Powhatan County, 15 March 1846.

COMMONWEALTH OF VIRGINIA VS. ADIE'S ADMR. 1859 (48)

ADIE, JAMES, of Hanover County, died in 1850, intestate. Thought to have been a native of Scotland. Estate consisted mostly of cash in the amount of between Five and Six Thousand Dollars and stock in Virginia Central Railway.

ALLEN VS. ALLEN &C., 1863 (1)

ALLEN, WILLIAM, dec'd, of Hanover County. Possessed land adjoining Bolling Talley, Richard Burnett, Wm. S. Tucker and Shepperson's Mill. Survived by widow, Nancy M. Allen, and issue:

1. EDMUND W. ALLEN.
2. JOHN W. ALLEN, of Kentucky.
3. ROBERT H. ALLEN, of Henrico County, Va.
4. MITCHELL F. ALLEN, of Henrico County, Va.
5. WILLIAM L. ALLEN.
6. JOSEPH H. ALLEN, of Henrico County, Va.
7. FRANCIS M. ALLEN.
8. JAMES B. ALLEN.

ANDERSON VS. CARPENTER & OTHERS, 1842 (1)

Genet Anderson's Will

ANDERSON, GENET. "I do hereby make my last will and Testament in manner and form following. I desire that all the perishable part of my Estate be immediately sold after my decease, and out of the monies arising therefrom, all my just debts to be paid. Should the perishable part of my property prove insufficient for the above purposes, then it is my desire that my Executors hereafter named may sell such of my negroes as to them may seem best and out of the monies arising therefrom pay and satisfy each of my just debts as shall remain unpaid out of the sales of the perishable part of my Estate. After the payment of my debts I give to my wife Maria D. Anderson the whole of my Estate both real and personal for and during the term of her life so long as she remain unmarried and after her decease or marriage, I give the same to my children, Mary Elizabeth, John Garland, Littleton Goodwin, Genet and Robert Semple equally to be divided among them and to be enjoyed by them forever. I do hereby constitute and appoint my friends Joseph Z. Terrell and John O. Harris, Executors of this my last will & Testament, hereby revoking all former wills and Testaments by me heretofore made. In witness whereof I have hereunto set my hand and affixed my seal this 19th day of December in the year of our Lord one thousand eight hundred and thrity-three". Genet Anderson
At a Court of Monthly Session held for Hanover County at the Courthouse on Tuesday the 26th of August 1834. This writing purporting to be the last will and Testament of Genet Anderson, dec'd was offered for proof by John O. Harris one of the Executors therein named, and Charles Thompson, Jr. and William Dabney being sworn and examined (there being no subscribing Witnesses to the said writing) declared that they are well acquainted with the hand writing of the said deceased, that they have examined the said writing and verily believe that the same was wholly written and subscribed by the said Genet Anderson, dec'd: Whereupon the same is ordered to be Recorded as the last Will and Testament of the said Genet Anderson, dec'd.
    Teste, Philip B. Winston, C.H.C.   A Copy, Teste, Wm. O. Winston, D.C.H.C.

GENET ANDERSON. Will dated 19 Dec. 1833, probated 26 April 1834. Considerable real and personal estate including some 25 slaves. Survived by widow, Maria D., and issue:

1. MARY ELIZABETH, wife of James C. Carpenter in 1842.
2. JOHN GARLAND ANDERSON.
3. LITTLETON GOODWIN ANDERSON.

4. GENET ANDERSON.
5. ROBERT SEMPLE ANDERSON.
6. MARIA THOMAS ANDERSON, posthumous.

All under age in 1842, Francis Blunt, Guardian.

Appraisers: M. M. Brown, Lancelot Phillips, and John C. Dickinson.

RICHARDSON & OTHERS VS. PULLIAM'S ADMR. &C., 1835 (33)
JOHNSON'S ADMR. VS. THOMAS' ADMX. &C., 1853 (21)

John Anderson's Will (Abstract)

ANDERSON, JOHN, of Hanover County. Will dated 19 April 1800. "In the name of God amen. I, John Anderson of Hanover County (Taylors Creek) being in perfect health and sound memory of mind, yet considering the brevity of this frail and transitory life, the certainty of death, and the uncertainty of the manner, do make and ordain this to be my last will and testament in manner and form following. Imprimis: I give my soule to God that gave it, hoping through the merits of my redeemer Jesus to receive full pardon of all my sins. Amen! Blessed be God. Next I commit my body to earth from whence it was taken in full assurance that it may be in the same manner as my beloved wife was, and as to my estate both real and personal I dispose of it in manner and form following:" Devises to his daughter Patsey A. Anderson 100 acres, the lower part, of land in Louisa County purchased of Joseph Hawkins, also two slaves, some live-stock, furniture and provisions. She being in "a single state" loans to her for life two rooms in the west end of his house called the hall and study, all out-houses, one-fourth of enclosed land for cultivation and pasturage, and one-fourth of all fruits from orchard. "I also lend her the use of Shadrack during her being in a single state, but should she marry or die then my will and desire is that Shadrack shall be at liberty and fully free in the same manner that free born persons are." Should she die unmarried and without lawful issue the estate given her shall return to his estate for equal division among all his children. To his son John B. Anderson the plantation where he now lives, his

desk, folding table and couch, and slaves. To his daughter Sally Pulliam he gives Fifty Lbs. current money. To daughter Susannah A. Johnson "all my right and interest in the tract of land my son Harmond died possessed of in South Carolina, Union County, also my right and interest in the negro woman Pegg and her present and future increase, that was my son Harmon's, also Five Lbs. current money of Virginia." Devises residue of his estate, including lands in Louisa County, negroes, etc. to daughters: Sally Pulliam, Matilda Richardson, Francisca Johnson, and Augusta Ann Johnson. "Item: And lastly I constitute nominate and appoint my son John B. Anderson, Jennings Pulliam, my friends Walter Chisholm, Jr., and David Chisholm, Jr., my Executors, hereby revoking all other or former wills heretofore made by me and publish and declare this to be my last will and testament. In witness whereof I have hereunto set my hand and seal this nineteenth day of April in the year of our Lord eighteen hundred."   John Anderson (Seal)
Witnesses: Thomas Chisholm, Sally Chisholm, Ann Chisholm, David Chisholm, Jr., Walter Chisholm,Jr.
Proved by their oaths, and by John B. Anderson and Jennings Pulliam, Executors, 19 November 1800.
Teste, William Pollard, C.H.C. A Copy,Teste Benjᵃ Pollard,Jr.

JOHN ANDERSON. Will dated 19 April 1800,proved 19 November 1800. Executors: John B. Anderson and Jennings Pulliam. Securities: Berryman and David Johnson. Later administrators with the will annexed were William Wingfield in 1841 and still later Francis Page, both Sheriffs of Hanover. Wife was deceased in 1800. Issue mentioned:

1. PATSEY A. ANDERSON, died unmarried prior to 1841 when William Nelson, Sheriff of Louisa County was Administrator with the will annexed.

2. JOHN B. ANDERSON. In 1801 deeded to George Underwood and Berryman Johnson of Louisa and Hanover Counties "land given by John Anderson, my father, 315 acres, 3 slaves. Witnesses: Wm. Spottswood Dandridge, Wm. Pulliam, Archᵈ B. Dandridge, and Robert Underwood. In 1814 conveyed to his son-in-law Robert Thomas of Fluvanna County, for $5,000 land in Hanover on Taylor's Creek, whereon the said John B. Anderson resides, 327 acres, 7 slaves, 4 horses, 17 cattle, 18 sheep, 30 hogs, and all of his furniture. Witnesses: Francis G. Taylor and Thomas Pollard.
He died intestate prior to 1835. Administrators were Francis Page, Sheriff of Hanover and John L. Swann, Sheriff of Louisa County. Only issue mentioned:

   1. PATSEY T., prior to 1814 wife of Robert Thomas of Fluvanna County.

3. SALLY ANDERSON, in 1800 wife of Jennings Pulliam. She survived and was Executrix of his estate. She is dead in 1835 and Robert J. Pulliam is Administrator. Jennings Pulliam's Administrator is 1835 is Joseph Starke of Henrico, in 1841 Philip B. Jones, and in 1853 Geo. W. Doswell is Administrator.

4. SUSANNAH ANDERSON, in 1800 wife of a Johnson. Probably removed to Union County in South Carolina.

5. BETTY MATILDA ANDERSON, in 1800 wife of Dudley Richardson. She survived and in 1841 Dudley Richardson, Jr. is her Administrator. Issue:

   1. DUDLEY RICHARDSON.
   2. DAVID RICHARDSON.
   3. SUSAN A., wife of Samuel Rountree.
   4. FRANCISCA, wife of Richard Rountree.
   5. BETSEY A., wife of Mr. Martin.
   6. MATILDA RICHARDSON, under age 1841.
   7. ALLEN RICHARDSON, of Hart County, Kentucky 1854. Wife, Judith F.
   8. SAMUEL A. RICHARDSON, deceased in 1853, Wm. O. Winston, Admr.
   9. THOMAS MANN RANDOLPH RICHARDSON, under age 1841.
   10. JUDITH T. RICHARDSON, under age in 1841, wife of David Rolston 1853.

6. FRANCISCA, wife of David Johnson in 1800. He is dead in 1802, James Holman, Admr. She is dead in 1841, Charles P. Goodall, late Sheriff, Hanover, Administrator. Survived by following issue:

   1. HARMON A. JOHNSON.
   2. DAVID A. JOHNSON.
   3. CHRISTOPHER JOHNSON.
   4. THOMAS B. JOHNSON.
   5. PATSEY, in 1835, wife of Mr. Glenn.

7. AUGUSTA ANN, wife of Berryman Johnson in 1800. He died in Louisa County prior to 1835. She married secondly, William L. Thompson, and both are dead in 1853

8. HARMON ANDERSON. Died prior to 1800. Had land in Union County, S. C.

THOMAS, ROBERT, of Fluvanna County, prior to 1814 married Patsey T., daughter of John B. Anderson of Hanover. In that year his father-in-law conveyed to him 327 acres on Taylor's Creek together with slaves, live-stock and furniture, for the consideration of $5,000. In 1835 he and Thomas Anderson "of Louisa County" are concerned in the Estate of Berryman Johnson. Thomas died in 1847 "possessed of a considerable real and personal estate in the Counties of Fluvanna and Hanover." Survived by his wife who is the Executrix, and by following issue:

1. ROBERT A. (S) THOMAS, dec'd in 1849, survived by a daughter named Mary, infant, living in Kentucky.
2. JOHN B. A. THOMAS, dec'd. Prior to his death had sold his interest in his father's land to John Sclater of Fluvanna County, who in turn had disposed of some of it to George T. Thomas. He died prior to 1859, leaving issue:
   1. ROBERT THOMAS.
   2. ELY THOMAS.

   3. MARION THOMAS.
   4. VICTORIA THOMAS.
3. RICHARD S. THOMAS.
4. GEORGE T. THOMAS.
5. WILLIAM J. THOMAS.
6. WILLIS C. THOMAS.
7. ELIZABETH F., married since 1847, Jefferson R. Noel.
8. SARAH A. THOMAS.
9. MARTHA B., wife of Silas B. Jones.

Robert and Patsey T. Thomas, in 1859, had a granddaughter, Mary W. Doss, infant, whose parent is dead. This, possibly, the daughter of Robert A. or S. Thomas, dec'd.

ANDERSON &C. VS. ANDERSON, 1869 (94)

John T. Anderson's Will

"ANDERSON, JOHN T., of Verdon, Hanover County do make and ordain this my last will and Testament. 1st. I desire that any debts I may owe may be promptly paid out of funds on hand. 2nd. I give to my beloved wife Ann Anderson $2,000 and the use of $5,000 during her life. I give her also the use of all houses at Verdon and 500 acres of land laid off as she may direct and the services of eight negroes, viz: Cook, Betsy, Fanny, Jack Morris, Henry, Jim Brown, Moses and Lucy Ann or Louisa. I give her my carriage and horses and one mule, all the meat, corn, flour and groceries on hand which she may desire for the support of her family, with such plantation utensils as she may deem necessary for the cultivation of her farm. I also give her one yoke of oxen, four milch cows and as many hogs and sheep as she may desire to keep on her farm. I also give her during her life such articles of household and kitchen furniture as she may deem it proper to select, my negroes together with the balance of my property including bonds, stocks &c. except my landed estate I wish divided among my children and so divided as that each of my children may receive an equal portion of my property, the advances which I have made or may hereafter make to any as seen by reference to their respective accounts in my book marked "Children's Accounts". I wish Kate, Betsy Holmes and old Betsy taken care of. The balance of land (after 500 acres for the use of my wife shall have been assigned to her) together with the mill, Tannery &c. I wish rented out until the death of my wife, when that with the 500 acres assigned to my wife, I wish may be equally divided among all my children. Should however a majority of my legatees at any time think it will promote the interest of all concerned that the land, mill, Tannery &c or any part of them should be sold they are privileged to do so & divide the proceeds as directed. In witness whereof I have hereto subscribed my name this 19th day of October 1863."

Signed & acknowledged in presence of: John T. Anderson
John H. Fox, Jos. P. Terrell, H. Stringfellow.
At a Court of Monthly Session held for Hanover County at the Courthouse on Tuesday the 27th of December 1864. This last will and Testament of John T. Anderson, dec'd was proved by the oaths of Jose. P. Terrell and H. Stringfellow two of the witnesses thereto and is ordered to be recorded.
Teste, R. O. Doswell, C.H.C.   A Copy, Teste, R. O. Doswell, C.H.C.

JOHN T. ANDERSON. Will dated 19 Oct. 1863, probated 27 Dec. 1864. Possessed of a "large and valuable estate" consisting of 1400 acres, many slaves, etc. Widow, Frances A. alive in 1865, deceased in 1869. Jos. T. Anderson their Admr. Survived by children and grandchildren:

1. J. M. ANDERSON.
2. JUNIUS H. ANDERSON.
3. LUCIUS C. ANDERSON, died circa 1896, widow Mabel, and two children survive, W. Newton, Jr., guardian of infants:
   1. ELLA ANDERSON.
   2. PEYTON ANDERSON.

4. EDMONIA T., wife of Dr. Linneaus B. Anderson in 1869.
5. ANN M. J., dec'd in 1869, wife of Joseph A. Clarkson (of Baltimore, Md. in 1874.) Issue:
   1. KATE CONWAY, wife of Richard D. Mundie.
   2. WALTER BERNARD CLARKSON, of Jacksonville, Fla., 1890.
   3. CHARLES TEMPLE CLARKSON.
   4. LYNDA PEYTON CLARKSON.
   5. JOSEPH ALBERT CLARKSON.
   6. JOHN PATTON CLARKSON
All infants in 1869.

6. ELIZABETH H., died intestate in Feb. 1888,
    wife of Edward O. Peyton. Survived by
    husband and three children:
    1. CHARLES S. PEYTON.
    2. JOHN A. PEYTON.
    3. WILLIE G., wife of John G. Sinclair.

7. OCTAVIA B., wife of Thomas P. Peyton.

8. CAMILLA C., nearly 21 in 1869, married
    A. W. Tinsley of Albemarle County.

9. OLIVIA C., dec'd, wife of Dr. Erasmus D.
    Booker of Richmond, Va. Issue:
    1. ANN D. BOOKER, married circa 1890,
        John M. Lyle (Lyell)
    2. ERASMUS C. BOOKER.
    3. JUDSON H. BOOKER.
    4. ADA M. BOOKER, married circa 1890,
        Robert Lyle.
    All infants in 1867.

(Others mentioned: James Lobban; Temple J.
Blunt's widow married a Mr. Dillard)

WOOLFOLK VS. ANDERSON & OTHERS, 1835 (49)

ANDERSON, THOMAS, dec'd of Hanover, died possessed of considerable estate, including
557 acres on North Anna River, adjoining
John T. Anderson, James Doswell, Thos. Trevillian and George Winston. Survived by his widow,
Lucy who has dower interest in 2000 acres for
life, then to two sons:

1. JOHN T. ANDERSON, and Frances Ann his wife
    in 1823 sells his interest dower to his
    brother. John T. Anderson keeps a Tavern.

2. THOMAS W. ANDERSON, (of Richmond, 1826) in
    1823 purchased brother's interest in the
    dower land of their mother and sold to
    their father-in-law, Pleasant Terrell.

Lucy, widow of Thomas Anderson, circa 1813, married Pleasant Terrell, who, in 1835 lives on
the dower land, and in 1836 have the following
issue:

1. SARAH ANN, wife of Edmund Winston.
2. LUCY T. TERRELL, "of lawful age."
3. JANE TERRELL.
4. JOSEPH P. TERRELL, aged 22.
5. MONTGOMERY TERRELL

Joseph Woolfolk, Sr. in 1823 (dec'd in 1835)
borrowed money of Pleasant Terrell. Securities
were his son Wm. H. Woolfolk, Hector Davis, Tho.
Doswell and John Thornton (dec'd in 1835, Sarah
Thornton, Executrix).

Others Mentioned: Charles Terrell's Tavern,
Nicholas Terrell, 1836; Bentley Woolfolk, 1827,

ANDERSON VS. BARKER'S ADMRS. &C., 1868 (1)

Richard C. Barker's Will

BARKER, RICHARD C. "I, Richard C. Barker,
being of Sound Mind & disposing Memory do
make this my last will and Testament in
manner and form following, to wit, hereby revoking all wills by me at any time heretofore made.
1st. I desire all my just debts paid. 2nd. I
give and bequeath to John H. Anderson and his
heirs Twenty-five hundred dollars in consideration of his services as executor of my estate.
3rd. The residue of my estate I devise and bequeath to be equally divided among the children
of William Anderson, Jr., dec'd. 4th. I appoint
John H. Anderson executor of my will. Witness my
hand and seal this   day of   1862.
                    Richard C. Barker (Seal)
Signed, sealed & published in the presence who
at the request of the Testator, in his presence
and in the presence of each other Subscribe our
names hereto as witnesses:
    A. J. Gouldman, A. O. Jones.
A copy, Teste, R. O. Doswell, C.C.

RICHARD C. BARKER "late of Hanover was killed
during the War, during 1862, a minor - over
the age of 18 - leaving a will which was probated soon after his death - which will was destroyed." "His estate consisted chiefly in his
interest in estate of his grandfather Richard
Anderson which was in suit at the time of his
death." Barker's Estate was claimed by his
uncles and aunts and their descendants, all of
whom may not be children and grandchildren of
Richard Anderson, dec'd:

WILLIAM ANDERSON, JR., dec'd, an uncle, who
    has issue:
    1. JOHN H. ANDERSON.
    2. RICHARD ANDERSON, JR., of Chesterfield
        County, Va., 1868.
    3. HORATIO S. ANDERSON.
    4. MARIA B., wife of John H. Patteson of
        Chesterfield County, 1868.
    5. EDGAR P. ANDERSON, infant, of Chester-
        field County, 1868.
    6. CHARLES C. ANDERSON, infant, of Ches-
        terfield County, 1868.

BENJAMIN E. ANDERSON, an uncle.

ARCHIBALD ANDERSON, dec'd, an uncle, who has
    issue, all infants, and non-residents of
    Virginia in 1868:
    1. ROBERT B. ANDERSON.
    2. WILLIAM H. ANDERSON.
    3. ALICE B. ANDERSON.
    4. MERIWETHER L. ANDERSON.
    5. LUCY THORNTON ANDERSON.
    6. ANN MARIA ANDERSON.

FREDERICK ANDERSON, dec'd, an uncle, who left infant issue:
1. ANN CORA ANDERSON.
2. MARRIAN ANDERSON.
3. THOMAS W. ANDERSON.
FRANCES A., an aunt, wife of Jacob Michaux.

E. MARION BARKER, an aunt, of Clarksville, Tenn.

The following persons were interested in Barker's Estate, but the connection is not indicated in the papers relating to this Chancery Cause:
R. C. BARKER, a resident of Kentucky.
R. H. P. ROBINSON, and Maria, his wife.

Guardian of the infant children mentioned:
Robert O. Doswell.

ANDERSON VS. SALE & WIFE, 1855 (43)

Robert Anderson's Will

ANDERSON, ROBERT. "In the name of God amen. I, Robert Anderson of the County of Hanover, State of Virginia, do make this my last will and testament hereby revoking all other wills by me heretofore made, in manner and form following. I wish my just debts and funeral expenses paid. I wish a head and foot stone put at my grave, and a head stone to my daughter Nancy Peasley and that of my deceased father and mother. I wish my Executor hereinafter named to sell the piece of land known as Parsons place and the land of Mrs. R. Jordans and also the 22 1/2 acres in Blackwells neck, public or private, as he may think best. I give the land on the road adjoining E. D. Waid and others to my sons Josephus and Robert P., which Josephus may sell if he thinks best, and put one half of the money at interest for the benefit of Robert P. in safe funds. I give the old place adjoining Elisha White and others to my son William Nelson to him and his heirs forever. I lend all the balance of my Estate to my beloved wife Mary F. during her life or widowhood; at her death or intermarriage I wish my Estate personal to be equally divided amongst all my children, except Susan E. Sale wife of Augustin W. Sale, to her I give what I have advanced to this time only, and the land on which I now live called "Hill Fork" I give to my children, namely: Mary Moone, Ann Henretta, Mary Ridley, Martha Robert, Neome Jane, and Robert Pen equally to them and their heirs forever. And it is my wish that a part of the negroes be hired out yearly for the schooling of the children &c. Richard Turner as he calls himself must pay $25. yearly secured by a bond annually for his hire. And lastly I appoint my son Josephus Anderson and my beloved wife Mary F., Executor and Executrix of this my last will and Testament with a request that the Court will please allow them to qualify without requiring security and that the Court will as I do appoint my son Josephus Guardian of his brothers and sisters without security also. In witness whereof I have hereunto set my hand and affixed my seal this the fifteenth day of May in the year of our Lord Christ eighteen hundred and fifty.

Robert Anderson (Seal)

Signed with my own hand and directed to the County Court of Hanover.

At a Court of Monthly Session held for Hanover County at the Courthouse on Tuesday the 23rd of August 1853. This Last will and Testament of Robert Anderson dec'd was offered for proof by Josephus Anderson the executor therein named and there being no subscribing witnesses thereto Robert Wade and Joseph H. Street were sworn and examined who declare they were well acquainted with the handwriting of the said Robert Anderson dec'd, that they have examined the said will and verily believe the same was wholly written and subscribed by the said Robert Anderson, dec'd, whereupon it is ordered that the same be recorded as the last will and Testament of the said Robert Anderson, dec'd. Teste, Wm. O. Winston, C.H.C. A Copy, Teste, Wm. O. Winston, C.H.C.

ROBERT ANDERSON, of Hanover, died in July 1853. Will dated 15 May 1850. Probated 23 August 1853. Possessed several tracts of land in Hanover and 13 lots near the City of Richmond. Was survived by his widow, Mary F., and issue:
1.
1. JOSEPHUS ANDERSON, removed to Tallahassee, Fla., prior to 30 August 1855.
2. SUSAN E., wife of Augustin W. Sale.
3. MARY M., married Lewis L. Smith.
4. ANN H., married J. M. White.
5. NANCY R., married C. W. Wright.
6. MARTHA R., married P. P. Moone
7. NAOMI J., married W. E. Rutherford.

8. ROBERT P. ANDERSON, died prior to 1 March 1869, under age and unmarried.
9. WILLIAM NELSON ANDERSON, died under age and unmarried.

FROM OLD WILL BOOK, PAGE 102

APPERSON, JOHN, deceased. Sarah Frances Apperson, orphan. Geo. W. Doswell appointed guardian 2 October 1851.

SHELTON & SUTTON VS. DOSWELL'S
EX. & OTHERS, 1833 (38)

ANDERSON, SAMUEL, of Hanover, died circa Jan. 1800, possessed of considerable real estate. James Doswell, Admr., now dead, and is succeeded by Thos. Price, Jr. Survived by four children, and his widow, Elizabeth, died in 1806, who married in 1801 Wm. L. Thompson.

1. LEONARD PRICE ANDERSON, born circa 1791, died unmarried circa 1812.

2. CHARLOTTE, born circa 1793, married in 1809 or 1810, John Pearson of Rockbridge County 1833, Augusta County in 1835.

3. ELIZABETH, born circa 1794, married circa 1817, Charles Vest.

4. SAMUEL ANDERSON, JR., born circa 1797. Non-resident of Virginia. In Chesterfield County, Va., 1824. Went to Washington, D. C. before he was of age. On 10 Dec. 1826 sold his undivided 1/3 interest in two tracts of land in Hanover, acreage unknown, - one of which was derived from Rachel Price, dec'd, adjoining Edmund Cameron, the heirs of Reuben Vest, dec'd and the heirs of Robert Bird, dec'd. The other tract dervied from Elizabeth Anderson, dec'd, being part of the land whereon Tarleton Pleasants now resides.

Others mentioned: James Doswell and Jane, his wife, conveyance 3 Dec. 1803 to Tarleton Price. Tarleton Pleasants also purchased land. Benja. Bates, Surveyor, 1800. William Mallory's Tavern at Negrofoot, Edwin Shelton, James T. Sutton.

ARNALL &C. VS. ARNALL'S EX. &C., 1836 (1)

Henry Arnall's Will

ARNALL, HENRY. "In the name of God amen. I, Henry Arnall of the County of Hanover, being in tolerable health but knowing that all persons are to die I wish to dispose of my property in the following manner. First my will and desire is that my wife Mary Arnall should have all my estate as long as she shall live. At her death I wish it divided in the following manner, to wit: I give to William Arnall my son twenty-five cents, to my son Henry Arnall's children twenty-five cents, to Joseph Arnall twenty-five cents, to Richard Arnall my son twenty-five cents. The balance I wish divided between Polly Davis, Nancy Moore, Susan Arnall to have two shares, Patsey Arnall, Ann, Sally Lemay one share. To Dabney Alvis children that he had by my daughter Rebecca twenty dollars. I will my Executors hereafter mentioned to hold in their hands one hundred Dollars to educate George Arnall son of my son Richard. My will is that my Grand Son John T. Arnall; Edmund Winston, John G. Harris and Wm. D. Taylor act as executors of this my last will. Witness my hand and seal this 30th day of August 1834."

Signed in the presence of:
  Francis A. Taylor, Jonathan M. Morris,
  Wm. D. Taylor.

his
Henry X Arnall   (Seal)
mark

CODICIL - "My will and desire is that I wish my wife to be supported well out of my estate as long as she may live and the Surplus of my estate to be divided between my daughters: Mary Davis, Nancy Moore, Susan Arnall, Sally Lemay and Patsey Arnall & to their legal heirs that may leave at their death. My wish also is that Nancy Moon, Sally Lemay, Susan Arnall and Patsey Arnall may have a home on my land during my wife's life if they wish it. And that neither of my Sons William B. Arnall, Joseph Arnall nor Richard Arnall shall have anything to do with or to live on any part of the land I may leave at the time of my death. In testimony whereof I have hereunto set my hand and affixed my seal this 15th of January 1835.

Signed Sealed and acknowledged in the presence of
  Claiborn Mallory.
  Wm. D. Taylor.
  Edmund H. Lowry.
  Henry Arnall, Junr.

his
Henry X Arnall
mark

At a Court of Monthly Session held for Hanover County at the Courthouse on Tuesday the 26th of May 1835. This last will and Testament of Henry Arnall, dec&d was proved by the oaths of Jonathan M. Morris, William D. Taylor, witnesses thereunto and the Codicil therewith returned was proved by the oath of William D. Taylor a witness thereto and at a Court of Quarterly Session continued & held for the said County at the Courthouse on Wednesday the 29th of July then next following the said Codicil was further proved by the oaths of Caliborn Mallory and Henry Arnall, Jr. two other witnesses thereto which will and codicil are ordered to be recorded.
  Teste, Philip B. Winston, C.H.C. A Copy, Teste, R. O. Doswell, D.C.H.C.

HENRY ARNALL, of Hanover. Will dated 30 Aug. 1834, Codicil 15 Jan. 1835. Probated 26 May 1835. Wm. D. Taylor, Executor, qualified 22 Dec. 1835, securities Joseph Patterson and Samuel Lemay. Taylor was dead in 1858, George K.Taylor his Admr. Widow, Mary Arnall died during the latter part of 1835. Arnall's will mentions a grandson, John T. Arnall, whose name does not appear in the suit. Their issue as given:

1. WILLIAM B. ARNALL, non-resident of Virginia. Made a deed 27 Feb. 1807 to Henry Arnall.
2. HENRY ARNALL, JR., dec'd, non-resident. Grantee, Thos. Price, Jr., who died prior to 11 Oct. 1844, Lucien P. Price, and Benja. Pollard, Jr. Exors. "Names of Henry Arnall's children are not known."
3. JOSEPH ARNALL. Grantee: Jos. M. Sheppard.
4. RICHARD ARNALL, had issue probably among others, a son, mentioned in Henry Arnalls will:
   1. GEORGE ARNALL.
5. MARY (POLLY), was wife of a Mr. Davis, survived him and died intestate prior to 1857.
6. NANCY MOORE, survived her husband, and in 1857 was dead, intestate. F. Patmon, grantee.

7. SUSAN (SUCKEY), married Dabney Alvis, survived him and died without issue, intestate prior to 22 Dec. 1857, when: "On motion of Thos. J. Mallory and Elizabeth his wife, James A. Harwood, Sheriff of Hanover, appointed Administrator."
8. MARTHA (PATSEY) ARNALL, died unmarried with will 1849, Henry Curtis, Admr.
9. ANN ARNALL, dec'd. probably the wife of Harrod J. Anderson. No issue.
10. REBECCA, wife of Dabney Alvis prior to the death of her father. He survived her. Their children are non-residents of this Commonwealth and their names are unknown. Dabney Alvis married secondly Susan, her sister.
11. SALLY, dec'd, wife of Samuel Lemay. He is dead in 1845 and Archibald B. Timberlake is Admr., and Edwin Shelton, his security.

———

Others Mentioned: Philip B. Jones, Special Commissioner; Festus Dickinson, dec'd, Samuel C. Dickinson and Woodson Wright, Exors.; Richard Archer, Teller, Bank of Virginia, 11 May 1836. Wm. R. Winn and White & Marye, Attorneys.

CLAIBORNE TRUSTEE, VS. ATKINSON & OTHERS, 1853 (7)

ATKINSON, JAMES, dec'd, on 6 August 1826 executed a Deed of Trust to Herbert A. Claiborne, the elder, Bowling Starke, and Charles Smith, Trustees (all dead) for the benefit of Elizabeth Atkinson, the wife of the said Atkinson, during life, and at her death, for the benefit of her seven children, and for a grandson, James McDaniel, on tract of land called "Cold Harbor" of 211 acres, and 103 acres in addition, also a Bond of Nathaniel and Charles Smith, dated 4 November 1820. The widow Elizabeth died 25 May 1853 in Richmond, survived by the seven children:

1. MARY, widow of William McDaniel.
   1. JAMES MC DANIEL. He and his mother live in Missouri.
2. JOHN S. ATKINSON, of Richmond, Va.
3. WILLIAM ATKINSON, of Richmond, Va.
   1. SARAH F., daughter over 16 in 1853.

4. FRANCES McALISTER, now widow of Robert Bailey.
5. TURNER ATKINSON, of Richmond, Va.
6. REBECCA, widow of Miles Carter, dec'd.
7. ROBERT ATKINSON, of Richmond, Va.

Others Mentioned:
Joseph Whiteside of Missouri, Mc Daniel, assignee.

PRICHARD VS. LEAGUE, ANDREWS & CO., 1841 (35)

ANDREWS, JOHN D., partner of Thomas League and Peter Wilson under style "League, Andrews & Co." late merchants at Houston, Republic of Texas. Samuel Andrews of Spotsylvania County, and Lewis Andrews, brothers of John D. Andrews.

BAKER & OTHERS VS. JOHNSON, 1874 (104)

Martin Baker's Will

BAKER, MARTIN. "I, Martin Baker of Gordonsville, Orange County, Va., possessing a sound mind and disposing memory do hereby make my last will and testament in manner and form following: 1st. I lend to my wife Mona during her life or so long as she remains my widow the following property and funds for her use hereafter mentioned and expressed, viz: I lend her my Gordonsville estate, lands, slaves, crops, stock, furniture, plantation furniture, utensils, &c &c. I wish my executors to lend out the amount of such bonds and money as may be in my possession at the time of my death to borrowers of good credit to be well secured to collect the interest thereon annually and pay it to my wife. I wish the tract of land I own in the County of Giles, a tract on Chickahominy Swamp in the County of Hanover, and a small lot adjoining Woodson Pleasants in Solomon Mark's plan in the County of Henrico sold by executors upon such credit as they may think desirable. The amount of such sales to be loaned out, the interest annually collected and paid over to my wife as heretofore directed. The amount of my interest or claim in the estate of my father I wish disposed of in the same manner. These funds, namely, the profits of my estate at Gordonsville, the interest accruing annually from the amount of bonds and cash on hand at the time of my death, the interest arising from the amount of sales of my lands, and my claims in the estate of my father, I lend to my wife Maria for the purpose of supporting herself, boarding, clothing and educating our children which is to be done without charge against any of them. 2ndly. If any of my servants should prove unsuitable I wish them sold or hired out, and the amount of such sales or hires reinvested in same kind of property or disposed of as the funds named in the first clause of this my will. 3rdly. I give to my son John M. Baker my gold watch which I imported and now wear. I also give to each of the rest of my children one hundred and fifty dollars to make them equal to him in this bequest. 4th. After the death of my wife my executors may use their discretion in selling or renting out my Gordonsville landed property until my youngest child arrives to lawful age at which time it must be sold upon such credits as they may think advisable. 5thly. I wish my daughter Marion to have a likely negro girl over and above the part and portion of the rest of my children. 6thly. The balance of my estate I wish equally divided amongst all my children to them and their heirs forever, except my daughter Marion whose part in the equal division as well as the negro girl extra, I lend to her during her life only, and at her death to be equally divided among all my children or their heirs. But if my daughter Marion should recover from her lameness, then her part before named is given to her and her heirs forever. 7thly. If my wife should marry a second time she is to forfeit all claim to my estate whatsoever. 8thly. If any of my children should become of age or marry before the final division of my estate, I wish my executors to advance them six hundred dollars. I nominate constitute and appoint my nephew Wm. M. Baker and Thomas Swift, Jr., executors to this my last will and testament hereby revoking all wills heretofore made by me. In witness whereof I have hereunto set my hand and seal this 15th day of June 1835.

                                        Martin Baker (Seal)

Teste: Leroy Chandler, George Parrott, James Quarles.

Probated Orange County 23 May 1836 by Wm. M. Baker, one of the Executors, with Clevears Baker, John R. Quarles and Richard S. Boulware, his securities. Teste, Reynolds Chapman, Clk.

MARTIN BAKER "formerly of Orange County died in 1836." Will dated 15 June 1835, probated in Orange 23 May 1836, Wm. M. Baker, Executor, dec'd. Possessed land in Counties of Orange, Giles, Henrico, and 100 acres on Chickahominy Swamp, called "Langston's Old Field" in Hanover. This latter tract, which adjoined the estate of Nancy Ford, was well timbered and subject to the depredations of one William Johnson and his wife C. M. Johnson. The widow, Maria Baker, survived but is dead at the time of this suit. Issue:

1. JOHN MARSHALL BAKER, SR., died between the year 1875 and 1889.
   1. JOHN M. BAKER, JR., Executor of his father. in 1891 of Columbia, Va.
   2. HENRY BAKER, of Geneva, Orange Co.Fla.

3. EARNEST G. BAKER, of Lovingston, Va.
4. ISABELLA V., wife of John R. Rogers of Nelson County, Va.
5. OCTAVIA (SALLIE V.) wife of John W. Freeman of Weiser, Washington Co., Idaho
6. FRANK B. BAKER, died 1888, widow, Edmonia married Mr. Shackelford.
   1. VIRGINIA BAKER.

2. MARTIN BAKER, unmarried in 1875.

3. CLEMENTINA V., died between 1875 and 1889, wife of Dr. C. William Beale who survived.
   1. CHARLES L. BEALE.
   2. MARION B., wife of F. B. Peyton of

Charlottesville, Va.
3. MARY LEE, wife of J. P. Kite of Som-
   erset, Orange County, Va.
4. JAMES G. BEALE, of Lee Hall, Va.
5. FRANK M. BEALE, of Charlottesville.

4. B. F. BAKER, died unmarried, intestate.

5. ANN MARION, married Reuben Morris, and
   died without issue.

Martin Baker, the testator, had a niece the
wife of Squire Nuckols.

WILLIAMS &C. VS. RHODES, 1867 (25)

BAKER, SAMUEL, deceased, of Hanover County.
Suit concerns a tract of land consisting of
50 acres adjoining property of Lucy T. Bowles,
James P. Woodson, and others. His heirs were
the following children:

1. ELIZABETH, wife of Charles L. Rhodes,dec'd

2. CLARATINA, wife of Major J. H. Baughan.

3. E. JANE, wife of John L. Williams.

BARLOW VS. SHELBURN &C., 1849 (4)

William K. Barlow's Will

BARLOW, WILLIAM K. "In the name of God amen. I, William K. Barlow of the County of Hanover do
make this my last will and Testament in the manner and form following, that is to say: 1st.
My will and desire is that all my just debts and funeral expenses be first paid. 2nd. I give
to my wife Lucy W. Barlow the whole of my lands on which I now reside together with the following
slaves and the future increase of the females thereof to wit, Peter, Sam, Joseph, William, Lucy,
George, Easter, Milly, John and Louisa, also the balance of my Estate of every description whatever to her and her heirs forever. Lastly, I do appoint my said wife Lucy W. Barlow Exetrix to
this my last will and Testament revoking all others heretofore made or subscribed by me and that
my said wife shall not be required to give security as Exetrix to this my said will. In witness
whereof I have hereunto set my hand and affixed my seal this 29th day of January 1836."

Signed sealed & acknowledged in presence of   William K. Barlow
   Francis Blunt, O. N. Bumpass.

At a Court of Monthly Session held for Hanover County at the Courthouse on Tuesday the 28th of
May 1844. This Last will and Testament of William K. Barlow dec'd was proved by the oaths of
Francis Blunt and O. N. Bumpass the witnesses thereto and is ordered to be recorded.
   Teste, Philip B. Winston, C.H.C.   A Copy, Teste, O. M. Winston, D.C.H.C.

WILLIAM K. BARLOW. Will dated 29 Jan. 1836,
probated 28 May 1844. Died on Easter Monday
April 1844, possessed of considerable real and
personal estate. Had purchased on 11 Oct. 1838,
for $1,550, 248 acres of land from Thomas J.
Johnson and Martha his wife. Survived by his
widow called Lucy W. Pleasants, who in 1849 is
the wife of Silas Shelburne. He left no children, and his next of kin was a brother and a
sister:

1. ALEXANDER BARLOW, a brother.

2. CATHERINE, a sister, widow of Charles
   Christian, who left three children:
   1. EDWARD CHRISTIAN, of Richmond, Va.
   2. SARAH CHRISTIAN, of Richmond, Va.
   3. MARTHA, wife of Philip Vermilra of
      Henrico County, 1850.

Depositions of J. W. Henry and James Higgason,
1852.

BARRICK'S DEVISEES VS. BARRICK'S DEVISEES & OTHERS, 1889 (55)

James B., and Martha Barrick's Wills (Abstract)

BARRICK, JAMES B., of Hanover. Will dated 19 Aug. 1854. Witnesses: Thomas Acree and Goalder W.
Puller. No probation. Devises to his wife, Martha, one half of estate; loans other half to
her during life or widowhood, then to be divided among his nearest relatives. Martha Barrick
made her will 22 Feb. 1886. Witnesses: Robert Gibson and George T. Talley. Devises her half of
land belonging to estate of late James B. Barrick to George H. Smith of Hanover. To niece,
Camilla A. Cowardin of Richmond, $50.00; bequests to nieces India Gary of Richmond and Clara
Gibson; nephew A. C. Gibson. Also to Clara Blackwell formerly White, and Mrs. Margaret Puller. To
Thomas R. Puller and T. F. Dillard, for benefit of Gothsemane Church.

JAMES B. BARRICK, dec'd of Hanover. Will dated 19 Aug. 1854. Widow, Martha's will dated 22 Feb. 1886. No endorsements of probation. They died without issue. Her legatees were several nieces, a nephew, and others. His estate in 1889 consisted mostly of 50 acres of land near Walnut Grove Church. His next of kin were five sisters and their heirs:

MARTHA ANN, a sister, married Carter New. Both are dead, leaving issue:
1. MARY J., widow of Mr. Sadle.
2. JAMES B. NEW, dec'd. Survived by his widow, who died prior to Mr. Barrick, leaving a son:
    1. WESLEY NEW, now deceased, who left a child six years of age in 1889:
        1. IDA M. NEW.
3 MARY, dec'd, married George W. Thomas, and left no issue.
4. COLUMBIA, wife of Franklin N. Manderville.
5. SARAH E., wife of Willett E. Weeks.
6. ADDISON F. NEW.
7. WALTER C. NEW.

LOUISA, a sister, married Wm. B. Turner, both are dead without issue.

SARAH S., a sister, married George H. Smith. She survived him, now a widow, and has issue, probably among others, a son:
1. GEORGE H. SMITH, aged 52 in 1889 and a farmer of Hanover.

JANE, a sister, married George W. Dow. Both are dead, leaving issue:
1. SARAH F., wife of William Blanks.
2. ERMANIA, dec'd, married a Mr. Price, and left issue:
    1. WILLIAM PRICE HARTWAG, aged 21 in 1889. Adopted by a Mr. Hartwag, whose name he assumed. Residence unknown.
    2. EDDIE B. PRICE, aged 19, 1889.

CATHERINE, a sister, married Thomas Dunn. Both are dead without issue.

Others mentioned: R. R. Horne, Treasurer of Hanover, and a farmer, aged 55 in 1889.

FROM OLD WILL BOOK, PAGE 36

BEAL, JOHN, of Hanover. Will dated 13 Feb. 1836. Witnesses: Richard G. Smith, George W. Rebineau, and J. H. Earnest. Proved on 6 April 1836 by Smith and Earnest. Executor, William Beal. No mention of wife. Issue:
1. WILLIAM BEAL.
2. ELIZABETH, wife of Miles H. Gardner.
3. LOUISA, wife of John R. Whiting.
4. JOHN BEAL.

BEAZLEY &C. VS. WHITE &C., 1851 (5)

BEAZLEY, SANFORD, died intestate 27 Nov. 1826 in Orange County. Col. Wm. L. White, Admr. Survived by his widow, Maria, who was a sister of Col. White, and seven children, all of whom at the time were very young - the youngest less than a year old:
1. MASSINA BEAZLEY.
2. MARIA LOUISA BEAZLEY.
3. FRANCES ANN BEAZLEY.
4. ELIZA, wife of William Frazier.
5. MARY JANE, wife of John N. Davis.
6. FERONIA, wife of William T. Kelley.
7. THOMAS L. BEAZLEY, lately dec'd (1851), leaving three infant children:
    1. MARY SANFORD BEAZLEY.
    2. MARGARET YOUNG BEAZLEY.
    3. THOMAS L. BEAZLEY.

CLARKE &C. VS. TRUEHEART, 1834 (6)
LADD VS. CLARKE & OTHERS, 1837 (23)
CLARKE VS. BELL'S ADMR. & OTHERS, 1840 (8)
LADD & OTHERS VS. CLARKE & OTHERS, 1844 (55)

BELL, NATHAN, dec'd of Hanover. Will was probated in the General Court 1807, abstract furnished by N. P. Howard, Clerk, under date 15 April 1835, for use in one of these suits. John Bell qualified as Executor. Anderson Bowles, Sheriff of Hanover, Admr. in 1840.

"Item: I give unto my son John Bell the tract of land whereon I now live containing by estimation four hundred acres with my mill called Brandy Mills together with the twenty acres reserved from the tract of land lent his mother during her life and also said tract of land at his mother's death, likewise a tract of land called Shepperson's containing one hundred and twenty acres together with my mill called Beaverdam Mills, also one other tract of land called Young's containing 128 acres and a piece of meadow ground adjoining containing twenty eight tracts, two half acre lots of ground in Hanover town together with all the rest and residue of my estate of what nature and kind whatsoever, to him and his heirs forever."

He was survived by his widow, Sarah, who is dead in 1835, and Thomas G. Clarke is her Admr., and by four children:

1. JOHN BELL, Executor of his father's Estate died intestate prior to 1837, Nathaniel Nelson of Charles City County, Admr. He was possessed of 1000 acres of land, and survived by his widow, Mary L. No issue.

2. MARY B., married Amos Ladd, survived him, and in 1840 has a daughter:
    1. ANN LADD.

3. ANN, married a Mr. Ladd. Their issue as of 1844:
  1. MARY LADD.
  2. JAMES M. LADD.
  3. NATHAN B. LADD.
  4. WILLIAM P. LADD.
  5. SEBELIA A., wife of Raphael M. Conn.
  6. SARAH B. LADD.
  7. BENJAMIN F. LADD.

4. REBECCA, dec'd, married Thomas G. Clarke, who survived, and is her Administrator in 1840. Their issue, all infants, in 1837:
  1. NATHAN B. CLARKE.
  2. JOHN W. C. CLARKE.
  3. ARABELLA G. CLARKE.
  4. THOMAS G. CLARKE.

Commissioners: Reuben Meredith, George W. Trueheart, Richard H. Johnson, Henry Curtis, and Edward B. Crenshaw, 1837.

WINSTON, ANTHONY, of Parish of St. Paul, and County of Hanover, on 17 March 1769 deeded to John Austin, Sr., of same Parish and County, for consideration of 538.15.0 Lbs, three tracts: 1st. "old plantation" where Isaac Winston, late of Hanover died, 247 1/4 acres on White's Mill pond, adjoining Trueheart and Barrett White. 2nd tract, 238 3/4 acres adjoining Craighead, Moore Bell, Whitlock and Richardson on Beaverdam Swamp, called Tarkiln Ridge. 3rd tract, 59 acres, low ground of Chickahominy Swamp, granted to said Anthony Winston and John East about the year 1756. One-half acre excepted where the graveyard now is at the old place. Witnesses: John Street, Nathan Bell, Moor Bell, Thos. Austin.
On 20 April 1771 he conveyed to Nathan Bell of same County and Parish, for 155 Lbs., 156 acres on Beaverdam Creek, reserving one acre adjoining on east side of mill dam. Witnesses: Barr. White, John Ellis, Moor Bell and Hezekiah Bowles.
On 22 May 1776, Anthony Winston of Buckingham County conveyed to Nathan and Moor Bell of Hanover for 49 Lbs. land below the causeway, corner Moor Bell, John Austin and said Winston. Witnesses: Barrit White, Elisha White and John White.

TRUEHEART, LEWIS, of Hanover, on 18 Sept. 1810 purchased of John Austin, Sr., 147 1/4 acres for consideration of $1.00, on White's Mill pond adjoing Trueheart and Barret White. Lewis Trueheart died with a will, but only an extract appears in this suit:

"I give and bequeath to my brothers Bartholomew Trueheart and George W. Trueheart, the land I purchased of John Austin, Sr., containing by survey 157 1/4 acres."

Bartholomew Trueheart of Powhatan County, on 13 Sept. 1817, for $3,687.25, deeds 147 1/4 acres to George W. Trueheart and Aaron Butler, moiety of a tract given by Lewis Trueheart in his last will and testament to the said Bartholomew Trueheart and George W. Trueheart. Witnesses: John H. Steger and Littlebury H. Mosby, Justices of the Peace of Powhatan County.

George Washington Trueheart of Louisa County on 15 April 1818, purchases of Dr. John Adams and Margaret his wife of City of Richmond, for $4,000, land in Hanover known as White's Mill on Beaverdam which was conveyed to John Adams by deed from William Trueheart and wife on ---- date. Also all the right &c conveyed by deed from William White and Mildred his wife on same date, to the said John Adams.

BIRD VS. BIRD & OTHERS, 1832 (2)
JAMES & WIFE VS. BIRD & OTHERS, 1834 (21)
BYRD VS. BYRD'S ADMR. & OTHERS, 1876 (42)

BIRD, ROBERT, of Hanover died intestate, possessed of considerable property, including 20 slaves. Survived by his widow who later married Edward Cameron, and four children:

1. THOMAS R. BYRD, of Chesterfield County.
2. FERONIA A., wife of Spotswood James, 1832. Sold her interest in father's Estate to Lemuel and Joseph Vaughan. Boling Vaughan, Security.
3. ARIADNE P. BIRD. Will dated 17 August 1849, (signs as Byrd) witnesses: L. H. Minor and J. Alonzo Smith. C. St.G. Noland on 20 Aug. 1860 stated she was capable of making her will. Will probated by these, and Geo. W. Doswell appointed Executor, W. R. Winn, Security. Devisees were the two daughters, Ann Maria and Susan E., of William Luck, in whose family she had been living. Will contested on grounds of non compos.
4. LOUISA M. BIRD, died unmarried 20 April, 1833, aged about 26.

CAMERON, EDWARD, married the widow of Robert Bird, dec'd (her name not stated), and had issue, all under 21 years of age in 1834:

1. ENSEBIA N. CAMERON.
2. MARY R. CAMERON.
3. JOHN D. CAMERON, of Henrico County 1836.
4. Wm. R. CAMERON, of Henrico County 1836.
5. FRANCIS D. CAMERON, died prior to 1840, leaving children:
  1. JOHN B. R. CAMERON.
  2. G. W. CAMERON.

Others Mentioned, 1832: Wm. D. Taylor, Curator, Thomas Bumpass and Nathaniel B. Thomposon, Sec.

COOKE & WIFE VS. BERKELEY &C., 1838 (8)
SMITH &C. VS. ROBINSON'S EXORS., 1867 (40)
BERKELEY & OTHERS VS. BERKELEY & OTHERS, 1879 (60)

BERKELEY, NELSON, of Prince William County in 1821, and of "Airwell" in Hanover containing 670 acres, of which he has a one-third interest. Married twice. Name of first wife not stated, by whom he had a son "half-brother" to his other children:

1. THOMAS NELSON BERKELEY, was married prior 16 June 1821 when he and his father made a contract to farm "Airwell" in which he had a two-third interest. Died prior to 1838, survived by his widow who shortly afterward married Rev. John Cooke, and by one daughter:
   1. MARY EDMONIA, under age and unmarried in 1850. Wife of St. George Noland in 1853, and his widow in 1879.

Nelson Berkeley married secondly prior to 16 June 1821, Lucy P., a daughter of John and Susan (Clements) Robinson of "Locust Level" in Hanover. Survived by his widow in 1850, and the following issue:

2. BETTY LANDON BERKELEY, died unmarried. Her will was dated 5 March 1866, and proved 27 Aug. 1867 by Robert O. Doswell, and Richard T. Berkeley who testified as to her handwriting. Henry Robinson Berkeley, Executor. Devisees: Sisters, Catherine R. Winston, Sally N. Berkeley; brother Edmund Berkeley for life then to his unmarried daughters; friend and relative Thos. W. Lewis in trust for brother Wm. H. Berkeley for life, then to his unmarried daughters; friend and relative, Rev. James A. Latane in trust for "my dear afflicted brother Carter Berkeley, D.M.", then to his unmarried daughters; Godsons Thomas N., eldest son of brother Edmund Berkeley, Gregory T. Bedell, eldest son of Carter Berkeley, Wm. Wilbefore, second son of Wm. H. Berkeley; Pastor, Rev. Joshua Peterkin. and his daughter Rebecca Peterkin; Mr. Samuel J. Harrison for Bibles for "my three precious children Caskie Harrison, Norvell Harrison, and Percy Harrison;" Nieces, Mary Edmonia, Noland, Lucy Robinson Lewis, and Mary Latane Berkeley.

3. CATHERINE R., married in December 1849, P. W. Winston. He is dead in 1863.

4. SALLY N. BERKELEY, died unmarried 1877.

5. EDMUND BERKELEY, "JR" Executor of his father's Estate. Overseer of "Airwell" in 1829, 1831, 1832 and 1833. Dec'd 1867. It is not stated to whom he married.

[Susan E., daughter of Lewis and Elizabeth Berkeley of "Montout" married an Edmund Berkeley.] Survived by issue:

1. THOMAS N. BERKELEY. Alive in Staunton 1895. Non compos mentis.
2. HENRY ROBINSON BERKELEY, of Orange, Va., 1895.
3. JOHN HILL BERKELEY.
4. BETTY L. BERKELEY, of Wingina, Nelson County, Va., 1895.
5. KATE T. BERKELEY, of 615 Princess St., Alexandria, Va., 1895.
6. LOUISA C. BERKELEY, of Newsoms, Southampton Co., Va., 1895.
7. MARY LATANE, wife of Wm. A. Aldrich, of Perryman, Harford Co., Md., 1895.
8. SUSAN D. BERKELEY, of Elko, Henrico County, Va., 1895, care T.F.Pollard.
9. EDMUND BERKELEY.
10. EDMONIA, died circa 1887, wife of H. B. Hooe, of Nokesville, Prince William County, Va., survived by her husband and one daughter:
    1. ELIZABETH B. HOOE.
11. FANNY, wife of Dr. Wm. B. Barham of Newsoms, Southampton County, Va., 1895.

6. WILLIAM H. BERKELEY, dec'd in 1879, survived by following issue:

   1. JOANNA R. BERKELEY.
   2. MARY A BERKELEY.
   3. EDMONIA C. BERKELEY.
   4. LUCY A., wife of William E. Briggs.
   5. MARIA H., under 21 and wife of Wm. P. Christian in 1879.
   6. WILLIAM WILBEFORE BERKELEY, called second son, of Roanoke, Va., 1895.
   7. ANN B., wife of Laney Jones, Jr.
   8. JOHN C. BERKELEY.
   9. GEORGE H. BERKELEY.

7. DR. CARTER BERKELEY, (non compos mentis) Married Ann B., daughter of Dr. Carter and Frances N. Berkeley of "Edgewood" Issue as of 1879:

   1. NANNIE C., wife of J. F. Brooke of Staunton, Va., 1895.
   2. GREGORY T. BEDELL BERKELEY, under age in 1842, died in Baltimore, Md., in July 1894.
   3. ISABELLA C. BERKELEY, under 21 in 1842.
   4. WILLIAM M. BERKELEY, under 21 in 1842, living in Staunton, Va., 1895.
   5. CATHERINE S. C. BERKELEY, under 21 in 1842.

8. MARY, married a Mr. Latane. Full name not
stated. [Her sister, Betty Landon Berkeley, in will, mentions "friend and relative Rev. James A. Latane", and "friend
and relative Thomas W. Lewis."] They had
issue, a daughter,
    1. LUCY ROBINSON LEWIS, widow in 1879,
       with one child:
          1. JOSIE LEWIS.

ROBINSON, JOHN, "President of the Council",
married Catherine, daughter of Robert Beverley, the first, and had issue:

1. WILLIAM ROBINSON, who married first, Miss
Beverley, and secondly, Miss. Smith.
Issue, two sons:

    1. JOHN ROBINSON, of "Locust Level" mar-
      ried Susan Clements, and had issue:"
      1. HENRY ROBINSON, died without
         issue, prior to 8 January 1856,
         when Ann C. Robinson executed
         a deed of trust to Wm. D. Win-
         ston to secure the payment of
         $500.00 due to John Pollard of
         King & Queen County "all the
         interest of the said Robinson
         in a tract of land devised to
         her and her two sisters Mary
         and Joanna Robinson by her bro-
         ther Henry Robinson, dec'd, -
         being one-third thereof - said
         tract contains 312 acres and
         adjoins the lands of William D.
         Winston, Edmund Winston and
         others.
      2. JOHN ROBINSON, of "Locust Level."

    3. CATHERINE, wife of Mr. Pollard.
      Issue:
      1. JOHN POLLARD, who has issue:
         1. THOMAS POLLARD, dec'd
           in 1869.
         2. HENRY ROBINSON POLLARD.
         3. SUSAN CLEMENTS, mar-
           ried prior to 1859,
            Richard H. Woodward,
            who is dec'd in 1869.
         4. SARAH, married Alfred
           Bagby.
      2. EDMUND POLLARD.
      3. WILLIAM H. POLLARD.
      4. JOSEPH POLLARD.

    4. LUCY P., wife of Nelson Berkeley
      of Prince William County, and
      of "Airwell," Hanover County.

    5. MARY ROBINSON, died unmarried.
      Will made in 1848. Devised her
      one-third interest in "Locust
      Level" to sisters.

6. JOANNA ROBINSON, died unmarried.
Will dated 20 Jan. 1845, Codi-
cil 16 June 1847, Probated 25
Sept. 1855. Devisees: Nieces,
Betty L., Catherine R., and
Sally N. Berkeley; Sisters,
Ann C. Robinson and Lucy P.
Berkeley; Henry R., son of
nephew Edmund Berkeley, Jr.;
Joanna R., daughter of nephew
Wm. H. Berkeley; Isabella C.
Berkeley daughter of nephew
Carter Berkeley; Susan C. Pol-
lard daughter of nephew John
Pollard; Nephews, Edmund, Wm.
H., and Joseph Pollard. In the
sale of her slaves desires tha
families to be kept together -
husbands not to be seperated
from wifes, or mothers from
children. Appoints Philip B.
Winston, Executor. Witnesses:
E. F., P. H., O. M., John R.
and Jane D. Winston, W. H.
Priddy and A. Hill.

7. ANN C. ROBINSON, died unmarried.
Will dated 31 Mar. 1856, Codicil 7 Feb. 1859, Probated 22
March 1859. Devises to Henry
Robinson Berkeley a son of
nephew Edmund Berkeley, her
portion of "Locust Level" she
holds under the will of her
brother Henry Robinson. The
slaves to be emancipated and
sent to Liberia or some free
state. Bequests to Mary L.,
Susan D., Kate T., and Edmonia
daughters of nephew Edmund
Berkeley; Susan Clements Pollard and Sarah Bagby daughters
of nephew John Pollard. John
Pollard, Executor. Witnesses:
Wm. D. Winston, John R. Taylor
Frans. G. Taylor, A. M. Morris.

   2. HENRY ROBINSON.

EMANCIPATED FAMILY OF NEGROES

SMITH, PLEASANT, dec'd. Widow Jane (and her
mother Fanny James) and their children,
emancipated Negroes by the will of Miss Ann C.
Robinson of Hanover County.

   1. ISABELLA, wife of Granville Saunders.
   2. CORNELIUS SMITH.
   3. ANN, wife of Philip Bowman.
   4. VIRGINIA SMITH.
   5. NANCY SMITH.
   6. WILLIAM SMITH.

BERKELEY & OTHERS VS. BERKELEY'S ADMR. & OTHERS, 1844 (4)

Carter Berkeley's Will

BERKELEY, CARTER. "I, Carter Berkeley of the County of Hanover and State of Virginia being of sound mind and disposing memory do make this my last Will and Testament. 1st. After paying my just debts I desire that what is left of my personal property may be kept together and with my farm called Edgewood to be used to the best advantage for the support of my wife Frances N. Berkeley and my four children Ann B. Berkeley, Park F. Berkeley, Catherine F. Minor and Carter N. Berkeley the annual nett proceeds of the whole to be divided in the following manner, to wit: One-third to be given to my wife F. N. Berkeley and the other two-thirds to be equally divided between my aforesaid four children Ann B. Berkeley, P. F. Berkeley, Catherine F. Minor and Carter N. Berkeley. 2nd. I give to my son Robert C. Berkeley my part of the tract of Land called Broom-field supposed to be two hundred and twenty-seven acres more or less, being the upper undivided part of what remained of the tract of Land (after the sale I made to William Fulcher) adjoining the said Fulcher's Land above it and my sister L. C. Berkeley's Land below it, for which Land I have given my said son Robert a Deed but which Deed is not recorded. I also give to my son Robert C. Berkeley ten and a half acres of Land lying on the New found river and adjoining the above men-tioned Tract which said 10 1/2 acres I bought of Wm. Fulcher who gave me a Deed for same, recor-ded in the Clerk's Office of Hanover County. The above two tracts of Land I give to my said son Robert & his heirs forever. 3rd. I do not give anything to my daughter Elizabeth W. C. Taylor because I gave her a full proportion of my property when she was married. I desire she may live at Edge Wood as Long as she remains Single and her daughter Kitty C. Taylor paying each a reason-able sum for board considering their food only, it being my wish that as long as she and her daughter continue single, they shall each or either of them have a home at Edge Wood and a cabbin for a servant or more convenient to the house and necessary to wait on them, the cabbin to be built or repaired at their expense. I have given my son Edmund Berkeley a full proportion of my landed property therefore I leave no Land to him. 4th. After the death of my wife Frances N. Berkeley I give all my Estate in Land with its appurtenances to be equally divided among my chil-dren Ann B. Berkeley, Park F. Berkeley, Catherine F. Minor and Carter N. Berkeley. 5th. After the death of my wife Frances N. Berkeley I give all the residue of my Estate to be equally divided among my children Edmund Berkeley, Robert C. Berkeley, Ann B. Berkeley, Park F. Berkeley, Catherine F. Minor and Carter Nelson Berkeley whatever advances of negroes or money that I have heretofore made to any of these my children last mentioned are to be taken as so much of their proportion of the said residue of my Estate: These advancements will appear on the account I have kept against each of them who have received any advances. I give to my wife Frances N. Berkeley one feather Bed, Two Mattresses, four pair of Sheets, two Blankets, and four pillows, two pair of blankets, a quilt and counterpane and two Bedsteads, all to be chosen by herself. I also give my silver Teapot and twelve silver Table spoons and twelve silver Tea spoons to be chosen by herself. I leave my wife Frances N. Berkeley Executrix and my sons Robert C. and Carter N. Berkeley Execu-tors of this my last Will and Testament. In Witness whereof I hereunto set my hand and affix my seal this 12th day of February in the year of our Lord 1835."

Carter Berkeley (Seal)

"Codicil to my Will on the preceeding pages of this sheet. I desire that no Security may be required of the aforenamed Executrix and Executors of this my Will, but that either any or all of them may be permitted to qualify and execute the business upon giving their joint Bond. Witness my hand and seal this 21st day of Sept. 1835."

Carter Berkeley (Seal)

Codicil to my Will —
"If my wife and children and my Executors think it will be best for the interest of those concerned, to sell my Land and distribute the money or other property received in pay for it, I hereby authorize them to do so and to make a perfect title to it. Witness my hand and seal this 20th February 1837."

Carter Berkeley (Seal)

I give to my Daughter Ann B. Berkeley her proportion of my Estate for her life only, and to her children after her death and I have done so because I fear it may be taken to pay the debts which Carter Berkeley her husband owes, and I hereby direct that all I have given to s'd Ann B. B. shall be for the separate use and maintenance of herself and children free from the claims of any or all her husband's creditors. And to carry this my intention into effect, I hereby appoint Robert C. Berkeley and Edmund Berkeley, Jr., of Hanover as Trustees to hold the property above given in trust for the above purpose, but that Dr. C. Berkeley, Jr., may keep it in possession and use it to the best advantage he can for the support of himself, his wife A. B. B. and her children. The above trustees may sell any or all the property at the request of Ann B. B. provided they vest the amount in safe fund or in such a way as to secure the Interest or profits annually to the exclusive support of Ann B. B. and her husband and children."

At a Court of Monthly Session held for Hanover County at the Court house on Tuesday the 28th of June 1842. On the motion of Robert C. Berkeley to admit to probat this Testamentary paper and the codicils thereto annexed, purporting to be the last Will and Testament of Carter Berkeley, dec'd. And it appearing that Carter N. Berkeley has departed this life since 23rd day of March last, and that the summons awarded against the widow and distributees of the said Carter Berkele dec'd have been duly executed except on the said Carter N. Berkeley and he having no personal representative, by consent of the parties, except the said Carter N. Berkeley, this motion is continued until the next Court. And at a like Court held for the said County at the Court house on Tuesday the 27th of December 1842, came Robert C. Berkeley, Frances N. Berkeley, widow of Carter Berkeley, dec'd, Edmund Berkeley, Elizabeth W. C. Taylor, Parke F. Berkeley, Carter Berke ley and Ann B. his wife, who was Ann B. Berkeley, Frances N. Berkeley, admx. of Carter N. Berke-ley, dec'd, Lucius H. Minor and Catherine F. his wife who was Catherine F. Berkeley, Ann C. C. Taylor and Edmund Berkeley, Guardian ad litem of Gregory T. B. Berkeley, William M. Berkeley, Isabella C. Berkeley and Catherine S. C. Berkeley by their Attorneys, and Philip B. Winston and Lucien B. Price being sworn and examined, deposed that this Testamentary paper and the Codicils thereto are in the proper hand writing of the said Carter Berkeley, and thereupon the said Testa mentary paper is admitted to probat as the Will of the said Carter Berkeley, in connection with the will of the said Carter Berkeley heretofore admitted to probat, as the will of the said Carter Berkeley.

Teste, Philip B. Winston, C.H.C.   A Copy, Teste, Philip B. Winston, C.H.C.

CARTER BERKELEY, M. D. of "Edgewood" made two wills, one of which was probated 26 November 1839, and the other, given above, was dated 12 Feb. 1835, codicils 21 Sept. 1835 and 20 Feb. 1837, probated 28 June 1842. Mentions a sister, L. C. Berkeley. Wife, Frances N., Executrix. Prior to this marriage she was the widow of Thomas Nelson, dec'd, and as such possessed 17 slaves in her own right. (Mrs. Thomasia Meade and heirs were also entitled to an interest in the Estate of Thomas Nelson.). Mention is made to "the late George W. Nelson" without further comment. Dr. Carter Berkeley possessed a con-siderable estate, including some 20 slaves. He died in 1839, survived by his widow, and issue:

1. ELIZABETH W. C. TAYLOR, widow in 1835.
   1. ANN C. C. (Kitty) TAYLOR.
2. EDMUND BERKELEY
3. ANN B., wife of Dr. Carter Berkeley,* who is sometime "Jr." - a relative. Issue as of 1842, all infants:
   1. GREGORY T. B. BERKELEY.
   2. WILLIAM M. BERKELEY.

3. ISABELLA C. BERKELEY.
   4. CATHERINE S. C. BERKELEY.
4. PARK F. BERKELEY.
5. CATHERINE F., wife of Lucius H. Minor.
6. CARTER NELSON BERKELEY, died 23 March 1842, leaving a widow, Ellen R., and on daughter:
   1. JOSEPHINE BERKELEY.
7. ROBERT C. BERKELEY.

*Dr. Carter Berkeley was a son of Nelson Berke ley of "Airwell" and his wife, Lucy P. (Robin-son) Berkeley of "Locust Level," which Estate consisted of 312 acres, being on Beaverdam Tur pike and on road from Newman's Mill to Fork Church, adjoining lands of Winston, Cooke and others. It was about a mile and a half from Hanover Academy, and Taylorsville, and about a mile from the Richmond, Fredericksburg & Potoma Railway, according to description circa 1880.

Commissioners appointed to divide land: James Fontaine, William C. Winston, Edmund Berkeley, Richard F. Darracott, and Patrick H. Price.

BERKELEY & WIFE VS. HERRING &C., BERKELEY &C., 1856 (4)

Lewis Berkeley's Will

BERKELEY, LEWIS. "I, Lewis Berkeley of the County of Hanover do hereby make my last will an Testament in manner and form following, that is to say: 1st. I desire that all my just debt be paid. 2nd. I give to my wife Elizabeth Berkeley one-third part of all my estate both rea and personal including in her third part the Montout house with all the household and kitchen fu niture also my Carriage and horses for and during her natural life and after her decease I give the same to my Children Susan E., Mary N., Nelson W., Landon C., Richard F., Francis E., Lewis and Lucy C. equally to be divided among them and to be enjoyed by them forever. 3rd. I give to all my children except Susan C. Berkeley two hundred dollars each. I have excluded my daughter usan from a participation in this legacy because I think she has an equivalent in the provision f Sally Marshall. 4th. All the rest of my estate both real and personal of what nature or Kind oever it may be not herein before particularily disposed of after deducting from the portion of y daughter Susan E. and my son in Law Edmund Berkeley the sum of one thousand dollars which I dvanced to them and from the portion of my daughter Mary N. and my son in law Richard F. Darra-ott the sum of four hundred dollars advanced to them I desire may be equally divided among my everal Children herein before named which I give to them and their heirs forever. And lastly I o hereby constitute and appoint my wife Elizabeth Berkeley Executrix and my son Nelson W. Berke-ey and my sons in law Richard F. Darracott and Edmund Berkeley executors of this my last will nd testament. In witness whereof I have hereunto set my hand and affixed my seal this the wenty second day of February in the year eighteen hundred & thirty six."

                                                                    his
                                              Lewis Berkeley + (Seal)
                                                                   mark
igned sealed & declared as & for the last Will and Testament
f the above named Lewis Berkeley, in the presence of us:
 Benjamin Vaughan (+), William G. King, J. W. Sheppard, Nelson Berkeley, Jr.

t a Court of Monthly Session held for Hanover County as the Courthouse on Tuesday the 28th of une 1836. This last will & Testament of Lewis Berkeley deceased was proved by the oaths of . W. Sheppard & Nelson Berkeley, Jr., witnesses thereto and is ordered to be recorded.
 Teste, Philip B. Winston, C.H.C. A Copy, Teste, R. O. Doswell, D.C.H.C.

EWIS BERKELEY, of "Montout" a 430 acre Estate in Hanover County. Will dated 22 Feb. 1836, probated 28 June 1836. Widow, Elizabeth, died n 1852. Their issue:

1. RICHARD F. BERKELEY, wife, Betty S.
2. SUSAN E., wife of Edmund Berkeley.
3. MARY N., aged 46 in 1856, wife of Richard F. Darracott, aged 49 in 1856.
4. LUCY C·, aged 30 in 1856, wife of James B. Shelton, aged 31 in 1856.
5. LANDON C. BERKELEY.
6. NELSON WILLIAM BERKELEY.
7. LEWIS BERKELEY.
8. FRANCIS E. BERKELEY.

"Some of these children have conveyed their nterest in Lewis Berkeley's Estate to George . Herring and wife Mary P. Herring, John Darra-cott of Richmond and William D. Winston of Han-ver County."

WALTHALL &C. VS. WILKINSON, 1833 (48)
BETHEL VS. BLAKEY'S ADMR. & OTHERS, 1835 (2)

BLAKEY, SMITH, of Henrico County, died pos-sessed of a large estate. In 1796 had been Executor of the Estate of Charles Hundley, ec'd of Hanover. Survived by his only child, a on, who was his Executor:

1. GEORGE BLAKEY of Henrico County, died 1824 intestate, possessed of a "considerable and valuable real and personal property" which included many slaves, 1000 acres in Hanover and two tracts of land in Hen-rico, one of which had a saw and grist mill on Stoney Run, rented to George Woodfin, being near John New and Joseph Starke. Commissioners to divide land were Parke Street, Richard G. Smith,

James Croxton, John New, Edward Hill, Ed-ward Govan, Richard Adams. Cary Wilkerson of Charles City County (at Lewisbury, Va. 1833, dec'd in 1835) Administrator and Guardian of his children. George Blakey was survived by his widow, Elizabeth B. Blakey, and five infant children:

1. ANN W., in 1833 wife of James H. Walthall of Richmond, Va.
2. MARY ELIZABETH, in 1833, wife of Bartholomew Mc. Tomlin.
3. THOMAS H. BLAKEY, in 1835, of Charles City County.
4. JOHN M. BLAKEY, in 1835, of Charles City County.
5. WILLIAM A. BLAKEY, died 1832, under age and unmarried.

William Tyler, Sheriff, Charles City County in 1835. John C. Tyler appointed his deputy in March 1835, succeeding John. S. Stubblefield.

Charles Hundley's Will

HUNDLEY, CHARLES, "In the name of God amen. I, Charles Hundley of the Parish of saint Paul & County of Hanover being sick and weak in body, but of sound and perfect mind & memory. Imprimis. I give and bequeath to Elizabeth A. Hundley and to her Heirs and assigns forever my negro girl named Annie. Item. I give and be-queath my negroe girl Sucky to Polly Hundley and her heirs and assigns forever. I give and bequeath my negro girl Fanny to Sarah Hundley and her heirs and assigns forever. Item. I give and bequeath my negroe boy Ben to Ransom Hund-ley and his heirs forever. Item. my wish & de-sire is that all the remainder of my estate both real and personal be sold by my executor hereafter named for the payment of my debts in such manner as he shall think best and if any

thing remains to be equally divided between Martha Freeman & Clarkeley Hundley & the survivor of them and their heirs forever, and lastly I do hereby constitute & appoint my good friend Smith Blakey of the County of Henrico, my whole and sole executor of this my last will and testament hereby revoking and making void all other wills by me Heretofore made. In witness Whereof I have hereunto set my hand ' affixed my seal this 25th day of May 1796."
                    Charles Hundley (Seal)
Signed sealed published & declared by the testator to be his last will and testament in presence of Bartt Anderson, John Edmundson, Nicholas Mills.
"ITEM as a Codicil to this my last will and testament the negroe girl Fanny which I have given to Sarah Hundley in this my will I desire it may goe with her mother, & in lieu thereof I give and bequeath to the said Sarah Hundley twenty-five pounds current money of Virginia & her heirs forever, witness my hand & seal this 19th day of November 1796."
                    Charles Hundley (Seal)
Wit - Bartt Anderson, Nicholas Mills.
    At a Court of monthly Session held for Hanover County at the Courthouse on Wednesday the 21st of December 1796. This last will and testament of Charles Hundley dec'd was offered for proof by Smith Blakey an Executor therein named and was proved by the oath of Bartelot Anderson one of the subscribing witnesses thereto, and also by the oath of the said executor. And at a Court of quarterly session continued and held for the said County at the Courthouse on Thursday the 16th of February 1797 the said will was further proved by the oath of Nicholas Mills another subscribing witness thereto, and is ordered to be recorded.
    Teste, William Pollard, C. H. C.
    A Copy, Teste, Philip B. Winston, C.H.C.

CHARLES HUNDLEY. Will dated 19 Nov. 1796, probated 21 Dec. 1796. Personal estate, including seven slaves, sold for 654.5.2 Lbs. Survived by his widow Elizabeth A Hundley. The surviving heirs in 1835 were two daughters:

1. CLARKELEY, wife of Elisha Bethell, whom she survived.
2. MARTHA, who married first a Mr. Ross, whom she survived, and married secondly a Mr. Freeman, and has survived him.

    CAUTHORNE VS. CAUTHORNE, 1866 (10)

FRAGMENT OF SUIT; Geo. Kelley & wife Elizabeth; John P. Woodson & wife Eveline; Martin Brittain; Mathew S. Davis? wife Mary; Rebecca A.and John J. Brittain; Charles Ellis; Wm. Sledd, admr. of B. Franklin, dec'd; & Sarah A. Snyder, Extx of Philip Snyder, dec'd, versus John Brittain and Gabriella, his wife. (Other papers missing.)

    BLACKBURN &C. VS. BLACKBURN &C., 1854 (5)

BLACKBURN, HENRY, of Hanover, died intestate in 1854. Survived by his widow, Harriet Blackburn, and by four brothers, as follows who were his only heirs:

EDWIN BLACKBURN.

FLEMING BLACKBURN.

BARROTT BLACKBURN.

DABNEY W. BLACKBURN.

    BUCKLEY &C. VS. BUCKLEY & OTHERS, 1860 (56)

BUCKLEY, LAWRENCE, of Hanover County, prior to 1842, married Frances E. S.(maiden name not stated) niece and legatee of Sarah Lankford, dec'd in 1842, and had issue:

1. MARIETTA, married William B. Slaughter.
2. MARTHA E. BUCKLEY.
3. JOSEPHINE J. BUCKLEY, aged 17 in 1860.
4. JULIETTA O. BUCKLEY, aged 15 in 1860.

            Sarah Lankford's Will

LANKFORD, SARAH. "The last will and testament of Sarah Lankford of the County of Hanover, Virginia. Imprimis. I lend to my niece Frances Buckley and her children that she now has or may hereafter have during their joint lives all my property of every description and at the death of the said Frances Buckley it is my will and desire that the said property be equally divided between such of her children as shall then be alive. 2ndly. I hereby appoint my friend Hector Davis Trustee for the said Frances Buckley and Children and Executor of this my will and enjoin on him to prevent the husband of the said Frances Buckley from having anything to do with the said property as far as possible. Given under my hand this 31st day of Augt. 1842."
Signed in the presence   Sarah Lankford (Seal)
of us: Hector L. Davis,
F. P. Harris, Frances(+)Shuley, Wm. M. Thomas.

At a Court of Quarterly Session held for Hanover County at the Courthouse on Thursday the 27th of October 1842. This last will and testament of Sarah Lankford, dec'd, was proved by the oaths of Frances Shuly and Wm. M. Thomas, witnesses thereto and is ordered to be recorded
    Teste, Philip B. Winston, C.H.C.
    A Copy, Teste, Wm. O. Winston, C.H.C.

The land of Sarah Lankford, in 1860, 268 acres, which adjoined lands of Patrick Perrin, John Brock, and James James, was sold to Joseph H. Snead for $1,609.50.

PHILLIPS VS. BLUNT'S EXORS &C., 1873 (49)

Francis Blunt's Will

BLUNT, FRANCIS. "I, Francis Blunt of the County of Hanover, do make this my last will and Testament in manner and form following, viz: 1st. I loan to my wife Elizabeth D. Blunt for and during her natural life the use of the west room in my dwelling house. Also my negro woman Betsey, One Choice Cow, Two best feather beds, bedsteads and furniture one bureau, one large chest, one press, six chairs, two walnut tables and as much of my other furniture as may be necessary for her convenience. 2nd. I give to my son Charles W. Blunt my negro man named John and my negro boy named Boston to him and his heirs forever. 3rd. I give to my son John H. Blunt the tract of land whereon I now reside containing by estimation two hundred and thirty-five acres be the same more or less, and at the death of my said wife, I give to my said son John H. Blunt, Betsey and her future increase from this time to him and his heirs. 4th. I give to my daughter Martha Ann Parr my negro boy named Joe and my negro girl named Ella and the future increase of said girl to her and her heirs. 5th. I loan to my daughter Ellen M. Phillips for an during her natural life my negro girl Bettie, And at the death of my said daughter my will is that the slaves so loaned her, and the future increase of said girl Bettie be equally divided among the children that she now has and those that she may hereafter have to them and their heirs. 6th. I give to my daughter Sarah F. Jones my negro boy named William and my negro girl named Amy and the future increase of said girl Amy to her and her heirs. 7th. I give to my five Grand-children, to wit Elizabeth A. Tiller, Mary E. Bumpass, Frances L. Bumpass, John S. Bumpass, and Francis B. Bumpass, children of Jesse F. Bumpass, my negro woman Mary and her two children Sam and Mary, to them and their heirs. 8th. I give to my son in law Jesse Bumpass my interest in a bond executed by him (and I believe I am security) to H. H. Wingfield appointed a receiver to rent out the mills owned by Thomas Perrin and myself. 9th. I give to my Grand daughter Elizabeth F. Phillips my silver tea spoons. To my daughter Martha Ann Parr's oldest daughter my silver kettle spoons. To my grandson Francis B. Bumpass my shot gun, and to my Grandson William F. Blunt my silver watch - to them and their heirs. 10th. It is my will and desire that all the property that I may own at the time of my death not heretofore disposed of, both real and personal be sold by my executors hereinafter named either privately or publicly as they may deem best, and the money arising from such sales, as also all the money that I may have , or may be owing to me at the time of my death be put out on interest. The interest of which to go to the comfortable support of my said wife during her life. 11th. After the death of my said wife my will is that all the money that may be on hand, or owing my estate, and the furniture and stock loaned her be equally divided among my five children, Charles W. Blunt, John H. Blunt, Martha Ann Parr, Ellen M. Phillips and Sarah F. Jones, to them and their heirs. 12th. I do appoint my friend William W. Mallory and my son John H. Blunt Trustees for Ellen M. Phillips, and her children. Lastly. I do appoint my friends Richard B. Hendrick, William W. Mallory and my son John H. Blunt executors to this my last will and testament revoking all others heretofore made or subscribed by me. In witness whereof I have hereunto set my hand and affixed my seal this first day of July 1851."

Signed and sealed in presence of us: Francis Blunt (Seal)
    William D. Winston, Joseph F. Hughes.

At a Court of Monthly Session held for Hanover County at the Courthouse on Tuesday the 26 of August 1851. This last will and testament of Francis Blunt, dec'd, was proved by the oaths of Wm. D. Winston and Joseph F. Hughes the witnesses thereto and is ordered to be recorded.
    Teste, Wm. O. Winston, C.H.C.   A Copy, Teste, Wm. O. Winston, C.H.C.

FRANCIS BLUNT, of Hanover, died 9 July 1851. Will dated 1 July 1851, proved 26 Aug. 1851 by the witnesses. Wm. W. Mallory and John H. Blunt qualified as Executors. Estate valued at $8,000. Survived by widow, Elizabeth D. Blunt who died circa 1 Oct. 1853. In this suit, only issue surviving in 1873 were involved, and no grandchildren stated, though several were mentioned in his will. Apparent issue:

1. CHARLES W. BLUNT.
2. JOHN H. BLUNT.
3. MARTHA ANN, wife or widow of a Mr. Parr.

4. ELLEN M., wife of William Phillips, and have issue perhaps among others:
    1. ELIZABETH F. PHILLIPS.
5. SARAH F., wife of Patrick H. Jones of Louisa, Va., who was born 23 Jan. 1818.
6. DAUGHTER, dec'd (mentioned in will) who married Jesse Bumpass, and left issue:
    1. ELIZABETH A TILLER (perhaps married)
    2. MARY E. BUMPASS.
    3. FRANCES L. BUMPASS.
    4. JOHN S. BUMPASS.
    5. FRANCIS B. BUMPASS.

MAHALA'S EXOR. VS. BOWE &C., 1832 (25)
PERRIN & WIFE VS. BOWE & OTHERS, 1837 (31)
BOWE VS. BOWE, 1837 (3)
BOWE'S ADMR. VS. WINSTON'S EXECUTOR & OTHERS, 1867 (59)

Nathaniel Bowe's Will

BOWE, NATHANIEL. "In the name of God amen, I, Nathaniel Bowe of the County of Hanover being of sound and disposing mind and memory do hereby make and declare this be my last will and testament hereby revoking all others by me heretofore made. Imprimis. I give and bequeath unto my wife Susanna Bowe one-third of my whole estate real & personal, the real estate to be allotted her so as to embrace the dwelling and other necessary out houses thereto attached. This bequest however is to terminate with the natural life of the said Susanna. Item. It is my will that the balance of my estate real & personal be divided into eleven equal parts, the real estate as conveniently as may be, having regard to its value, one equal part of my said estate real and personal I give and devise in trust to Benjamin Wingfield, Esqr. for the sole and exclusive benefit of my daughter Susanna N. Perrin wife of Samuel Perrin and her children which she now has or may hereafter have by her marriage with the said Perrin. And I hereby invest the said Trustee with power to sell or exchange any of the said property as he may think conducive to the interest of the said Susanna N. Perrin and her children. This trust however is to terminate with the death of the said Saml Perrin when the property hereby bequeath and devised shall become the absolute estate in fee simple of the said Susanna N. Perrin, or of her children should the said Susanna have departed this life. Item. I give and devise one other equal part of my estate real & personal to my daughter Polly Cross wife of Oliver T. Cross to her and her heirs forever. Item. I give and devise one other equal part of my estate real & personal to my daughter Martha Davis wife of Nathaniel Davis to her and her heirs forever. Item. I give and devise one other equal part of my estate real & personal to my daughter Nancy Yarbrough wife of Jesse Yarbrough to her and her heirs forever. Item. I give and devise to my daughter Sophia Wingfield wife of Hudson M. Wingfield one other equal part of my estate real & personal to her and her heirs forever. Item. I give and devise unto my daughter Elizabeth Green wife of John B. Green one other equal part of my estate real and personal to her and her heirs forever. Item. I give and devise one other equal part of my estate real and personal to my daughter Amanda Goddin wife of Thomas H. Goddin to her and her heirs forever. Item. I give and devise one other equal part of my estate real & personal to my daughter Harriett Bowe to her & her heirs forever. Item. I give and devise to my daughter Emily R. Bowe one other equal part of my estate real and personal to her and her heirs forever. I give and devise unto my son Nathaniel F. Bowe one other equal part of my estate real & personal to him and his heirs forever. Item. I give and devise unto my son Hector Bowe one other equal part of my estate real & personal to him and his heirs forever. Item. It is my will that that part of my estate left my wife during her life shall at her death in like manner be divided into eleven equal parts one part whereof I give and devise in trust to Benjamin Wingfield Esq. for the sole and exclusive use and benefit of my daughter Susanna N. Perrin wife of Saml Perrin and her children, upon the same limitations and conditions as are contained in the second clause of this my will - the residue I give and devise in equal parts to such of my children as may then be alive or to the children of those who may have died. Item. I hereby constitute and appoint my sons Nathaniel Fleming Bowe and Hector Bowe Executors to this my last will. In testimony whereof I, Nathaniel Bowe have hereunto set my hand & seal this 21st day of Novr. 1829."

Witnesses: James King and German R. Glenn.   Nath¹ Bowe (Seal)

At a Court of Quarterly Session held for Hanover County at the Courthouse on Friday the 26th of February 1830. This last will and testament of Nathaniel Bowe dec'd was proved by the oaths of James King and German R. Glenn the witnesses thereto & is ordered to be recorded.
   Teste, Philip B. Winston, C.H.C.   A Copy, Teste, Philip B. Winston C.H.C.

NATHANIEL BOWE. dec'd. Will dated 21 November 1829, proved 26 Feb. 1830 by witnesses. Nathaniel F. Bowe, Executor. Testator, jointly with his brother, William Bowe, dec'd were administrators of their brother John Bowe, dec'd, who was one of the Securities of John Ragland, Executor of Pettus Ragland, dec'd, and the said John Ragland has departed this state. Fendall Ragland was Executor of Pettus Regland circa 1827. Nathaniel Bowe, who was sometime called "Captain" died "about the last of December 1829." He left "a considerable real and personal estate." The division of his slaves was made by Reuben Meredith, Felix Winston, and William W. Michie. Survived by his widow, Susanna, and by many children and grand-children.

1. NATHANIEL FLEMING BOWE, Executor of his father's Estate. He was in Petersburg, Va.
   in 1836. During the years 1832 and 1833,
   in partnership with his brother, Hector,
   in the tobacco manufacturing business, conducted in Nathaniel F. Bowe's name, in the
   City of Richmond, Va.

2. HECTOR BOWE, born in Hanover 29 Nov. 1811,
   died 8 Feb. 1858, "Married on Thursday the
   26th of March 1835 by the Rev. James B.
   Taylor, Hector Bowe to Mary W. Ellis, both
   of Hanover County." He was in Petersburg,
   Va. in 1835, and had been in partnership
   with his brother, Nathaniel F., in the
   tobacco manufacturing business, 1832 and
   1833 in Richmond, Va. Issue:

   1. ROBERT BRUCE BOWE, born 1 March 1836 in
      Petersburg, Va.
   2. AMANDA STUART, born 25 Nov. 1837 in Han-
      over, married John F. Cross.
   3. VIRGINIA SELDEN, born 26 May 1840 in
      Hanover, married William M. Wingfield.
   4. NATHANIEL WOODSON BOWE, born 4 Nov.1842
      in Hanover.
   5. EMILY RUSHBROOK BOWE, born 27 Feb. 1849.
   6. MARY ANN BOWE, born 22 August 1851.
   7. ALICE MAUDE BOWE, born 18 July 1856.
   8. BOLER W. BOWE.

3. SUSAN N., wife of Samuel Perrin. Benjamin
   Wingfield, Trustee. Children:

   1. ARIADNE B. PERRIN.
   2. EUGENIA N. PERRIN.

4. POLLY V., in 1837 widow of Oliver T. Cross,
   his Administrator and Guardian of her children:

   1. ARAMINTA CROSS.
   2. MARTHA B. CROSS.
   3. MARY A. CROSS.
   4. JOHN F. CROSS.
   5. FRANCES CROSS
   6. CHARLES P. CROSS.

5. ELIZABETH, wife of John B. Green.

6. SOPHIA D., wife of Hudson M. Wingfield.

7. NANCY, wife of Jesse G. Yarbrough.

8. AMANDA, died prior to her father, survived
   by her husband, Thomas H. Goddin, Sr., who
   is Guardian of their children: Infants.

   1. MORTIMER GODDIN.
   2. THOMAS H. GODDIN, "the younger"

9. EMILY R., dec'd, survived by husband Archibald B. Timberlake, who is Guardian of
   their infant children:

   1. DAVID ALGERON TIMBERLAKE.
   2. JOHN H. TIMBERLAKE.

10. MARTHA, wife of Nathaniel Davis.

11. HARRIET, wife of John. J. Wingfield, in
    1836, of Albemarle County.

John Bowe's Will

BOWE, JOHN. "Hanover 20th Augt. 1809. Cap.
John W. Ellis. D⁻ Sir. I am about starting
down the Country and never having made a
will & should anything happen to prevent my
making one, my wish and desire is that William
the son of Nancy Tinsley shall be entitled to
fifty Virginia bank shares standing in my name
on the books of the bank. The first dividen̲t
arising from the s⁰. fifty share I wish given to
Nancy Tinsley, the next four dividen̲ts I wish
my admr. to lay out in the purchase, schooling,
clothing & having Emancipated a mulatto girl
named Mahala now the property of Col. Thomas
Tinsley. The two next I wish laid out in schooling and clothing a mulatto girl that I purchased of Mrs. Bowler & emancipated her in Hanover
Court the eighth, tenth & twelvth, the same as
the first dividen̲t provided she is living at
the time of their becoming due, the ninth, eleventh & thirteen to be equally divided between
the two mulatto girls before mentioned. The
bal̲lance of the dividen̲ts & the interest of the
money arising from said shars I wish applied towards clothing schooling & boarding William the
son of Nancy Tinsley or so much thereof as shall
be necessary. If the said William should die before he gets married or shall arrive to the age
of twenty one or die without an heir The fifty
shares or the money arrising from them shall be
divided amongst my relations agreeable to law
as all the rest of my estate will of course be.
             Yours respectfully,
                     John Bowe."
"P. S.
   I wish Nath Bowe, Benj. Brand of Hanover Town
or yourself my be appointd Guardian to the boy
Wm.   J. Bowe."

At a Court of Monthly Session held for Hanover
County at the Courthouse on Wednesday the 27th
of December 1809. This writing purporting to
be the last will & testament of John Bowe,
deceased was offered for proof by John W. Ellis
whereupon the said John W. Ellis, Samuel Richardson were sworn & examined & the said John W.
Ellis declares that the deceased in his lifetime delivered the said writing to him sealed &
informed him that it was his will & the said
Ellis further declares that he verily believes
that the same was wholly written & signed by
him the said deceased. And the Court being
well acquainted with the handwriting of the
said deceased and believing that the said

writing was wholly written and signed by him do
thereupon order the same to be recorded as his
last will and testament.
     Teste, William Pollard C.H.C.
     A Copy, Teste, Philip B. Winston C.H.C.

William Bowe's Will

BOWE, WILLIAM. "I, William Bowe of the Coun
ty of Hanover do constitute this my will.
I give Polly the daughter of Susanna Jones,
a negro girl called Mary extra. I give William
the son of the said Susanna two hundred dollars
for the purpose of assisting him in his schooling, also extra. I lend to Susanna Jones a
negro man called Dick, a cow & my house yard &
garden where I now live with the privilege of
getting wood and fruit. I now give my land on
Totopomoy Creek together with the land I got by
my brother John and a tract called Butlers to
be equally divided among Susanna Jones six children known and called by the following names,
to wit, Fredric, Salley, Polley, Nancy, Albert
and William. I then give the ballance of my estate of every description to be equally divided
among the before mentioned six xhildren. What I
lent Susanna Jones at her death is to be for
her children. I appoint Samuel Jones of Richmond and Henry W. Timberlake of Hanover my Executors to execute this my last will. Given under my hand and seal this 17th day of June in
the year of our Lord one thousand eight hundred
and sixteen."
                              William Bowe (LS)
Signed sealed acknowledged
and delivered in the presence of
     Chapman Timberlake, Benjamin A. Timberlake,
     Elisha Jones.

At a Court of Monthly Session held for Hanover
County at the Courthouse on Wednesday the 28th
of August 1816. This last will and Testament
of William Bowe dec'd was proved by the oath of
Benjamin A. Timberlake one of the witnesses
thereto. And at a Court of Quarterly Session
held for the said County at the Courthouse Wednesday the 23rd of October next following, the
said will was further proved by the oath of
Elisha Jones another of the witnesses thereto,
and is ordered to be recorded.
     Teste, William Pollard, C.H.C.
     A Copy, Teste, Philip B. Winston, C.H.C.

Included in these suits:

WINSTON, WILLIAM O., of Hanover County, died
on 15 March 1862, survived by his widow,
Sarah A. Winston, and the following children,
the last five of which are infants in 1867:

1. BETTY B., wife of Thomas L. Rosser.
2. PHILIP B. WINSTON.

3. SALLY M. WINSTON.
4. FENDALL G. WINSTON.
5. FANNY A. WINSTON.
6. WILLIAM O. WINSTON.
7.   BICKERTON L. WINSTON.

Mahala's Will

MAHALA. "In the name of God amen, I, Mahala a
free woman of color of the County of Hanover
and parish of Saint Paul being in sound mind
and memory do make and ordain this to be my
last will and testament hereby revoking all former wills. Imprimis. It is my will and desire
that my children that I purchased of the estate
of Colo. Thomas Tinsley deceased shall be free
& all the children that I may have hereafter
together with those I had previous to my emanci-
pation shall participate equally in whatever I
may died possessed of either in money, stock or
other personal property or real estate. It is
my wish that my daughter Clara be bound to her
former Mistress, Susanna Tinsley until she arrives at the age of twenty-one or as long as
the said Susanna Tinsley may live. In witness
whereof I have hereunto set my hand & affixed
my seal this 16th day of February 1824."
                                       her
Signed sealed in presence   Mahala +
of Susanna Tinsley   mark
     Saml. Tinsley.

Codicil to this my last will. I hereby constitute and appoint Thomas G. Tinsley Executor to
this my last will. In witness whereof I have
hereunto set my hand and affixed my seal this
17th day of February 1824."
                                       her
                                 Mahala +
Signed sealed & acknowledged   mark
in presence of Susanna Tinsley
     Saml Tinsley.

At a Circuit Court of Law & Chancery, continued
& held for Hanover County at the Courthouse, on
Wednesday the 28th of September 1831. This
last will and testament of Mahala a free woman
of colour & the codicil thereafter written were
offered for proof by Thomas G. Tinsley the
Executor in the said Codicil named, and were
proved by the oaths of Susanna Tinsley & Samuel
Tinsley the witnesses thereto and are ordered
to be recorded.
     Teste, Philip B. Winston, C.C.
     A Copy, Teste, Philip B. Winston, C.C.

RANDOM NOTES:
     Wm. W. Mallory died in 1877. Was in Rappahan-
nock County 1874, in Louisa 1875 "very feeble
and does not expect to again attend Hanover
Court." Wm. D. Winston dec'd in 1873. George W.
Doswell, rep. James Winston, dec'd, Edmund Winston and A. M. Morris, representatives.
     --from Berkeley Suits.

BOWLES VS. BOWLES' ADMR. & OTHERS, 1833 (3)

Thomas Bowles' Will

BOWLES, THOMAS. "I, Thomas Bowles do make this my last will and testament: To wit - My first request is that all my just and lawful debts be paid. The ballance of my estate I give in trust to my two sisters Mary and Chrischania so that they may receive the yearly profits thereof. To them and their heirs forever But if either shall die without lawful issue, in that case my intention is that all shal go to the survivor. In the event of both's dying without lawful issue my intention is that my estate shall go to my brothers Davy, Isaac and Iray and my half sister Emelia equally in the manner above directed. My will and desire further is that if either shall have lawful issue in that case she or he shall have her or his part free from trust in the manner first above written. John Jones and Oliver T. Cross I leave my executors. "

Thomas Bowles
8 June 1817

At a Court of Quarterly Session held for Hanover County, at the Courthouse on Wednesday the 26th of July 1820. This writing purporting to be the last will and testament of Thomas Bowles, dec'd was offered to proof by Peter Bowles and the said Peter Bowles and Oliver T. Cross and John Jones being sworn and examined, declare that they are well acquainted with the handwriting of the said deceased, and verily believe that the said Will was wholly written and signed by him whereupon the same is ordered to be recorded. And John Jones and Oliver T. Cross the executors therein named in open Court relinquished their right of Executorship thereto. Whereupon on the motion of Peter Bowles a certificate is granted him for obtaining Letters of Administration on the estate of the said dec'd, with this his said will annexed, he having performed what the law in such cases require.

Teste, William Pollard, C.H.C.

A Copy, Teste, Benjª Pollard, Jr., D.C.H.C.

Elizabeth Bowles' Nuncupative Will

BOWLES, ELIZABETH. "26 December 1804. Henry Perrin and Edmund Tyler were sworn in Court on the motion of Peter Bowles guardian of Christiana Bowles, to prove the nuncupative will of Elizabeth Bowles dec'd, who whereupon declared that the said deceased in their presence, three of four days before her death, which happened some time in November last, devised her wearing apparel to her three sisters Polly, Christiana and Emela Bowles and the residue of her estate after the payments of her debts, she devised to the said Christiana and called upon them to take notice that that was her last will

and testament."

A Copy, Teste, Tho. Pollard, D.C.H.C.

BOWLES, THOMAS, of Hanover, died intestate circa 1800, possessed of a considerable personal estate. Survived by his widow, Jemima, who was his Administrator. She is since deceased and Peter Bowles is her Admr., and the Admr. of Thomas Bowles. Thomas and Jemima left issue; together with issue of former marriage:

1. THOMAS BOWLES, JR., dec'd. Will probated 26 July 1820.
2. PETER BOWLES.
3. *AMELIA H., in 1833 wife of Ara P. Gardner.
4. ISAAC BOWLES.
5. CHRISTIANA, in 1833 wife of Martin Woodworth.
6. POLLY BOWLES, living in Henrico in 1833.
7. BETSEY BOWLES, died unmarried, intestate.
8. DAVID BOWLES, in 1833 living in Fluvanna County.
9. IRA S. BOWLES.

*Half sister to Thomas Bowles, Jr.

Others Mentioned: John Shore, Commissioner.

BLACKBURN & WIFE VS. ANDERSON, 1858 (59)

BOWLES, WILLIAM. of Hanover, died intestate some years ago. Estate included two tracts of land - 23 2/3 acres adjoining Thomas Cocke (formerly Joseph Bowles) James Stone and others; and 21 acres on Stony Run, adjoining Wm. Nelson, Waldrop, and others. Survived by his widow, Susan Bowles, now deceased, and issue:

1. JAMES R. BOWLES, who sold his interest in land circa 1850 to William Anderson, Jr.
2. MARY A BOWLES, who sold her interest in land circa 1850 to William Anderson, Jr.
3. WILLIAM E. BOWLES, dec'd, survived by his widow, Mary Ann, now wife of Washington G. Blackburn, and one daughter:
   1. JANE EDMONIA BOWLES.

SOUTHWORTH VS. BROOKS' ADMR &C., 1838 (39)

BROOKS, NANCY, of Hanover, died intestate. She was the widow of John Brooks. Her Administrator in 1838 is Anderson Bowles, the Sheriff of Hanover County. Survived by following issue:

1. ELIZABETH, wife of James B. Southworth.
2. JOHN BROOKS, of Henrico.
3. JAMES BROOKS, of Henrico or Chesterfield.
4. WILLIAM BROOKS, of Henrico.
5. MARIA BROOKS, infant, Anson Richards, Gdn.
6. THOMAS BROOKS, of Campbell County.
7. HENRY A. BROOKS, of age 2 Oct. 1841.

Mentioned: Thos. Baker of near Chesterfield.

DUKE VS. BURNLEY, 1811 (12) - DUKE'S ADMR. VS. BURNLEY, 1823 (16)
BURNLEY VS. BURNLEY, 1837 (4)

John Burnley's Will (Abstract)

BURNLEY, JOHN, of "Hanover County, York river, Virginia." Will dated London, England, 26 Oct. 1778. Real and personal property to be sold. To brother Zachariah Burnley Six Hundred Lbs. Virginia Currency. Executors to put Six Hundred Lbs. Virginia Currency for each of sisters, Elizabeth Duke, Keziah Duke, and Ann, wife of Thomas Littlepage, and their heirs, "to interest, and the interest arising to be annually paid to my Sisters, and their heirs." To the three sons, David, James. and William Meriwether, "sons of my Sister Judith, late wife of James Meriwether, Four Hundred & Fifty Pounds to be equally divided between them, or if any are dead, to the survivors or survivor." To apprentice George Ellsworth "one Hundred Pounds currency, if he be living, otherwise the amount to be put to interest for the benefit of the poor children of Hanover county." Residue of estate to brothers Hardin and Richard Burnley, who are designated Executors. Witnesses: Samuel Gist, Aiskew Birkett, and Henry Rogers. (Extracted by Messrs. Crispagny & Greene, proctors in Doctors Commons.)

"Frederick by divine providence Archbishop of Canterbury, primate of all England and Metropolitan do by these presents make known to all men that on the Sixteenth day of February in the year of our Lord one thousand seven hundred and eighty at London before the right Worshippul Peter Calvert Doctor of Laws, master Keeper or Commissary of our Prerogative Court of Canterbury Lawfully constituted, the last will and Testament of John Burnley late of Hanover County York river in the providence of Virginia in North America Deceased, hereunto annexed, was proved, approved and Registered; the said Deceased having whilst living and at the time of his death, Goods, Chattels, or Credits in divers dioceses or Jurisdiction by reason whereof the proving and registering the said Will, and the Granting administration of all and singular the Goods, Chattels and Credits and also the auditing, allowing and final discharging the accounts thereof are well known to appertain only and wholly to us and not to an inferior Judge: and that administration of all and singular the Goods, Chattels and Credits of the said deceased and anyway concerning his will was granted to Hardin Burnley the Brother of the said deceased and one of the Executors named in the said will, he having been already sworn by Commission will and faithfully to administer the same and to make a true and perfect Inventory of all and Singular the said Goods, Chattels and Credits and to exhibit the same into the Registry of our said Court on or before the last day of August next ensuing, and also to render a just and true account thereof, power reserved of making the like Grant to Richard Burnley the Brother also of the said Deceased an other Executor named in the said will, when he shall apply for the same. Given at the time and place above written and in the twelfth year of our Translation". Henry Stevens, Geo. Gostling, Jr., Jno. Greene, Duputy Register.

"At a Court continued and held for Hanover County on Saturday the 5th day of March, 1785. This transcript of the last Will and Testament of John Burnley, deceased, with the Probat thereon, certified under the hands of Henry Stevens, George Gostling, Junr., and John Greene Deputy Register of the prerogative Court of Canterbury under the proper Seals of Office in the Said Court and dul stamped according to the Laws of Great Britian, were produced in Court and are ordered to be recorded". Teste: William Pollard, Jr., C.H.C. A Copy, Teste, Thomas Rogers, D. C. H. C.

CAPTAIN HARDIN BURNLEY, the first of the name in these suits, acquired by deed 17 May 1753 recorded in the General Court, an estate called "To Ink" of 1000 acres from James Skelton, adjoining his son Meriwether Skelton, on Pamunkey River at mouth of Mangohick Creek, St. David's Parish, King William County. James Burnley was overseer for Captain Hardin Burnley and his son John during the years 1764, 65 and 66, when the land was processioned by James Beadles and Thos. Shepherd, Captain Francis Smith being present. Captain Burnley died prior to 1778 when "ToInk" had passed to John. In the Executor's deed 1783 disposing of this property, it is stated that: "Richard Burnley was John's eldest brother of the whole blood." Capt. Burnley's issue follows:

JOHN BURNLEY. Will dated London, 26 Oct. 1778, probated in Prerogative Court of Canterbury 16 Feb. 1780; in Hanover County, 5 March, 1785. Similar, earlier will dated 10 July, 1771, probated in Hanover, 4 Nov. 1779. Witnesses: John Wingfield, William and Daniel Clarke, Richard Dabney. Hardin Burnley qualified in Great Britain, Richard Burnley in Virginia, as Executors. The latter dying soon afterward, Zachariah Burnley appointed Administrator. He was possessed of a large estate, part in Great Britain, and a considerable part in this Commonwealth. Was associated with Hardin and Richard Burnley, and John Wingfield in the mercantile business. It is stated that John Burnley "died at sea." His estate "To Ink" was sold to Benjamin Temple.

RICHARD BURNLEY, Merchant of Hanover County, "eldest brother of the whole blood, and heir at law of John Burnley, deceased." Qualified as Executor of his brother's estate, but died before the Estate could be administered and prior to 4 Sept. 1783. Survived by his widow, Eliza Swann Burnley, his Administrator 1785 in Orange County. His issue, if any, were not involved in these suits.

HARDIN BURNLEY. Qualified as Executor of his brother's Estate in Great Britain. On 4 Sept. 1783 described as "merchant of Hanover County, and heir at law of John Burnley,dec'd." In 1798 "a resident in and subject of the King of Great Britain . . that Edmund Littlepage of this Commonwealth had effects in his hands belonging to the said Hardin Burnley." He purchased "To Ink" privately for cash on the day of its advertised public sale, but retired in favor of Col. Temple.

JOHN COCKE deposed 14 March, 1798 before Hay Battaile and David Coleman, Justices of Caroline County: "Was present at the sale of John Burnley, dec'd in King William County on 29 July, 1802, when the land advertised as a Public Sale was sold by Zachariah Burnley to Hardin Burnley, privately for 2000 Lbs. to which many of the prospective buyers protested. Colo. Temple and Colo. Hickman and many others swore that Hardin Burnley was a dam'd Tory and had no right to hold land in this Country and that he should not stay on the place, and was actually driven off the land. Zachariah Burnley was told he should not have sold the land privately, replied: Why Gentlemen, he bought it to secure a debt due him from the Estate of John Burnley, but that anyone might have it at the same price, upon which Colo. Temple agreed to take it." The deponent further saith that he lived upon the land adjoining the said tract for several years before.

John and Richard Burnley had executed a bond to Hardin Burnley, Jr., on 5 Nov. 1773, in the sum of 2463.17.5 Lbs that they would pay unto Hardin Burnley 1231.18.10 Lbs. Henry Punter, and James Landrum were witnesses to this paper.

"Richard K. Tyler personally appeared before me, William Foushee, a magistrate of Henrico County and made oath that Hardin Burnley, Executor of John Burnley, dec'd is not an inhabitant of the State of Virginia. 31 May, 1798."

On 25 April, 1816, he is again described as of the Kingdom of Great Britain. Hardin Burnley,Jr. apparently remained there.

COLONEL ZACHARIAH[2] BURNLEY. Qualified 6 June, 1782 as Administrator of John Burnley, dec'd with John Wingfield and Samuel Redd,Securities. Owned land in Hanover and Orange Counties, the latter he sold circa 1800 to Thomas Macon, formerly of Macon Mill, Madison County, and went to live with Robert and Archibald Wilson, bachelors of the adjoining place, across the road from Reuben[3] Burnley's. Shortly afterward, not being in good health, and "upwards of 70 years of age" he removed to his son Hardin's home in Hanover, where he died intestate during the Summer of 1800. He possessed no real estate at the time of his death. Hardin[3] qualified as Administrator in Hanover, and William D. Taylor, on 26 Jan. 1820, qualified as such in Orange County. Of his issue, only three sons are mentioned: Hardin[3], Reuben[3], and James[3], as follows:

HARDIN[3] BURNLEY lived at "Bear Island" Hanover, described as being in "the Forks" and about a mile and a half from the farm of Thos. Price, Sr. He died in 1809 intestate. Administrators being at various times: John L.Swann,Sheriff; John M. Shepherd, Henry Pendleton and John H. Steger. Survived by his widow, Mary B. who married Henry Pendleton in 1815. He died 1823 and was the Testator of Edmund and Joseph W. Pendleton, who, with Philip B. Winston, were his Executors. His surviving issue were: Hardinia[4], Mary[4], Edwin[4], Judith[4], Hardin[4], Elizabeth[4], and Hardinia M[4] , [the younger].

HARDINIA[4] BURNLEY, wife of Dr. James Maury Morris on 28 Jan. 1824. On 1 Nov. 1819, Wm. D. Taylor and wife executed a Deed of Trust to Henry Robinson and Richard Morris, Trustees for the benefit of Dr. Morris. In 1848 he is dead, William Overton and Jacquelin P. Taylor, Executors.

MARY[4] BURNLEY, married Dr. Thomas J. Meaux, prior to January 1819. In 1834 they have a daughter, probably among others: Ann[5] Meaux.

EDWIN[4] BURNLEY, in 1822, was allotted eleven slaves from his father's Estate. Under age in 1823. One of the Executors of Hardinia M[4] Burnley's Estate in 1837.

JUDITH[4] BURNLEY, wife of John H. Steger in 1822, when she was allotted nine slaves,her share in her father's Estate. On 26 Oct.'27 John H. Steger qualified as Administrator of Hardin[3] Burnley's Estate, with Thomas J. Meaux and Hardin Burnley, Jr., Securities. In 1828 Steger had removed to Cumberland County, Va., where he was one of the Justices of the Peace.

HARDIN[4] BURNLEY, JR., "Owner of one-sixth of a tract of land called 'Bear Island'" in Hanover County, on which he borrowed of his sister, Hardinia M.,1832 and moved to Miss.

ELIZABETH[4] BURNLEY, in 1834 was the wife of a Gwathmey, probably Dr. William Gwathmey. Her youngest daughter was named Hardinia Morris Gwathmey. Names of other issue not given.

HARDINIA M[4] BURNLEY, "the younger." Her will dated St. Augustine, Fla., 21 Feb. 1834 was probated in Hanover Co., 23 June, 1835. The witnesses, Charles J. Richards and Eliza L. Van Lew proved it. She appointed Mr. John H. Steger and brother Edwin Burnley her Executors. To "my beloved mother, Mary B. Pendleton, my lands, slaves and property of every description, subject to the direction and management of Mr. John H. Steger." At the death of her mother, "desires slaves to be manumitted, and sent to Liberia on the coast of Africa furnished with such clothes and comforts for the voyage, and for their introduction to said place, but should any of them prefer to remain in slavery at home they are at liberty to do so." Directs that her mother pay Dr. William Gwathmey within four years, Five Hundred Dollars "as a compensation for his kind attention to me at this and other times." To sister Elizabeth's youngest daughter, Hardinia Morris Gwathmey she gives her watch. To niece, Ann Meaux, she gives her piano forte.

REUBEN[3] BURNLEY, of Orange County. Justice of the Peace on 8 March, 1798.

JAMES[3] BURNLEY. Overseer of "To Ink" the estate in King William County of Captain Hardin and John Burnley, for three years, 1764,- 65,-66. Thereafter lived mostly on his father's lands in Hanover and Orange Counties.

ELIZABETH[2] BURNLEY, widow of [*   ] Duke 1771. Legatee of her brother, John Burnley: "It is my will and desire that my Executors put Six hundred pounds Virginia Currency to Interest, and the Interest arising to be annually paid unto my Sister Elizabeth Duke, and after her decease, it is my will that the said Six Hundred pounds to be equally divided betwixt her, the said Elizabeth's then surviving Children." She died intestate prior to 15 April, 1820. Richard Keeling Tyler was her Administrator. In 1852, Fleming Terrell, the Sheriff of Caroline, administered her Estate. Survived by the following issue: Burnley[3], Ann[3], Elizabeth[3], Mary[3], and Patsey[3].

BURNLEY[3] DUKE. Died circa 1846, when Francis Blunt, Sheriff, Hanover County, his Administrator. Blunt appears to have died shortly thereafter, for in 1852, Henry Curtis, then Sheriff, is the Administrator.

———
*Bill of 1793, name "John" is faintly written.

ANN[3] DUKE, was the wife of William Smith 1811. In 1846, survived him, but died in the same year. Patrick Michie, Sheriff of Louisa Co., her Administrator.

ELIZABETH[3] DUKE, wife of Reuben Smith of Louisa prior to 1811. He died circa Nov. 1823, and she was dead 1851, when Patrick Michie, Sheriff of Louisa Co., her Administrator.

MARY[3] DUKE, wife of Richard Keeling Tyler in 1811. He was dead 15 Aug. 1832, when Caroline County Court ordered that the Estate of Richard K. Tyler, dec'd, administered by John Taliaferro, late Sheriff, be committed to Fleming Terrell, Sheriff for administration. Order signed by John L. Pendleton. In 1846 Mary Tyler is also dead, and Pichegrue Woolfolk, Sheriff of Caroline, her Administrator.

PATSEY[3] DUKE, married after 1813 and prior to 1823, Ambrose Madison. Both alive in 1851.

KESIAH[2] DUKE. Legatee of her brother John Burnley: "It is my will and desire that my Executors put Six hundred pounds Virginia currency to Interest and the Interest arising to be annually paid to my Sister Keziah Duke and after her decease it is my will that the said Six hundred pounds be equally divided betwixt her the said Keziah Duke's then surviving Children." No mention of Mr. Duke, who was dead, apparently, before 1771. She married Samuel Redd prior to 4 Nov. 1791. In 1791 William Redd and Samuel Temple were his Executors. She died circa November 1823, when Hardin Duke was her Administrator. In 1852, Patrick Michie, Sheriff, Louisa Co., was her Administrator. The issue, by Mr. Duke only: Hardin[3], Cleviers[3], James[3], and Amy Dyer[3].

HARDIN[3] DUKE. Administrator of his mother's Estate from 1823 to 1846 and later. Administrator of Cleviers Duke's Estate in 1843. In 1851, is deceased, and Garland Duke is "his personal representative."

CLEVIERS[3] DUKE. Died circa Nov. 1823, Richard Duke, Sheriff of Albemarle County, Administrator. In 1850 Estate committed to Thomas Brown, Sheriff of Albemarle.

JAMES[3] DUKE. Died shortly before 1846, Hardin Duke, his Administrator. He had disposed of a part of his interest in Burnley's Estate on 27 May, 1826, to Wm. Dabney, recorded in Spotsylvania County, who assigned to Festus Dickinson "who died since April, 1829, and his Executors, Samuel C. Dickinson and Woodson Wright, qualified in Caroline County.

AMY DYER[3] DUKE, married prior to 15 Feb. 1813 Hugh Pettus, and died circa Nov. 1823.

ANN[2] BURNLEY. Legatee of her brother John Burnley: "It is my will and desire that my Executors put Six hundred pounds Virginia Currency to Interest and the Interest arising to be annually paid unto my Sister Ann Littlepage wife of Thomas Littlepage, and after her decease it is my will and Desire that the said Six Hundred pounds to be equally divided betwixt her the said Ann Littlepage's then Surviving Children." She died prior to 1813, James B. Littlepage her Administrator. No further mention of her husband. Their issue were: Thomas[3], Mary[3], James B[3], John B[3], Frances[3], Ann K[3], Edmund[3], Hardin[3], Burnley[3], and Catherine[3].

THOMAS[3] LITTLEPAGE. Deceased in 1813. Isaac Quarles, Administrator. Widow, Sarah Coleman Littlepage, alive in 1852. Issue as of 1813:

1. ISAAC B[4] LITTLEPAGE.
2. SARAH C[4] LITTLEPAGE, under age in 1813.
3. THOMAS[4] LITTLEPAGE,under age in 1813,and deceased on 26 Feb. 1817, Sarah C. Littlepage, Administrator in King William County. Isaac and John S. Quarles, her Securities. In 1823 his Administrator was Philip Aylett, Sheriff of King William County.

MARY[3] LITTLEPAGE, wife of James R. Pannill in 1813. In 1846: "James R. Pannill is dead, leaving his wife surviving him, and who has since died, and Thomas Starke is her Administrator."

JAMES B[3] LITTLEPAGE. Died before 1826,Mary C. Littlepage, Administrator. Ambrose Edwards, Edmund Littlepage, and Fendall Gregory were her Securities. On 26 Aug. 1826, James C. Edwards qualified as Administrator, and in 1846 he is dead and Telemachus B.Littlepage is the Administrator.

JOHN B[3] LITTLEPAGE. Alive in 1813, died prior to 1846, when Richard Wilroy, the Sheriff of King William County is his Administrator.

FRANCES[3](FANNY) LITTLEPAGE,wife of James Mill circa 1822. He was granted letters of Administration on her Estate in King William Co., 28 Nov. 1825, with Christopher Johnson and Sterling Lipscomb,Securities. In 1847 James Mill is dead, and William N. Gregory, Administrator. Her Estate was in the hands of George Mill in 1852.

ANN K[3] LITTLEPAGE wife of William Bagby after 1822. Deceased prior to 1823 when he is her Administrator. In 1846 he is dead, and John Bagby is Administrator "de bonis non"of Ann K. Littlepage.

EDMUND[3] LITTLEPAGE. Deceased in 1823. John B. Richardson, Executor. In 1848 James B. Littlepage is Administrator.

HARDIN[3] LITTLEPAGE. Died with will. Eliza S. Littlepage, Executrix on 15 April 1820, and until her decease in 1847, when Sarah C.Littlepage is Administrator.

BURNLEY[3] LITTLEPAGE. Mentioned in 1813, and in 1852.

CATHERINE[3] (KITTY) LITTLEPAGE. Mentioned 1813 and in 1852.

JUDITH[2] BURNLEY. The will of her brother, John Burnley: "I give and bequeath to the three Sons of my Sister Judith Meriwether, late wife of James Meriwether, vizt: David, James and William four hundred and fifty pounds Virginia Currency to be equally divided betwixt them but if either of them should be dead then the money to be divided betwixt the two Survivors and so if two of them should be dead then the money to go to the Surviving one though should all of them be dead the said four hundred and fifty then to be equally divided betwixt my Sisters Elizabeth, Keziah and Ann." She was dead prior to 1771, and no mention is made of James Meriwether anywhere in the papers of these suits. The sons:

1. DAVID[3] MERIWETHER. Mentioned only in 1827.
2. JAMES[3] MERIWETHER. "   "   "   "
3. WILLIAM[3] MERIWETHER. "   "   "   "

———

COSBY, WINGFIELD, deposed in Louisa County, 17 Mar. 1798, that he lived on the estate "To Ink" in 1770 and 1771.

MADISON, JAMES, of Caroline County, one of the Securities on 26 Jan. 1820 of William D. Taylor of Orange Co., Zachariah Burnley's Administrator. In 1852 Lawrence Battaile, Sheriff of Caroline County was deceased, who had been an Administrator of Zachariah Burnley and of James Madison, dec'd, and Lawrence Battaile was Administrator of Lawrence Battaile, Sheriff, deceased.

SHEPPARD, ALEXANDER, dec'd of Culpeper County, Dr. Wm. Sheppard, dec'd 1827 had been his Administrator, and James Sheppard and Reynolds, are Executors of the latter. John M. Sheppard, dec'd in 1828 (late Administrator of Hardin Burnley), Dr. Joseph M. Sheppard, his Executor.

TAYLOR, William D., qualified in Orange County 26 Jan. 1820 as Administrator of Zachariah Burnley, dec'd. His Securities were John Darracott, and James Madison. He had received on 12 May, 1821, from Dr. William Sheppard, Administrator of Alexander Sheppard, dec'd of Culpeper County a former Administrator of Zachariah Burnley deceased, bonds due the Estate by R. L. Taliaferro and Henry Taliaferro, Philip Roberts and Henry Field, Robindoh Yancey and Henry Field, S. Sanford and Lawrence Taliaferro, and Uriah Terrell, and placed them for collection with Robert Taylor, Attorney of Orange County. On 21 Sept 1827 Robert Taylor, Jr. testifies as to his father's handwriting, and Garland B. Taylor testifies as to his father's William D. Taylor's handwriting.

THORNTON, ANTHONY, 1847 Deputy Marshall of the 18th District of Virginia, and designated Collector for the State of Virginia.

WINGFIELD, JOHN, Burnleys' partner. Obtained, on 4 Jan. 1782, receipt from Hardin Burnley for all accounts remaining in his hands. In 1823 it is stated that he removed to Georgia many years ago and died without property in Virginia

John Darracott's Will (Abstract)

DARRACOTT, JOHN, of Hanover Co. Will dated 8 Aug. 1835. "I give and bequeath unto my beloved wife, Mary A. Darracott all my Estate of every description to be held by her for the mutual benefit of my wife, and such of her children as are now under the age of twenty-one, and the schooling of such of them as have not received their education, and for those purposes, it is my wish that my wife either hire out my negroes rent out my lands grist and saw-mills or retain them in her possession, or manage the said property in such other way as she may think best, and out of the profits ensuing therefrom that she should apply the same to the objects above specified." "It is my will and desire that in case of the marriage of any of my children or their arriving at the age of twenty-one years that my said wife should make such advancements to them as she may think proper and that they be charged with the same and at the division of my Estate at the death of my wife that they account therefore before they participate in any part of my Estate. It is my wish and desire at the death of my wife that all my Estate should be equally divided among all my children except those to whom I have made advancements and those to whom my wife may make advancements in order thereof that Justice may be done to such of my children as have not received any advancements." Directs that Elizabeth S. Winston be charged with $2,000, son Wm. P. with $1,365, son Richard F. with $430.00, and son George W. Darracott with $265.00, "which they are to account for to my Estate before they are at liberty to participate in the division thereof." Appoints his wife sole Executrix. Desires that she consult with his friends Dr. Joseph M. Sheppard, William D. Winston, and sons William P., and Richard F. Darracott in the management of the Estate. Witnesses: Elizabeth S. Sheppard, Sally Sheppard and William D. Winston. Probated on Tuesday the 28th of May 1837 by Sally Sheppard, William D. Winston and Richard F. Darracott who proves the signature of Elizabeth S. Sheppard, dec'd. Teste, Philip B. Winston, C.H.C. O. M. Winston, D.C.H.C.

JOHN DARRACOTT. Will dated 8 Aug. 1835, probated in Hanover County, 28 May 1837. He had been one of the Securities of William D. Taylor, and Administrator of Col. Zachariah Burnley. On 27 July 1825, John and Mary A. Darracott deeded to Joseph M. Sheppard, William D. Winston, and Lewis Berkeley, a tract of land containing 1800 acres, which came to them as her portion of her father's land; also a tract called "Kimbroughs!" After John Darracott's death, his widow Mary A. and children, on 8 June 1839 sold to Robert Ellett a tract of 50 acres called Darracott Mills for $4,000, on South Anna River, R.F.&P.Ry., and adjoining William D. Winston. Mary A. Darracott died in October 1858, leaving issue:

1. ELIZABETH S., dec'd in 1837, survived by her husband, William D. Winston.
2. WILLIAM P. DARRACOTT.
3. RICHARD F. DARRACOTT.
4. GEORGE W. DARRACOTT.
5. SUSAN DARRACOTT.
6. BENJAMIN F. DARRACOTT, of Caroline Co. 1852.
7. MARY P., wife of George J. Herring in 1852.
8. JOHN DARRACOTT.
9. CHARLES H.; 10. ANN W.; 11. ROBERT DARRACOTT
Last three infants 1847, Phil. B. Winston, Grdn.

ELLETT, ROBERT, of Hanover County, died intestate, survived by widow Susan G. Ellett, and seven children. In 1839 had purchased of Darracott's heirs the property, Darracott Mills. His heirs in 1852 were his widow, and issue:

1. JAMES T. ELLETT.
2. THOMAS C. ELLETT.
3. MARY E., wife of John Dobson in 1852.
4. CHARLOTTE C., wife of John Beale in 1852.
5. R. T. ELLETT.
6. ROSA N. ELLETT
7. BETTIE ELLETT.

OTHERS MENTIONED CONCERNING JOHN BURNLEY'S EST.: Cash paid to: 1782 John Taylor, fees, Wm. Toler, John Smith; 1783 Wm. O. Winston, Dr. Riddick, Wm. Johnson; 1784 Elisha Talley; 1786 T. Shore; 1787 Dr. Bowdoin, Dr. Quinlin, John Ingram; 1795 Corns. Calvert, John Minor. Received from: 1784 Benj. Temple, Hardin Burnley; 1785 Elizabeth Burnley act. Judgment vs. Richard Burnley, dec'd; Richard Goodall, Austin Webber, Newman & I. Baylor, Wm. Arnold, Stephen Johnston, John Tilman, M. Terrell, Thomas Dickerson, John Lawrence, Jonathan Ware, Isaac Perrin and J. Cocke.

ROPER VS. TAYLOR & OTHERS, 1849, (36) - ROPER'S EXOR. &C. VS. TAYLOR & OTHERS, 1858 (33)

MARSHALL, WILLIAM. Died circa 1815 possessed "of a large personal and real estate" including "Ratcliffs," 612 acres near Negrofoot, purchased of Jos. F. Price. Survived by five children and his widow, Maria O., who married Roper.

1. ELIZABETH A., wife of Wm. D. Taylor, who died prior to 1858, she surviving him.
2. THOMAS G. MARSHALL, of Fauquier Co., 1849.
3. WILLIAM MARSHALL, JR., died unmarried.
4. JOHN J. MARSHALL, died 1844, will, single.
5. LUCY, died circa 1837, wife of Edmund Burnley, who with two sons, survived her and are non-residents of Virginia:
   1. HARDIN BURNLEY (called Jr.)
   2. WM. M. BURNLEY, born circa 1837.

ROPER, GEORGE, married Maria O., widow of Wm. Marshall. She died on 4 March, 1858, survived Mr. Roper and left two children of this union:

1. ANN ELIZA, wife of John D. Munford in 1849 and residents of Henrico County. In 1858 he and four infant children survive her, and are residents of Williamsburg, Va.:

   1. MARIA O. MUNFORD.
   2. SALLY MUNFORD.
   3. NANNIE MUNFORD.
   4. JOHN D. MUNFORD.

2. WILLIAM W. ROPER, of Caroline County, and Executor of his mother's Estate in 1858.

SHEPPARD'S ADMR. VS. TRUEHEART & OTHERS, 1835 - SHEPPARD'S ADMR. VS. SHEPPARD'S ADMR. &C. 1836 (39)

Philip Sheppard's Will (Abstract)

SHEPPARD, PHILIP, of Hanover County. Will dated 4 Nov. 1815. "In the name of God amen. I, Philip Sheppard. being of sound and disposing mind and memory, do dispose of my estate in manner and form following:" Desires that his Executors pay his debts and "do and act in any and every way that they may think best in order to discharge the same and to "do and act in the same manner as if I were living should & ought to do and act." Devises to brother Mosby Sheppard, Nancy Sheppard, Joseph Sheppard James, Joseph Sheppard Leake and Philip Jefferson Leake, each, one-fifth part of his personal and real estate for their lives, then to their lawful heirs. Failing in issue, such parts to return to the survivors of the decisees and their lawful heirs. Joseph S., and Philip Jefferson Leake not to receive their inheritances until twenty-five years of age, but are to draw interest on the same until that time. Appoints Mosby Sheppard, and Joseph Sheppard James, his Executors. Witnesses: Nathl. Glenn, Thomas Owen, and John Hendrick. Probated on Wednesday, 27 December 1815, by Mosby Sheppard, Nathaniel Glenn, Thomas Owen, and John D. Hendrick.

Teste: William Pollard, C.H.C. Benjᵃ Pollard, Jr., D.C.H.C.

BENJAMIN SHEPPARD, of Hanover County. In 1836: "has been dead many years." *He left a will; Austin Morris, Edmund James and Mosby Sheppard, qualified as Executors. Survived by his widow, Elizabeth Sheppard and eight children:

1. PHILIP SHEPPARD, dec'd. Will dated 4 Nov. 1815, probated 27 Dec. 1815. Unmarried.
2. MOSBY SHEPPARD, dec'd, Jesse Winn, Admr.
3. JOHN SHEPPARD, of Henrico County in 1836.
4. MARY, wife of Austin Morris, deceased.
5. SUSANNA, dec'd. Survived by husband Edmund James, and probably among others a son:
   1. JOSEPH SHEPPARD JAMES.
6. LUCY, wife of Austin D. Leake. Both are dec'd in 1836, leaving issue probably among others, two sons:
   1. JOSEPH SHEPPARD LEAKE.
   2. PHILIP JEFFERSON LEAKE, of Chesterfield County, Va., 1836.
7. ELIZABETH, wife of John Starke. Survived him in 1836, living in Henrico Co. 1837.
8. NANCY, married William Trueheart.
* No will found among these papers.

COLLINS VS. COLLINS, 1863 (39)

COLLINS, LEWIS J. Wife, Martha A., aged about fifty-four years in 1853, and married "about twenty years ago." In 1852, Robert Ellett and Sarah, his wife, executed a Deed of Trust, with William D. Winston, as Trustee, for the benefit of Lewis J. and Martha A. Collins, a tract containing 45 3/4 acres of land.

Lewis J. Collins, apparently, was the second husband of Martha A., she having issue prior to their marriage.

Her issue, as of 1863:

JOHN T. CREW

MILDRED J. COLLINS
JAMES B. COLLINS, aged 21 years
SARAH E. COLLINS, aged 18 years
WILLIAM D. COLLINS, aged 15 years
ROBERT F. COLLINS, aged 12 years.

SWIFT &C., BURCH &C. VS. BURCH'S ADMR.
& OTHERS, 1838 (4)

BURCH, ISHAM, of Hanover, died in 1827 intestate. "Left no wife, children or descendants." His brother, Peter Burch qualified as Administrator. The heirs were his sisters and brothers, six in number, and their descendants:

PETER BURCH, of Hanover, died in 1837 possessed of 102 acres of land and some personal property, including 15 slaves. Milton M. Brown qualified as his Administrator in Nov. 1837. "Left no wife, children or descendants." His heirs were his sisters and brothers and their descendants:

BENJAMIN BURCH, died prior to 1838, survived by an only child and daughter:
1. ANN, wife of Thomas Swift.

ELISHA BURCH, In 1838 "sole survivor of his sisters and brothers."

CHEADLE BURCH, died prior to 1838, leaving the following issue, all residents of Tennessee.

1. MARY C., dec'd, married John Edwards.
2. JUDITH VIRGINIA C., wife of James K. White.
3. BERNARD M. BURCH.
4. SARAH E., wife of a Mr. Hodge. (Receipt for the interest in her uncles' estates witnessed by Joseph T. Hughes,Tennessee.

JOHN BURCH, deceased in 1838, survived by issue:

1. THOMAS C. BURCH.
2. ELIZABETH P. BURCH.
3. MARIETTA S. BURCH.
4. EMMA C., wife of Wm. B. Hay. In Shelby Co., 1839, Wm. A. Dietrick, witness.
5. CLEMENTINE M. BURCH.
6. SARAH I., married Thomas B. Spence. Both are dead in 1838 without issue.
7. MARY, married Robert Chewning, both are dead, leaving issue as of 1838:

   1. LUCY, wife of Alexander Whitlow.
   2. SARAH, wife of Mr. Robards.
   3. ELIZABETH CHEWNING.
   4. ELIZA, wife of Mr. Taliaferro.
   5. ISHAM CHEWNING.
   6. ELISHA CHEWNING.
   7. MARIA CHEWNING.
   8. HARRIET CHEWNING.
   9. ALBERT G. CHEWNING.
   10. MARY CHEWNING.

ELIZA, married Nathaniel Breedlove. Both are dead in 1838, leaving issue.
1. FRANCES, wife of Aaron R. Hall.
2. ISHAM B. BREEDLOVE.
3. JAMES M. BREEDLOVE, non-resident of Va.

BARKER VS. STARKE & OTHERS, 1835 (3)

BURNETT, RICHARD, of Hanover. Will dated 4 Aug. 1829, proved by witnesses John R.Whiting and Isaac Burnett on 27 Aug. 1833. He devised his "considerable estate" to his wife for life, then to his nephew Richard Burnett, Jr. Under date 26 July 1798 had made a marriage agreement with Peggy or Margaret Hughes in which Patrick Anderson and Billy Talley were Trustees. Witnesses, Edmd Barker, George Burnett and Corns. Burnett.

Margaret Burnett's Will

BURNETT, MARGARET. "I, Margaret Burnett of the County of Hanover being sick but of sound mind and memory do make this my last will and testament. I give and bequeath unto Tazewell Barker, Sally Barker, Elizabeth Barker, Emily Barker and Ira Barker my negro man Tom and his wife Milley and their children Suckey and Moses and also my young negro man Zack,with the future increase of the females of the said negroes, to be equally divided among them respectively and their heirs forever. I give and bequeath to my niece Ann Hughes the widow of my nephew John Hughes dec'd my old negro woman Tamer and forty dollars and also the tract of land whereon I now live to be valued by respectable gentlemen and accounted for as hereinafter expressed, to her and her heirs forever. I lend unto my niece Margaret Talley during her natural life my tract of land lying near the Rawleigh which I purchased of Billey Talley and the land which I purchased of my nephew David Hughes being a part of the tract which formerly belonged to my Brother John Hughes dec'd to be valued to her in the manner above stated, and to be accounted for as hereinafter expressed and at the death of said Margaret Talley I give and bequeath the said tract of land above named unto the children of the said Margaret Talley: James Talley, Mary Talley, Frances Talley, Louisa Talley and Martha Talley, to them and their heirs forever. And all my estate which is not herein before disposed of, being ascertained to that amount the value of the land aforesaid is to be divided into two equal parts one of which part I give and bequeath unto my niece Ann Hughes. And the other part I lend unto my niece Margaret Talley, and at the death of the said Margaret Talley, I give and bequeath the same unto the children of the said Margaret Talley by name - James, Mary, Frances, Louisa and Martha Talley forever. Witness my hand and seal this 10th day of July 1834.
                                              her
                        Margaret + Burnett
                                            mark

Witnesses: John Pate, John M. Mills, Cobbit Richardson. (No endorsement of probation) Others Mentioned: Susan L. Starke, Adx of Wm. Starke 1836; Bowling Starke Surv.Ex. Tho.Starke. Wm. Allen, Thos Phillips, Tazewell Barker.

PARSLEY VS. BURNETT & OTHERS, 1834 (31)

BURNETT, FOSTER, and Patsey his wife of Han-
over County, on 21 Feb. 1832, sold to John
P. Parsley 48 acres of land near the said
Parsley's Grocery (Parsley's land formerly John
Johnson's) on Richmond road adjoining Walter
Turner's Estate and Henry Hughes. Some years
previously Burnett had been Guardian for the
infants Nancy Via and Gilson Burnett, of whom
Gilson Via was Trustee. In 1834, Patsey, wife
of Foster Burnett is dec'd, leaving issue:

1. MARTHA ELEANOR BURNETT.
2. MARGARET ELIZABETH BURNETT.

BURNETT-VS. CLARKE & OTHERS, 1879 (43)

BURNETT, G. RUFUS, of Hanover, an infant, by
his grandmother, the late Mrs. Eliza Skelton, purchased of the late Thomas G.Clarke
58 1/2 acres adjoining lands of Lucien King and
others in Henry Magisterial District, and occupied the land until her death in 1863. No deed
was executed.

CLARKE, THOMAS G., died many years ago leaving a widow, Martha M. Clarke, and two chil-

1. N. B. CLARKE.
2. JOHN W. CLARKE, of Louisiana.

3. THOMAS A. CLARKE, of North Carolina.
4. ARABELLA G., wife of P. H. Starke.

WADDILL VS. BURNETT, 1846 (49)

BURNETT, PLEASANT R., of Hanover, died circa
1841, intestate, possessed of 137 acres of
land. Survived by his widow, Tabitha, and
six children:

1. MARGARET, wife of Miller Brown in 1846.
2. MALENDA, wife of William Hollins in 1846.
3. WALLER BURNETT.
4. PLEASANT BURNETT.
5. AMERICA BURNETT, died under age and
   unmarried.
6. WHITING BURNETT.

The last four of whom are infants in 1846.

Others mentioned: Wm. Acree, neighbor of Burnett; Elizabeth Cook; Wm. A. Curtis, constable
before 1847; John Dobson 1853; John H. Earnest
1848; John C. Hughes 1850; George Johnson 1853;
Wm. E. Martin 1850; Samuel M. Moody, merchant
of New Kent County since 1839; Grandison Wade,
Leadwell Wade 1853; Matilda Wade; Robert Wade,
owner of a Grist Mill since 1834; John Waddill,
owner of a Grist Mill; James White, Wm. West in
1820 neighbor of Burnett; Ann F. Wright who
lived on Mrs. Burnett's land; also Richard Morris 1853, and Joseph Parsley 1853.

CATLIN & OTHERS VS. CATLIN'S ADMR. & OTHERS, 1882 (23)

William England's Will

ENGLAND, WILLIAM. "In the name of God Amen. I, William England of the County of Cumberland in
the State of Virginia in feeble health but of sound and disposing memory knowing that it is
appointed that all shall die and being desirous of disposing of the little property I possess do make and ordain this to be my last will and testament (revoking all previous wills & testaments if any there should be) in manner and form following that is to say. first I desire all
my just debts and funeral Expenses paid. I have heretofore given to my son Wm. C. England a negro
woman Harriett and her two children and a bed and furniture. I have also given to my son John L.
England (now dead) a negro woman Martha and her two children and a bed and furniture and I have
also given to my daughter Sally who first married Parker and then Catlin and who is since dead a
negro woman Eliza and her three children and a bed and furniture which said property I estimate
as being of equal value to each of my three named children and confirm the same to them and their
heirs in the manner it is now held with the contingency placed upon the property held by my son
William C. England. I have also put into the possion of my son Wm. C. England a negro boy Isham
of the value of seven hundred dollars to be held in trust for the benefit of his children to be
estimated without interest as to so much advanced to my son Wm. C. at the final division of my
estate. I give to my grandson Benjamin A. England son of Wm. C. a negro boy Robert to be valued
if alive at the division of my estate and to constitute so much of the portion of my estate
designed for the children of my said son Wm. C. I give to the children of my dead son John L. a
negro boy Dick to be valued (if alive) at the division of my estate and estimated as so much
designed for them. I give to the children of my dead daughter Sally a negro boy Albert to be
valued if alive in the same manner as the boy to the children of my dec'd son John L. and to constitute a part of their portion of my estate. My bed and furniture & brass kettle I give as a
seperate & special legacy to my granddaughter Sarah E. England , daughter of my dec'd son John L.
To my three oldest sisters (if living at my death) I give fifty dollars each for three years to
be raised from the hire of the negroes Robert, Dick and Albert before distribution as herein

directed, that is, if there should not be sufficient means of my other estate not specially given away and not otherwise. My old and faithful servant Clary to be at liberty to choose her master and be sold at valuation and in no event if it can be avoided to be exposed to public sale. My boy Henry I wish valued and the privelege given to either of the representatives of my grand-children to take him so as to keep him in the family and to avoid a public Sale which I wish avoided if it can be arranged. My tract of land I wish sold upon such terms as my Executor here-inafter named may think most to the interest of my estate. It is my further wish that the bal-lance of my estate that may remain after the payment of all legal demands against it, all lega-cies & expenses of administration, be equally divided giving to the children of each of my three children before named, one equal third part thereof. Taking into the estimate the negroes specially given to my grandchildren by valuation so as to make them equal considering the property given in my life time (except Isham to be accounted for) of equal value. Lastly, I con-stitute and appoint my friend Creed D. Coleman my Executor to carry this my last will and testa-ment into execution hoping that he will take upon himself the burthen of administration. In wit-ness whereof I have hereunto set my hand and affixed my seal this 1st day of May 1854.

Signed and sealed in presence of   his
  Hez. Ford, Wm. Ranson, Susan A. Ranson.   Wm + England (Seal)
                                                      mark

Probated Cumberland County 22 May 1854 by witnesses, Hez. Ford and Wm. Ranson. Creed D. Coleman, Executor. Securities, Wm. D. Talley, John P. Woodson, Ferdinand G. Coleman. Bond $11,000.00

WILLIAM ENGLAND, of Cumberland County. Will dated 1 May 1854. Proved 22 May 1854 by Hez. Ford and Wm. Ranson. Executor, Creed D. Coleman. Securities, William D. Talley, John P. Woodson, and Ferdinand G. Coleman. Bond $11,000. Wife is not mentioned. Will names three children and two grandchildren:

1. WILLIAM C. ENGLAND, who has among other children, a son:
   1. BENJAMIN A. ENGLAND.

2. JOHN L. ENGLAND, died prior to his father. Had issue, among whom, a daughter:
   1. SARAH E. ENGLAND.

3. SALLEY, who married first a Mr. Parker and secondly William Catlin who died during the lifetime of her father, leaving chil-dren. She was the second wife of William Catlin of Hanover County, who died in 1882 intestate survived by his widow Rebecca R., of his third marriage. Suit concerns tract of land "Beaverdam" of 140 acres in Henry District, adjoining Crutchfield, Whitlock and others, of which all of his children and heirs are interested. The issue of his various wives are not segregated:
   1. WILLIAM N. CATLIN, of Hanover.
   2. EDWARD A. CATLIN.
   3. JOHN E. CATLIN.
   4. MOLLIE J., widow of a Mr. Pate.
   5. HALLIE, wife of Robert C. Davis.
   6. MARTHA H., wife of Dr. Charles R. Cullen.
   7. JAMES T. CATLIN.
   8. HERBERT M. CATLIN.
   9. BENJAMIN R. CATLIN, "nearly 21 years of age in 1882."
   10. ELLA CATLIN, "under 21 years in 1882."

11. ELLA V., dec'd, married a Mr. Sydnor, and had infant children in 1882:
    1. WILLIAM A. SYDNOR.
    2. IDA L. SYDNOR.
    3. EUGENE R. SYDNOR.
    4. STANLEY SYDNOR.
    5. PEARL G. SYDNOR.
    6. RUBY O. SYDNOR.

12. ANN, dec'd, married P. H. Butler, and died leaving issue:
    1. OTHO L. BUTLER, non-resident.
    2. FRANK S. BUTLER, non-resident.
    3. WILLIAM C. BUTLER.
    4. LELIA E., wife of Robert Gills.
    5. MARY, wife of George A. Wiley.
    6. NANNIE, wife of Wm. E. Payne.

13. SARAH J., wife of T. W. Pemberton. She is evidently dec'd in 1882. She had one daughter:
    1. SALLIE, wife of J. G. Penn, and has infant children:
       1. MARY K. PENN.
       2. JOHN PEMBERTON PENN.
       3. JAMES G. PENN.
       4. ANNIE L. PENN.

PRICE VS. AMERON, 1833 (32)

CAMERON, EDMUND, of Hanover, on 27 Oct. 1826 deeded to his mother Catherine Cameron 225 acres adjoining Thomas Price, Jr., on the north, Reuben Vest on the west, Samuel Anderson and Elizabeth Thompson on the South, and by Nathaniel Bumpass on the east. On 15 Oct. 1830, Catherine Cameron and Edmund Cameron made a Deed of Trust to Thomas Price, Jr., for benefit of Patrick H. Price, on 240 acres where the Camerons reside, adjoining lands of Thos. Price,

Jr., Charles Vest, and others.

Edmund Cameron's wife, Fanny D., is deceased in 1833. She left five infant children, one of whom was "at the breast," which were cared for by Catherine. Catherine Cameron's address in 1840 was Taylorsville. She "sold land she got from her mother, to Ambrose Brooks." The Deed was written by James W. Henry, son of Mrs.Elizabeth Henry, a sister of Catherine Cameron.

BROOK'S, PHILIP, son, Ambrose Brooks, purchased land of Catherine Cameron. He had married Elizabeth, one of the children of John Gentry "who had no special place of residence."

Others Mentioned: Cosby Duke and wife Elizabeth; Hugh N. Thompson; Albert Lane who "was born near the place where William W. Mallory lived"; William W. Mallory "taught school" and is a Constable; John J. Taylor; Major Baughan's land adjoined Catherine Cameron's. Depositions of: Spotswood James and Thos. R. Byrd 1834; James Stodgel, John Norman and William Cameron, Jr. at home of John Holland in Fluvanna County, 1835; Elizabeth Duke, John T. Duke, Marshia Terrell 1836; James Higgason and Thomas Bumpass.

CARVER VS. CARVER'S ADMX. & OTHERS, 1866 (9)

CARVER, DR. ROBERT M., of Hanover, died 15 Jan. 1862, intestate. Widow, Frances Parke Carver, Admx. On 18 March 1847, in a seperation agreement, Carter Braxton and William T. H. Pollard were Trustees for property in her right from the Executor of Parke Street, Sr.; from the Admr. of Charles P. Street, dec'd, and from the Executor of Parke Street, Jr., dec'd - the last two, late brothers of the said Fanny, who had another brother, Samuel G. Street. Issue of the Carvers in 1866, infants:

1. THOMAS PARKE CARVER, of "Bellevue" Hanover County, who is represented in this suit by his next friend, H. G. Cross. He is of age in 1868, and Admr. for the Estate of his aunt, Elizabeth R. Carver.
2. CHARLES STREET CARVER, who died prior to 26 May 1868.

Dr. Robert M. Carver, dec'd, had sisters:

ELIZABETH R. CARVER. Will dated 9 April 1868, probated 26 May 1868. Thos. P. Carver, Admr.

CHARLOTTE H. WALDROP.

MARY A., died after 26 May 1868, wife of Samuel M. Baker, leaving issue:

1. SUSAN M. BAKER.
2. SAMUEL M. BAKER, JR.
3. CHARLOTTE A. BAKER, infant in 1868.
4. THOMAS O. BAKER.

KING'S ADMR. VS. CARY, 1817 (23)

CARY, WILSON MILES, ESQ., in 1787 executed a Deed of Trust covering slaves and other personal property to his kinsman, Miles King, Sr., whose Executor was Dr. Miles King,Jr. Also indebted to Betheoh? Smith, Executor of Wm. Smith, dec'd, in 1794. His estate had suffered considerably at the hands of the British, and he was greatly annoyed by his creditors. He wrote Miles King that he had no straw for the making of brick, no money for postage, and no wine in his cellar. Correspondence shows that he was in Elizabeth City County on 23 April 1789 and during 1798; at "Rich Neck" on 9 July 1789; during 1801 and on 21 Jan. 1809, and in 1813, he was in Williamsburg. On 4 Sept. 1812, and 21 Feb. 1816, at "Carysbrook" Wilmington P. O., Va., when on the latter date he addresses Dr. Miles King "In Assembly" Richmond, Va., which letter was forwarded to Norfolk. Wilson Miles Cary died prior to 1817, when his Executors were Miles Cary and Wilson Jefferson Cary, dec'd. Walker Timberlake of Shadwell Mills, Administrator of Wilson Jefferson Cary. Horace Timberlake, late Sheriff of Fluvanna County, Administrator of Wilson Miles Cary, dec'd. In 1825, Miles Cary, who had been one of the Executors of Wilson Miles Cary was in Elizabeth City County.

Wilson Cary of Warwick County, mentioned 25 September 1786.

William Cary, in 1786 was Guardian of Caty Dudley, orphan of James Dudley, dec'd. His Securities were John Langhorn and Wilson Miles Cary.

KING, MILES, SR., a kinsman of Wilson Miles Cary, had been an original member of the firm of William Hylton & Co., merchants. Sold his interest. David L. Hylton and David Hylton two other members are deceased. Dr. Miles Cary, Jr., Executor of Miles King, Sr., was at Hampton, Va., on 4 Sept. 1812, and in Norfolk, Va., 21 May 1838, when he gives power of attorney to John C. Pryor of Elizabeth City County.

Others Mentioned: James Govan of Richmond, 1786 and 1792; Archibald Govan 1786.

CHRISTIAN VS. CHRISTIAN, 1856 (88)

CHRISTIAN, WILLIAM BROCKENBROUGH, of Hanover, deceased. Land, 163 to 196 acres adj. Thomas King. Survived by his widow, Sarah B. Christian, now dec'd, and issue:
1. HORACE B. CHRISTIAN.
2. EMMUELLA CHRISTIAN.

TAYLOR VS. COCKE, 1871 (55)

COCKE, I. N., formerly of the City of Richmond, Va., removed to Augusta Co.

CHICK'S EXORS. VS. CHICK & OTHERS, 1854 (57)

Pettus W. Chick's Will

CHICK, PETTUS W. "In the name of God amen. I, Pettus W. Chick of Hanover County being in my natural mind do make this to be my last will and testament in manner and form, viz: First I commit my Soul to God and my body to be decently buried. My will and desire is that all my Just debts be paid and funeral expenses. Item: I give to my wife Mary Ann Chick negroes namely: Betty, Charlotte, James Monroe, James, Amagilla, Manuel, Queen, James Robertson, and Rose, and their increase. My land to be divided say to begin at the foot way leading to John Swift's on Locust Creek, Starting at a willow at the crossing place making two small Persimmon Tree Standing on the drain about twenty yards this side the willow mentioned on the creek to be the line, from thence along the old school path to my Spring Branch thence up the Spring Branch to the Gum Spring to run to the right hand along the ditch to the west until it comes to two Persimmon trees on the said Spring branch thence up the first fork which I make the corner from thence a Straight line due South to John B. Jones' line, the land on the west side from Locust Creek to the above said Jone's line I give to my wife Mary Ann Chich, on the east of said line I lend to my brother Davis S.Chick one-half the land during his lifetime, at his death my desire is that it shall be equally divided between my niece and nephew John R. Chick and Rebecca Ellen Turner, the other half on the east side of said line I give to Nancy L. Jones. Item: I lend to my brother Davis S. Chick the negroes namely: Maria, Amanda, Wilson, Elizabeth and their increase during his lifetime after which I give to Wm. J. Chick, his son, Maria and her daughter Elizabeth and their increase. Wilson, the above named boy I give to my nephew Robert Jones, my sister Patsey's son. Amanda, the above named girl to Ann Selden Ragland, my niece. Item: I give to Nancy L. Jones negroes namely: Louisa, Alexander, Lucion and Charles Berkeley and their increase. I give her one feather bed and furniture, one cow and calf, five sheep, one sow and pigs, one black mare called Flint, five barrells corn. Item: I lend to my Brother Davis S. Chick named above one black mare called White foot. Item: I give to my wife Mary Ann Chick my riding horse Blacky, one gray mare called Pat, one bay colt called Stuck. The balance of my stock Hogs Sheep and Cattle Buggy Ox Cart Household and Kitchen furniture plantation tools. Item: I give to my nephew Burwell P. Jones one negro man named Robertson my Blacksmith and my Gun and no more of my estate. Item: I give to Nathaniel H. Turner, William Cocke, James Turner and their heirs negroes to be equally divided, namely: Clarissa, Montgomery, Henry, Bunans and Chapman. Item: I give to the rest of my Brothers and Sisters, namely: Burwell

Chick, William Chick, Ambler Chick, John R. Chick, Patsey Selden Jones, Nancy Bluford Phillips and their heirs except my nephew Burwell P. Jones who is to have no more of my estate, Negroes (namely) Fountain, Wyatt, Solomon, Sally, Susan, Queen, John, Parke, Leta, Billy, Emila, Randolph, Jacob, Richmond, Lewis, and their increase to be equally divided. Item: I give to Cousin William Bagby one negro girl named Martha. Item: I give to his son, William Chick Bagby one mare colt called Nim. Item: I give to Wm. J. Chewning and John R. Chick my nephews, each twenty dollars. Any property not named or mentioned in the above will I give to my Brothers and Sisters last named above this is my will. I do constitute and appoint my Brother in law William Bagby my lawful Executor of this my last will and Testament this 11th day of March 1854.

Witnesses: Pettus W. Chick
  Frederick H. Thompson
  Richd M. Bagby
  Edwin B. Sharp

At a Court of Quarterly Session held for Hanover County, at the Courthouse, on Tuesday 25th of April 1854. This last will and Testament of Pettus W. Chick dec'd was proved by the oaths of Frederick H. Thompson and Edwin R. Sharpe, witnesses, and is ordered to be recorded.
  A Copy, Teste, Wm. O. Winston, C.H.C.

PETTUS W. CHICK, dec'd of Hanover. Will dated 11 March 1854, proved 25 April 1854. Executor was his cousin and brother-in-law William Bagby of Louisa County. Left considerable personal estate. His heirs were his widow, Mary Ann nee Turner, sister of James Turner, dec'd, and brothers and sisters, or their descendants:

DAVIS S. CHICK, a brother, of Henrico County, who has issue, perhaps among others, a son mentioned in Pettus' will:
  1. WILLIAM J. CHICK, of Richmond, Va.

BURWELL CHICK, dec'd, who was another brother. His children, all non-residents:
  1. PETTUS W. CHICK.
  2. W. B., wife of George W. Chapline.
  3. MARIA H., wife of Theodore B. Thompson.
  4. LOUISA V., wife of William R. B. Farr.
  5. CAROLINE L., wife of Asa Hodges.
  6. REUBEN S. CHICK.

COL. WILLIAM M. CHICK, dec'd, who was another brother. He died in Jackson County, Missouri, where he had been located for many years, survived by his widow, Ann E., and children and grandchildren, all of Missouri:
  1. MARY JANE, wife of John T. Peery.
  2. WILLIAM S. CHICK.
  3. WASHINGTON H. CHICK.
  4. JOSEPH S. CHICK.

5. PETTUS W. CHICK. (Ann E. Chick, Guardian).
6. VIRGINIA CHRISTIANA, died 1849, survived
   by husband, John C. McCoy, Guardian of
   their children. (Jos. S. Chick, Security)
   1. VIRGINIA McCOY.
   2. JULIET McCOY.
   3. ELLEN McCOY.
   4. SPENCER McCOY.
7. SARAH A., dec'd, who was wife of John W.
   Polk, dec'd. They were survived by one
   child, a son, under 21, but over the age
   of 14 in 1858:
   1. HENRY CLAY POLK. (Jos. S. Chick, Gdn.)
8. MATILDA M., wife of Nathan Scarritt.

AMBLER CHICK, Sr., a brother, of Logan County,
Kentucky. His attorney-in-fact in 1855 was a
son: (Probably other issue)
1. AMBLER CHICK, JR.

JOHN R. CHICK, dec'd, another brother, whose
heirs were his children and grandchildren:
1. JOHN R. CHICK, whose wife is Martha S.
2. ELIZABETH, wife of Samuel Pleasants, of
   Hanover County, 1855.
3. REBECCA ELLEN, wife of Benjamin F. Turner.
4. ANN SELDEN, wife of John S. Ragland of
   Richmond, Va.
5. LITTLETON CHICK, dec'd, survived by widow,
   Ann D. Chick, and five children of Albemarle County, 1855: (Orphans in 1849)
   1. MERIWETHER L. CHICK.
   2. ELIZABETH A. CHICK.
   3. EUGENE L. CHICK.
   4. CHARLES W. CHICK, infant in 1855.
   5. OTHO B. CHICK, infant in 1855.

PATSEY SELDEN, dec'd, a sister, who married
Samuel B. Jones, dec'd. Surviving issue:
1. ROBERT J. JONES, of Richmond, Va.
2. DAVID N. JONES.
3. PETTUS B. JONES, of Sevier Co., Arkansas.
4. SAMUEL B. JONES, of Hanover County, Va.
5. NANCY B., wife of Frederick H. Thompson of
   Hanover.
6. L. M. H., wife of John W. Moody, of Hanover
   (C&O Ry. employee in 1855)
7. MARTHA A. (or S.), wife of John E. Kelley.
8. JANE, wife of Hardin D. Nuckols of Hanover.
9. PAULINA SIMS, widow.
10. NANCY LEWIS, wife of Thomas W. Hope of
    Louisa County. (She is mentioned as a
    daughter of Patsey Selden Jones, but is
    not included in the final settlement of
    the Estate. There may be some confusion
    here.)
11. BURWELL P. JONES, of Hanover.

NANCY BLUFORD, another sister, wife of William
Phillips of Forsythe County, Georgia.

(   ) another sister, dec'd, married
William Bagby, cousin and brother-in-law of
Pettus W. Chick, and his Executor. Issue in

1855, perhaps among others, and infant son:
1. WILLIAM CHICK BAGBY.

(   ), another sister, dec'd, who
married a Mr. Chewning, and has issue, perhaps
among others a son, mentioned in Pettus's will
as William J. Chewning, but in suit as:
1. JAMES W. CHEWNING.

MARTHA, another sister, married William Cocke,
who is deceased, leaving children and grandchildren:
1. CATHERINE S., wife of James M. Bagby.
2. CHARLES H. COCKE, of Louisa County.
3. WILLIAM COCKE, dec'd. No issue.
4. NATHANIEL JAMES COCKE, non-resident of Va.
5. (   ), dec'd, who married John Johnson, leaving issue:
   1. MARY ANN, wife of George A. Strong of
      Louisa County, Va.
6. MARTHA, wife of Thomas Johnson. Non-residents of Virginia.
7. LEWIS COCKE, dec'd, who is survived by
   children: (Widow not mentioned)
   1. PETTUS M. COCKE, of Richmond, Va.
   2. THOMAS COCKE, of Louisa County, Va.
   3. ANN ELIZABETH COCKE, of Louisa.=Ford
   4. VIRGINIA M. COCKE.
   5. LEWIS T. COCKE, infant 1855.
   6. SAMUELLA, married circa 1856, John
      Shepherd.
   7. SARAH L. COCKE, infant 1855.

(   ) another sister, dec'd, who was
wife of James Turner, dec'd, of Louisa, whose
"sole surviving children" are:
1. JOHN H. TURNER, of Louisa.
2. BENJAMIN F. TURNER, of Hanover County, who
   married Rebecca Ellen Chick, his first
   cousin, daughter of John R. Chick, dec'd.
3. LEWIS TURNER, (probably dec'd in 1855.) ?
4. ELIZABETH, wife of George W. Timberlake of
   Richmond, Va.

(   ) dec'd, another sister, married
Nathaniel H. Turner, of Louisa. No issue.

Commissioners: Edward Morris, George Fleming,
Thomas Hardin, John Terrell and John Swift.

CHICK & OTHERS VS. COCKE'S ADMX. &C, 1833 (7)

COCKE, BENJAMIN, JR., of Hanover, died intestate, possessed of considerable real and
personal estate. Survived by widow, Elizabeth, Admx., and issue:
1. POLLY, wife of Davis S. Chick. Sold interest in Estate to John D. Andrews.
2. JOHN A. COCKE, sold interest in Estate to
   John D. Andrews.
3. BENJAMIN J. COCKE, sold interest in Estate
   to John D. Andrews.
4. WILLIAM A. COCKE, dec'd, married Elizabeth

S. Nuckols, who survived, with two children:
1. WILLIAM B. F. COCKE.
2. MARY E. COCKE.
5. ELIZABETH W., dec'd, married John C. Pulliam, who with two children, survive her:
1. MARTHA W. PULLIAM.
2. E. J. PULLIAM.
6. MARTHA J., married Shandy Perkins.
7. ROBERT P. COCKE.
8. FRANCES A., married Seneca T. P. Digges.
9. VIRGINIA C. COCKE, died unmarried.
10. EDWIN B. COCKE.

CHISHOLME'S EXOR. VS. HADEN & OTHERS, 1838 (10)

Hugh Chisholme's Will

CHISHOLME, HUGH. "In the name of God amen. I, Hugh Chisholme of the County of Hanover & State of Virginia do make this my last will and Testament in manner and form following: Viz, 1st I desire that all my just debts be paid by my Exors. here after named. 2nd I lend to my sisters Nancy Haden and Sally Chisholme who are now living with me all my estate both real & personal during their natural lives. 3rd: After the death of my two sisters Nancy Haden and Sally Chisholme I desire that all my Estate loaned them by the 2nd clause of this my last will be sold by my Exors. on such terms as they may think best and the money arising from such sales I give and bequeath to the children of my brother John R. Chisholme or their legal representatives to them and their heirs forever. 4th: I constitute and appoint my two friends Edmund C. Goodwin & Charles Thompson, Jr., Exors. of this my last will as Witness my hand & seal this 24th day of March 1835."
                              Hugh Chisholme (Seal)
Signed, sealed and delivered as the last Will and Testament of the above named Hugh Chisholme in the presence of C. W. Dabney and Wm.O.Winston

At a Court of Monthly Session held for Hanover County at the Courthouse on Tuesday the 22nd day of August 1837. This last will and Testament of Hugh Chisholme dec'd was duly proved by the oaths of C. W. Dabney and William O. Winston, the witnesses thereto and is ordered to be recorded.
    Teste, Philip B. Winston, C.H.C.
    A Copy, Teste, Wm. O. Winston, D.C.H.C.

HUGH CHISHOLME, of Hanover. Will dated 24 Mar. 1835, proved 22 Aug. 1837. Charles Thompson, Jr. qualified as Executor. His heirs were two sisters and a brother:
NANCY HADEN, a sister, who died without issue.
SALLY CHISHOLME, a sister, died unmarried.
JOHN R. CHISHOLME, a brother, in 1838 had three sons under age, living in Albemarle County. These sons, whose names are not stated, sold

on 4 September 1848 their property to Benjamin Sneed, witnesses by J. E. Dawson and Benjamin J. Shepherd. On 4 February 1851 William Dawson Chisholme sold to Benjamin Sneed his interest in his uncle Benjamin Sneed's Estate after the death of his aunt Nancy Haden.

ANDERSON &C. VS. ANDERSON, 1869 (94)

CHRISTIE, CHARLES J., of Borough of Wilkes-barre, County of Luzerne, State of Pennsylvania. Will dated 16 July 1835, Codicil 18 Jan. 1838. Probated at Wilkesbarre, 6 April 1838 by Elizabeth Christie, Executrix. Desires his body to be interred in burying ground of Saint Stephen's Church in Wilkesbarre. Just debts to be paid. Devises to his wife, Elizabeth, an estate during her widowhood. Mentions daughters and grandchildren:
1. LUCINDA, wife of Henry Cady, who purchased land of John T. Anderson's Estate.
Issue:
1. CHARLES CHRISTIE CADY.
2. MARY ELIZA CADY.
2. AMANDA E., wife of Augustus C. Laning, and have issue:
1. ELIZABETH LANING.
2. MARY ANN LANING.

CLOUGH &C. VS CLOUGH'S ADMR. &C., 1858 (22)

CLOUGH, JOHN, SR., of Hanover, died in 1840. Had possessed considerable real and personal property, but becoming financially involved, on 22 September 1822, executed a Deed of Trust for the benefit of himself and family, to a son of a former marriage, George N. Clough, of all of his estate to be operated, and "Surplus to be used to pay Dr. Nathaniel Nelson, Joel Crenshaw for a coffin, Hugh McDonald for smith's work, and William Pollard for tuition for two children, then to children of the said John Clough, Sr. he had by Sarah Clough, jr, deceased", as follows:

1. MARY, married Chapman Crenshaw, who is now dead and she has transferred her interest to Milton Crenshaw. In 1847 her issue:
1. HARRIET, wife of H. G. Pollard.
2. AMANDA, wife of James M. Pollard.
3. SARAH CRENSHAW.
4. INDIANA, wife of David J. Shepperson.
5. LUCY H. CRENSHAW.

2. LEONARD J. CLOUGH.   On 22 March 1825, Judith C. Clough and Elizabeth A. Clough of Hanover, deeded to Leonard J., and George N. Clough, one tract of land and Grist Mill on the same, in Hanover, containing 400 acres, which said land was devised to them by the will of Edward N. Clough, dec'd, dated 29 June 1813. Land

adjoining the property of John Clough,Sr. the Estate of Edmund James, dec'd, Nathaniel Thompson, Lemuel Vaughan, Henry Pollard, and Estate of John Harris,dec'd. The consideration being that the said Leonard J. and George N. Clough will pay and discharge the amount of two Deeds of Trust: one payable to Charles Crenshaw, and the other payable to Edmund Crenshaw.

On 1 November 1828, Leonard J. (or I.) Clough of Hanover, deeded to George N. Clough, consideration $415.00, Grist Mill and seven acres of land bequeathed by Edward N. Clough, dec'd, to his sisters, Judith C. Clough and Elizabeth A. Clough, and by them conveyed to Leonard J. and George N. Clough, by deed dated 22 Mar. 1825, being on South side of Cedar Creek on which said Mill is situated, adjoining William Sydnor, dec'd, Henry Pollard and Clough's. Witness: Nath[l] Cross.

3. LAVINIA S., married William Pollard, and both are dead without issue.

4. JOHN T. CLOUGH, dec'd in 1830.

5. REBECCA F., married Richard F. Thomas. On 25 September 1831, Richard F. Thomas and Rebekah, his wife, formerly Rebekah F. Clough of the City of Richmond, deeded to George Nelson Clough of Hanover, for consideration of $100.00, all their interest "in land in Hanover which was the property of where John Clough, Sr., now resides," on North Fork of Cedar Creek, adjoining Dr. Hargraves, Edmund James, dec'd, and others, being one undivided 7th in tract estimated to contain 214 acres. In 1858, Rebekah and her husband are both dead, leaving issue:
1. MISSOURI THOMAS.
2. VIRGINIA W., married Botts Childress, who, with two infant children survive her in 1858:
   1. MARY E. CHILDRESS.
   2. VIRGINIA CHILDRESS.

6. LUCY T. CLOUGH, dec'd in 1830.

7. SARAH E. A., married Dabney C. Waller. On 1 July 1830, Dabney C. Waller and Sarah his wife, formerly Sarah A. Clough of Louisa, and John C. Dickinson and Martha A. H., his wife, formerly Clough, the said Waller and Dickinson having married two daughters of John Clough, Sr., each entitled to 1/7th of land in possession of John Clough, Sr., who has a life estate in same... George N. Clough being desirous to buy the 2/7ths - of his two sisters Martha A. H. Clough and Sarah A. Clough - which they are entitled at the death of their father, John Clough, Sr., - their two interests deeded to George N. Clough for consideration of $200.00. In 1858 "Sarah and Dabney C. Waller are both dead, leaving unknown heirs in the West."

8. HARDINIA B., married John Swift, Sr. On 8 March 1830, John Swift, Sr., and his wife Hardenia B. Swift, formerly H. B. Clough, both of Henry County, State of Tennessee, conveys to George N. Clough for $105.00, all right title, etc. in the Estate of real and personal property of John Clough, father of the said Hardenia, of Hanover County, Virginia.

9. MARTHA A. H., married John C. Dickinson. She and her sister, Sarah A. Waller sold their respective 1/7th interests to their brother, George N. Clough, 1 July 1830. In 1858 Dickinson is deceased. Survived by his wife and issue:
1. REGINA DICKINSON.
2. ROSINA DICKINSON.
3. MARTHA DICKINSON.

John Clough, Sr., by a former marriage had, perhaps among others, two sons; and two daughters:

10. B. A. CLOUGH, died unmarried prior to 1858.

11. GEORGE NELSON CLOUGH, died in 1847, with a will. Estate to wife, Martha B. Clough. John D. G. Brown, Admr. Martha, the widow, in 1858, has married B. T. Stanley. Clough had no issue. He and Leonard J. Clough, on 22 March 1825 bought of Judith C. Clough and Elizabeth A. Clough 400 acres left them by Edward N. Clough, dec'd, in his will dated 29 June 1813, and on 1 November 1828, George N. Clough purchased Leonard's interest for $415.00. (No information to identify Edward N. Clough, dec'd.) George N. Clough also purchased other interests in his father's property from his half sisters. On 23 March 1831, John Wight, Admr. with the will annexed of Jedidiah Leeds, dec'd of Richmond, conveyed to George Nelson Clough of Hanover, for consideration of $168.75, 27 acres, being the same tract of land conveyed by John Crew and Margaret his wife to Jediah Leeds by deed 23 Dec., 1816, bounded on the East and North by lands of John Clough, on West by Chas. Crenshaw, and on South by Elizabeth Harris, being 6/10ths of 45 acres formerly belonging to Susanna Harris, dec'd. And, on 6 June 1841 George N. Clough deeds to Hugh N. Pendleton and Gordon H. Pendleton, to manage for the benefit of Edmund A. Pendleton and Mildred, his wife, 106 acres, including 1/4 acre, which is

reserved for the Graveyard, on the North of the dwelling house. Tract being on the North side of Cedar Creek, a short distance below lands of Gordon H. Pendleton, Thomas Bumpass and Harmon W. Davis. On 20 April 1830, George N. Clough purchased of William G. Maddox of Hanover, and Richard Harris of Chesterfield, and Samuel Harris of King & Queen County, 4 1/2 acres each - making 13 1/2 acres, being part of a tract of land in Hanover on the North Fork of Cedar Creek, formerly belonging to Susanna Harris, dec'd, and bounded by the lands of John Clough, Sr., Joseph Vaughan, and Dr. Samuel Hargrave. Consideration being $60.00. The witnesses were James Higgason, A.M.Brooke and David Harris. Other witnesses in 1825 were Spotswood James, Wm. Pollard, and Plummer Harris.

12. JUDITH C. CLOUGH, on 22 March 1825 sold land devised to her by the will of Edward N. Clough, dec'd, to Leonard J., and George N. Clough.

13. ELIZABETH A. CLOUGH, on 22 March 1825 sold land devised to her by the will of Edward N. Clough, dec'd, to Leonard J. and George N. Clough.

EDWARD N. CLOUGH, dec'd. It is said that his will was dated 29 June 1813. Devised land to Judith C., and Elizabeth a. Clough, who were sisters of Leonard J. Clough. The identity of Edward N. Clough is not disclosed in the papers of this suit.

PHILLIPS VS. COCKE'S EXOR., 1835 (29)
COCKE'S EXOR. VS. COCKE'S ADMR., 1859 (56)

William Cocke's Will

COCKE, WILLIAM. "In the name of God amen. I, William Cocke of the Parish of saint Paul in the County of Hanover do make this my last will and Testament. Imprimis: I lend unto my Daughter Sarah Camp the four negroe slaves David, George, Pegg & Hannah and at her death it is my will and desire that the said slaves with the increase of the females may be equally divided among the children of my said daughter which may be alive at her death, but in case any of her children shall died in her lifetime leaving issue that such issue shall have the part of their parent had she or he been alive at the time of the death of my said daughter. Item: I give and bequeath unto my son in law Richard P. Camp five head of sheep. Item: I give and bequeath unto my son in law Henry Fleet my three negro slaves, towit, Billy, Betty and Lewis, one horse, one cow, five head of sheep

to him and his heirs forever. Item: I give and bequeath unto my son William Cocke my three slaves, towit, James, Robert and Alfred, one horse, one cow, five head of sheep, and a bed and furniture to him and his heirs forever. Item: I lend unto my beloved wife, during her life the tract of land whereon I now live, all the plantation utensils, the crops of all kinds, the household and kitchen furniture and the stock not before mentioned, and the following slaves, towit, John, Nat, Charles, Nelson, Stephen, Ben, Aggy, Rhoda, Grace and Maria and it is my will and desire that my wife pay my debts out of the crops, stock and furniture lent her aforesaid. At the death of my said wife I give unto my Grand daughter Dianna Cocke, daughter of my son Joseph Anderson Cocke four hundred dollars to be raised out of that part of my estate lent to my wife. My tract of land aforesaid I give and bequeath unto my son William and to his heirs forever, and the balance of my estate lent to my wife as aforesaid, I give and bequeath unto my three children Sarah Camp, Elizabeth Fleet and William Cocke to be equally divided between them to them and their heirs forever. And whereas it is uncertain whether my said son Joseph Anderson Cocke be now alive or not, but in case he shall return, then I give him at my wife's death one-half of my said tract of land and the said slaves, Nat, Charles and Nelson to him and his heirs forever, and in the event of his returning I do hereby revoke the devise to the said Daughter as aforesaid. Item: Whereas I have heretofore given unto some of my children some property by way of advancement, I do now hereby confirm such gifts to them and their heirs forever. Lastly, I do hereby constitute and appoint my son William Cocke and my sons in law Richard P. Camp and Henry Fleet Executors of this my last will and Testament. In Witness whereof I have hereunto set my hand and affixed my seal this eighth day of December one thousand eight hundred and fifteen!"

                     William Cocke.

Signed, sealed & published by
the Testator as & for his last
will and Testament in presence of
Joseph C. Wingfield,
Tho. Pollard,
Benjn Wingfield

At a Court of Monthly Session held for Hanover County at the Courthouse, on Wednesday the 27th of March 1822. This last will and Testament of William Cocke dec'd was offered for proof by William Cocke one of the Executors therein named and was proved by the oaths of Thomas Pollard & Benjamin Wingfield two of the witnesses thereto, and also by the oath of the Executor, and is ordered to be recorded.
    Teste, William Pollard, C.H.C.
    A Copy, Teste, Benjn Pollard, Jr., D.C.H.C.

Joseph Anderson Cocke's Will

COCKE, JOSEPH A. "I, Joseph A. Cocke of the County of Hanover and Parish of Saint Paul do hereby make this my last will and Testament in manner and form following, That is to say: 1st. I desire that all the perishable part of my Estate be amediately Sold after my decease and out of the moneys arising therefrom: all my Just Debts be paid. Should the perishable part of my property prove insufficient for the above purposes then I desire that my administrators hereafter named may sell my Plantation pay and Satisfy Such of my Just Debts as Shall remain unpaid out of the sale of the perishable part of my Estate. 2nd. After the payment of my Just Debts all the rest of my estate both real and personal together with the moneys arising from the said Sale I desire may be equally divided between my nephews and nices and therrs heirs forever in absolute phesimple. Lastly do hereby Constitute and appoint my friends Joseph C. Wingfield and Samuel Perrin my administrators of this my last will and testament hereby revoking all other or former wills or Testaments by me heretofore made in testimony whereof I have hereunto set my hand and affixed my seal this Seventh day of March one thousand eight hundred and twenty-three."

Jos. A. Cocke (Seal)

Signed Sealed published and declared as and for the last will and Testament of Joseph A. Cocke in the presence of us -
Thos Wingfield.
Benjn Wingfield.

At a Court of Monthly session held for Hanover County at the Courthouse on Wednesday the 24th of December 1823. This last will and testament of Joseph A. Cocke dec'd was proved by the oath of Benjamin Wingfield, one of the witnesses thereto.
Teste, William Pollard, C.H.C.
A Copy, Teste, Benjn Pollard, Jr., D.C.H.C.

WILLIAM COCKE, of Hanover. Will dated 8 Dec. 1815, proved 27 March 1822. He possessed a tract of land on South branch of Mechumps Creek, containing by estimation 241 acres, described as being three miles south east of the Courthouse, upon which there was a brick dwelling of three stories with one large room and hall on each floor, and on the ground floor was a frame addition and porches. The property was sold to James T. Sutton. William Cocke was survived by his widow, Susanna, who died in 1827 or 1828, and by the following issue:

1. WILLIAM COCKE. Executor of his father's Estate. Married Elizabeth Talbot of Norfolk County where he lived after his marriage, and where he died intestate after 4 Dec. 1833, and prior to 2 June 1835.

John Riggins of Norfolk, Administrator. Their children were:
1. WILLIAM KADER TALBOT COCKE. In 1835 "at sea". Died in 1855 of Yellow Fever, survived by children, of whom William Morrison of Alligator Post Office, St. Mary's Parish, La. was Guardian in 1860.
2. THOMAS ISAAC COCKE. In 1835 in Norfolk. Address in 1860 was Alligator Post Office, St. Mary's Parish, La.
3. MARY DIANNA TABB COCKE of Norfolk in 1835. Address in 1860, Mrs. Mary D. T. Wofford of Brashear City, Saint Mary's Parish, Louisiana.
4. SALLY ELIZABETH COCKE of Norfolk in 1835. In 1860, Mrs. Sarah E. Pugh of Paincourtville, Assumption Parish Louisiana.(In 1843, "Mrs. Diana Talbot certifies that Sarah Elizabeth, daughter of Colo. William Cocke, late of the County of Norfolk, and his wife Elizabeth Talbot, was born 17 October 1822, and died 19 March 1826.) She was William Cocke's first daughter of the name. Mrs. Sarah E. Pugh was the second daughter of the name.

2. JOSEPH ANDERSON COCKE. Will dated 7 March 1823, probated 24 December 1823. Inherited land on Mechump's Creek and personal property from his father. Being indebted to his brother, Col. William Cocke, in the amount of $318.12, under date of 5 April 1822, executed a Deed of Trust for his benefit to Philip B. Winston, Trustee, covering the said land. Jos. A. Cocke married circa 1804, Judith Talley, but they lived together only two or three years, after which he went to his father's to reside, and she to her father's in the New Castle neighborhood. In 1813 he enlisted for five years in the U.S. Army, after which he went to Canada, from which he returned to his father's home. He was subject to "drinking" and his wife would not live with him. "Thomas Wingfield lived with him about half the time." His widow, Judith, after his death married Thomas Phillips and survived him. She and Joseph had one daughter who died prior to her father:
1. DIANNA COCKE.

3. MARTHA SARAH, married first Richard Pollard Camp, dec'd, and had issue:
1. WILLIAM C. CAMP, formerly of Richmond, died prior to 12 May 1857.
2. RICHARD POLLARD CAMP, unmarried in New Orleans in 1855, when he sells his interest in his uncle Joseph's Estate to Willis Wilson Wingfield "being the property bequeathed to

to his mother Martha Sarah Camp,
now the wife of Joseph C. Wingfield".
3. JOHN C. CAMP, of Richmond, Va., on 1
May 1855, sells his interest in his
Uncle's Estate to Shelton S. Wingfield.
4. PAUL G. CAMP.
5. SARAH T., "formerly Graham, married
John T. Samuel of Caroline County.

MARTHA SARAH CAMP, married secondly Capt.
Joseph C. Wingfield, and had issue:
6. MARY E. S. WINGFIELD.

4. ELIZABETH, married Henry Fleet. In 1835 a
resident of Matthew County, Va. Issue:
1. WILLIAM HENRY FLEET.
2. MILDRED S. FLEET.
3. SARAH C. FLEET.
4. MARY F. FLEET.

Others mentioned: Henry T. Duke; John D. Andrews' Tavern at the Courthouse; Deposition of
Ralph Wingfield.

COLEMAN VS. COLEMAN, 1872 (1872-1873)

Lewis M. Coleman's Will

COLEMAN, LEWIS M. "I, Lewis M. Coleman of
Hanover County, Virginia do make this my
last will and testament. 1st. I desire that
my wife Mary A. Coleman be left sole guardian of
my children according to her will and executrix
of my estate without security, but to be subject
to the advise and control of my executors hereinafter named. 2nd. I desire that my executors
shall pay to the poor of the County of Albemarle the balance due on my promise of two hundred dollars. 3rd. I appoint Wm. LeRoy Brown.
Robt. T. Coleman, Malcolm N. Fleming, James D.
Coleman and Dr. George Fleming as joint executors. In the event of the second marriage of
my wife Mary A. Coleman, I desire that the
executors above named shall have the exclusive
control and management of my estate. Witness my
hand & seal this 19th day of March 1863. Edge
Hill, Caroline County, Virginia, 19 March 1863".

                              L. M. Coleman (Seal)
Thomas H. Welsh
H. Black, M. R. Coleman, Geo. Fleming,
M. E. Schooler, Jas. D. Coleman.

"My wife and the executors above named shall
have full power to sell any portion of my
estate real or personal if they think it con-
ductive to the interest of my children & invest
the money in other securities. I also desire
that my subscription of one hundred dollars towards shoeing my Regiment (1st Va. Artillery)
to be paid.Witness my hand & seal this 19th day
of March 1863.   Lewis M. Coleman."

LEWIS M. COLEMAN, dec'd. Will dated 19 March
1863, Codicil same date. Died from wounds he
received in battle. Had an interest in tract of
land called "Landora" in Caroline County, which
he had sold just before his death, to his brother, Dr. Robert T. Coleman. Survived by his
widow, Mary Ambler Coleman, Executrix, and by
three children:
1. MATILDA M. COLEMAN.
2. CLAUDIA B. COLEMAN.
3. LEWIS M. COLEMAN. (Jr.)

       CORBIN VS. BOYD'S ADMRS &C., 1835 (7)
          WELLFORD & WIFE VS. ARMISTEAD
                & OTHERS, 1833 (50)

CORBIN, RICHARD, of King & Queen County,
died with will in June 1819, "possessed of
a considerable quantity of valuable furniture and a considerable quantity of valuable
plate and silver which he loaned to his widow
Rebecca for life or until his son James P. Corbin attains the age of 21." The son, James P.
was residuary devisee of his Estate, real and
personal, consisting of various plantations,
numerous slaves, large debts due to him, etc.
His plantations were "White Hall," "Corbin Hall"
"Green Branch," "Nesting," and "Laneville" also
"Moses Neck," and "Farley Dale." In the deposition of Benjamin Boughton taken in 1836 at the
office of Thomas B. Barton, he estimated the
annual net profits of these estates from $8,000
to $10,000 "when he was Agent for Mr. Corbin
and visited these estates at his direction."
His widow, Rebecca Parke Corbin was Executrix
until her death, when John Faunteleroy and Wm.
Boyd were appointed Administrators de bonis non

Rebecca Parke Corbin's Will

REBECCA PARKE CORBIN. "I, Rebecca Parke Corbin
of Laneville in the County of King & Queen
do make this my last will and testament as follows: I give to my son James Parke Corbin one
negro boy named Richard White and a choice horse
from White Hall when he arrives at the age of
twenty-one. I give to my daughter Elizabeth
Farley Carter one-third of all the money that I
am or may be entitled to from my mother's estate
to her and her heirs forever. I leave my old
servant Sally free and to receive from my estate
fifty dollars annually for her support. All the
balance of my estate both real and personal
except my watch I give to my two daughters
Rebecca Parke Farley Faunteleroy and my daughter
Catherine Carter Corbin to be equally divided
between them and their heirs lawfully begotten
living at the time of their death, if any of my
daughters Rebecca P. F. Faunteleroy or my daughter Catherine Carter Corbin should die without
lawful heirs of their bodies the part that I
have given to go to their survivors. I give my
watch to my daughter Catherine Carter Corbin.
Lastly I appoint my friend William Boyd, and Jno

Faunteleroy Executors to this my last will and testament, and it is my will and wish that the Court will permit them to qualify as such without giving any Security. Witness my hand and seal this 29th day of November 1821."

Rebecca P. Corbin (Seal)

Signed and acknowledged
in presence of
    Saml Harris
    Ann M. Dudley.

Rebecca Parke Corbin, the widow of Richard died in March or April 1822. The value of her personal estate was $7,960. John Faunteleroy qualified as Executor, and he is deceased. Wm. Boyd qualified as Executor on 11 October 1824. He is also deceased and William Armistead is Administrator of Mrs. Corbin and of William Boyd. Richard and Rebecca P. Corbin survived by issue:

1. JAMES PARKE CORBIN, an infant of tender years at the death of his father.

2. REBECCA PARKE FARLEY, called Faunteleroy in her mother's will of 1821, probably then the wife of John Faunteleroy, her mother's first Executor, who it is said lived with Mrs. Corbin. He was also one of the Executors of Richard Corbin's Estate. John Faunteleroy is deceased in 1824 (probably died in 1824) when Thomas William Faunteleroy is his Administrator. In 1833 she is the wife of William N. Wellford.

3. CATHERINE CARTER, in 1833 she is the wife of a Mr. Faunteleroy.

4. ELIZABETH FARLEY CARTER CORBIN, mentioned in her mother's will, but not involved or mentioned in the suits.

ARMISTEAD, WILLIAM, JR., of Gloucester County qualified in King & Queen County as Administrator with the will annexed of William Boyd, dec'd, with George B. Poindexter, William Chamberlayne, J. Francis Row and Thomas Lumpkin as Securities. William Boyd had qualified as the Executor of Mrs. Rebecca P. Corbin on 11 Oct. 1824, giving bond in the amount of One Hundred Thousand Dollars. (He was also Executor in 1823 of John Boyd, dec'd.) "Certificate of qualification of William Armistead as Administrator of Mrs. Corbin and Wm. Boyd not found in office - order book burnt by burning of office. No Inventory or appraisement or Administration of Wm. Boyd's Estate returned by Wm. Armistead."- R.Pollard, Jr., 11 June 1833. (Robert Pollard, Jr., Clerk of Court, King & Queen County.) William Armistead, in 1833 was in Huntsville, Madison County, Alabama. Deceased in 1859, George W. Doswell, Sheriff, Hanover County, Administrator.

Others mentioned: William Robbins, John Dixon, and Ptn R. Nelson, who with William Boyd, Exor., inventoried Estate of Mrs. Corbin in 1825; Richard Randolph Corbin, Guardian of C. C. Faunteleroy; William B. Boyd, William Boyd & Co., and Robert Boyd's Estate; William Chamberlayne of Gloucester County, dec'd, Edward C. Mosby, Executor in 1833; Col. Moore G. Faunteleroy. W. T. Shackelford who repaired a carriage for Mrs. Corbin; George Ross, a creditor of Richard Corbin and witness in 1836; Commissioners, 1829: William Garrett, John Southgate, John W. Fleet, Ro. M. Spencer - King & Queen County; Justices of King & Queen 1824: James H. Henry, Benjamin Pollard, Robert M. Spencer and Alexander Fleet; In 1833: Reuben M. Garnett, Lee Boulware, John Motley, and Temple Walker; George B. Pendleton, Deputy Clerk of Court, King & Queen County 1833. Thomas F. Spencer, Coronor, King & Queen 1833.

Reference is made to a Law Suit in Williamsburg in which the Estate of Richard Corbin is involved.

COSBY VS. BROWN, 1837 (9)

COSBY, AZE GAD, of Louisa County, bricklayer, on 1 Dec. 1827, purchased 106 1/8 acres of land known as the "Howard Tract," from Walter Crenshaw and Martha, his wife, adjoining James McDaniell, Absolum Pate, Austin Morris, John Donnely, and Crenshaw for consideration of $212.25. On 28 May 1828, "for love and affection he bears to the children of his sister Eliza Donalla, conveys to them this land, one mare and colt, etc." James Donella "had intermarried with Eliza Cosby sister of Izzad Cosby and has [in 1837] seven children now alive, the eldest of whom is twelve years of age." On 1st Jan. 1837,"Izad Cosby, brick-layer, is in the County of Goochland." [Note variations in spelling of these names].

Others mentioned: Samuel Heritage who "worked for James Donelly for twelve months; Mrs. Martha Gentry; George Pitman; Fleming Brown and his son Peter W. Brown, both of whom had taught school at Walter Crenshaw's gate; Depositions of Dr. Callom B. Jones, Thomas B. Bowles, Barret White, and James McDowell in 1839.

CRENSHAW'S ADMR. VS. POLLARD &C., 1871 (41)

Chapman Crenshaw's Will

CRENSHAW, CHAPMAN. "In the name of God amen. I, Chapman Crenshaw doth make this my last will and testament, in the first place it is my woush that all my just debts shall be paid, and in the second plaice I lone to my wife Mary Crenshaw al my estate boath real and personal so long as she remains my widow, and

in case she shal marry or die then I give to
each of my Darters that I had by the said Mary
Crenshaw that may be alive fifty dollars each
to be rased first out of my estate and then the
ballance of my estate I give to all my children
that I had by the said Mary Crenshaw to be
equally divided between them equal or thir airs
lawfully begotten of the body. I also appoint
my sons Leonard A. Crenshaw and Tomolion B.
Crenshaw or either of them my Exetors to this
my last will and testament As witness my hand
and seal this 12th day of October 1840.

Teste,   Chap^m Crenshaw (Seal)
   Washington C. Crenshaw
   Leonard J. Clough
   Edward J. Crenshaw

At a Court of Monthly Session held for Hanover
County at the Courthouse on Tuesday the 26th
January 1841. This last will and testament of
Chapman Crenshaw dec'd was proved by the oaths
of Washington C. Crenshaw, Leonard J. Clough
and Edward J. Crenshaw, the witnesses thereto,
and is ordered to be recorded.
   Teste, Philip B. Winston, C.H.C.
   A Copy, Teste, Wm. O. Winston, D.C.H.C.

CHAPMAN CRENSHAW, of Hanover. Will dated 12
October 1840, Probated 26 January 1841. Tomeleon Crenshaw qualified as Executor. Possessed
220 acres of land adjoining W. C. Crenshaw, Wm.
P. Stone, dec'd, and others; also 12 or 14
slaves. Survived by his widow, Mary, who died
intestate in February 1871. She had a sister,
Miss Lucy Clough. Chapman Crenshaw's issue:

1. TOMELEON CRENSHAW, was Executor of his
   father's Estate. Died intestate leaving
   issue:
   1. ELDORUS CRENSHAW, aged 20 in 1871.
   2. HENRIETTA CRENSHAW, aged 16 in 1871.
2. MILTON C. CRENSHAW.
3. HARRIET, wife of Hezekiah G. Pollard. They
   live in Illionis.
4. AMANDA, wife of James M. Pollard of Hanover.
5. THOMAS H. CRENSHAW, of Henrico. Lived for
   eight years in Mississippi. In 1872 he is
   47 years of age, and his wife is Catherine Crenshaw.
6. RICHARD G. CRENSHAW. Left Virginia in 1844
   or 1845, lives in New Orleans, La., where
   his address in 1872 was 625 Moreau St.
   His infant name was Freeborn G. Crenshaw.
7. JOSEPHUS W. CRENSHAW, died in 1868, survived by his widow, Irene, and children:
   1. ANNA G. CRENSHAW.
   2. CORA E. CRENSHAW.
   3. MARY J. CRENSHAW.
   4. ROBERT E. CRENSHAW.
   Who are infants in 1872. Irene, the widow has intermarried with Joseph Bowles.
8. INDIANA H., wife of David A. Shepperson of
   Richmond, Va.

9. LUCY HASSIE, wife of George W. Trimmer of
   Richmond, Va.
10. SARAH E. CRENSHAW, of Hanover County.
11. LEONARD A. CRENSHAW.

SARAH E. CRENSHAW, who is not the daughter of
Chapman Crenshaw, in her deposition, speaks of
"Uncle Nat. C. Crenshaw," and "Uncle Milton
Crenshaw."

   CRENSHAW VS. STANLEY & OTHERS, 1873 (2)
   CRENSHAW VS. CRENSHAW, 1856 (10)

CRENSHAW, THOMAS, dec'd of Hanover County,
had devised 188 acres to Sarah Crenshaw
for life, and at her death, to her children by her deceased husband, Joel Crenshaw,
who are, in 1873:

1. WASHINGTON C. CRENSHAW, died unmarried,
   intestate in 1872. Edward J. Crenshaw,
   a brother, Administrator. They had been
   partners in the farming and milling business.
2. EDWARD J. CRENSHAW, Administrator of his
   brother, Washington C. Crenshaw's Estate.
   Circa 1836 he entered in partnership
   with this brother for conducting a farming and milling business, and continued
   until the latter's death in 1872. They
   purchased on 30 April 1839 lands of
   Hamilton A. Crenshaw and John Stanley
   lands adjoining Henry Pollard and Joseph
   Vaughan's Estate, and other tracts, among
   them, that of Thomas Crenshaw, dec'd,
   also a tract of land, 188 acres, devised
   by Thomas Crenshaw to Sarah Crenshaw for
   life, then to her children by her dec'd
   husband, Joel Crenshaw.
3. HAMILTON A. CRENSHAW, of Richmond, Va. in
   1840, when on 9 May he executed a Deed of
   Trust to Richard M. Crump, Trustee of
   Richmond, for the benefit of Washington
   C. Crenshaw, and Nathaniel Cross of Han-
   over, and Dr. William Winturn of Henrico.
   It is said that his father was Joel Crenshaw, dec'd, and his mother was Sarah
   Crenshaw, dec'd, and his grandfather was
   Thomas Crenshaw, dec'd, all of Hanover.
   He had been Executor of the Estate of
   Thomas Crenshaw, dec'd, and Guardian of
   Edward J., Eliza A., and Virginia T.
   Crenshaw. Securities were Washington C.
   Crenshaw, Chapman Crenshaw, James McDowell and Walter Crenshaw. In 1873 it was
   stated that Hamilton A. died some years
   before Washington C., leaving two children, who died in infancy.
4. MARY C., dec'd, married John Stanley, who
   survived, with their five children:
   1. JOEL T. STANLEY.
   2. CLARENDA W, wife of Fabius H. Hen-
      drick.
   3. LOUISA A., wife of Samuel S. Wingfield.

4. MARY STANLEY.
5. SALLY, dec'd, married Mr. Anthony.
   1. MARY ANTHONY, infant daughter.

Others mentioned: Benjamin W. Green, who had been in partnership with Hamilton A. Crenshaw under the trade name of "Green & Crenshaw" in the Coal and Grainnery business; Mehitabel Dabney, dec'd, William B. Dabney, Admr. [Reference is made to a Suit in Hustings Court of Richmond 26 September 1836, in which Sarah E. Dabney and Lucy H. Dabney were plaintiffs, and Martha Stuart, defendant.]

CROSS' HEIRS VS. CROSS & OTHERS, 1835 (8)
  PERRIN VS. STARKE & OTHERS, 1843 (29)
SMITH'S ADMR. VS. CROSS' ADMR., 1858 (53)

John Tinsley's Will

TINSLEY, JOHN, "In the name of God amen. I, John Tinsley of Hanover County being sick and weak of body but in perfect mind and memory thanks be to Almighty God, and Knowing it is appointed unto all men once to die, Do make this my last Will and Testament as touching my temporal concerns in manner and form following. But principally and first of all I recommend my Soul to Almighty God who gave it hoping through the merits of my blessed Savior and redeemer Jesus Christ to find redemption and forgiveness of my sins - my body I recommend to be buried in a Christian like manner. Imprimis, my will and desire is that my son David Tinsley - and Sarah Starke shall maintain my wife Sarah Tinsley during her natural life. Item: I give to my son David Tinsley two hundred and thirty-eight acres of land whereon he now lives, being part of two hundred and eighty acres that I purchased of Bowler Cocke and I lend unto my said son David Tinsley during his natural life the following negroes to wit - Joe, Nan, Judy,George Fanny, Reuben, Winny, Amey, Beck, Daniel, Charles, Beck, Teanor, John, Lewis, George, Mordecai & Lucy which said negroes and their increase I give to the surviving children of my said son David Tinsley to be equally divided between them at his death - but in case any of his said children should die and leave issue in his lifetime, it is my will and desire that that issue should have what its parent would have been entitled to, provided he or she had survived his, her or their father David Tinsley. Item: I lend to my said Daughter Sarah Starke two hundred acres of land being the plantation whereon I now live and nineteen negroes of the following names: Pompey, Fondey, Bradley, Moll, Judy, Betty, Milley, Fanny, Maria, Gilley, Mima, Claiborne, Hannah, Frank, Polly, Robin, Beck, Oney, and Dick. I give the said land after the death of my said Daughter to my Grandson Thomas Starke to him and his heirs forever the negores that I have lent her, I desire they and their increase

may be equally   amongst my said Daughters surviving children at her death, but in case any of her children should die in her lifetime, leaving lawful issue, then it is my will and desire that that issue should have what its father or mother would have had, provided he, she or they had have survived his, her or their said mother Sarah Starke. I also give her one sorrel horse. Item: I lend to my Daughter Lucy Cross ten negroes, namely - Sukey, James, Jane, Bartlet, Phebe, China, Ned, Joseph, Beck and Sarah, - and I give her two young Cattle, - the negroes and their increase, I give to the surviving children of my said daughter Lucy Cross, to be equally divided between them at her death, but in case any of her children should die in her lifetime, leaving Lawful issue, then it is my will and desire that, that issue should have what its father or mother would have been entitled to provided he, she or they had survived his, her or their said mother Lucy Cross. I lend to my son William Tinsley fifty acres of land being part of the 288 acres purchased of Bowler Cocke, being at the mouth of a lane at a Hickory running down to Peter Lyons' line, as far as will take in fifty acres, running thence up the fork - a course that will take in 50 acres from thence to his own line, - during his natural life and after his death I give the aforesaid fifty acres of land to my granddaughter Elizabeth Tinsley, daughter of my son David Tinsley, to her and her heirs forever. I give to my son William Tinsley five pounds cash, and to my grandchildren by my son Philip Tinsley, dec'd, I give to each of them one Dollar being Polley, Patsey, William, John, Burwell and Nancy - my crop that is now growing or on the ground I desire may be equally divided between my son David Tinsley and my daughter Sarah Starke. I appoint my son David Tinsley my whole and Sole executor to see this my will executed. It is my will and desire that my estate should not be appraised. In testimony whereof I (having heard this will distinctly read) do make & ordain it my last will and testament & in consequence thereto have hereunto set my hand and seal 13th day of October 1795."

Witness present reading   John Tinsley (Seal)
and signing:
  Thos Tinsley
  Christopher Butler
  Nathl Bowe.

At a Court held for Hanover County at the Courthouse on Thursday the 3.^d of December 1795. This last will and testament of John Tinsley, dec'd was offered for proof by David Tinsley the executor therein named and was proved by the oath of Thomas Tinsley, Christopher Butler, and Nathaniel Bowe the witnesses thereto and is ordered to be recorded.
  Teste, William Pollard, C.H.C.
  A Copy, Teste, Philip B. Winston, C.H.C.

JOHN TINSLEY, dec'd of Hanover. Will dated 13 October 1795, Probated 3 December 1795. Survived by his widow Sarah, and children and grandchildren, among whom:

1. PHILIP TINSLEY, died prior to 1795, leaving children as mentioned in John Tinsley's will:
    1. POLLY TINSLEY.
    2. PATSEY TINSLEY.
    3. WILLIAM TINSLEY.
    4. JOHN TINSLEY.
    5. BURWELL TINSLEY.
    6. NANCY TINSLEY.
2. DAVID TINSLEY, who had issue in 1795 perhaps among others:
    1. ELIZABETH TINSLEY.
3. WILLIAM TINSLEY.
4. SARAH, married in her 23rd year a Mr. Starke. On 11 February 1835 deposed that she was sixty years of age. Issue perhaps among others:
    1. THOMAS STARKE.
    2. JANE, wife of a Mr. Bowles in 1835.
5. LUCY "ran away and married Samuel Cross some eight or nine years before the death of her father. They were married at Captain Macon's. Samuel Cross lived at Major Timberlake's. She had three children before her sister Sarah was married to Starke." Samuel Cross died prior to 1806, survived by his widow, Lucy who was alive in 1831, but deceased in 1835, leaving four children:
    1. OLIVER T. CROSS, dec'd in 1835 survived by widow Mary V. (Polly),Admx. and Guardian of her infant children. She is dec'd in 1858, leaving issue:
        1. ARAMINTA C., married Wm. Smith. He survived her in 1842 and is her Admr. No issue.
        2. MARTHA B., married Edward Griffin Living in Henrico Co. in 1858.
        3. MARY ANN, married James H. Smith. He survived her in 1845, and is her Admr. No. issue.
        4. JOHN F. CROSS. After his mother's death was Admr. of his father's Estate.
        5. FRANCES (FANNY) R., wife of Joseph T. Priddy.
        6. CHARLES P. CROSS.
    2. THOMAS CROSS.
    3. ELIZABETH, married nearly 20 years in 1835 to Benjamin Hazlegrove, who owned a Tavern in Hanover. "No issue and probably never will."
    4. CATHERINE, dec'd, married David Lyle, "Departed this life without issue."

Commissioners: Reuben Meredith, Laney Jones, Edwin Shelton, Benj. Wingfield, Edward H. Mc Gehee. Robert Michie, witness 1825. Catherine Ellis, Michael Jones, Albert G.,&Susanna Bowe.

PERRIN VS. STARKE & OTHERS, 1843 (29)

CROSS, OLIVER, of Hanover, and his wife, Sarah Cross, separated circa 1807, when he executed a Deed of Trust conveying 600 acres of land and six slaves for her benefit. Samuel Day, Trustee, dec'd in 1811, and John Glazebrook, Acting Trustee, under the decree of Hanover Court of 28 February 1811 for selling the lands belonging to Oliver Cross and Sarah his wife of Hanover. Others involved in this transaction were Samuel Perrin, John Starke, Francis Blunt and Nathaniel Cross. In 1819 Sarah Cross is deceased. Oliver Cross who had "been in Tennessee" survives. Their issue in 1843:
1. JOHN CROSS, "JR.", whose wife is Nancy.
2. ELIZABETH, wife of Clayton Coleman.
3. JOSEPH CROSS.
4. WILLIAM CROSS.

Oliver Cross had a brother, Joseph Cross. "Sam'l Perrin was indebted to the late Mrs. Mary Ann Jones, the grandmother of the late Wm.W.Michie, Esq., who was her principal heir and legatee." Thomas Perrin was her close friend and neighbor

Others mentioned: Fleming B. Cross; Samuel T. Pulliam; John Priddy; Edmund Taylor's Tavern; James P. Tyler; William S. White; Benjamin Wingfield; Horatio Gates Winston, an Attorney; Gervias S. Trueheart of Amelia County, and Henry P. Southall, Justice of the Peace of Amelia County, 1843.

DAVIS & OTHERS VS. CROSS & OTHERS, 1850 (10)

CROSS, FLEMING B., of Hanover died intestate circa 1830, without issue "leaving some real estate - a number of slaves and personal property. Shortly after his death, Nancy Cross his widow (who has since married William H. B. Campbell) qualified as Administratrix." She died without issue and intestate, and having only a life estate, her dower and distributable share passed to his brothers and sisters:

FINCH CROSS, dec'd, a brother, died intestate. Jordan Harris, Admr. Survived by widow, Nancy Cross, and issue:
1. MARGARET E., wife of Jordan Harris.
2. SHELTON V. CROSS.
3. BETSY ANN, wife of Walter T. Gilman.
4. HENRY G. CROSS.
5. ELDRIDGE CROSS.
6. ANN, wife of Charles McDowell.
7. SUSANNA CROSS, under 21 years of age.
8. THOMAS F. CROSS, under 21 years of age.
9. JOSEPH CROSS, under twenty-one years of age.

JOHN F. CROSS, dec'd. Widow, Ann N., Admx., who was another brother. Issue:
1. JAMES F. CROSS.

2. WILLIAM I. CROSS.

3. EDWIN O. CROSS.

4. SARAH H., wife of James Wortham.

5. JOHN F. CROSS.

6. SHELTON H. CROSS, an infant.

USANNA, a sister, widow of Tinsley Davis, no
surviving issue.

LIZABETH, wife of William L. White. Joseph
Starke, Trustee.

amuel Perrin sold land to Fleming B. Cross.

UNNINGHAM'S ADMR. VS. BASSETT'S ADMR., 1853 (6)

CUNNINGHAM, WILLIAM, dec'd of Hanover Co.,
died intestate in 1831. Richard G. Smith,
Administrator. Bonds in Cunningham's
ffects: John Bassett, dec'd, late of Hanover.
G. W. Bassett promised to pay; Wm. Cunningham,
s Administrator of J. W. Tomlin, dec'd; Benja-
en Brand, Executor of Joshua Drinkard.

CASON VS. CASON &C., 1867 (23)

CASON, WILLIAM, of Spotsylvania, died intestate in 1851 or 1852. James B. Cason, Admr.
His securities were Jane P. Cason and Lucy
ickinson. (Lucy is dec'd and Burwell B. Dickin-
on is her Administrator). At the death of Wil-
iam Cason "had neither father, mother, brothers
r sisters - only the children of four brothers
ho were his heirs."

DWARD CASON, dec'd, who was a brother, who left
issue:
1. ROBERT CASON.
2. ELIZABETH CASON.

HOMAS CASON, dec'd, who was a brother, who left
issue:
1. NELSON CASON.
2. GRANVILLE CASON.
3. EDMUND CASON.
4. NANCY, wife of Alexander Fitzhugh.
5. MARY, wife of a Mr. Wilkerson.
6. LUCINDA, dec'd, who married John Estes,
   who is her Administrator.
7. JOHN CASON, dec'd, whose children are unknown.

AMES CASON, dec'd, who was a brother, who left
children whose names are unknown.

OHN CASON, dec'd, who was a brother, who left
children whose names are unknown.

he children and heirs of John Cason, dec'd son
f Thomas, a brother, and of James Cason, dec'd
brother of William Cason, dec'd, are not dis-
inguished, but who are as follows:

Richard W. Pierce and Susan, his wife, Miles
Wigglesworth and Amelia, his wife, and William,
Edward and Nancy Cason; also Edward M. Cason;
Hobson O. Gentry and Jane, his wife; William A.
Baughan and Lucy Ann, his wife; Joseph H. John-
son and Jane, his wife; Addison Hall and Eliza-
beth, his wife; and Silas, Hardenia and Horatio
Gentry, infants, John J. Chew, their Guardian.

DABNEY VS. WASH & OTHERS, 1847   (13)

DABNEY, CORNELIUS, dec'd. "Several years
ago returned from the State of Kentucky
to which he had emigrated in a very infirm
state of health and bringing with him only your
orator, Charles C. Dabney, of all his children
- then under 21 years of age - and went to reside with Nathaniel C. Wash of Hanover who had
intermarried with a relative, and in whose kindness he had much confidence, and where Cornelius
Dabney died, possessed of a considerable sum of
money." "He left surviving him only the following children."
1. CHARLES CORNELIUS DABNEY.
2. ANN E., wife of William H. Jones.
3. CAROLINE C. DABNEY, under 21 years of age.

Depositions, 1847 of: John L. Owing, John C.
Pulliam, Peter Johnston, Edmund Wash, Robert P.
Clements.

WHARTON'S TRUSTEES, DABNEY'S TRUSTEES
VS. WHARTON, 1854 (25)

Mehetabel Dabney's Will

DABNEY, MEHETABEL. "I, Mehetabel Dabney of
County of Henrico and State of Virginia,
do make this my last will and testament.
I give to my daughter Martha Stuart three shares
in the bank of Virginia. I give to my daughter
Sarah four shares in the said bank, and also to
my daughter Lucy four share in said bank. The
remaining two I give to my son Wm. Beverley Dabney and in consideration of deficency of shares
I give him my watch. My lots and houses I wish
sold and an equal devesion made of the proceeds
to each of my children. The negroes also to be
devided and an equal distribution made of them,
with the priviledge to Lucy Jackson of chusing
to which of my children she wishes to belong.
The part of my property that falls to my daughter Martha to be put in trust by her brother
for the benefit of herself and children. The
money arising from the sale of the lots to be
laid out in bank stock or anything else thought
more advantageous, for her benefit, and her
brother is to remit to her every half year the
dividend of said shares, and he is also to hire
her negroes and send her the heir at the end
of every quarter. This property for Martha to
be subject to no debt of her husband's that may

have been or shall hereafter be contracted by
him and subject only to her own order, and kept
for the entire benefit of herself and children.
I give also my servant Judith to my daughter
Sarah and leave the property of my daughter
Sarah and Lucy entirely for their benefit not
to be subject to the debts of any husband. I
leave also to my daughter Martha my largest bed
now in the House. I leave to my daughter Martha
and Lucy my old woman Clarinda to be taken care
of as long as she lives, and hope they will not
be unmindful of her comfort. Written with my
own hand, in testimony of which I subscribe my
name."
                              Mehetabel Dabney
Teste:
  J. B. Fergusson
  Robt. H. Fergusson.

At a Court of Hustings held for the City of
Richmond at the Courthouse on the 25th day of
September 1835. This last will and testament
of Mehetabel Dabney late of the City of Richmond deceased was proved according to law by
the oaths of James B. Ferguson and Robert B.
Ferguson the subscribing witnesses thereto, and
ordered to be recorded and on the motion of
William B. Dabney, who made oath in the form
prescribed by the act to amend the act entitled
an act reducing into one the several acts concerning wills, the distribution of intestate's
estates and the duty of executors and administrators passed the 16th day of February 1825
and with Sarah E. Dabney and Lucy H. Dabney his
securities entered into and acknowledged a bond
in the penalty of eighteen thousand dollars conditioned as required by the aforesaid act, certificate is granted the said Wm. B. Dabney for
obtaining letters of administration on the
estate of the said decedant, with the said will
annexed in due form.
    Teste, N. P. Howard, Clk.
    A Copy, Teste, Ro Howard, Clk.

MEHETABEL DABNEY of Henrico County. Will not
    dated. Probated 25 September 1835. William
    B. Dabney qualified as Executor. He was sur-
vived by the following children:
  1. WILLIAM B. DABNEY, Executor.
  2. MARTHA, wife of a Mr. Stuart in 1835.
  3. LUCY JACKSON, married after 1835 Robert H.
     Wharton. She and her children were lega-
     tees of Charlotte A. Wharton, who died
     in Goochland County with will dated 15
     February 1841. Her children were:
     1. WILLIAM A. WHARTON, aged 16 in 1856.
     2. RICHARD G. WHARTON, aged 14 in 1856.
     3. CHARLES D. WHARTON, under 14 in 1856.
     4. LUCY H. WHARTON, under 14 in 1856.
     5. ROBERT H. WHARTON, age not stated.
  4. SARAH DABNEY.
Depositions 1856 of: John F. Cross, George Wm.
Pollard, Archibald B. Timberlake, Hector Bowe.
William C. Wickham, Justice of the Peace.

DABNEY VS. NORVELL & OTHERS, 1848 (13)

DABNEY, WILLIAM B., married Martha Frances,
    daughter of Mrs. Ann Norvell, a widow of
    Richmond, Va. Mrs. Norvell owned land in
Hanover County which was generally known as the
place of birth of Honorable Henry Clay, which
adjoined the lands of Henry M. Hudson and others
William B. Dabney executed a Deed of Trust to
Mrs. Norvell in 1840. His issue in 1848 were:
  1. ANN MEHETABEL DABNEY.
  2. FRANCES BEVERLEY DABNEY.
  3. ALICE MARY DABNEY.
  4. CATHERINE ELIZABETH DABNEY.
All of whom were under age in 1848. Philip B.
Jones of Orange County mentioned.

DARRACOTT & OTHERS VS. U. S. & OTHERS, 1826 (12)
        DARRACOTT'S ADMR. VS. DARRACOTT
              & OTHERS, 1847 (14)

DARRACOTT, JOHN, of Hanover, dec'd. Left a
    considerable real and personal estate. He
    had been one of the Securities of William
D. Taylor, Administrator of Zachariah Burnley.
Darracott's land was purchased by Robert Ellett.
He was survived by his widow, Mary A. Darracott
and by eleven children:
  1. RICHARD F. DARRACOTT, who lived at Mill-
     ford in 1852.
  2. ELIZABETH L., wife of William D. Winston.
  3. WILLIAM P. DARRACOTT.
  4. JOHN DARRACOTT.
  5. GEORGE W. DARRACOTT.
  6. MARY P. DARRACOTT.
  7. SUSAN DARRACOTT.
  8. BENJAMIN F. DARRACOTT.
  9. CHARLES R. DARRACOTT, an infant in 1847.
 10. ANN W. DARRACOTT, an infant in 1847.
 11. ROBERT H. DARRACOTT, an infant in 1847.

TAYLOR, WILLIAM D., of Hanover, owned "Taylorsville" an estate of between five and six hundred
acres, which in 1819 he conveyed to Richard Morris, Jr., and Henry Robinson, Trustees for the
benefit of James Maury Morris. Afterwards became Administrator of the Estate of Zachariah
Burnley [his wife being Burnley's daughter] and
John Darracott and James Madison were his Securities. In 1822 he is Collector of the Revenue
of the United States "for this District." In
1825, makes a deposition in Goochland County.

Others mentioned: Charles Morris; A. R. Thornton, United States Deputy Marshall 1822.

DAVIS' EXOR. VS. DAVIS & OTHERS, 1852 (13)

DAVIS, TINSLEY, of the State of Tennessee,
    died in January 1850, intestate. Philip B.
    Winston qualified as Administrator. The
intestate had resided in Shelby County, Tenn. He

was survived by children:
1. ROBERT R. DAVIS.
2. BEVERLY S. DAVIS.
3. SYCURGUS DAVIS.
4. MARIA A. R. PETTUS.
5. WATSON D. DAVIS, an infant, John H. Van-
   hook, Guardian.
6. ANGELINA H. DAVIS, an infant.
7. TINSLEY DAVIS, an infant.
8. HUGH DAVIS, an infant.

Others mentioned: Susanna Davis; J. M. Stanard of Mobile, Alabama testifies to some writing of Henry Davis who lived in Pensacole, Fla., and is now dead. In his letter of 19 January 1846, Stanard suggests that "George Willis could present an original document proving Davis' signature." Connection of Susanna and Henry Davis to the intestate is not stated.

DEALS VS. DEALS, 1860 (13)

DEALS, PEYTON, married in 1860 Parmelia, daughter of Edmund L. Hall and Mary Corker of Hanover, and lived together until he entered the Army. She had married Larkin James Harlow, son of William Harlow and Elizabeth McGraw.   Divorce.

TALLEY & OTHERS VS. DEJARNATTE'S EXORS 1836 (41)
   WINSTON VS. WILLIAMSON &C., 1869 (52)
      William Y. DeJarnatte's Will

DEJARNATTE, WILLIAM Y. "I, William Y. De-Jarnatte of Hanover County and State of Virginia being in perfect health, mind and memory do hereby make my last will and testament in manner and form following, that is to say. First I desire that all my just debts be paid out of my personal estate . 2ndly I desire that my interest in the tract of land called "Fall Point" late the property of John Harris, dec'd be sold and conveyed by my exors hereinafter named on a credit of twelve months provided they can get as much as nine dollars pr acre; one half of the money arising therefrom I give to my loving wife to her and her heirs forever, the other half to be equally divided amongst my three children. 3dly Should my wife marry I do desire that my exors put my children with some respectable female teacher to be by her brought up and educated under the directions of my sd executors, whom I do appoint guardians to my children; this request I hope they will punctually attend to indeed should they qualify as my exors (which I trust in God they will) they would be purjured did they not do so. My reason for this request is that it is the most unpleasant thing I never thought of, to have my children domineered over by - a step father, but when they arrive to such an age as to be capable of judging for themselves, if be their

and my executors should have no objection and it should be the wish of their mother and father in law that they should live with them, they may be permitted to do so. 4 I do by this my last will and testament emancipate and set free Maria the mulatto girl I bought out of the estate of David Richardson, dec'd & her two children. 5thly. I desire that my executors do carry or cause to be carried to the State of Ohio the s^d negroes within twelve months from my decease at the charge of my estate ofcourse; and endeavor to put them under the care of some respectable family (a quaker family would be prefered.) 6thly. I desire that my exors do for the first year furnish the s^d negroes with an ample support of bread & meal & a place to live at. 7thly As soon as the situation of my estate will admit and not exceeding twelve months after the s^d negroes shall have been carried to the sd state it is my desire that my Exors do purchase one hundred acres of land in the sd state in the County or some adjacent County to that in which the quakers from the Cedar Creek settlement in the State of Virginia have removed to wit Littleberry Crew and others for the sd negroes to reside and to have a comfortable log house made on the said land for them one forth sd land to be cleared & arable at least. 8thly I lend the land thus to be purchased to Maria during her life and after her death to be equally divided between her two children to them and their heirs forever. 9thly I desire that my exors do take out of my personal estate any sum not exceeding four hundred Dollars for the purpose of purchasing the sd land, though I expect a much less sum will do. 10thly As to the residue of my estate I wish it divided according to the statute directing the distribution of intestates estates believing that the law makes an equitable distribution with this exception that the one third of. my estate to which my loving wife will be entitled be selected by her and not allotted that is she is to make choice of such negroes as may think proper so as to make up her share & take her dower in the lands where she pleases, the other two thirds to be equally divided amongst all my children. Lastly I appoint Thomas Doswell and Paul T. Doswell my brothers in Law and my friends Thomas Price, jr. exors of this my last will and testament. I hope they will all qualify if they have that regard for me and my family which I have for them. I do hereby revoke all former will by me heretofore made. In witness whereof I have hereunto set my hand and affixed my seal this twenty fourth day of June in the year of our Lord one thousand eight hundred and fifteen."
                    W. Y. DeJarnatte (Seal)

      Codicil to the annexed will
First my will and desire is that my exors heretofore named shall in twelve months after my death sell at Public Sale, on a credit of one,

two and three years the tract of land on which
I at present reside. 2ndly I give to my much
beloved-wife five hundred dollars value in my
household furniture to be selected at her own
discretion. 3rdly It is my will that the second
clause of my will directing a sale of that part
of the land called Fall Point which I purchased
of the heirs of the late Jno Harris be revoked,
and it is my desire that my exors (if in their
discretion they may think proper) do proceed to
purchase out the balance of the said heirs as
they arrive to lawful age and that the profits
of my estate after the support of my wife and
family (and if necessary) any part of my personal estate be disposed of to enable them to
affect so desirable an object. 4thly The debt
due me from Elkanah Talley Secured by a deed of
trust duly recorded, I desire should be assigned
to my sister Catherine and her children injoin-
ing on my exors by all means to put it in such
a situation as not to be made subject to the
payment of his debts or for his use - and
should my said Sister determine to remove to
the Westward, that my exors should from the
property conveyed in trust aforesaid raise the
sum of two hundred dollars for the purpose of
defraying the expences of moving &c. 5thly
Having purchase out all the reversionary interest in the personal estate of William Cocke,
dec'd except George Richardson Cocke's interest,
my exors are at liberty to exercise their discretion in the purchase of his interest also.
6thly and Lastly. It is my will and desire that
my brothers in law Thomas and Paul T. Doswell
and my friend Thomas Price, jr. should act as
sole exors to this my last Will and that my
friend Francis Blunt's name has been erased at
my request. In witness whereof I have hereunto
set my hand and affixed my seal this 19th January 1817."

                                W. Y. DeJarnatte

Witnesses -
  Chas Morris
  Josiah Holt
  John D. Thilman

At a Court of Monthly Session held for Hanover
County at the Courthouse on Wednesday the 26th
of March 1817. This last will and testament of
William Y. Dejarnatte dec'd and the Codicil
thereafter written, were offered to proof by
Thomas Doswell and Thomas Price, jr. two of the
executors therein named & Samuel Richardson and
Richard Morris, junr. being sworn and examined
declare that they are well acquainted with the
hand writing of the said deceased, and that
they verily believe that the said will was wholly written signed and sealed by him; and the
said Codicil being proved by the oaths of
Josiah Holt and John D. Thilman two of the witnesses thereto; and the said Will and Codicil
being also proved by the oaths of the said
Executors, are ordered to be recorded. Teste,
William Pollard C.H.C. Copy,Ph.B.Winston, C.H.C.

WILLIAM Y. DEJARNATTE, of Hanover. Will dat-
4 June 1815, Codicil 19 January 1817. Prov-
26 March 1817. Appointed "brothers in law Thom-
Doswell and Paul T. Doswell" and friend Thomas
Price, Jr., Executors. Mentioned Catherine hi-
sister. Survived by his widow, Sophia Jane (wh-
afterwards married Henry Winston, both decease-
in 1836) Thomas Doswell was her representative
in this suit. Issue:
  1. JANE MARIA, wife of Roscow Lipscomb.
  2. ELIZABETH S., died intestate prior to
       1869, wife of a Mr. Williamson, by whom
       she had issue:
       1. DABNEY WILLIAMSON.
       2. LUCY B. WILLIAMSON.
       3. THOMAS D. WILLIAMSON.
       4. MARY J., died prior to 1869, married
            Thomas H. Fox, who with an infant
            son, whose name is not stated,
            survive her.
  3. WILLIAM Y. DEJARNATTE, died with a will
       prior to 1869. John G. Harris and Wm. D-
       Winston (the latter dec'd) Executors.
       Survived by his widow, Cora, who is als-
       dec'd. Issue, an only daughter:
       1. WILLIE F, wife of Edmund P. Winston.

TALLEY, ELKANNA, of Spotsylvania County 1836
married prior to 1817, Catherine, sister of
William Y. DeJarnatte, Sr., who was mentioned
in his will. She did not remove from the state
Her issue, all infants in 1836:
  1. ALEXANDER W. TALLEY.
  2. SARAH E. TALLEY.
  3. JANE S. TALLEY.
  4. CATHERINE Y. TALLEY.
  5. MARTHA D. TALLEY.
  6. MARGARET V. TALLEY.
  7. DANIEL D. TALLEY.
  8. ELIZA ANN TALLEY.
  9. VIRGINIA T. TALLEY.
  10. AMANDA M. TALLEY.

        HANCOCK & WIFE VS. DICKINSON'S
               EXORS. &c., 1843 (18)
   THOMPSON &C. VS. DICKINSON &C., 1843 (46)
     THOMPSON'S TRUSTEES VS. DICKINSON
               & OTHERS, 1846 (43)
   CASON VS. DICKINSON'S ADMR. &C., 1853 (9)
   DICKINSON &C. VS. DICKINSON &C., 1857 (31)

           Nathaniel Dickinson's Will

DICKINSON, NATHANIEL. "I, Nathaniel Dickinson of the County of Hanover and State
of Virginia do make ordain and publish
and declare this my last will and Testament in
Manner and form following, Viz - 1st. I desire
all my Just debts be paid they are few in number and of Small amount. 2nd. I give to my so-
John C. Dickinson and his heirs forever one
eighth part of my estate. My Said Son is to be
charged with four Hundred dollars which Sum or

early that amount I paid Thomas B. Cosby Exor f Wingfield Cosby dec'd for a Negro Man for him. I also desire that my Said Son John C. Dickinson who has been for the last Nine or Ten years living on a tract of land of Mine Shall not be accountable or chargeable for any rent from the Same on conditions that he brings no charge against my estate for any repairs to House or for building done by him while he continues to reside on the same. 3rd. I give in Trust to my four sons Viz John C., William T., Burwell B. and Charles Dickinson one other eighth part of My estate for the benefit and use of My daughter Hardenia Arnold suring her Natural life if my said daughter Hardina Should have a child or children I desire that the said eighth part of my estate by the 3rd clause in this my will given in Trust to her four brothers for her benefit and use Shall at the death of my said daughter Hardena go to her child or children in fee simple but should my said daughter Hardena die leaving no issue I desire the same be equally divided between all the rest of my children or their legal representatives under the restrictions or Trust as regards my daughter Susan H. Graves as I shall here in after provide for that portion of my estate which I intend for her use and benefit. My said daughter Hardena Is to be charged with four hundred dollars for a Negro boy given her. 4th. I give to my four sons Viz. John C., William T., Burwell B., and Charles Dickinson in Trust one other part of my estate for the benefit and use of my daughter Susan H. Graves during her natural life, and at her death I give the said eighth part of my estate to her children in fee simple if any of her said children should marry and have issue and died before their Mother then I desire that the issue of such child or children may take that portion which their Father or Mother would have been entitled to if they had survived their Mother. I have paid some money and been at some expense in furnishing my said daughter Susan H. and her family but I desire that no charge be made for the same having received nearly so full compensation in Services she has rendered me. 5th. I give to my daughter Frances Hancock and her heirs forever one other eighth part of my estate. My said daughter Frances to be charged with four hundred dollars for a negro Girl given her. 6th. I give to my son Burwell B. Dickinson and his heirs forever one other eighth part of my estate. 7th. I give to my son William T. Dickinson and his heirs forever one other eighth part of my estate. 8th. I give to my son Charles Dickinson and his heirs forever one other eighth part of my estate. 9th. I give in Trust to my said four sons Viz - John C., Wm. T., Burwell B. and Charles Dickinson the remaining eighth part of my estate for the benefit and use of My daughter Minerva Dickinson during her natural life if my said daughter Minerva Should marry and have issue I desire that the said eighth part of My estate go to

her issue in fee Simple. Should my said daughter die without issue then I desire that the said remaining eighth part of my estate hereby given in Trust for her benefit and use be equally divided between all my children or their legal representatives, with the same restrictions or Trusts as are contained and made in this my will in the third and fourth clauses of the same relative to my Two daughters Hardena Arnold and Susan H. Graves. 10th and lastly I appoint my four sons John C., Wm. T., Burwell B., and Charles Dickinson Executors of this my last will and Testament with the hope that all of them will if living act as such also my earnest wish that they all act as Trustees for their sisters and have that portion of this my will which relates to their Sisters executed according to the true intent and meaning thereof. In testimony Whereof I have hereunto set my name and affixed my seal this the 17th day of August 1840.

[This will was not signed, nor were there endorsements of probation.]

NATHANIEL DICKINSON, of Hanover, died circa 1843. Will dated 17 August 1840. No date of its probation on copy. Sons, William T., and Burwell B. Dickinson qualified as Executors. Possessed "a large real and personal estate" - including three tracts of land -"part in Hanover and part in Louisa" consisting of 900 acres. His home plantation was called "Green Bay." He "possessed twenty-six slaves - eighteen males and eight females." His personal estate was valued at $9,000.00. Was survived by his widow, Frances, who died on the 19th or 20th of January 1857, and by eight children:

1. JOHN CALVIN DICKINSON, of Hanover, was dec'd in 1857. Lived on land belonging to his father. Possessed land near Anderson's Bridge called "Woolfolk's" 213 1/4 acres, adjoining Edward A. Rowzie; two tracts in Caroline County, one called "Mason's" 317 1/2 acres, adjoining Richard B. White, and one moiety of a tract held in joint tenancy with Joseph Z. Terrell, 110 1/4 acres, adjoining James Gatewood, Samuel Luck and others; "also had a life interest in the Estate of Mrs. Salley Ashley's tract of land called 'Ashley's', adjoining Nathaniel Dickinson and James Seay and others." He had been Administrator of the Estate of William Ashley. Besides other crops he was a large grower of tobacco, of which he also purchased from other growers and sold, usually at a loss, in Richmond, where he transported it usually by wagon, and where he was a patron of the "Faro Bank." He was survived by his widow, Martha A. H., daughter of the late John Clough, Sr., deceased, and by five infant

children:
1. MARCELLUS DICKINSON.
2. ALBERT G. DICKINSON.
3. REGINA DICKINSON.
4. ROSE DICKINSON.
5. MARTHA ANN DICKINSON.

2. HARDENIA M., wife of Hugh B. Arnold of
   Richmond, Va. Sold their interest in
   Estate to Edward J. Rouzie.

3. SUSAN H., wife of William H. Graves of
   Richmond, Va. Assigned her interest in
   her father's estate to their son Herbert.
   Issue as of 1857:
   1. WILLIAM H. C. GRAVES.
   2. HERBERT V. GRAVES.
   3. MARIETTA A., wife of John R. Moore.
   4. HARDENIA M. L., wife of William T.
      Coghill.
   5. BERNARD B. GRAVES.
   6. EMMA C. GRAVES, under 21 in 1857.
   7. JOHN B. GRAVES, under 21 in 1857.
   8. ELIZABETH W. GRAVES, under 21 in 1857.

4. LUCY FRANCES, widow of William Hancock,
   dec'd in 1857, when she is in Louisa
   County. Sold her interest in her father's
   Estate to Herbert V. Graves. Her issue
   in 1857:
   1. MARGARET A., wife of William J. Han-
      cock of Caroline County.
   2. NATHANIEL J. HANCOCK.
   3. WILLIAM W. HANCOCK.
   4. FLEMING J. HANCOCK.
   5. JANE F. HANCOCK.
   6. OTERA E. HANCOCK.
   7. LUCIETTA M. HANCOCK.
   8. GEORGE W. HANCOCK.
   The last four of whom are infants 1857.

5. CHARLES P. DICKINSON, infant in 1843,
   dec'd in 1848, intestate, and without
   issue. Dr. E. A. Rowzie, Admr. He had
   sold his interest in his father's Estate
   to William Hancock.

6. CAROLINE MINERVA DICKINSON, infant in 1843,
   dec'd in 1848, intestate and unmarried.

7. WILLIAM T. DICKINSON, of Beaver Dam, Va.,
   in 1857.

8. BURWELL B. DICKINSON, of Beaver Dam, Va.,
   in 1857. Deceased in 1862.

Nathaniel Dickinson, dec'd, was also survived
by two sisters:

LUCY DICKINSON, a sister, of Hanover, died
circa 22 June 1853, intestate and unmarried.
On 25 February 1843 she conveyed to James B.
Cason for $200.00, one-half of a tract of
land held by her and sister Jane P. Cason,

wife of James B. Cason. Her only heirs were
the children of a brother, Nathaniel Dickinson
deceased, and an only sister, Mrs. Jane P.
Cason.

JANE P., another sister of Nathaniel Dickinson,
dec'd, wife of James B. Cason. They have
issue in 1854, perhaps among others, a son:
1. JAMES B. CASON. "nephew of Lucy Dickinson".
   In 1854 he was Administrator of William
   Cason, dec'd, who was non compos mentis.
   Those interested in William Cason's
   Estate were, perhaps among others, Wm.
   Cason, Robert Cason and Robert Wilkerson
   and Mary his wife. Louis A. Boggs had
   been Committee for William Cason, the
   decedant, in 1852.

TERRELL, JOSEPH Z., and Mrs. Martha Terrell,
his wife, on 31 March 1843 executed a Deed of
Trust to his brother, Dr. Nicholas Terrell, who
was dec'd in 1854, and Maria B. Terrell was his
Executrix. Joseph Z. Terrell's creditors were
Dorothy D. Crawford, William Hancock, a Merch-
ant, Peter Burch's Admr., Wm. D. Dickinson,
Garnett Lowry and Albert Lowry.

CLOUGH, JOHN Sr., and Sarah his wife, on 2
November 1819 executed a Deed of Trust to
Leonard J. Clough and John T. Clough. On 12 Sept.
John Clough, Sr. alone, executed a Deed of
Trust to George N. Clough. John Calvin Dickinson also had executed a Deed to George N. Clough
who was his brother in law, covering loans made
from time to time to Dickinson by Clough said
to have amounted to over $10,000.00. No copy of
such deed is exhibited. Dickinson was insolvent.
George Nelson Clough caused a number of depositions to be taken in his effort to prove that
he was financially capable of making such a
loan, which fact had been questioned in court:

ALVIS, JOSHUA, in 1844 at the Bell Tavern in
Richmond, deposed that he had known George N.
Clough for forty years, and as a business man
for twenty years. When he first knew him, he
was engaged in receiving tolls on the Brook
Turnpike Road; afterwards as a clerk for William Boatright on Shockoe Hill, during which
time he was running street wagons for himself.
After he left Mr. Boatright "I think he got married to a Miss Timberlake and I understood he
got property by her. I understood he got property also from his uncle Edward N. Clough - a
mill, land and negroes." He understood that he
was a man who could command money. Dealt largely
in negroes - transactions in them amounting to
four or five thousand dollars. He was in merchandising business in Hanover, built his store
and kept a Tavern. Good credit. Did not know
when he removed to Hanover. Lives now 24 or 25
miles from Richmond.   Joshua Alvis said that
he, Alvis, resided in Richmond until last year,
for three years lived in Chesterfield County,

some six miles from Richmond. "I was engaged in buying up negroes in Louisa, Orange and Spotsylvania."

GREEN, BERNARD W., in 1844 at the Bell Tavern in Richmond, deposed, that he had known Geo. N. Clough since 1819-20. Knew him as toll keeper, as clerk at Boatright's. He married Miss Caroline Timberlake and got in the neighborhood of four or five thousand dollars by that marriage. That he also received from Emily and Hardinia Timberlake, dec'd, two legacies of $500.00 each, and from Mrs. Martha Timberlake a legacy of between $700.00 and $1,000.00. He likewise had the use and management of the money of Miss J. E. Timberlake, Harriet Timberlake, Mary Timberlake and of Mrs. Martha Timberlake during her lifetime. He attended to their business generally. Was a thrifty, money-making man and possessed of a good estate and good credit. He considered Clough to be worth $20,000 to $25,000. "My mother was a Timberlake, sister of Clough's first wife." Said he had heard that Clough received two or three thousand dollars from Edward N. Clough.

TILMAN, EDWARD, in 1843, deposed that he was an acquaintance of George N. Clough for the past fifteen or eighteen years. Lived in his neighborhood. Believe he received legacies from Benjamin Timberlake's Estate, William E. Harris' Estate, Edward N. Clough's Estate, and John Clough's Estate.

HALL, ZACHARIAH, in 1846, deposed at Hatch's Store: Has known George N. Clough all his life. He lives at "old Mr. John Harris' place, and I do not know whether that is in Hanover or Louisa. I married his sister."

HALL, LITTLETON A., in 1846, deposed that he would be 45 years of age on the 11th of this month, March, 1846, and that he lives at the old John Harper place. In 1844 lived at a place Calvin Dickinson's called "Woolfolk's", for Richard Rowzie. Was waggoner for Dickinson. Says he cannot read or write. Lived with John Calvin Dickinson for four or five years, and has known him for twenty to twenty-five years. Has known George N. Clough for twelve or fifteen years.

WHITE, COL. WILLIAM L., in 1846, deposed that he has known George N. Clough since he was a boy. Clough is about 40 years old. That Benjamin Timberlake's Estate was worth between $11,000.00 and $15,000.00. William E. Harris' Estate was worth $15,000.00

GOODALL, CHARLES P., in 1844 deposed that Geo. N. Clough received 1/7th part of Benjamin Timberlake's Estate, his first marriage being to Timberlake's daughter. Benjamin Timberlake had a daughter Hardenia who died single, also a daughter Emily who died single. Clough received

1/5th of the Estate of Martha, widow of Benjamin Timberlake."Clough's second wife was a daughter of my neighbor William E. Harris."

LEADBETTER, ISAAC, in 1843, deposed that he had known George N. Clough for twenty years. That Edward N. Clough left to George N. and Leonard J. Clough all his real estate.

VAUGHAN, LEMUEL, deposed that he had known George N. Clough nearly all of his life. Stated that Clough was in the service of Brook Turnpike Co. for two years. That he had received of Benjamin Timberlake's Estate, Martin Timberlake's Estate, Emily Timberlake's Estate, Hardenia Timberlake's Estate, Edward N. Clough's Estate and William E. Harris' Estate, legacies. Clough merchandised in Hanover 14 or 15 years.

HARRIS, MOSES, in 1844, at Henry Leadbetter's Tavern in Hanover, deposed that he was Executor of his father, William Ely Harris' Estate. That George N. Clough had married his sister, Martha B. Harris, and that Charles C. Tinsley, Francis Muncass and Charles Harris was indebted to her.

MCDOWELL, JAMES, in 1844, at Henry Leadbetter's Tavern, deposed that George N. Clough had a sister in law, Elizabeth J. Timberlake. That Clough lives on land left to him by his uncle, Edward N. Clough.

DOSWELL, H. C., in 1844, at William Hatch's Store, deposed that Edward N. Clough had died with a will, and that his estate went to two sisters and two nephews, George N. Clough and Leonard J. Clough

CROSS, NATHANIEL, in 1843, at Henry Leadbetter's Tavern, deposed that he had known Geo. N. Clough since Clough was a small boy.

TERRELL, JOSEPH T., in 1843, at William Hatchs Store, deposed that he lived about 13 miles from George N. Clough's, and about 3 1/2 miles from John C. Dickinson, and that Clough had married Dickinson's sister.

HARDYMAN, JAMES E., in 1843, at Wm. Hatch's Store, deposed that John C. Dickinson was Calvin or John Calvin Dickinson.

DUNN, JAMES, a shoe-maker, in 1844, at Henry Leadbetter's Tavern, deposed that John C. Dickinson's sister married George N. Clough, whose father was John Clough, Dec'd.

WOOLFOLK, BENTLEY B., deposed in 1844 that he was Overseer for John C. Dickinson in 1836 and 1837.

SIMS, WILLIAM E., deposed in 1844 that he lived on Mrs. Pleasants place 1840 to 1843.

PHILLIPS, LANCELOT, in 1844, deposed that he had known Mr. William E. Sims since he was a boy. That he knew Mr. Joseph T. Hughes when he came to Beaverdam to live, as Agent for Louisa Railroad.

MASON, CLAIBORN R., in 1844 deposed that Jos. T. Hughes was Sub. Agent and for two years Agent at Beaverdam Depot. That John C. Dickinson in latter part of 1842 or beginning of 1843 told him, at Beaverdam Depot, that his father had just died.

DUKE, ALFRED, in 1844, at Will Hatch's Store, stated that he was acquainted with Joseph T. Hughes for five years "one of which he was in my employ as Sub Agent at Beaverdam Depot." "Always looked upon him as a man upon whose varacity I could rely, also his honesty."

HANCOCK, LARKIN B., in 1846, at Negrofoot, deposed that he was Superintendent of Capt. Charles Thompson's farm for eight years. His wages were $170.00 annually and a share of tobacco.

Others who made depositions were: Judith, daughter of George Bumpass; William S. Bagby; George W. Doswell, Deputy Sheriff, and Security of John C. Dickinson; Henley C. Doswell; Major Thomas Doswell; Edmund Fontain; Judson B. Lowry; Charles H. Mallory; Edward Phillips; Dr. John Philips; Lancelot Philips who married G. Cosby; Sally Philips; P. H. Price; Garland B. Sims; Bowling Vaughan and William C. Winston.

George N. Clough was unmarried in 1822. Died in 1852. "Had a little daughter."

THOMPSON, CHARLES, and Sarah A., his wife, on 15 July 1843, executed a Deed of Trust to William O. Winston, for the benefit of his creditors. He had become much embarassed as the result of becoming Security for persons who became financially insolvent. The Deed covered: 560 acres "where he now lives," hoes, axes, one wagon and gear, two ox carts, a pair of new ox cart wheels, one wheat threshing machine, horse carts, harness, wheat fan, two stills and worms, four work mules, three bay mares, and one mare "now in possession of Arthur Payne of Fauquier, two sorrell horses, two yearling colts, one yearling mule, 26 head of cattle, among which are three yoke of oxen, 45 sheep, 45 hogs, one four wheel carriage and harness, and one old sulkey, all household and kitchen furniture, 35 slaves, and one undivided moiety of 160 acres in Carroll County, Missouri, also twelve shares of the capital stock of the Louisa Railway Company.

Commissioners to divide land in 1843: Col. Geo. S. Netherland, Joseph F. Price, Milton W. Brown, Nicholas Terrell and Edmund Fontaine. In 1853:

Charles Morris, William C. Winston, Robert Nelson, William Hatch, John D. G. Brown, William Carpenter and George W. Hall.

Others mentioned: Chastain White 1846; Genet Anderson, dec'd, Maria D. Anderson, Extx. 1862; Wyatt Seay, John T. Gileson, Wm. T. Sims.

ROY VS. EDWARDS & OTHERS, 1834 (35)

Barbara Dickie's Will

DICKIE, BARBARA. "I, Barbara Dickie formerl of the County of King & Queen now residing with James Edwards in the County of King William, being of sound mind & disposing memory thanks be to God & knowing the uncertainty of death & the uncertainty of life do make and ordain this my last will & Testament in manner & form following, Viz - Item - I Give & bequeath unto my sister Jannet Roy wife of Beverley Roy a horse of her choice out of my stock. Item - I give & bequeath unto Marianna Dickie daughter of my brother James Dickie a negro woman by the name of Hannah and another by the name of Eve. Item - I give & bequeath unto Frances Dickie another daughter of said James a young woman by the name of Philidelphia. Item - I give and bequeath unto William Dickie son of said James, a negro boy by the name of Beverly. Item - I give & bequeath unto Anah Dickie a daughter of said James Dickie a negro girl by the name of Fenton. Item - I give and bequeath unto Janet Dickie daughter of said James, the following negroes, to wit, by the name of Caroline, Winny and boy Jake. Item - I give & bequeath unto Elizabeth G. Dickie another daughter of s^d James my horse & gigg, the above named children being the children of my brother James Dickie, the property I have given them specificily I give them & their heirs each, instead of give it to my brother. Item - I give & bequeath unto Jennet Edwards daughter of James & Mary Dunbar Edwards my plantation in King & Queen County lyeng dragon swamp containing to the best of my knowledge eighty nine acres, be it more or less, also a negro woman named Fanny & four children namely William, Eliza, Martha & Roberte. Item - I give & bequeath unto Barbara Edwards daughter of said James & Mary Dunbar Edwards a negro fellow by the name of Bob & woman by the name of Mary & four children namely Antony, Lucy, Henery and Jacob. Item - I give and bequeath unto James Butler Edwards son of sd James & Mary Dunbar, a negro fellow by the name of London. Item - I give & bequeath unto Anah Edwards daughter of sd James & Mary Dunbar a woman of the name of Mariah and two children namely, Susan and Parthena. Item - I give & bequeath unto Dunbar Edwards son of sd James & Mary Dunbar a fellow by the name of Antony & Scy (the blacksmith) I loan him upon conditions that should his mother (and my sister) Mary Dunbar

Edwards wife of James Edwards be a widow, then its my will and desire that my said sister have hold use and occupy the said fellow Scy as long as she lives and at her death I give the said Scy to Dunbar Edwards. Item - I give and bequeath unto Mary Edwards another daughter & the last of James & Mary D. Edwards a negro boy named Richmond and a girl Jane. Item - its my will and desire that all the residue of my Estate after paying of all my just debts, I give & bequeath unto Barbara Edwards daughter of James & Mary D. as above mentioned lastly I do constitute & appoint my friends James Edward & his son in law Ambrose Edwards my Executors, to this my last will & Testament, revoking all wills or bequeaths heretofore made by me. In witness whereof I do hereunto sit & affix my hand and seal this seventh day of May in the year of our Lord 1817."

Barbara Dickie (Seal)

Teste:
Christopher Johnson.
Ro Hill, Senr.
J. C. Edwards

The foregoing is a true copy of a paper purporting to be the last Will & Testament of Barbara Dickie dec'd filed in a suit lately depending in the Circuit Superior Court of Law & Chancery for the County of Hanover in which Augustus G. D. Roy Committee of Barbara Dickie was plaintiff & Hancock D. Edwards surviving Exor. of James Edwards dec'd were defendants.

Teste, Philip B. Winston, C.C.
18th April 1845

Received of Philip B. Winston, Clerk of the Circuit Superior Court of Law and Chancery for the County of Hanover the original will of Barbara Dickie of which the foregoing is a copy.
James Lyons, Counsel
for B. Dickie heirs, Syne &c.
April 18 1845

BARBARA DICKIE, spinster, of King & Queen Co., died at the home of her brother-in-law, James Edwards in King William County, where she had made her home since 1820. Her will was dated 7 May 1817. No date of probation. James Edwards was appointed Administrator. She had been adjudged non compos mentis and Augustus G. D. Roy assigned as her Committee.

John Clark deposed at his home in King & Queen County in 1835 that he noticed in 1814 change in mind of Barbara Dickie. "She was entirely deranged - without fear or dread of consequences."

Her heirs were two sisters and a brother and some of their children:

JENNETT, a sister, wife of Beverley Roy in 1817, mentioned in will. Not involved in suit.

JAMES DICKIE, a brother, who was not involved in suit. Mentioned in will of 1817, along with the following children:
1. MARIANNA DICKIE.
2. FRANCES DICKIE.
3. WILLIAM DICKIE.
4. ANNA DICKIE.
5. JANET DICKIE.
6. ELIZABETH G. DICKIE.

MARY DUNBAR, a sister, wife in 1817 of James Edwards. Edwards is deceased in 1833. Issue:
1. JAMES BUTLER EDWARDS, who was Executor of his father's Estate.
2. HANCOCK DUNBAR EDWARDS.
3. MARY, wife of Robert B. Syne in 1834.
4. MARIA EDWARDS, mentioned in the suit, but not in the will.
5. BARBARA EDWARDS, mentioned in the will, but not in the suit.
6. JANET, wife in 1817-1834 of Ambrose Edwards
7. ANNA, wife in 1834 of Theophilus Tatum of Richmond, Va.

Others mentioned: Miss Nancy Bird and Miss Polly Bird, and Mrs Martha C. Claybrook of Middlesex County, 1835; Thomas Dickie, Overseer in 1818 for Miss Dickie, Sam Stone, whose father lived at home of Miss Dickie, John Richards and John Richards, Jr., all of King & Queen County 1834; George R. Carlton who has a store in King William County, Isaac B. Edwards, Mary W. Howard who lived in the family of James Edwards, Robert Hill and Wilson C. Pemberton, all of King William County 1834. Edward Pollard, a Justice of the Peace, King William County 1834.

DOSWELL VS. PAGE, 1863 (14)

Lilly Ann Doswell's Will

DOSWELL, LILLY ANN. "I, Lilly Ann Doswell being of sound mind a disposing memory make and ordain this my last will and testament hereby revoking all former wills at any time heretofore made by me. 1st. I will and desire that all of my property of every kind after the payment of my debts be equally divided into two parts. One equal part I give to John Page, Esq. of the County of Hanover to be held by him in trust for the following uses and purposes: for the joint maintenance and support of my son James M. Doswell and his wife Martha E. Doswell and their children during the joint lives of the said James M. & Martha E. and after the death of the one who shall first die, for the joint maintenance and support of the survivor and the children during the life of such survivor and after the death of such survivor to be divided among the lineal descendants of the said James M. & Martha E. Doswell and their heirs forever according to the Virginia law of descents, but should the said James M. &

Martha E. die leaving no such lineal descendants, then to my son Benjamin T. Doswell and his heirs forever. But in no event to be any manner subject to the disposal or liable for the debts or contracts of the said James M. Doswell. 2nd. The other equal part I give to the said John Page in trust for the use support and maintenance of my son Benj^a T. Doswell so long as he shall remain single or unmarried and upon his marriage for the joint maintenance & support of the said Benjamin T. Doswell and his wife and their children during the joint lives of the said Benjamin T. and his wife and after the death of the one who shall first die for the joint maintenance and support of the Survivor and the children during the life of such survivor and after the death of such survivor to the lineal descendants of the said Benjamin T. Doswell to be divided amongst them according to the Virginia Law of descents and to their heirs forever. But should the said Benjamin T. Doswell die leaving no such lineal descendants then to my son James M. Doswell subject to the trust declared in the next proceeding Clause. But in no event to be in any manner subject to the disposal or liable for the debts or contracts of the said Benjamin T. Doswell. I hereby nominate John Page Esquire my Executor of this my will. Witness my hand and seal this 16th day of January 1861."

                      L. A. Doswell
Signed, sealed & published as the last will of L. A. Doswell in our presence who in her presence and in the presence of each other have subscribed our names as Witnesses thereto: C. G. Griswold, H. C. Doswell, W. J. Kimbrough.

"Codicil to my will dated 16th January 1861. After the payment of my debts I give two thousand dollars to John Page in trust for the use of my son Benjamin T. Doswell to be held by him upon the same trusts - for the same purposes, and under the same limitations as are expressed in the second clause of my will above. The residue of my estate is to be divided and distributed as directed in the first and second clauses of this my will. Witness my hand and seal this 23rd day of October 1861."

                      L. A. Doswell (Seal)
Signed Seal & published
in our presence:
  William Spicer
  Thos Doswell
  James T. Doswell.

    A Copy, Teste, Wm. O. Winston, C.H.C.

LILLY ANN DOSWELL, of Hanover. Will dated 16 January 1861, Codicil 23 October 1861. Died in November 1861. Possessed a life estate in one-half of a tract of land called "New Market" on Little River, containing 537 acres. The other half was owned in fee simple by Benjamin T. Doswell, purchased under a Deed of Trust from James M. Doswell. Her issue were these son

from James M. Doswell. These were her sons:
1. BENJAMIN T. DOSWELL, who married Laura C. Doswell, marriage contract dated 28 December 1863.
2. JAMES M. DOSWELL, deceased in 1863, survived by his widow Martha E., and three infant children:
   1. THOMAS DOSWELL.
   2. JOHN C. DOSWELL.
   3. LILLY B. DOSWELL.

          DUKE VS. DUKE, 1857 (13)

DUKE, RICHARD S., "long dead" William Duke qualified as his representative. Thomas H. Duke on 23 July 1850 qualified as Guardian of orphans of Richard S. Duke:
1. JAMES L. DUKE.
2. SARAH C. DUKE.

Tazewell L. Barker, deceased, had been Security for Thomas H. Duke. Ira Barker and Henry Tucker, Administrators.

   DUNN VS. DUNN'S REP. & HEIRS, 1869 (60)

          Thomas B. Dunn's Will

DUNN, THOMAS B. "In the name of God, amen. I, Thomas B. Dunn of the County of Hanover and State of Virginia do make this my last will and Testament hereby revoking all the wills by me made. Item 1st. It is my wish and desire that my Executors hereinafter named shall pay all my just debts. Item 2^d. After the payment of my debts when my youngest child Thomas B. Dunn shall arrive at the age of twenty-one years it is my will and desire that the residue of my estate real and personal should be equally divided between my three children, John H., Robert S., and Thomas B. Item. I hereby appoint my friend John B. Patterson Executor of this my last will and testament. Witness my hand and Seal this   day of April 1859."
                  Thomas B. Dunn (Seal)

Signed sealed and acknowledged
in the presence of:
  John Gibson
  John T. Mills

    (No endorsement of probation)

THOMAS B. DUNN, of Hanover. Will dated "April 1859". No endorsement of probation. John B. Patterson of King William County qualified as Executor. Testator possessed 200 acres on road leading from Richmond to Old Church, which he had purchased of his brother Charles C. Dunn, dec'd, but no Deed executed. Testator's issue:
1. THOMAS B. DUNN, dec'd. Widow, Mary C.
2. ROBERT S. DUNN.

3. JOHN H. DUNN, dec'd, survived by his
   widow, Maria J. D., whose address in
   1871 is Lock 9, Goochland County.

CHARLES C. DUNN, a brother of Thomas B. Dunn,
Sr., was deceased in 1866, survived by a
daughter:
1. Lucy James Dunn.

ROLPH, SAMUEL J., a "repairer of time pieces"
and traveling through Caroline County met a
widow, a daughter of Captain William Harrison,
who had a small son, and married her. She furnished Rolph money with which to purchase the
Dunn land. This suit resulted over the fact
that title could not be given.

HALL VS. ELLIOTT &C., 1866 (73)

ELLIOTT, GEORGE W., deceased of Hanover.
Died in December 1865, intestate, survived
by his widow, Fanny C. Elliott, and by two
children:
1. BETHENIA L., wife of P. H. Hall.
2. ALBIN N. ELLIOTT.

BLUNT VS. ELLETT, 1864 (45)

ELLETT, ROBERT, and Susan G., his wife, on
21 April 1851, conveyed to Semple Ellett,
for consideration of $1,250.00, a tract of
land consisting of 252 1/10 acres located on
both sides of Falling Creek in Hanover, being a
part of the land conveyed to Robert Ellett by
William O. Winston on 28 May 1850.   Semple
Ellett was living in Chesterfield County, Va.,
in 1844, '45 and '46. His wife was Elizabeth J.,
daughter of John and Elizabeth Poindexter of
Christian County, Ky. William R. Poindexter who
appears to have been Elizabeth J. Ellett's brother, and John Ellett were Trustees for land
held for her benefit.

Others mentioned: William A. Dick, formerly of
Hanover, in 1864, a resident of Challahoochie
County, Ga.

EUBANK & OTHERS VS. TINSLEY, 1836 (14)

EUBANK, THOMAS SR., of Hanover, wife dec'd,
on 31 October 1825, conveyed real and personal property to his children:
1. ROYAL H. EUBANK.
2. JULIA ANN EUBANK.
3. SARAH EUBANK, under 21 years of age.
4. THOMAS EUBANK, JR. under 21 years of age.
5. JAMES EUBANK,   "   "   "   "   "
6. WILLIAM EUBANK,   "   "   "   "   "
7. PETER EUBANK,   "   "   "   "   "
8. JOHN EUBANK,   "   "   "   "   "
9. REUBEN BASSETT EUBANK,   "   "   "   "

10. GEORGE W. EUBANK, under 21 years of age.

Samuel H. Tinsley purchased land of Thomas Eu-
bank, Sr. Witnesses: James F. Huffman, Richard
Davis, James McDowell, and Philip B. Jones.
Deposition of John W. Bowles. Other witnesses
were Nathan Hanes, Fendall Ragland and George
B. Hanes in 1825. Hector Davis, of Taylorsville,
Attorney at Law in 1842.

GAINES & OTHERS VS. FLEMING & OTHERS, 1856 (17)

FLEMING, WILLIAM, late of Hanover, died 10
February 1856, intestate, possessed of a
large estate, including 800 acres of land
in Hanover, also a Land Warrant #10895 for 160
acres, issued 29 November 1855. Survived by his
mother, Elizabeth Fleming, and brothers and sisters:

LUCY GUNNELL, dec'd, who was a sister. William
J. Pendleton, Executor.

NANCY, wife of Charles Glinn, who was another
sister.

MARIA E. FLEMING, a sister.

LEWIS D. FLEMING, a brother, non-resident.

THOMPSON FLEMING, a brother, non-resident.

MATILDA, dec'd, a sister, who married a Mr.
Davis, leaving issue:
1. FREDERICK H. DAVIS, a non-resident, purchased of his brother, James O. Davis,
   his interest in their uncle William
   Fleming's Estate, late of Hanover County.
2. JAMES O. DAVIS, a resident of Tallahatchie
   County, Miss., sold to his brother Frederick H., his interest in the Estate of
   "our deceased uncle William Fleming,
   late of Hanover County, Va."
3. MARTHA ANN, married first, John Baker,
   dec'd (Will dated 18 March 1847, proved
   14 June 1847 in Louisa County. Robert T.
   Bibb, Executor) and had issue:
   1. JOHN M. M. BAKER.
   2. WILLIAM H. BAKER.
   3. JAMES BAKER.
   4. BENJAMIN T. BAKER.
   She married secondly, Albert T. Spicer,
   Deed of marriage settlement dated 17
   June 1853. Nathaniel W. Harris, Trustee,
   of Louisa County. Clayton G. Coleman was
   also a Trustee in 1853.
4. AMELIA F., wife of Dudley Hall.
5. JANE ELIZABETH, wife of a Mr. Hall and has
   a daughter, under twenty-one years of
   age:
   1. MARTHA FRANCES, wife of John S. Scott,
      and non-resident in 1856.
Others mentioned: John Stanley, a deponent 1856.

FORD VS. FORD &C., 1860 (29)

Reuben Ford's Will

FORD, REUBEN. "I, Reuben Ford of the County of Hanover make and ordain this my last will and Testament. I lend to my wife during her widowhood all my landed estate, my stock of every kind together with the household and kitchen furniture and plantation utensils but upon the marriage or death I devise the whole of the property above mentioned to my two sons Patrick H. Ford and Reuben J. Ford and in the event of either Patrick or Reuben dying under age or without issue the said property is to go to the Survivor of them. I desire that the one-quarter of an acre of the land in which I now reside shall be reserved around the Grave-yard for funeral purposes. I give my Carpen-ters tools of every kind to two sons Patrick and Reuben. I give to my daughter Melinda Browne and Lucinda Slaughter five dollars each. All other money of which I may die possessed in lands, notes or otherwise I bequeath to my two sons Patrick and Reuben to be expended by my Executor in a Judicious manner upon their educa-tion. I appoint my wife Lucy Ford Executrix and my friend Joseph Harris Executor of this my will. Given under my hand this 17th day of Febry 1852."

                                    Reuben Ford
Witness -
  Joseph Wingfield
  Bushrod W. Wingfield

At a Court of Quarterly Session continued and held for Hanover County at the Courthouse on Thursday the 1st of March 1855. This last will and Testament of Reuben Ford deceased was proved by the oaths of Joseph Wingfield and Bushrod W. Wingfield the witnesses thereto and is ordered to be recorded.
    Teste, Wm. O. Winston, C.H.C.
    A Copy, Teste, R. O. Doswell, D.C.H.C.

RUEBEN FORD, of Hanover. Will dated 17 Febru-ary 1852, probated 1 March 1855."Possessed considerable real and personal estate." Sur-vived by his widow, Lucy, and four children:
  1. MELINDA, wife of James T. Brown prior to 1852.
  2. LUCINDA, wife of Pleasant Slaughter, prior to 1852.
  3. PATRICK H. FORD, under 21 in 1860.
  4. REUBEN J. FORD, under 21 in 1860.

Others mentioned: James A. Harwood, late Sheriff of Hanover County, resident of Chesterfield 1860.

DAVIS &C. VS. FRANCIS' ADMR. &C., 1860 (11)

John B. Francis' Will

FRANCIS, JOHN B. "I, John B. Francis of the County of Hanover and State of Virginia do hereby make my last will and Testament in the manner and form following, that is to say - Item - 1st. I desire that immediately after my decease so much of my perishable property as may be sufficient to pay all my just debts and funeral expenses Shall be Sold and Should the perishable part of my property be insufficient for the above purpose then I desire that Execu-tors hereafter named Shall Sell my real Estate and out of the money arising therefrom pay and Satisfy Such of my just debts as may remain un-paid out of the perishable part of my Estate. Item - 2nd. after the payment of my debts and funeral Expenses I lend to my beloved Wife Jane Mildred all my Estate both real and personal during her widowhood but I desire that She Shall educate Such of my Children who have not received three years tuishon So as to make the equal of those who have received that much. Item - 3. Should my Wife die or marry or neglect to educate my Children above named then I desire that my Executors hereafter named Shal Sell so much of my personal Estate as will enable them to board and educate my children as above before any division of my Estate shall take place. Item - 4th. If my wife Should marr then my desire is that my Estate both real and personal be divided between my Wife and Chil-dren, giving my Wife only an equal Share with the Children to dispose of as she may think pro per but if my wife Continue my widow until my Children or any one of them become o age or marry She Shall be at liberty to make such Child or Children such advancement out of my Estate as she may think proper not exceeding their supposed proportion. Item - 5th at the death of my wife I desire that my Executors Sell all my personal Estate whatsoever Kind it may be and divide the proceeds equally among all my Children - namely Mary E., James H., Martha W., Emeline J., Charles R., John B., S. Eli., William W., and W. H. Francis. Item - 6th at the death of my wife I give my real estate to my Children and their heirs for-ever to be equally divided among them. Item -7t I do hereby Constitute my brother James G. Fran cis and my friend Samuel Davis Executors of this my last will and Testament hereby revoking all former Wills by me made in Witness whereof I have hereunto Set my hand and affixed my Seal this 17th day of August 1843."
                                    John B. Francis
Signed Seal & delivered as
the last will & Testament of John B. Francis in our presence: R. Carver, John Sneed, John J. Winn, John. J. Davis. (No endorsement of pro-bation).

JOHN B. FRANCIS, of Hanover. Will dated 17 Aug 1843. No endorsement of probation. He pos-sessed with other property, 296 acres on Chick-ahominy Swamp, adjoining John D. Lively, James

Hill and others, and seven slaves. His widow, Jane M. qualified as Executrix and continued as such until her death circa 1860. At her death, Charles R. Francis qualified as Administrator. Issue of John B. Francis and his wife:
1. MARY E., wife of John J. Davis.
2. JAMES H. (JAMES I. in suit) FRANCIS, married Sarah Harris.
3. MARTHA W. (MARTHA L. in suit), married James G. Jenkins.
4. EMELINE J., married Charles Terrell.
5. CHARLES R. FRANCIS, Administrator of his father's Estate in 1860 after the death of his mother.
6. JOHN B. (JOHN T. B. in suit) FRANCIS.
7. SAMUEL ELI FRANCIS, infant in 1860, John J. Davis, Guardian.
8. WILLIAM W. FRANCIS.
9. W. H. FRANCIS, died before his father, but after the date of the will.

CARPENTER VS. FULCHER'S ADMR., 1869 (51)

Mary Fulcher's Will

FULCHER, MARY. "In the name of God amen. I Mary Fulcher of Hanover and state of Virginia being weak of body but of a sound and discriminating mind do make and ordain this to be my last will and Testament hereby revoking all others. First I wish all my property to be sold both real and personal as soon as my executor herein after named shall think it will sell to the best advantage and after paying all my just debts and after collecting what is due to me I give to William G. Woodfin of the State of Georgia five hundred dollars. I also give to Susan M. Carter of the City of Richmond, Nannie J. Clarkley of Petersburg, Va., Amanda M. Jones of Powhatan, Judith W. Jackson of Hanover County and Milly Jaques of Petersburg the sum of five hundred dollars to each of them. I also give my brother George Woodfin without in any manner to be subject to the payment of his debts or the control of his creditors the sum of five hundred dollars annually in quarterly payments during his lifetime. The remainder of my estate I give to my three Grandchildren, towit - Sally Fulcher, Waller Carpenter & Wm. W. Fulcher, Jr., and I wish my executor to manage this bequest for my three Grandchildren until they shall respectively arrive at the age of twenty-one years and should one more of them my Grand Children die before attaining the age of twenty-one years then I wish the survivor or survivors to inherit the whole of this bequest to my grandchildren and lastly I constitute and appoint my beloved son William W. Fulcher Executor of this my last will and Testament, and it is moreover my wish that he should not be required by the Court to give Security for the faithful performance of his duties. Witness my hand & seal this 8th

day of Feb. 1861."
                           Mary Fulcher
Witness, Teste:
   F. M. Barker
   Hugh Brown

At a Court of Quarterly Session held for Hanover County at the Courthouse on Wednesday the 26th of Feb. 1861. This last will and Testament of Mary Fulcher deceased was proved by the oaths of F. M. Barker & Hugh Brown the witness thereto and is ordered to be recorded.
   Teste, Wm. O. Winston, C.H.C.
   A Copy, Teste, R. O. Doswell, C.H.C.

MARY FULCHER, of Hanover, died in February 1861. Will dated 8 February and probated 26 February 1861. She was the widow of William Fulcher. Estate valued between $20,000 and $25,000. Son, William W. Fulcher, Executor. Issue:
1. WILLIAM WALLER FULCHER, died 25 December 1868, intestate. James P. Carpenter, Administrator. Possessed land in Richmond and 1500 acres in Hanover including the "Springfield" tract whereon he lived. Was considered a man of unusual financial ability. He left issue:
   1. SALLY, wife of James P. Carpenter, died under age of twenty-one in May 1870.
   2. WILLIAM WALLER FULCHER, JR., died under age of twenty-one in 1874.
   3. JACKSON FULCHER, under age in 1869.

2. [   ] a daughter, dec'd, married W. J. Carpenter, who survived, with issue:
   1. WALLER CARPENTER, "of age in 1872, died 2 July 1874."

Others mentioned: J. N. Woodfin, aged 57 of Powhatan in 1869, a cousin of William Fulcher, and brother-in-law: Mary Fulcher was his sister. George Johnson: "lived on adjoining plantation to William Fulcher. Knew him all his life. I was Overseer for Col. Fontain for 31 years."; Geo. W. Doswell; Edward Vaughan; J. Preston Cocke, Attorney-at-Law.

GARDNER VS. GARDNER'S ADMR., 1860 (41)

Thomas Gardner's Will

GARDNER, THOMAS. "In the name of God amen. I, Thomas Gardner of the County of Hanover do make this my last will and testament in manner and form following. 1st. I give to my son Thomas Gardner all bonds and notes and other evidences of debt and whatever may be due me on the settlement of my account as his gudn amounting principal and interest to upwards of two thousand dollars. 2. I give to my daughter Sallie M. Norment the proceeds arising from the sale of my negro girl Amy loaned to her soon after her marriage which proceeds were used by her husband Wm. E. Norment in the purchase of another girl. 3 I leave to my son James B. Gardner during his the said J. B. Gardners life boy John son of Caroline and at the death of the said James B. Gardner I do give and bequeath the said boy John to the lawful heirs of the said James B. Gardner. 4 I give to my son Reuben E. Gardner the plantation called Hogs containing two hundred acres of land, also whatever may be due me on the settlement of my account as his Guardian. I do also loan to him negro boy Walker during the life of the said R. E. Gardner and at his death I do and bequeath the said boy Walker to the lawful heirs of the said Reuben E. Gardner. 5th I loan to my daughter Harriet N. Gardner negro woman Caroline and her daughter Ellen and their increase during the life of my said daughter Harriet N. and at her death I do give and bequeath the said Caroline and her daughter Ella and their increase to the lawful heirs of my said daughter Harriet Gardner. 6th. I do loan to my daughter Mary E. Gardner girl Louisa daughter of Caroline during the life of said Mary E. Gardner and at her death I do give and bequeath the said girl and her increase to the lawful heirs of the said Mary E. Gardner. 7 I do loan to my son Thomas Gardner my boy Charles son of Frances during the life of the said Thomas Gardner I do give and bequeath the said boy Charles   lawful heirs of the said Thomas Gardner. 8 I do give and bequeath to my daughter Harriet A. Gardner and Mary E. Gardner the farm on which I reside together with one hundred and forty acres purchased of the trustees of Washington Henry Academy making a tract of three hundred and seventy-one acres (371) but with the understanding that the said Harriet N. Gardner and Mary E. Gardner shall consider themselves by the above bequest as fully paid for whatever may be due them by me as their Guardian but should they not accept of this bequest on the terms upon which it is granted, It is my will and desire that the said Farm at such time and on such terms as my Executor may think best and two thousand dollars arising from the sale I do give and bequeath to my daughter Harriet A. Gardner and two thousand to my daughter Mary E. Gardner and the balance to be applied to the payment of whatever may be due the said Harriet N. and Mary E. Gardner by me as their Guardian and should anything be remaining it shall be equally divided among all my children. 9 I give to my son Thomas Gardner old man Christi. 10 I give to my daughter Sallie Norment old woman Janny. 11 I give to my son James B. Gardner old woman Betty. 12 I give to my daughter H. N. Gardner old woman Aggy. 13 I give to my son R. E. Gardner old woman Fanney. 14 I give to my daughter Mary E. Gardner woman Eliza. 15 It is my wish and desire that any remaining servants be equally divided among all my children to wit - Thomas Gardner, Sally M. Norment, James B. Gardner, Reuben E. Gardner, Harriet N. Gardner and Mary E. Gardner with request that they treat them with great kindness and humanity. 16 It is my will and desire that the proceeds of the residue of my estate be equally divided among all my children. 17 I do constitute and appoint my trusty friend E. P. Meredith executor of this my last will and testament with the desire that no security be requested of him in his administration bond. Given under my hand and seal this 19th day of August 1857."

                                    Thomas Gardner

No witnesses.

Hanover County -

At a Circuit Court continued and held for said County at the Courthouse on Tuesday the 28th of September 1858. This last will and Testament of Thomas Gardner deceased was offered for proof by Edward P. Meredith the Executor therein named and there being no subscribing witnesses to the same, Edwin T. Shelton and Billy W. Tally were sworn who declared they were well acquainted with the hand writing of the said Thomas Gardner and on the motion of the said Meredith therein named it is ordered that this be recorded as the last will and testament of the said Thomas Gardner, deceased. Given under my hand this 28th September 1858,

                        Jas. D. Christian, Clk.
    A Copy, Teste, George L. Christian, D.C.

THOMAS GARDNER, of Hanover. Will dated 19 August 1857. Probated 28 September 1858. E. P. Meredith qualified as Executor. Possessed a large real and personal estate. He was a son of Reuben Gardner. Thomas Gardner was survived by six children:

1. THOMAS M. GARDNER, dec'd in 1860, R. E. Gardner, Admr. Survived by his widow and three children, residing in Kanawha County, Va.:
    1. JAMES BERNARD GARDNER.
    2. WILLIAM P. GARDNER
    3. CHARLES P. GARDNER.
2. SALLY M., wife of W. E. Norment.
3. JAMES B. GARDNER, died unmarried prior to 1860.
4. REUBEN E. GARDNER.
5. HARRIET NEWELL, wife of Wm. Nelson Gardner in 1860.
6. MARY E. GARDNER, under age in 1858.

Others mentioned: Thomas E. and Mary E.Meredith.

FROM OLD WILL BOOK, PAGE 79

GREEN, WILLIAM B., dec'd. Nathaniel C. Lipscomb appointed Guardian of Jane S., orphan of Wm. B. Green, dec'd, 5 October 1847.

SELDEN VS. BRAXTON'S TRUSTEE, 1867 (27)

Mary G. Garlick's Will

GARLICK, MARY G. "In the name of God Amen. I, Mary G. Garlick of New farm King William County with gratitude to my heavenly father for having preserved me through many years, and though somewhat enfeebled in body by the weight of years, yet being of sound mind do now make and constitute this my last will & testament revoking all others. Item 1st. I give and bequeath to my dear daughter Mildred C. Garlick who has devoted her life to my comfort and welfare the following property - viz. my servants Richard, Billy, Robert, Susan and her children Sophia, Sarah, Reuben, Winny, Tommy and Walter, Dorinda and her children, James, Nat, Robert and Eliza, and Lucinda with the increase of the females. These servants are intended to make Mildred equal to my other children for what they have already received. I also give to my daughter Mildred C. the following servants - Joe, Henry, Octavia, George, and the increase of the females. 2nd. I give and bequeath to my said daughter Mildred C. all the interest I have in and to a parcel of land sixty acres more or less called Terrysfield To the said land the two first children of my late Husband by a former marriage were entitled to a child's portion; to one of these children, Mrs. Mary Semple wife of Mr. James Semple, I gave one negro Girl named Maria for her portion in the said land and to Mrs. Josiah Burruss and Mary Hill the children of Elizabeth Ryland the wife of William S. Ryland who was the eldest daughter I shall herein bequeath one hundred dollars for their portions of the said land, also I give to my nephew William P. Braxton in trust for the benefit of my daughter Sarah Selden and her children two thousand dollars on condition that she relinquish all her right and title to the lands called Terry's field and New farm to my daughter Martha C. Garlick. 3rd. I give to my daughter Mildred C all my household and kitchen furniture, one half my silver spoons, my silver ladle, all my farming implements, wagons, horse and ox carts, ploughs and gear of all kinds, my carriage & harness, all my stock of horses, mules, cattle, sheep and hogs. 4th. I also give to my said daughter Mildred C. twenty-six shares of the stock of the Bank of Virginia & one-third of all the servants not herein specifically devised or given away. 5th. I have some years ago given in trust to Mr. A. Brown and my son Braxton for the use of my daughter Sarah Selden and her children, servants, to wit Eliza & her children Maria, Lucy, Shirley, Reuben, James, Henry, Emma and Susan, Nelly and her children Robert, Sophia and Armistead, Martha and her children Ann and an infant, Sally and her child Juliet, Ellen and her child, William and Nat, Andrew and Martin with the increase of the females.

I now give and bequeath in trust to my dear nephew William P. Braxton for my said daughter Sarah Selden and those of her children living at her death, provided none of her children die before she does leaving children, then such child or children to take the parents share the following servants, To wit - Anne, Jerry and James and the increase of the females, the last named now hired in Richmond. 6th. I give to said William P. Braxton also in trust for my said daughter Sarah Selden and her children living at her death or if any should die before the mother leaving issue then to such issue its parents share, two thousand five hundred dollars in State Stock upon condition that she the said Sarah Selden surrender and convey to Mildred C. Garlick all the right title and interest in and to the land called Terry's field and Newfarm without which then this bequest and devise shall be void. 7th. I also give to my nephew William P. Braxton in trust for my said daughter Sarah and such children as she may have living at her death with the provisions made as above in regard to any that may be dead at her death, one-third part of all the servants I may leave at my death not specifically bequeathed or given away - to be kept in the hands of the trustee, should he think it advisable so to do and the hires only given to the maintenance of the objects of the trust and this condition is attached to this bequest that one hundred dollars shall be paid out of this bequest to Braxton Garlick (for that sum he loaned to his sister Sarah) before my said daughter Sarah & her children receive the use & benefit of this gift. I further direct & will that if my said daughter Sarah Selden & her children or any of them claim of Mr. A. Brown and Braxton Garlick (who are trustees for the property mentioned in the fifth item in this will) the value of one of these servants named Robert who was conveyed by me in trust and who was sold improperly by Mr. Selden (Sarah's husband) with the knowledge of any one interested, that then these servants last herein devised in trust to Wm. P. Braxton for Sarah & her children shall be liable to pay whatsoever may be claimed for the said servant Robert. I also give to my daughter Sarah half of my silver spoons. 8th. I have heretofore given to my dear son Braxton the following servants, to wit: Delphia and her children Milly, Joe, Beck, Owney and Reuben and Bernard, Robert. I do hereby give and bequeath to my nephew William P. Braxton for my son and his children in trust one-third part of all the servants I may have at my death undivided and not given away herein, upon the following conditions, that my said son Braxton pay a bond off with all the interest due thereon that Mr. Ottoman Slaughter holds with myself as the principal or obligee, of said bond executed some ten or twelve years ago for the sum of eleven hundred dollars or thereabout. I executed the bond to raise money for

Mr. Selden the land Selden sold in King William paid the amount to take up the bond aforesaid to my son B. Garlick and he used the money for other purposes and did not pay off the bond as he should have done should he fail to pay said bond and interest, then it is to be paid out of the servants herein last bequeatted in trust to Wm. P. Braxton for said Braxton Garlick and his children. 9th. I give and bequeath to Mrs Catherine Burruss and her sister Mary Hill one hundred dollars for their right in the land called Terrys field which I consider a fair equivalent for the same should it not be so considered then whatever is a fair valuation. 10th I give to my nephew William P. Braxton for his many kind services my servant man Carter. 11th My servant Maria, Nat's wife I leave to whichever of my daughters she may choose for her mistress, hoping she may be well taken care of. Should she choose my daughter Sarah then she is to be considered as given in trust to William P. Braxton as the other property given him in trust. She is to express her election before disinterested gentlemen. 12th. I do hereby leave to my dear nephew Wm. P. Braxton my sole executor of this my last will & testament should it please God to remove him before he qualifies then I do hereby constitute and appoint my friend Mr. Josiah Burruss my executor and the trustee in every instance in which my nephew is appointed herein and I desire that neither shall be required to give security. My undivided servants are Owney and her children, Martha, Anne, Ben, Frank, Johnny, Beverly, Louisa, Sallie and her children, Agnes, Bolla, Mortimer, Infant, Katy and her children Charlotte, Venus, Andrew, & Bartlett, Lena & Addison Richard, Jr. In testimony to the foregoing I have hereunto put my signature and seal this 19th day of March 1856."

                                Mary C. Garlick (Seal)
In presence of
    A. H. Perkins
    & L. Trant
who were present together when the testratrix acknowledged the above contents to be her last will.

At a Court held for King William County at the Courthouse on Monday the 22nd day of Sep. 1856. This last will & testament of Mary C. Garlick dec'd was produced proved by the oaths of A. H. Perkins and Lawrence Trant the subscribing witnesses thereto & ordered to be recorded. And on the motion of Wm. P. Braxton the Executor therein named, who made oath thereto acknowledge a bond in the penalty of forty-eight thousand dollars conditioned according to law. Certificate is granted him for obtaining a probate of said will in due form, which bond is ordered to be recorded.
    Teste, A. Shield, D.C.
    A Copy, Teste, William D. Pollard, Clerk
                    April 24th 1860

MRS. MARY G. GARLICK, widow, of King William County. Will dated 19 March 1856. Probated 22 September 1856. Dr. William P. Braxton, a nephew of Stanley, King William County qualified as Executor, also Trustee for Mrs. Sarah Selden, who, with her children are the only ones concerned in this suit. From Mrs. Garlick's will it is learned that she was the second wife of her deceased husband, whose name is not stated. Issue of Mr. Garlick by a former marriage:
1. MARY, wife of James Semple.
2. ELIZABETH, dec'd, who married William S. Ryland, and had issue:
    1. CATHERINE, wife of Josiah Burruss.
    2. MARY HILL

Issue of Mr. Garlick and his wife Mary G.:
3. MILDRED CALL GARLICK, spinster.
4. BRAXTON GARLICK.
5. SARAH, wife of Edward B. Selden. Her cousin Dr. William P. Braxton, Trustee for her interest in her mother's Estate, invested the proceeds of 25 shares of the capital stock in the Bank of Virginia, devised in trust, in the 6th clause of her mother's will, in a farm in New Kent Co. called "Cool Well" which was purchased of Wellington Goddin and Eliza P., his wife. Issue of the Seldens:
    1. GEORGIANNA K., widow of B. A. Curtis in 1867.
    2. LELIA W. SELDEN.
    3. ALFRED F. SELDEN.
    4. MILDRED C. SELDEN.
    5. BRAXTON SELDEN, dec'd in 1867.
    6. EDWARD B. SELDEN, dec'd in 1867.
    7. ST. GEORGE SELDEN, dec'd in 1867.
    8. VIRGINIA C. SELDEN.

CHARLES WEBB VS. RICHARD GAINES &C., 1833 (16)
(From Chancery Court, King William County)

GAINES, HARRY, died with will prior to 8 July 1805. He had purchased of the Trustees of the late Ralph Wormley the estate "Piankatank" of 853 1/4 acres, adjoining the "Springfield" tract, and lands of Mrs. Hudgins, Mrs. Bristow, Mrs. Wortham and Dragon. Some years later, a son, Robert B. Gains, under a Deed of Trust dated 24 September 1827 and of record in Middlesex County, conveyed "Piankatank" to Richard Gaines. There were proposals for trading this property for "Beverley Plain" in Caroline County, owned by the Woodwards. Harry Gaines, (Sr.) dec'd was survived by his widow Betty, and the following children:
1. JOHN GAINES, of King & Queen County, an infant in 1805, student of William and Mary College in 1808. Administrator of his brother Wm. F. Gaines.
2. ELIZABETH, infant in 1805, married prior to 1833, Thomas Miller.

3. BENJAMIN GAINES, deceased in 1836, leaving
children:
1. WILLIAM GAINES.
2. RICHARD GAINES, married prior to 1833,
Mary Ann C. (Mira) Gaines.
3. JANE, in 1833, wife of John M. Steger.
4. HARRY GAINES, (Jr.) deceased in 1833,
leaving children:
1. MORTIMER GAINES.
2. CORNELIA, wife of Thomas Meaux.
3. JUDITH, died circa 1836, survived by
husband, Thomas Carter of King William County.
4. MARTHA GAINES.
5. SARAH GAINES, died unmarried, and
under age.
5. ROBERT B. GAINES, on 24 September 1827 in
Deed of Trust recorded in Middlesex Co.,
conveyed "Piankatank" to Richard Gaines.
In 1831 his wife is Lucy G. Gaines.
6. MARTHA F., died prior to 8 July 1805 survived by her husband Captain Robert B.
Hill who died circa 1836.
7. WILLIAM FLEMING GAINES, died in infancy,
prior to 8 July 1805.

Robert Thurston, late Sheriff of Gloucester Co.,
and Committee of Harry Gaines.

Dr. Charles Webb of King William County calls
"brothers" Benjamin and Harry Gaines (Jr.) and
"sister" Martha F., who married Capt. Hill.

John and Richard Bagby assignees of Dr. William
F. Gaines. (Suit does not show the latter's connection).

WOODWARD, HENLEY, married Fanny B. Streshley,
a sister of Moses Streshley, late of Caroline County (will dated 29 March 1825) by which
she was devised the tract of land called "Beverley Plain." There were proposals for trading
this land for "Piankatank" belonging to the
Gaines. Henley and Fanny B. Woodward had issue,
perhaps, among others:
1. THOMAS H. WOODWARD, of age in 1831.
2. WILLIAM WOODWARD.

Harry B. Sthrishley (note spelling) apparently
a brother of Fanny B. Woodward.

Others mentioned: William Armistead; George H.
Dabney; Thomas Dew 1827; Reuben Dugar; Thomas
Faunteleroy, dec'd, John Faunteleroy, Executor;
John Faunteleroy, dec'd, Henry A. Christian,
Trustee for Thomas Faunteleroy, Surviving Exor;
James Frazier assignee of John J. Carpenter;
William Fulcher of Hanover; Mourning Johnson,
Guardian of Richard Coleman; Thomas Jordan;
David Palmer, dec'd, Henry C. Palmer, Executor;
Beverley Robinson, dec'd, Robert Pollard and
Thomas W. New, Admrs. John Williams and John J.

Willis, Securities; Martha Roy; Joseph Stewart,
dec'd, Christopher Tompkins, Admr.; Thomas
Street, Justice of the Peace of Middlesex Co.,
in 1834; William Taylor, dec'd, Robert Campbell,
Administrator.

GENTRY VS. GENTRY, 1857 (10)

Henry D. Gentry's Will

GENTRY, HENRY D. "I, Henry D. Gentry of
the County of Hanover in infirmity of
body, but in perfect soundness of mind
and memory desirous before my death of making a
disposition of my estate in accordance with my
views of propriety and of the true interest of
my beloved wife and children, I do make this my
last will and Testament in manner and form following. 1st I give unto my son David A. Gentry
my slaves Robin and Spencer & one bed and furniture. 2nd. I give unto my son John H. Gentry
my slaves Jesse & ben. 3rd I give unto my
daughter Martha V. A. Gentry my slaves Pate,
Rachael and Thomas and one bed and furniture.
4th. I give unto my daughter Elizabeth I. Gentry my slaves Scinthy, Sarah and William and
one bed and furniture. 5th. it is My will and
desire and I hereby direct that the tract or
parcel of land which came to me from my father's
estate, situate beaing and lying near the farm
of Garland Tinsley and Samuel Overton be sold
and the proceeds of the sale thereof to be
equally divided between my children. 6. I lend
unto my wife Martha Gentry, with the exception
of the Slaves land &c herein before bequeathed
as long as she may remain my widow the whole of
my estate both real and personal, but in the
event of my wifes marrying again, and after her
death, I give the whole of that estate both
real and personal to my children to be equally
divided between them, with the only reservation
that my plantation on which, and the mansion
house in which I now reside, shall be a home
for either of my daughters Martha and Elizabeth and for my son David A. Gentry (if they
choose it so to be) as long as either of them
may remain unmarried, and that the said mansion
House and plantation shall at their option
never be sold as long as either of them may
remain single. 7 - It is my will and desire
and I hereby so direct that my wife Martha in
the event that any of my slaves be disobedient,
or conduct themselves in such a way as in her
opinion require it have the privilege and power
of selling them and that she have the choice of
either dividing the proceeds of the sale
between my children or appropriating it to the
purchase of other slaves to be still considered
as part of my estate loaned her. 8 And lastly
in Confirmation of this my last will and testament I hereby subscribe my name and affix my
seal this 6th day of January, in the year of
our lord 1851."   Henry D. Gentry (Seal)

Acknowledged as his last will and Testament before us witnesses by the request of and in the presence of the Testator:
    Ezekiel S. Talley
    Thomas W. Edwards
    Richard E. Atkinson

At a Circuit Court held for Hanover County at the Courthouse on Wednesday the 17th of November 1853. The last will and Testament of Henry D. Gentry dec'd was proved by the oaths of Ezekiel S. Talley and Richard E. Atkinson witnesses thereto and is ordered to be recorded.
    A Copy Teste, Jas. D. Christian, Clk.

                David A. Gentry's Will

"I, David A. Gentry make my last will and testament in manner and form following. I give unto my three nephews - Henry Thomas Gentry, John Henry Cox, & Washington Jones Sledd the whole of my Estate real and personal to be equally divided between them and with their respective portions of my money to be appropriated to the education of each respectively. I appoint my friend Ezekiel S. Talley Exor of this my last will and testament revoking all other wills heretofore made. Witness my hand and seal this 7th day of August 1853."
                            D. A. Gentry (Seal)
Acknowledged in the
presence of Witnesses:
    Ezekiel S. Talley
    Wm. S. R. Brockenbrough

At a Court of Monthly Session held for Hanover County at the Courthouse on Tuesday the 27th of November 1853. This last will and testament of David A. Gentry dec'd was proved by the oaths of Ezekiel S. Talley & Wm. S. R. Brockenbrough the witnesses thereto and is ordered to be recorded.
    Teste, Wm. O. Winston, C.H.C.
    ACopy Teste, Wm. O. Winston.

HENRY D. GENTRY, of Hanover. Will dated 6 Jan. 1851. Probated 17 November 1852. Survived by his widow Martha, who in 1857 "remains a widow very aged, paralytic and bed-ridden." and the following children:
    1. DAVID A. GENTRY, dec'd. Will dated 7 Aug. 1853, probated 27 November 1753.
    2. JOHN H. GENTRY, who is married and has issue in 1857, probably among others:
        1. HENRY THOMAS GENTRY, an infant.
    3. MARTHA A. V., married between 17 November 1852 and 7 August 1853, John P. Sledd, and had issue, probably among others:
        1. WASHINGTON JONES SLEDD, dec'd in 1857.
    4. ELIZABETH I., married between 17 November 1852 and 7 August 1853, E. J. Cox, and has issue, probably among others:
        1. JOHN HENRY COX, under 14 years of age.

Henry D. Gentry's land, 204 acres, was near Hanover Town, 16 miles from Richmond, adjoining William B. Newton, Dr. William R. Nelson, and others.

Others mentioned: John Haw and Pleasant E. Wooddy, 1857.

        JOHNSON & WIFE VS. GENTRY &C., 1866 (9)

GENTRY, TURNER W., of Hanover, died in 1864 with a will which was destroyed by fire - no copy extant. Possessed 185 acres adjoining Charles B. Richardson, Mary J. Goodman, Col. Edmund Fontaine and Benjamin L. Smith. Survived by his widow Louisa A. Their issue:
    1. HARDINIA R., wife of John L. Johnson.
    2. ELIZABETH, wife of Addison Hall.
    3. ELIZA, wife of George B. Stone.
    4. FRANCES T., widow of William T. Yarbrough, deceased.
    5. SILAS L. GENTRY.
    6. LUCY ANN, married William A Baughan. Both are deceased, leaving an only child:
        1. TAYLOR BAUGHAN.
    7. JANE M, appears to have first married a Mr. Glasgow, by whom there was issue:
        1. HARDINIA RICHARD GLASGOW, infant.
        In 1866, Jane M. is the wife of Joseph H. Johnson, and have issue, infants:
        2. ELIZABETH JOHNSON.
        3. ELLA JANE JOHNSON.
        4. MARTHA JOHNSON.
    8. TIMOTHY GENTRY, under 21 years of age in 1866.

Others mentioned: Dr. Charles E. Thompson; Chas. P. Higginson.

    GILMAN VS. ELLETT'S ADMR. & OTHERS, 1853 (17)
        GILMAN VS. ELLETT'S ADMR., 1856 (17)
            GILMAN VS. GILMAN, 1867 (17)

GILMAN, EDMUND, of Hanover, died possessed of 148 acres of land which descended to his only children, three daughters:
    1. ANN GILMAN, died with a will in 1858. She gave certain special legacies to certain persons therein mentioned, and the residue of her Estate to her two sisters for life, then to Richard B. Gilman in fee. At the time of her death she was possessed of an undivided third part in a tract of land containing 148 acres.
    2. PRISCILLA GILMAN, died with a will a few weeks after her sister Ann, and in the same year. She devised $100.00 to Robert G. Gilman and the residue of her estate to sister Mary F. for life, with remainder in fee to Richard B. Gilman. She was possessed of a undivided third part of the tract of land aforesaid.

3. MARY F. GILMAN, died with a will sometime after her sister Priscilla, but in the same year. She devised to Walter T. Gilman $100.00 and the residue of her Estate to Richard B. Gilman in fee. She possessed another third undivided part of the said tract of land.

"All of the wills were duly admitted to probat in the County of Hanover in October 1858, but they have together with the record thereof, been destroyed by fire, and no official copies thereof are, or either of them, is now in existence." Richard B. Gilman qualified as their Executor. The only persons known to the Executor who can be affected by the re-establishment of the said wills are the devisees and heirs at law of Mary F. Gilman:

DICKIE GILMAN, dec'd, a brother of Edmund Gilman, whose children are:
1. SUSAN G., wife of Robert Ellett.
2. ROBERT G. GILMAN, non-resident.
3. WALTER T. GILMAN, non-resident.
4. ELVIRA E., wife of William N. Hendrick.
5. LUCY A., wife of James R. Horsley, and are non-residents.
6. SARAH GILMAN, non-resident.
7. MARGARET C., dec'd, who married Philip N. Mallory, and has issue:
  1. CATHERINE MALLORY.
  2. ELIZABETH MALLORY.
  3. RICHARD W. MALLORY.

JOHN GILMAN, dec'd, a brother of Edmund Gilman. Children:
1. WILLIAM A. GILMAN.
2. EDWIN GILMAN.
3. ELIZABETH C., wife of James Blunt.
4. JAMES W. GILMAN.
Grandchildren of John Gilman. Parents' names are not stated:
  1. JOHN W. GILMAN.
  2. MARTHA E. FORD, widow.
  3. LUCY, wife of Thomas H. Goddin.
  4. MARIA, wife of Albin Duke.
  5. MARY S., wife of Thomas Blunt.
  6. WILLIAM J. GILMAN.

DUDLEY GILMAN, dec'd, who was a brother of Edmund Gilman. (Dudley also called Duke Gilman). His children:
1. DUDLEY GILMAN.
2. JAMES GILMAN.
3. GRANVILLE GILMAN, dec'd. Heirs unknown.
4. SAMUEL GILMAN, dec'd. Heirs unknown.
Grandchildren of Dudley (or Duke) Gilman:
  1. GRANVILLE MONTELLE, non-resident.
  2. ELLEN, wife of William E. Wade.
  3. CLARA, wife of John Bowles.

NANCY, dec'd, a sister of Edmund Gilman, married a Mr. Gentry, and had children:
1. HARMAN GENTRY, non-resident.

2. FLEMING GENTRY, dec'd. Widow is Elizabeth.
Grandchildren of Nancy Gentry:
  1. ELIZA, wife of Mosby Ford.
  2. MARIETTA, wife of William R. Brock.
  3. MARIA ANN, wife of Robert H. Brock.
  4. CATHERINE, wife of William H. Walker.
  5. PATRICK H. GENTRY.
  6. JAMES GENTRY.
  7. FLEMING GENTRY.
  8. JOHN GENTRY.
  9. THOMAS GENTRY.
  10. ALEXANDER GENTRY.

JAMES GILMAN, dec'd, who was a brother of Edmund Gilman. Heirs unknown.

AUSTIN GILMAN, dec'd, who was a brother of Edmund Gilman. Heirs unknown.

WILLIAM GILMAN, dec'd, who was a brother of Edmund Gilman. Heirs unknown.

ELLETT, JOHN, of Hanover, died many years prior to 1853, intestate. Nathaniel Alexander Thompson, Sheriff of Hanover, his representative. Possessed of considerable property. Survived by his widow, Frances K., who died prior to 1853, and by children:
1. THOMAS ELLETT, died since his father. Thompson, Sheriff, his representative. In 1844, Francis Page, Sheriff of Hanover was his representative. He was survived by infant children of whom Edwin Ellett is Guardian in 1856, and by:
  1. VIRGINIUS ELLETT, of age.
2. RICHARD ELLETT, died since his father.
  1. ALEXANDER ELLETT, representative of his father, and Guardian of:
  2. WILLIAM H. ELLETT, under age in 1856.
3. SARAH W., wife of Nathaniel Hardin Davis. Residents of Knox County, Ill., in May 1856.
4. NANCY C., under age in 1835, wife of Richard B. Gilman in 1856.
5. MILLICENT, dec'd, married prior to 1824 or 1825, Benjamin C. Coghill, who for several years lived adjoining John Ellett, Sr., in Hanover. Millicent died during the lifetime of her father. Coghill and children removed from Hanover County to Warren County, Ill., where they were residents in 1837. In 1856 he and his children were residents of Henderson County, Ill. (which had been cut from Warren County.) Benjamin C. Coghill is married again. Issue by Millicent Ellett:
  1. JOHN WALLER COGHILL, of Illionis.
  2. MILLICENT C., under age in 1857, and wife of James Duke of Henderson County.
6. JOHN ELLETT, under age of 21 in 1835.

Thomas C. Ellett, Security 1856 for Alex. Ellett.

Commissioners in 1835: Charles P. Goodall and William Patman; in 1837: Charles C. Tinsley, Edmund Mills and Jesse Winn. Anthony Street, mentioned

GLENN VS. GLENN'S ADMR., 1834 (16)
GLENN VS. GLENN & OTHERS, 1835 (16)

GLENN, JOHN Sr., of Hanover County, died in 1784, possessed of some real estate which descended to his son, John, Jr. by whom he was survived, probably among other children.

John Glenn's (Jr.) Will

GLENN, JOHN. "In the name of God Amen: I, John Glenn of the County of Hanover being weak of body but of sound mind and memory thanks be to God, do make and ordain this my last Will and Testament in manner and form following, Viz. First I commit my soul to God and my body to be decently buried. My will and desire is that all my just debts and funeral expenses be paid. Item: I give and bequeath to my beloved wife Hannah Glenn all my estate both real and personal consisting of the land whereon I now live, my negroes both young and old, stocks of every kind, household and kitchen furniture, Crops of every sort, together with everything I possess to be by her disposed of among my Children as she shall think proper to them and their heirs forever. Lastly I appoint my beloved wife Hannah Glenn Executrix of this my last will and Testament. In Witness whereof I have hereunto set my hand and seal this twenty-ninth day of September eighteen hundred and eleven."

                                    his
                    John Glenn   +   (Seal)
                                   mark
Signed & Seal in the
presence of
    William Chick.
    Ambler Chick
    Walter Chisholm

At a Court of Quarterly Session held for Hanover County at the Courthouse on Wednesday the 28th of July 1813. This last Will and Testament of John Glenn dec'd was proved by the Oaths of Ambler Chick & Walter Chisholm witnesses thereto, and is ordered to be recorded.
    Teste, William Pollard, C.H.C.
    A Copy, Teste, Tho Pollard, D.C.H.C.

Hannah Glenn's Will

"In the name of God amen. I, Hannah Glenn of the County of Hanover State of Virginia being of sound mind memoy thanks be to almighty God for the same do make and ordain this my last will and Testament, in the manner and form following (that is to say). Imprimis. I desire that all my just debts and funeral expenses to be paid.

Imprimis. I give to my son William Glenn the sixty-three acres of land on which he was put in possession of by his Father, also I give or confirm a title to thirty-eight acres more land which he had purchased of his father John Glenn in his lifetime, and which he has never had a deed for the same fully executed, also I give him the following negroes to wit Jenny, Fanny Mat, William, Owen, John, Martha and her two children William and Mary with their future increase to him and his heirs forever. Imprimis. I give to my son John T. Glenn sixty-three acres of land including his improvements also the following negroes - to wit - Michael, Ned, Celia, Lucy, Burwell, John, Eliza and Reuben, with their future increase to him and his heirs forever. Imprimis. I give to my son James R. Glenn sixty-three acres of land to include the buildings where I now live and the Spring of water during his natural life, should he depart this life and leave no lawful heirs after marrying, in that case I desire that the sixty-three acres of land given him to be equally divided between my two sons William Glenn and John T. Glenn and their heirs forever and also the excess of any there be, also I give to my son James R. Glenn the following negroes to wit Elisha, Mary, Mourning, Peter, Milley and Watson with their future increase to him and his heirs forever. Also I give him one Yoke of oxen and ox cart, one cow and calf, one feather bed and bed Stead, two figured counter pains, three bed quilts, one pair of Sheets and all the Tables, Chests, Knives and forks, pewter, earthen ware that I may possess at the time of my death. Imprimis. I give to my executors herein after named for the benefit of my grandchildren (the children of my son Archibald Glenn dec'd) sixty-three acres of land which is to be at the discretion of my exors during their minority but when they shall arrive at lawful age I give it to be equally divided amongst them. Also I had given to my son Archibald H. Glenn in his lifetime the following negroes to wit Jordan, Cuzza, Fanny, Tally, Charles and Betty to which said negroes and their future increase, I have no claim whatsoever, he having sold them during life. Imprimis. It is my desire that if upon survey of the whole tract of land it should be found to contain more than the sixty-three acres as devised to each legatee, together with the thirty-eight acres sold by my husband John Glenn to his son William Glenn as before named, that, in that event that each shall have his equal part of such excess so laid off as to be adjoining to their respective lots as divided and may be laid off. Imprimis. It is my will that all the residue of perishable property not herein before disposed of be sold by my executors hereinafter named and the proceeds of such sale together with any money which may be collected on account of debts due me at the time of my death be forthwith applied by my Exors to the payment of the Just debts which I may owe at the time of my death, then it is my will that my exors hire out my negroes Sam and Watson and annually apply the sums which may be raised by their hire to the payment of said debts, but if my creditors will not wait to be thus paid my said exors are hereby directed to sell my said negro man Sam at private sale, and that he may choose his master provided they will give a fair price for him, and apply the money thus obtained to the payment of the said debts, should these funds prove insufficient for the payment of the said debts my Executors are hereby directed to sell my said negro man Watson at private sale or as prescribed above for Sam. Whereas William Glenn and John T. Glenn has formerly become bound for Archibald Glenn as security in a debt whatever amount it may be, it is my desire that they shall be reinstated from the proceeds of the hire of said negroes above named. It is also my desire after all my just debts are paid that my executors shall raise from the hire or sale of the above named negroes two hundred dollars for the support of my grandchildren, the children of Archibald H. Glenn - and to be applied by my said Exors at their discretion for the support of said children. Imprimis. Also I give to my Son William Glenn after all the money heretofore mentioned be raised and all my debts heretofore named are discharged, my negro man Watson to him and his heirs forever, also I give to my son John T. Glenn after all my just debts heretofore named are discharged my negro man Sam to him and his heirs forever. Lastly, I do hereby constitute and appoint my sons William Glenn and John T. Glenn Executors of this my last will and testament hereby revoking all other written testaments by me made or heretofore made. In witness whereof I have hereunto set my hand and affixed my seal this 15th day of Sept 1830. Signed sealed and declared as & for the last will and testament of the above named

her
Hannah + Glenn
mark

In presence of
    Richard A. Woodson
    Stephen T. Hope
    George Gammon."

At a Court of Monthly session held for Hanover County at the Courthouse on Wednesday the 22nd of December 1830. The last will and Testament of Hannah Glenn dec'd was proved by the oath of George Gammon as witness thereto. And at a Court of Quarterly session continued and held for the said County at the Courthouse on Friday the 25th of February then next following, the said will was further proved by the oath of Richard A. Woodson another witness thereto and is ordered to be recorded.

    Teste, Philip B. Winston, C.H.C.
    A Copy,
            Teste, Benj^a Pollard, Jr., D.C.H.C.

JOHN GLENN, (JR.) of Hanover. "Died 3 November 1812 at the age of more than 80. His father, and the grandfather of Wm. Glenn, died in 1784." Will dated 9 September 1811, probated 28 July 1813. Possessed a considerable personal Estate. Survived by his widow Hannah, who died in Oct. 1830. Her will was dated 15 September 1830 and probated 22 December 1830. Wm. P. Anderson qualified as her Administrator with the will annexed. John and Hannah Glenn had issue:
1. WILLIAM GLENN.
2. JOHN T. GLENN
3. JAMES R. GLENN "who was in bad health and lived with his mother till her death."
4. ARCHIBALD H. GLENN, dec'd, who has issue in 1832:
    1. JOHN H. GLENN.
    2. FRANCES ANN, wife of John W. Loyall in 1842, who is Guardian of her brothers and sisters who are minors in 1842:
    3. DAVID GLENN, under 21 years of age.
    4. NANCY GLENN, under 21 years of age.
    5. ARCHER GLENN, under 21 years of age.

Others mentioned: William P. Anderson died prior to May 1833, Mary Ann Anderson Admx.; William R. Irby, Security, 21 Sept. 1835; P. V. Daniel, Attorney 1836. Depositions of: John D. Andrews 3 Oct. 1836; Agnes Baily at the Poor House in Goochland County before G. Woodson Payne, Justice of the Peace "Was acquainted with Mrs. Hannah Glenn's family for 15 or 16 years." A. P. Bowles 3 Oct. 1836; Edmund D. Ford at the home of Archibald Anderson, Justice of the Peace, Louisa County, 29 Sept. 1836; John Hope at same place and time "Known James R. Glenn for 40 years, who since his father's death lived with his mother." Richard Woodson at Wilson Bracket's Tavern in Richmond before R. Bradley a Notary Public, on Wednesday 26 Sept. 1836 "I wrote Mrs. Hannah Glenn's will." Tye Harris and Stephen T. Pulliam at William W. Pulliam's on 17 April 1834; Evan O. Ragland at Factory Mills, Louisa County, 5 Sept. 1833. Samuel A. Guy, Justice of the Peace, Louisa Co. Lemuel Crew, Master Commissioner, Hanover 1834.

STARKE'S ADMR. VS. HARRIS, 1826 (38)

GLAZEBROOK, RICHARD, SR., of Hanover Co., died in 1827. He was survived by his mother, whose name is not stated, also by his widow, who is not named, and by two children.
1. [   ] daughter wife of Benjamin Thomas.
2. RICHARD GLAZEBROOK, JR.

STARKE, JOHN, died circa 1827 with will. He appointed William Starke and John Head, Exors. Joseph Starke appointed Admr. Others mentioned: Sam'l J. Bagby, out of State; Moses Harris, son of William E. Harris, dec'd; Garland Harris; Wm. Tinsley; John T. Priddy; Isaac Leadbetter.

GOODALL VS. NELSON & OTHERS, 1833 (16)

Parke Goodall's Will

GOODALL, PARKE. "In the name of God amen. I, Parke Goodall of Co. of Hanover and Parish of St. Paul being of sound mind and memory thanks be to God for it do make and ordain this to be my last will and testament. Item. I give and bequeath unto my son Charles Parke Goodall the land that I live on known and called by the name of Travelers Rest to him and his heirs forever. If I should die before a Deed is got for the land that I bought of Col. Hugh Nelson it is my desire that the deed should be made to him & his heirs forever. I likewise give unto my son Charles P. Goodall two negro men to wit by the name of Billy and James. Item: I lend to my wife during her life all the rest of my negroes not heretofore given, all my stock of horse, cattle, hogs and sheep. I likewise lend unto my wife three Beds and furniture one dozen chairs such as she may chuse. Item: I give unto my son Charles P. Goodall nine Beds and their furniture and all the rest of the furniture that I have let it be of whatever kind it may. Item: I lend unto my wife my riding carriage during her life, and at her death, I give it to my son and it is my will and desire that my son and his mother shall live together during his life and at her death it is my desire that all the negroes and furniture heretofore lent my wife be equally divided between my son and his two sisters Mary Trevilian and Patsey B. Street and their heirs. It is my desire that the stock of all kinds heretofore lent to my wife during her life at her death whatever shall be left I give to my son. It is my will and desire that my three daughters, Jane M. Goodall, Susan Goodall and Eliza Goodall shall have no part of my estate whatever as I have given them Five hundred pounds each as will more fully appear by a certain writing to that effect. I leave the land given me by the Assembly of Virginia in the County of Caroline, my land in Louisa, and the place called Glinn in Hanover and my five Lotts in the City of Richmond to be sold for the payment of my debts, and the Land I swapt for in the County of Fauquier with Charles Purcell which agreement is in the hands of Samuel McCraw, I likewise leave to be sold for the payment of my debts. It is my desire that it shall be equally divided between my son Charles and my two daughters Mary Trevillian and Patsey P. Street shar and shar alike to them and their heirs forever. And I do hereby constitute and appoint my son Charles my Executor of this my last will and Testament, but he is not to give any security as an Executor. In witness whereof I have hereunto set my hand and seal this 15th day of January 1804."

Parke Goodall (Seal)

(No witnesses)

At a Court of Monthly Session held for Hanover County at the Court House on Wednesday the 24th of January 1816 this last will and Testament of Parke Goodall dec'd was offered for proof by Charles P. Goodall the Executor therein named and the Court being well acquainted with the handwriting of the said deceased and upon a view of the said will are well satisfied that the same was wholly written, signed and sealed by the said deceased and the same being proved by the said Executor is thereupon ordered to be Recorded.

Teste, William Pollard, C.H.C.

A Copy, Teste, Philip B. Winston, C.H.C.

PARKE GOODALL, of Hanover. Will dated 15 Jan. 1804, proved 24 Jan. 1816. On 6 March 1795 had purchased of Col. Hugh Nelson a tract of land called "Travelers Rest" adjoining other lands of Goodall. Title Bond dated 15 March 1799 with J. Nelson, Security. This cause in Chancery resulted over this transaction. Parke Goodall was survived by his widow, whom he does not name, and by children: (From will:)
1. CHARLES P. GOODALL, Executor of his father's Estate.
2. MARY, in 1804 wife of a Mr. Trevilian.
3. PATSEY, in 1804, wife of Mr. Street.
4. JANE M. GOODALL.
5. SUSAN GOODALL.
6. ELIZA GOODALL.

NELSON, COL. HUGH, dec'd of Hanover County. On 6 March 1795 he sold to Parke Goodall a tract of 251 acres of land adjoining Goodall, John Sledd and others, called "Travelers Rest" - the consideration being 150 Lbs. He and J. Nelson executed a Title Bond under date of 15 March 1799 to the said Goodall covering this property, with Richard Overton as Security. The witnesses being P. Street and J. Street. Col. Hugh Nelson had issue:
1. THOMAS NELSON, of Richmond, Henrico County in 1833.
2. LUCY, wife of Edmund Pendleton. Living in Caroline County 1833.
3. FRANCES EDMONIA NELSON, living in Knoxville, Tenn., in 1833.
4. JANE BYRD, married Francis Walker and both are deceased in 1833, leaving issue:
   1. JANE FRANCES, wife of Dr. Mann Page.
   2. JUDITH C., wife of William C. Rives.
5. NATHANIEL NELSON, dec'd in 1833, survived by his widow who is in Gloucester Co., and children:
   1. MANN PAGE NELSON, of Frederick Co.
   2. ELIZABETH MANN PAGE NELSON, non-res'dt
   3. JUDITH CARTER NELSON, in Caroline Co.
   4. THOMAS NELSON, a minor, Gloucester Co.
   5. HUGH NELSON, in Pennsylvania State
   6. NANCY P. NELSON, of Gloucester Co., Va.
Most of these last six children were minors.

Hugh G. Street, Commissioner in 1833.

GOULDIN VS. GOULDIN, 1849 (17)
GOULDIN VS. TYLER &C. 1872 (40)

GOULDIN, CARTER W., deceased, of Hanover County, died intestate, possessed of property including 9 slaves and 200 acres of land on Goodlyhole Creek, near Chickahominy Creek. His children in 1849:
1. SAMUEL H. GOULDIN.
2. ELLERSON GOULDIN, wife in 1855 is Sally, a daughter of William E. Tyler
3. WILLIAM E. GOULDIN, Admr. of his father's Estate.
4. SUSAN GOULDIN.
5. MARY GOULDIN.
6. REBECCA GOULDIN.
7. MARGARET ANN, wife of Benjamin Gathright.

In 1872 Ellerson Gouldin was "Goulding"

TYLER, WILLIAM E., of Hanover County, made a Deed in November 1855, of which Wat H. Tyler was a witness. William E. Tyler's children in 1855, were:
1. JOHN H. TYLER.
2. SALLY, wife of Ellerson Goulding
3. ANN ELIZABETH, wife of George W. Barker in 1872.
4. WILLIAM E. TYLER.

Others mentioned: William Parsley, 1849; Robert Wade, Bentley Wicker, Henry Curtis, Spotswood Liggan.

GOVAN'S EXOR. VS. TURNER'S EXOR. &C., 1849 (17)

Archibald Govan's Will (Abstract)

GOVAN, ARCHIBALD, of Hanover. "I, Archibald Govan considering the uncertainty of life and the duty of being prepared for death, and being of sound and disposing mind and memory, do make and ordain this my last will and Testament hereby revoking all former wills by me at any time made." Directs that his just debts to be paid. Mentions a family of slaves given by his father-in-law, William M. Waller to his wife, Lucy Ann Govan, for her and her children's benefit. Devises to his wife one-third of his Estate (not specifically bequeathed) both real and personal and of every description, expectancy or action, including his interest in Estate of his sister Mary Hill. His wife's portion of the land where he now lives to include the dwelling house and all the outhouses, barns, stables, etc., also the dwelling standing in the yard apart from the main dwelling house and known as "the office," which she is to have in addition to her one-third, but subject to the restriction that if one or both of his sons, on the arrival of the youngest at age of twenty-one, wish to divide and cultivate, or cultivate together the Estate, she shall

allow them to purchase her interest at fair valuation. Directs that his library, prints, and maps shall be divided in value between his two sons, William Waller Govan and James Govan, he hopes "they will keep them if not compelled by necessity to part with them." Devises to eldest son, William Waller Govan one-half of his Estate both real and personal. Also devises to him his watch and appendages which he may wear at the time of his death - it to be intrusted to his mother who is to give it to him when he arrives at age of twenty-one, or sooner if she thinks he has discretion enough to take care of it. Also gives him his double barrel gun. Desires that his Executors purchase for his second son, James Govan a similar watch to that given to his eldest son, also the appendages usually belonging to such a watch, the whole not to cost more than $195.00 "the initials of my name to be engraved on it as on his brother's and is to be kept by his mother and to be given him when he arrives at age of twenty-one, or sooner if he should manifest discretion sufficient to take care of it." Also devised to him the remaining half of his Estate both real and personal. "I also give and devise to him my rifle, my small pocket pistol and my brace of silver mounted flint pistols which formerly belonged to my father and which I hope he will keep not because of any intrinsic value they possess but because of the estimate I put on them." Hopes his wife will consider it to her interest to allow her portion of the real estate and also of the personal estate to be worked together with the portions of his sons, under direction of his Executors who are in such case to equalize the profits and expenses. Appoints his brother-in-law Alexander Duval and nephew George William Richardson, Executors and Guardian of his infant children. It is his desire that his children shall have their studies directed as to qualify them to enter the military school at Lexington in the State of Virginia "when they leave it, should it be before they arrive at legal age, they shall be free to choose what profession they will devote themselves to, and I earnestly beg of them not to spend a day of their lives in idleness." "Should the payment of my debts so reduce my estate as to make such an education unwise, I wish them to receive at least the rudiments of a plain english education and I positively enjoin it upon their Guardians the necessity of putting them at some business or labor by which they can make an honorable livelihood." Dated 21 day of November in the year 1844.

Archibald Govan (Seal)

Signed sealed, published and declared by the Testator Archibald Govan as & for his last will and Testament in the presence of us who in his presence and at his request have hereunto set our names as witnesses thereto: John Mutter
Edw. Govan.

At a Court of Quarterly Session continued and held for Hanover County at the Courthouse on Wednesday the 26th of July 1848. The last will and testament of Archibald Govan deceased was proved by the oath of John Mutter a witness thereto. And at a Court of Monthly Session held for the said County at the Courthouse on Tuesday the 22nd of August then next following it appearing to the satisfaction of the Court that Edward Govan one of the subscribing witnesses to the said will is dead, and Henry Curtis and James G. Turner being sworn, state that they are well acquainted with the handwriting of the said Edward Govan and that they verily believe that the signature of the said Edward Govan as a subscribing witness to the said will is his genuine signature. Thereupon the said will is ordered to be recorded as the last will and testament of the said Archibald Govan dec'd.

    Teste, Wm. O. Winston, C.H.C.

    A Copy, Teste, Wm. O. Winston, C.H.C.

ARCHIBALD GOVAN, of Hanover. Will dated 21 November 1844. Probated 26 July 1848. Died in March 1848. Possessed a tract of land consisting of 405 acres of land on Chickahominy Swamp, about eight miles from Richmond, and adjoining the lands of William G. Overton and Dr. William F. Gaines. Appointed his brother-in-law, Alexander Duval and his nephew George William Richardson, Executors of his Estate and Guardian of his two infant children. He mentioned the Estate of his sister Nancy Hill. Was survived by his widow, Lucy Ann, who after his death visited in Amelia and Amherst Counties. In 1850 she was in New Kent. Also survived by two sons:

1. WILLIAM WALLER GOVAN, living in Henrico in 1850, under age.
2. JAMES GOVAN, living in Henrico in 1850, under age.

Others mentioned: Thomas Turner, dec'd in 1849, Thomas G. Turner, Executor. George Via, Trustee. Dr. Littleton W. Starke. Commissioners 1851: Henry Curtis, William F. Gaines, William G. Overton, Edward Sydnor and William B. Sydnor.

GREEN VS. GREEN & OTHERS, 1833 (16)

GREEN, MACON SR., of Hanover, died intestate 22 March 1816. Sons Fleming and Thomas F. Green appointed Administrators. Survived by children:

1. FLEMING GREEN.
2. THOMAS F. GREEN.
3. ELEANOR, married after the death of her father, John B. Tinsley.
4. NANCY, dec'd in 1833, married after the death of her father, John Nash, who survived her and is living in Henrico.
5. FRANCES, married after death of her father Thomas Carter.

6. MACON GREEN, (Jr.) under age in 1833.

Commissioners in 1816: Thomas Tinsley, Benjamin Pollard, Benjamin Timberlake, George R. Smith and Thomas Oliver.

GREEN VS. TINSLEY'S EXECUTOR, 1863 (15)

William B. Green's Will

GREEN, WILLIAM B. "In the name of God Amen I, William B. Green of the County of Hanover do make and declare this writing my last will and Testament hereby revoking any and all others heretofore made by me. In the first place - I wish all my just debts to be paid and for that purpose, I wish such articles of personal property other than slaves as may be necessary to that end and as my wife can best spare to be sold, but I do not wish any slaves sold if the effects of paying any debts can be affected without. If the payment of my debts cannot be affected without the sale of slaves, then I wish such of the following slaves sold for that purpose as my wife can best spare and as may be necessary to pay what remains unpaid after the sale of the personal property other than slaves as aforesaid, to wit Sam, Fleming, Taylor, Joe, Martha and two of her children named William and James. Secondly - After the payment of my debts, I lend all the remainder of my estate both real and personal to my wife to be held by her during her natural life or widowhood for the comfortable support of herself and my children, and for the education of such of the latter as may not have completed their education at the time of my death but in case she should marry again it is my will that she shall from and after the time of such marriage have no interest whatsoever in my estate real or personal other than such interest as the laws would give her in case I died intestate. Thirdly - I will and bequeath to my wife my carriage and harness to be held by her as her own property unconditionally. Fourthly - At the death of my wife I will and bequeath to my four youngest children, Mary Wesley, William Corbin, Fanny Burwell and John Lewis, the following slaves, namely - Miles, Pharoah, Spotswood, Diley, Lucy Ann, Adeline, Frances, Charlotte and her child Emuella and their increase to be equally divided among them, My four youngest children aforesaid with this condition however that such of the above named slaves as shall on a division fall to the lot of my two youngest daughters, Mary Wesley and Fanny Burwell shall be held in Trust for their proper use and benefit during their natural lives by Charles Corbin Tinsley my wife's brother whom I hereby appoint Trustee for that purpose and in case of his death it is my will and desire that some proper person be appointed by the County Court of Hanover to act as Trustee in his place until the objects of said Trust are fulfilled and completed. My object and purpose in constituting this trust being to secure to my daughters aforesaid the entire use and benefit of their portion of the above named slaves as far as possible during their lives through the agency of a Trustee in case either of my sons should die under age (lawful age) or without lawful issue I wish his part of the above slaves to be equally divided between the survivors of my four youngest children and in case either of my young daughters aforementioned should die without Lawfull issue I wish her part divided equally among the survivors, My four youngest children. If my sons or either of them die over lawfull age he or they will dispose of his or their property as he or they may please but if either of my youngest aforesaid die leaving lawfull issue it is my will that her part of the above mentioned Slaves be equally divided among such lawfull issue left by her. Fourthly - At the death of my wife, I will and bequeath and devise to all my children namely - Jane Lipscomb, Mary Westley, William Corbin, Fanny Burwell and John Lewis all the remainder of my estate both real and personal to be equaly divided among them. The personal property falling to all my daughters in the devision I desire to be held in trust for each of them according to her part and for the individual benefit of each during her natural life in the same way and under the same conditions and provisions and to be finally disposed of in the same manner as recited in the fourth clause of this my will as in regard to the slaves these willed to my youngest daughters Mary Westly and Fanny Burwell with the ' single exception that I hereby appoint Roscow Lipscomb to act as Trustee for my eldest daughter Jane Lipscomb which said daughter Jane is to have a home in my house and live as one of the family as long as she remains single and unmarried. Sixthly - In regard to the real Estate that may fall to my daughters I desire that it may be sold at the discretion of the Trustee that acts for each or either of them and the money arrising from such sale invested in any description of property that he may think will be most beneficial to each or either of them and held in trust for her benefit and finally disposed of as directed in regard to the slaves willed to my youngest two daughters in the fourth clause of this will in case the death of either of my sons without lawfull issue or under (lawfull age) I wish all his property both real and personal equally divided among the survivors of my four youngest children. Lastly - It is my will and desire that my wife Lucy F. Green shall act as executrix to this my last will and Testament. I have hereto set my hand & affixed my seal this second day of May in the year of our Lord Eighteen hundred and forty-six."

Wm. B. Green (Seal)

Witnesses -
  Jos. M. Sheppard
  Charles L. Tinsley
  John H. Blunt
  Samuel Bumpass

At a Court of Quarterly Session held for Hanover County at the Courthouse on Tuesday the 28th of July 1846. This last will and testament of William B. Green dec'd was proved by the oaths of Charles L. Tinsley and John H. Blunt witnesses thereto and is ordered to be recorded.
  Teste, Wm. O. Winston, C.H.C.
  A Copy, Teste, R. O. Doswell, C.H.C.

WILLIAM B. GREEN, of Hanover. Will dated 2 May 1846, probated 28 July 1846. Appointed his wife Executrix. After her death, George W. Doswell, Sheriff of Hanover, was Administrator de bonis non. Testator possessed about 360 acres of land. Survived by his widow, Lucy F. (nee Tinsley), who died prior to 3 October 1856, and children:
  1. JANE LIPSCOMB, married prior to 1853, John B. Glazebrook, who was appointed her Trustee in place of Roscow Lipscomb who declined to act. She died since 3 Oct. 1856, leaving one child:
    1. WILBERT B. GLAZEBROOK, under 14 years of age in 1863.
  2. MARY WESLEY GREEN, died since 3 October 1846, a minor, unmarried.
  3. WILLIAM CORBIN GREEN.
  4. FANNY BURWELL. Over 14 years of age in 1863. Married between 15 March and 25 April 1866, T. H. Ellett, who was substituted as her Trustee in place of John H. Blunt.
  5. JOHN LEWIS GREEN. William J. Tinsley qualified as his Guardian in 1863. Became of age between 15 March and 25 April 1866.

Charles Corbin Tinsley, Lucy F. Green's brother, who was Trustee for some of her daughters, has since died and in 1863 Sophia E. Tinsley is his Executrix. Commissioners for the division of Green's Estate were John Ellett, Thaddeus Leake, B. B. Litman, Henry G. Cross, Andrew McDowell, T. C. Leake and J. T. Priddy.

GROSJEAN VS. SMITH &C., 1850 (57)

GROSJEAN, JOHN J., of Hanover, died intestate in January 1805. Final settlement of Estate in 1818. Survived by his widow, Mary (= Cunningham) and one son:
  1. DR. JOHN GROSJEAN, born 31 May 1791 in Hanover, died with will dated 23 Jan. 1819, probated in Feb. 1819, Burbon County, Ky. Studied medicine in Philadelphia and removed to Kentucky soon after attaining age of 21, and where he died without issue, survived by his widow, Julia Ann.

CUNNINGHAM, WILLIAM, of Hanover, died in June 1831. He married Mary, widow of John J. Grosjean of Hanover, soon after the latter's death. She was about 70 years of age in 1844, and died in November 1848, survived by a daughter:

1. [   ] who married Richard G. Smith. His will was probated circa 1855. William C. Smith, Executor.

Others mentioned: Miller Brown, who made a deposition in 1844.

TOLER VS. HALL &C., 1873 (39)

Dickinson Wash's Will (Abstract)

WASH, DICKINSON. "I, Dickinson Wash of the County of Louisa and State of Virginia do make the following my last will and testament." Debts and funeral expenses to be paid. Lends to his wife Matilda for life all lands except 45 acres which he devised to his sister, Nancy Wash, where she now lives, also gives her one slave. Lends to his wife the ballance of his property not otherwise disposed of. Gives her three slaves "to her and her heirs forever." To his nephew Edward S. Wash he gives one slave; and to nieces Sarah H. Spicer and Nancy S. Hall, he gives one slave each. Devises to William C. Stanley a slave, and "at the death of my wife I give to him all my land lying south of the Cooper tract . . to a corner to John R. Quarles and Misses Michie, to him and his heirs forever." Gives to John D. Binns and William D. Binns a slave each. "10th. At the death of my wife I give to John D. Binns and William D. Binns the land bounded by the Cooper tract, the land willed to William C. Stanley, the land of John R. Quarles, the Overton land and a line running the same course of the Overton line from Pine in the red bottom to Edward S. Wash's land and the said Edward S. Wash's land to them and their heirs forever. I also give to them all my wearing apparel and watch and if at the death of my wife there shall be any horses belonging to my estate I give to each of them one horse." Gives to Sarah E. Binns and Mary C. Binns a slave each. "13th. At the death of my wife I give to Sarah E. Binns & Mary C. Binns the Cooper tract of land supposed to contain about fifty-nine acres to them and their heirs forever." "14th. I give to John B. Smith in trust for the benefit of Mrs. Mary Binns a negro boy named Sam. It is my will that the said John B. Smith shall hold the said slave in trust for the benefit of the said Mary Binns during the lifetime of her husband Daniel K. Binns. I give to the said Mary Binns the right to dispose of said slave by will and if she shall survive her said husband I give the said slave to the said Mary Binns at his death, the said slave not in any manner to be liable for any debts which the said Daniel K. Binns

may have contracted or may hereafter contract. "16th. At the death of my wife I give the ballance of my property mentioned in the second disposing clause of this my will and lent to my said wife during her life and not herein particularly disposed of to my nephews and nieces to be equally divided among them, among the number William C. Stanley is included." "Lastly, I constitute and appoint John R. Quarles, John B. Smith and Edward S. Wash Executors of this my last will and testament and it is my will that they shall qualify as such without giving security. As witness my hand and seal this 28th of April 1855."

                                Dickinson Wash (Seal)

Signed and acknowledged as his will in presence of
    James M. Vest
    Charles Quarles, Jr.
    Charles H. Michie
    M. Wm. Michie

"In the 5th disposing clause of my foregoing will I have given unto my niece Sarah H. Spicer a negro woman named Fanny and in the 14th disposing clause of the said will I have given to John B. Smith a negro boy named Sam, son of Fanny. In this Codicil to my will I now declare it to be my will that my executor named in my will shall sell the said negores Fanny and Sam with the express provision that they are to be kept together and in this neighborhood for twenty-five years. And it is my will that my said executors shall pay to my said niece Sarah H. Spicer for her use and benefit the proceeds of the sale of said woman Fanny and that they shall pay to John B. Smith the proceeds of the sale of said boy Sam to be held by him for the benefit of Mrs. Mary Binns in the same manner as by the 14th clause of my will he is directed to hold the said boy Sam. Witness my hand and seal this 20th day of May 1856."

                                Dickinson Wash (Seal)

Signed and acknowledged as his will in presence of
    James M. Vest
    M. Wm. Michie
    Charles Quarles, Jr.

Probated in Louisa County 10 August 1857.

DICKINSON WASH, of Louisa County, Va. Will dated 28 April 1855, Codicil 20 May 1856, probated 10 August 1857. Executors named in will qualified. Widow, Matilda Wash. Devised property to his sisters, Nancy Wash, dec'd in 1873, and Mary, wife of Daniel K. Binns, and their children: John D., William D., Sarah E., and Mary C. Binns. Also to nephews Edward S. Wash and William C. Stanley, and nieces Nancy S. Hall and Sarah H. Spicer. The latter had perhaps among other children, a daughter Minerva A. Hall :

HALL, JESSE B., married four times, one of his wives, apparently the third, was Minerva A., daughter of Sarah H. Spicer, who was a niece of Dickinson Wash, dec'd of Louisa County, Hall and his wife Minerva A., had issue prior to 21 November 1868:
1. GEORGE F. HALL, a resident of Cabell Co., West Virginia in 1875.
2. JULIAN L. HALL.
3. SALLIE B. HALL, a minor in 1875.
4. JOHN R. HALL, a minor in 1875.
5. WARNER L. HALL, a minor in 1875.
6. MILISSA A. HALL, a minor in 1875.

His present wife, the fourth one, whom he married prior to 21 November 1868, was Susan M., by whom he had issue:
7. SAMUEL E. HALL, a minor in 1873.

Others mentioned: Jackson S. Valentine, Trustee. William H. Winston, aged 58 in 1873, and who lives about 2 1/2 miles north of Ashland.

JOHNSONS VS. CHILDS & DABNEY
1842 (21)

Sarah Hambleton's Will

HAMBLETON, SARAH. "In the name of God Amen. I, Sarah Hambleton of the County of Louisa and State of Virginia do make and publish this my last will and Testament in the manner and form following (that is to say) First - I give and devise to my Grandson David Richardson a negro woman named Amy and her future increase to him and his heirs forever but it is my will that his mother my daughter, Ann Richardson shall be supported by him during her natural life. I also give him my Cupboard. I give and devise to my son David Hambleton one negro woman named Dinah with the future increase to him and his heirs forever. I also lend him a negro man named Nat during his natural life and at his death, I give and devise the said negro Nat to my two grandsons Oliver Elsworth Hambleton and James Madison Hambleton, to them and their heirs forever, but in case either of my grandsons Oliver Elsworth Hambleton or James Madison Hambleton or both of them should die without lawful issue their part or parts so dying I give and devise to my granddaughter Polly Hambleton and her heirs forever. I give and devise to my granddaughter Rebecca Harris one negro woman named Biny with the future increase to her and her Heirs forever but it is my will that she shall let her mother Jane Harris have the use of the said Negro Biny, and her increase during her natural life but in case my Granddaughter Rebecca Harris should die without lawful issue then and in that case I give and devise the said Negroe Biny with her future increase to the children of her sister Ann Johnson that may be living at the time of

such death to be divided among them share and share alike which I give to them and their heirs forever, but it is to be distinctly understood that the said children are to let their mother Ann Johnson have the use of the said negro Biny and her future increase during her natural life. I give and devise to my daughter Mourning Plant one negro Boy named Dick and to dispose of him at her death in any manner she may think proper. I give and devise to my grandaughter Sarah Hoggard one feather Bed with furniture to her and her Heirs forever. All the residue of my Estate of every description whatsoever I give and devise to my two daughters Susanna Richards and Elizabeth Sharp to them and their Heirs forever. I hereby constitute and appoint my son David Hambleton Executor of this my last will and testament hereby revoking all former wills by me made. In Witness whereof I have hereunto set my hand and affixed my seal this first day of January one thousand Eight hundred and sixteen."

her
Sarah + Hambleton (Seal)
mark

Signed Seald & published as the last will & testament of the said Sarah Hambleton in the presence of us
    John Waddy jr
    H. M. Burnley
    James Burnley, Jr.

Probated in Louisa County 9 December 1816 by the oaths of Henry M. Burnley and James Burnley, Jr., witnesses.

SARAH HAMBLETON, of Louisa County. Will dated 1 January 1816, probated in Louisa 9 December 1816. David Hambleton, Executor. This suit is over the slave Biny or Bing which she purchased in 1790:

"David Hambleton of Louisa County and John Harris of Hanover County sells to Sarah Hambleton of Louisa, one negro woman Dinah and her child named Bing. Consideration 50 Lbs. Witnesses: Richard Richardson, Jesse Hagard, Nathan Pulliam. 26 Oct. 1790."

From her will and information given in the suit her heirs were:
1. DAVID HAMBLETON, Executor, who may have been the father, among others, of the grandchildren mentioned in will:
    1. OLIVER ELSWORTH HAMBLETON.
    2. JAMES MADISON HAMBLETON.
    3. POLLY HAMBLETON.
2. ANN, wife of a Mr. Richardson, and has perhaps among others, a son:
    1. DAVID RICHARDSON.
3. JANE, wife of a Mr. Harris, issue probably among others:
    1. REBECCA, wife of Thomas Childs of Hanover. No issue, aged 50 in 1838.

2. ANN H. wife of a Mr. Johnson, has
   issue in 1842, who are greatgrand-
   children of Sarah Hambleton,dec'd.
   1. ABIMULUK JOHNSON, "next friend
      of some of his brothers and
      sisters, who are infants."
   2. HARRIS JOHNSON.
   3. WILLIAM H. JOHNSON.
   4. JANE L. JOHNSON.
   5. NANCY H. JOHNSON.
   6. JURUSHA, wife of Albert G. Davis.
   7. JOHN L. JOHNSON.
   9. HENRY H. JOHNSON.
4. MOURNING PLANT, mentioned in will.
Depositions taken in this suit of the following:
Hardin Duke at the house of William W. Anderson
in Louisa 1839 "Lived about a mile from Sarah
Hambleton from 1782 until her death."; Wm. Hall
in 1840 "Was living at Beaverdam Depot in 1838.
Joseph F. Dabney a regular slave trader.";
Elijah Harris at Beaverdam Depot in 1838 "Mrs.
Childs is my Aunt."; Solomon Harris at store of
William W. Anderson in Louisa 1840; William
Thompson and Captain Charles Thompson.

ELLIS VS. HARRIS, 1861 (14)

Martha Ann Harris' Will

HARRIS, MARTHA ANN. "In the name of God
amen. I, Martha Ann Harris of the County
of Hanover and State of Virginia being of
sound mind but of infirm body, do make the following my last will and testament. First - I
wish all my just debts to be paid. Second - I
will and bequeath all my personal property consisting of one-half the value of the negro
woman Maryetta & her children as a loan to Mrs.
Harriet G. Thompson so long as the said Mrs.
Harriet G. Thompson Shall live at her death it
is my will that the said negroes Shall be divided with her property equally between her children Caroline V. Bumpass, Mary E. Thompson,
Thadius S. Thompson, Sarah A. Thompson, Nathaniel B. Thompson, to them and their heirs forever provided it is necessary to make a sale of
the above mentioned negroes to effect a division it is my will that after a Sufficient Sum
has been deducted to pay my just debts the remainder shall be equally divided between the
above mentioned Caroline V. Bumpass, Mary E.
Thompson, Thadius S. Thompson, Sarah A. Thompson and Nathaniel B. Thompson. Aug. 8, 1859."

                                    her
                     Martha Ann + Harris
Witnesses: mark
  A. N. Beackett
  B. B. Bumpass

At a Court of Monthly Session held for Hanover
County at the Courthouse on Tuesday the 16 of
June 1860. This last will and testament of
Martha Ann Harris dec'd was proved by the oaths

of A. N. Beackett and R. B. Bumpass the witness-
es thereto and is ordered to be recorded.
   Teste, Wm. O. Winston, C.H.C.
   A Copy, Teste, Wm. O. Winston, C.H.C.

MARTHA ANN HARRIS of Hanover. Will dated 8
August 1859, probated 26 June 1860. She died
of consumption, under age, and unmarried.

   "Martha Ann Harris came to the house of
   Mr. Charles Vest of Hanover with her mother
   and sister from one of the Western States
   in the year 1841, then four or five years
   of age. Continued to reside with Mr. Vest
   who was her uncle for several years, and
   has since resided in the family of Mrs.
   Thompson, her aunt, the mother of Mary E.,
   Nathaniel B., Thadius S., and Sarah A.
   Thompson."

She was survived by two sisters:

ELVIRA, wife in 1861 of Reuben S. Ellis.
CAROLINE, wife in 1861, of Thomas G. Bumpass.

Others mentioned: Dr. Brackett.

HARRIS' ADMR. VS. HARRIS' ADMR. &C., 1866 (19)

HARRIS, WILLIAM ELI, of Hanover died "with
a will in August 1835" (no copy extant).
Moses Harris qualified as Executor as such
he served until his death, when Testator's widow
qualifed as Administrator. His Estate included
about 1720 acres of land which was divided in
1835 among his widow and surviving children. He
also possessed 24 slaves. Ann Harris, the widow, died intestate in January 1852, possessed of
57 acres of land and "considerable personal
property." Jordan Harris qualified as her Administrator. Issue of Wm. Eli & Ann Harris:
1. JORDAN HARRIS, Administrator of his mothers
   Estate. Assigned 44 1/2 acres of tract
   called "Walker's", 223 1/2 acres adjoining Ground Squirrel Bridge "on which is
   the dwelling house."
2. SARAH D., married after 1835, Joseph Talley; assigned 251 acres called "Carson's"
3. MARTHA B., formerly wife of a Mr. Clough,
   whom she married after 1835. After 1852,
   wife of Benjamin T. Talley. Assigned 249
   acres called "Gentry's" on South Anna
   River.
4. SOPHIA E., married prior to 1835, Charles
   C. Tinsley, dec'd. She survived. Assigned
   283 1/2 acres being the tract called
   "Lacey's" and part of "Walker's."
5. JANE W., married prior to 1835, Edwin Snead
   Assigned 201 acres called "Crew's" which
   adjoined Edmund F. Wickham. She is dead
   in 1867, and Philip B. Snead is her Admr.
6. MOSES HARRIS, was Executor of his father's
   Estate. Assigned "the balance of the

tract called "Walker's", and 243 1/2 acres called "Hampton's". Died in Cumberland County prior to 1866.

7. ELIZABETH A. (DEBORAH ANN), dec'd, married after 1835, John Ellett, who survived, with infant children, of whom he is Gdn. in 1866:
   1. EDMONIA J., wife of Robert T. McNeal. "removed with her husband to Kansas prior to 1866."
   2. WILLIE ANN ELLETT.

Commissioners to divide land in 1835: Nathaniel Crenshaw, Chas. P. Goodall, Wm. Wingfield, Jr., Nath. Cross and Robert Ellett. Others mentioned: Joseph Harris and Burwell Toler appointed as Guardians of Emily Jane Thornton, orphan of Oliver Thornton, 18 January 1869.

HARRIS & OTHERS VS. WOODDY'S ADMR. &C. 1836 (19)

HARRIS, JOHN* of Hanover, died 23 November 1814, intestate. "Possessed considerable estate." His widow, Martha W., Admr. George Mason, her Security.

George Mason, on 22 March 1820 qualified as Guardian of Harris' infant children, with Arthur Bowles and James M. Higgason, Sec'tys.

Issue of John and Martha W. Harris:
1. RICHARD O. HARRIS.
2. SAMUEL B. HARRIS.
3. JOHN P. HARRIS.
4. MARTHA, married John D. Owen, and died without issue, a minor.
5. MELVINE HARRIS.
*John Harris,C.C. [No explanation of the "C.C."] Martha W. Harris, the widow, married David Wooddy, and both died prior to 1836, intestate. Their Estates committed to Anderson Bowles, Sheriff of Hanover. Others Mentioned: Edward N. Clough, Joel Crawford and Anderson Hopkins.

LAWRENCE &C. VS. HARRIS' EXOR. &C., 1837 (24)

Thomas Harris' Will

HARRIS, THOMAS. "I, Thomas Harris of Hanover County in a state of Soundness of mind but weakness of Body do constitute and appoint this my last will and testament in manner following. I desire that all my Just debts may be fully paid and that my Dear daughter Sarah Ann should have five hundred dollars given her, and then my whole estate should be divided into four equal lots, to be loted drawn for, and that my Grand Son Robert Barclay Lawrence and his Father Thos Lawrence shall take one lot Equally between them but Tho Lawrence shall hold the real estate of his lot, only for life, and at his Death it shall be equally divided between my three Daughters who shall take the other three lots to them and ther heirs forever, and lastly I do appoint my son in law Joel Cook my executor of this my last will and testament desireing that he my not be required to give security for his performance and I hope he may not charge more than will well pay himself for his Trouble."

Thos Harris (Seal)
2nd Mo. 18th 1826

Charles Vest
James Hunnicutt
John P. Kimbrough

"Richmond Jail 9 Mo. 18th 1826 I, Thomas Harris, make this codicil to my will. That whereas I have been for sometime past considering by many to be in a state of derangement and whereas I have had several trials before the Magistrates of the City of Richmond and declared by them to be of sound mind except that of believing it my duty in obedience to divine impression on my mind to undress . . . and exhibit my self naked before a congregation as a prophetic sign. Now therefore failing and believing myself to be of sound mind it is my will and desire that my will now in the hands of James Honeycut of Goochland County be continued except in the particulars herein mentioned, Viz: my will and desire is that my dear Daughter Sarah Ann Harris should be given in addition to that will five hundred dollars out of my estate therein mentioned, and that my Grand children who have lost their mother, towit Deborah Cook's children and Isabella Lawrence's son Robert Barclay Lawrence shall each receive five hundred dollars in addition to what is given them in the will now in the hands of James Honeycut of Goochland County. I wish no other alteration to be made in my said will. Given under my hand and seal this 18th day of 9th Month 1832."

Thos Harris
Signed in the presence
of Philip Courtney
   David White
   Robert H. Branch.

At a Court of Monthly Session held for Hanover County at the Courthouse on Tuesday the 27th of November 1832. This last will and testament of Thomas Harris dec'd was proved by the oath of Charles Vest and by the affirmation of James Hunnicutt two of the witnesses thereto: and the Codicil thereafter written was also proved by the oaths of David White and Robert H. Branch witnesses thereto, which will and codicil are ordered to be recorded.

Teste, Philip B. Winston, C.H.C.

A Copy,
   Teste,
      Philip B. Winston, C.H.C.

THOMAS HARRIS, JR., of Hanover. Will dated 18 November 1826, Codicil 18 September 1832. Probated 27 November 1832. Owned land in Hanover County and in the State of Ohio. "Possessed considerable real estate and a small personal estate." Joel Cooke qualified as Executor. Issue, of whom only two survived the Testator:
1. SARAH ANN, wife of Nathan Parker.
2. REBECCA, wife in 1837 of Joseph Jordan, of the State of Ohio.
3. ISABELLA, dec'd, married Thomas Lawrence, survived by an only child:
   1. ROBERT BARCLAY LAWRENCE, an infant in 1837.
4. DEBORAH, dec'd, married Joel Cooke who survived, with five infant children:
   1. CLOTILDA COOKE.
   2. JONAH T. COOKE.
   3. LYDDIA COOKE.
   4. ISABELLA COOKE.
   5. JOEL COOKE.

Others mentioned: Robert Ellett and William Priddy who purchased land of the Harris Estate. J. M. McDowell, who auctioned the land; Nathan C. Crenshaw and Wm. O. Winston, Commissioners. Samuel Crew, Master Commissioner of Chancery. James D. Kimbrough.

HAW & OTHERS VS. HAW'S ADMR. &C., 1878 (11)

HAW, RICHARDSON T., of Hanover, on 13 April 1838, recorded 30 April 1838, executed a Deed of Trust to John Haw, Trustee, for the benefit and "In trust for the use of his wife Margaret M., and at her death to be divided among all her children or heirs." a tract of land containing 315 acres where Richardson T. Haw now lives, bounded on the north by the road leading from Salem Church to Hanover Town, on the east by lands of Messrs. Anderson, Reuben Gardner and Judge Brockenbrough, on the south by Dr. Talley, and on the west by Reuben Gardner. Consideration $700.00 [This suit, instituted in 1878, continued too late to be of interest in this volume.]

FROM OLD WILL BOOK, PAGE 89

James Hill's (Sr.) Will (Abstract)

HILL, JAMES SR., of Hanover. Will dated 12 July 1849. Witnesses: Andrew C. Attkisson, Miles Macon, Nath[l] King. Proved by last two on 1 October 1849. Survived by widow Mary Hill, and issue:
1. JAMES HILL, Jr. Testator confirms gift to him of a plantation in Henrico County. Was one of the Executors of his father's Estate.
2. WALKER HILL. Appointed by his father as one of his Executors.

3. SALLY, dec'd, who was a daughter by her father's first marriage, whose name is not given, married David Timberlake, and had issue:
   1. EMILY TIMBERLAKE.
   2. ARCHIBALD TIMBERLAKE.
   3. WILLIAM TIMBERLAKE.
4. WILLIAM HILL. His father devised to him "my plantation 'Thompson's' for life, then to his children."
5. SUSAN B., wife of George B. Read, who have issue, not named.
6. NEWTON HILL, who has issue, who are not named.

BAUGHAN VS. HINES' ADMR. &C., 1844 (5)
HINES & OTHERS VS. HINES' ADMR. &C., 1844 (18)

HINES, CHARLES B., of Hanover "died many years ago seized of considerable personal estate." He left no will and Charles Thompson was appointed Administrator, and Milton W. Brown, was his Security. Thompson's certificate of Administration was revoked, and Benjamin F. Thomas was appointed in his place, also as the Guardian of the infant children, which included all except Susan. He was survived by his widow, Mary, whose age in 1845 as judged to be between forty and forty-five, and by issue:
1. SUSAN, in 1844, wife of Leander Baughan, who is of age, and the following infants in 1844:
   2. MARY J. HINES.
   3. JOSEPH H. HINES.
   4. MARTHA C. HINES.
   5. MARGARET W. HINES.
   6. MARIA F. HINES.
   7. CHARLIE C. HINES.
   8. ELIZABETH HINES.

FROM WILL BOOK 1852, PAGE 142

HOGG, STERLING, of Hanover County. Will dated 10 February 1860. Probated 26 September 1865. Witnesses: William Harris, Anderson Thorp. Bequest to his wife, Rebecca Hogg, and to William Chiles.

MONTAGUE & WIFE & OTHERS VS. WINSTON'S
EXECUTORS & OTHERS, 1882 (13)
Dr. Robert Honyman's Will (Abstract

HONYMAN, ROBERT. "I, Robert Honyman, Doctor of Physic, Hanover Co., State of Virginia." Devises to son, Robert Bruse Honyman "all the tract of land whereon I live." 900 acres, also slaves. To daughter Jane wife of Rev. Andrew Broaddus "now separated." Daughters: Cornelia, wife of Dr. Samuel Oldham; Helen, dec'd, who was wife of Thomas Nelson; and Catherine "if she recovers use of her reason." Grandson, Robert Carter Nelson. Mentions his claim against Thomas Macon, and the Estate of Thomas Norvell. Executors: Son, Robert Bruce Tonyman, son-in-law Thomas Nelson, son-in-law Dr. Samuel Oldham, son-in-law Rev. Andrew Broadus, Mr. William Nelson, his son William Nelson, Jr., Garland Thompson, Jr., and David Bullock of Richmond. James Fontaine one of Executors in the Codicil to his will. Will dated 22 June 1821, proved in April 1824, when Robert H. Nelson, Pleasant Terrell and James Byars certify to Testator's handwriting. [Suit filed in 1870 and is too late to be included in this volume].

FROM OLD WILL BOOK, PAGE 76

HOPKINS, WILLIAM F., of Hanover County, was appointed Guardian of his children, named below, on 7 October 1845.
1. WILLIAM A. HOPKINS.
2. JAMES M. HOPKINS.
3. KITURAH A. HOPKINS.
4. MARY J. HOPKINS.
5. DELPHIA HOPKINS.

EARNEST VS. HUGHES' EXOR., &C., 1850 (29)
EARNEST'S GDN. VS. HUGHES &C., 1857 (30)

John Hughes' Will

HUGHES, JOHN. "In the name of God amen. I, John Hughes of the County of Hanover and Parrish of Sant Pauls being in ill state of helth doo make and ordain this my last will and Testament in manner and form following, First I commend my Soul to God, and my boddy to the dust to be intered in that manner as my surviving friend may chose to direct. Item 2nd. I request thall my Just depts should be paid. Item 3rd. I give to my loveing wife Nancy Hughes during her natural life or widdowhood all my estate both real and personal with this consider ation that if she should never marry again I wish her my said wife Nancy Hughes to enjoy all the benefits of my estate during her natural life, but if she should think proper to marry again it is then my desir that my estate should be divided into three equal parts and that my wife as aforesaid should onlley have one third dueing her natural life and the other remaining two thirds should be equally divided between my children Charles Hughes, Sarow Hughes and Agness Hughes to them and their heirs forever. Item 4. I do apoint my loveing wife Nancy Hughes my onley executrix to this my last will and testament revoking and disernuling all other. In witness whereof I have hereunto set my hand and affixt my seal this the 2d day of Jany 1815".

Signed sealed & delivered in presence of Thomas Melton, Moses (+) Talley, Charles Talley, Junr.

John + Hughes (Seal)
his
mark

At a Court of Monthly Session held for Hanover County at the Courthouse on Wednesday the 22nd day of March 1815. This last will and testament of John Hughes dec'd was offered to proof by Nancy Hughes the executrix therein named and was proved by the oaths of Moses Talley and Charles Talley junr witnesses thereto and also by the oath of the said executrix, is ordered to be recorded.
Teste, William Pollard, C.H.C.
A Copy, Teste, Wm. O. Winston, C.H.C.

HUGHES, JOHN, of Hanover. Will dated 2 Jan. 1815, probated 22 March 1815. Estate included 100 acres of land in lower end of Hanover, about eleven miles from Richmond. Survived by his widow, Nancy, who died in July 1857, and by three children:
1. AGNESS, died in 1842, survived by her husband George L. Earnest, her Administrator (Thomas Ruskell, Security) and by two infant children:
   1. AGNESS, who was two or three years of age in 1842, and deceased in 1850.
   2. GEORGIANNA MILDRED, aged three or four years in 1842, and over 14 in 1857.
2. CHARLES R. HUGHES.
3. SARAH, wife of Isaac Burnett in 1850.

Appraisers in 1815: Absolom Melton, Nicholas Talley, Edwd G. Sydnor, Rowland Tucker. Others mentioned: John H. Ernest 1850; C. B. Hill 1850; Francis W. Johnson 1854; P. N. Powell 1857; Samuel White 1828 and 1857; Robert White 1828; W. H. Lyons, Attorney, 1857.

HUGHES VS. TIMBERLAKE & OTHERS, 1838 (18)

HUGHES, JOSEPH T., "at present resident of Hanover" purchased of James B. Smith and Ann B., his wife, two certain tracts of land in Hanover County, on Mechanicsville Turnpike, for consideration of $500.00 cash and the further consideration of $1,000.00. Hughes sues for possession.

HESTER ANN JONES VS. ELISHA JONES, 1835 (22)

JONES, ABSOLOM, of Hanover, died intestate. Private in the State Line during the Revolution. For such services was issued Revolutionary Bounty Land Scrip #6908, dated 10 May 1831 for 33 1/3 acres of land. One of his heirs was Ella Jones, of whom the following grandchildren of the Intestate, are heirs:
1. HESTER ANN JONES, who sues by Absolom Jones, her next friend.
2. ISABELLA JONES.
3. ELI JONES.
The last two are infants in 1835, Elisha Jones, Guardian. Philip B. Winston Guardian ad litern.

JONES VS. BALL, 1854 (22)
JONES VS. CURTIS, 1853 (21)

Joel Jones' Will

JONES, JOEL. "In the name of God Amen, I Joel Jones of the Parish of St. Paul and County of Hanover, in State of Virginia being of sound disposing mind and memory do make and ordain this my last Will and Testament in manner and form following. Imprimis. I lend to my beloved wife Catherine Jones during her life her choice of either of the dwelling houses upon the plantation whereon we now live and ten acres of Land to be laid off convenient thereto in any manner she may direct, and as much of my household and kitchen furniture as she may think necessary for her use. I also lend to her my Gig and harness and a good carriage horse, one to be purchased if none answering her views should belong to me at the time of my death. I also give unto her my said wife during her natural life an annuity or clear yearly income of two hundred Dollars lawful money of Virginia to be paid in equal proportions half yearly by my sons Washington Jones and Albert Simms Jones respectively; And it is my will and intention that the said annuity of two hundred Dollars be chargable in equal sums on the bequests herein made respectively to my sons Washington Jones and Albert Jones. Item. I give and bequeath to my daughter Maryan Simms Jones one feather bed and furniture. And I lend to my Daughter all the money due from her husband John H. Jones (on bonds now in my possession) to me together with an additional thousand Dollars to be raised from any part of my Estate not specifically disposed of. The above sums of money are loaned upon the following conditions that my said daughter Maryan Simms Jones shall receive annually from my Executor or Executors the interest of the said money during her life and at her death I desire that the principal shall be equally divided between all of her children. Item. I lend unto my daughter Paulina America McLaurie during her life the following slaves and their increase, to wit, old Soloman, Nelson, Solimon, George, Andrew, Jack, William, Sealey, Charlotte, Nancy, Jacob, Isaac, Chancy, Sedwell, Armistead, and Martha and at the death of my said daughter Paulina America, I give and bequeath all the said slaves and their increase to her children and their heirs to be equally divided between them. But should my saud Daughter Paulina America die leaving no lawful issue, upon that happening I then lend all the negores and their increase herein lent to her my daughter Maryan Simms Jones during her life and at her death I give and bequeath all the said negroes and their increase to her children and their heirs to be equally divided between them. Item. I give and bequeath unto my son Washington Jones and to his heirs the plantation on which I now reside together with all the lands added thereto by my different purchases, the whole tract estimated to contain from 650 to 700 acres be the same however more or less. I also give unto my said son Washington, the following slaves and their increase, to wit James, Abraham, Henry, Benjamin, Joe, Claiborne, Archer, Caroline, Judith, Eliza, Fanny, Silvia, Milly, Sophia, Paulina, Zion and Miles - all the said property is given with the reservation of the house and ten acres of land to his mother for her life - and subject to and chargable with the one moiety of the annuity or yearly sum to his mother as herein before mentioned. But should my son Washington die leaving no lawful issue upon that happening, I do by this my will give and bequeath all the property herein given to him unto my son Albert Simms Jones and his heirs, saving the wife of the said Washington, should he have one, her thirds in the said estate during her widowhood. Item. I give and bequeath unto my son Albert Simms Jones and to his heirs the tract of Land on Chickahominy swamp called the Meadowbridge Plantation recently purchase by me of Joshua Storrs and the following slaves and their increase, to wit - David, Ceaser, Frank, John, Shadrack, Absolem, Garland, Emily - - - Lucy, Maria, Oliver, Suck, Rachael, Oliver, Sam, Iverson, Harriett, Maria Jones and Mary, all the said properties is given subject to and chargable with the one moiety of the annuity or yearly sum to his mother, as herein before mentioned. But should my said son Albert Simms die leaving no lawful issue upon that happening I do by this my will give and bequeath all the property herein given to him unto my son Washington Jones and his heirs, saving to the wife of Albert Simms Jones should he leave one, her thirds in the said estate during her widdowhood. Item. I give and bequeath to my two sons Washington Jones and Albert Simms Jones all the plantation utensils, household & Kitchen furniture (including at the death of their mother that, that may be remaining herein reserved to her use) together with forty head of choice sheep, all my hogs, and four choice horses (exclusive of bay horse given to Washington and a grey mare given to Albert and now in their respective possessions) to be equally divided between the my said sons. Item. It is my will and desire that as soon after my death as may be proper that the tract of land purchased by me of Talley and others containing about 210 acres be sold in such manner and on such terms as my Executrix and my Executors, or those qualifying as such may deem in their judgments best and they are hereby authorized to make such full and ample conveyance or conveyances in fee simple to the purchaser or purchasers as may be requisite & proper. Item. It is my will and desire that all the rest of my Estate both real and personal of what nature and kind so ever it may be not herein before particularily disposed

may be equally divided among my several chil-
en hereinbefore named which I give to them,
eir heirs Executors, administrators and
signs forever. And lastly I do hereby consti-
te and appoint my beloved wife Catherine
nes Executrix and my sons Washington Jones
d Albert Simms Jones Executors of this my
st Will and Testament hereby revoking all
lls by me heretofore made. In Testimony
ereof I have hereunto put my hand and affixed
 seal this 24th day of March in the year of
r lord one thousand eight hundred and twenty-
ne."

Joel Jones (Seal)
gned, sealed published and
clared by Joel Jones as his
d for his last Will and
stament in the presence as hearing of us who
 his request and in his presence have sub-
ribed our names as witnesses -
lliam A. Jones, Ezekiel S. Talley, Mildred P.
lley.

 a Circuit Superior Court of Law and Chancery
ntinued and held for Hanover County at the
urthouse on Wednesday the 29th of April 1835.
is last Will and Testament of Joel Jones dec'd
s proved by the oaths of Ezekiel S. Talley
d Mildred P. Talley witnesses thereto and is
dered to be recorded.
   Teste, Philip B. Winston ,C.C.
   A Copy, Teste, Philip B. Winston, C.C.

JONES VS. BALL, 1854 (22)
JONES VS. CURTIS, 1853 (21)
BURKE & EGGLESTON VS. JONES &C., 1861 (56)

OEL JONES, of Hanover. Will dated 24 March
 1829, probated 29 April 1835. Possessed con-
derable personal and real estate including a
act called "Meadowbridge Plantation" on
ickahominy Swamp. Survived by his widow, Cath-
ine, Executrix, and issue:
1. WASHINGTON JONES.
2. ALBERT SIMMS JONES, married after 25 Feb.
   1831 and prior to 1853, Frances Clopton,
   a daughter of Patrick Clopton, dec'd and
   his wife, Harriet, a daughter of Thomas
   Brown. Inherited "Meadowbridge Plantation" from his father, of which there
   are plats and maps of the vicinity in
   the papers of these suits. In 1861 it was
   the place of his residence and described
   as "situated in the County of Hanover on
   Chickahominy Swamp bounded on one side
   by the road leading from said swamp to
   Richard Johnson's, and on the other side
   by a tract of 280 acres surveyed by William Clopton in 1847." In 1861 the grandchildren of Thomas Brown, who were the
   children of "Albert S. & Frances Jones
   by his first marriage," were:
   1. ANN MARIA JONES.
   2. JOHN HAW JONES.

3. MARYAN SIMMS, married prior to her father's
   will, John H. Jones.
4. PAULINA AMERICA McLAURIE - evidently her
   married name - not involved in suits.

CLOPTON, PATRICK, of Hanover, died prior to
 1831. Widow, Harriet, on 25 February 1831,
for consideration of $1.00 and the further con-
sideration of $330.00 paid by Francis Ellett of
Henrico, sells to William Clopton two slaves,
of which Susan Turner "has a life estate." William Clopton "to hold slaves in trust for the
benefit of Frances Clopton until she is twenty-
one years of age, but should she die before
that time, then in trust for Ann Clopton, sister of Frances, and should she die without
issue, then to surviving children of Patrick
Clopton, dec'd, father of the said:
   1. FRANCES, married prior to 1853, Albert S.
      Jones.
   2. ANN CLOPTON."

Others mentioned: John B. Clopton, William Cunningham, J. H. Ernest, William S. Cheatham, and
W. N. Yarbrough (Coroner) 1853; Thos. W. Talley.

JONES & OTHERS VS. POLLARD, 1838 (21)

JONES, LANEY, deceased of Hanover County, was
 survived by his widow Martha L. Jones prior
 to 1838, and the following issue:
1. LANEY JONES.
2. JOHN JONES.
3. WILLIAM W. JONES.
4. ELIZABETH C. JONES.
5. PHILIP B. JONES.
6. MARTHA W. JONES.
7. HENRY R. JONES.
8. MERIWETHER JONES.
9. ANN B. JONES, under 21 years of age
10. MOLLY T. JONES, under 21 years of age
11. THOMAS N. JONES, under 21 years of age.

KING VS. JONES' WIDOW & HEIRS, 1858 (23)

JONES, MERIWETHER, deceased, of Hanover Co.,
 was survived by his widow Kitty Ann Jones,
 prior to 1858, and by the following issue:
1. MARTHA ELLEN, in 1858, widow of Hector L.
   Davis.
2. WILLIAM JAMES JONES.
3. DAVID ROBARD JONES.
4. JOHN JONES, under 21 years of age.
5. HENRY JONES, under 21 years of age.
6. MERIWETHER JONES, under 21 years of age.

SAUNDERS VS. MANN &C., 1866 (53)

JONES, MICHAEL, dec'd of Hanover County. Will
 destroyed. Was possessed of "large landed
 estate." Survived by widow, Martha, who died
in June 1866, and issue:

1. WILLIAM R. JONES.
2. DAVID G. JONES.
3. THOMAS JONES.
4. MICHAEL G. JONES, dec'd, survived by two
   infant children:
   1. WILLIAM A. JONES.
   2. MICHAEL JONES.
5. FRANCES E. JONES.
6. AMANDA, wife of Edward T. Mann.
7. ELI M. JONES.

WALTON VS. JONES' EXOR. & OTHERS, 1872 (38)

Thomas Jones' Will

JONES, THOMAS. "I, Thomas Jones of the County
of Hanover & State of Virginia, of sound
mind & memory do make & ordain this my last
will and testament hereby revoking all others.
1st. It is my will & desire that after my death
all my just debts & funeral expenses be first
paid by my executors hereinafter named. 2nd. It
is my will & desire that my beloved wife Elizabeth Jones after my death shall hold and possess during her life all my landed estate on
which I now reside with all the stock of every
description, all the horses, mules, plantation
utensils, household and kitchen furniture, my
carriage, wagon, cart & ten such slaves as she
may select out of my servants and that she be
at liberty to use, manage & employ the said
property (land & slaves) as she may think
proper & to take to her self all the profits
arising therefrom & at her death all the said
property (except the land) is to be divided as
hereinafter directed. 3rd. It is my will &
desire that my son Thomas L. Jones shall after
the death of myself & wife have & possess the
tract of land on which I now reside estimated
at six hundred acres or more to him & his
heirs forever & I desire that said land shall
be estimated to him at five dollars per acre.
4th. I give to my son Thos. L. Jones my man
Robin bought of Miss Nancy Showalter & require
him to pay in consideration therefor twenty
dollars to each of my daughters, Viz: Frances
W. Hope, E. A. D. Lumpkin & S. H. Spindle. 5th.
It is my will and desire that after my wife
shall have selected ten such servants as she
may prefer from among my slaves, the remainder
of my slaves shall be appraised by George Fleming, E. W. Morris, & Charles Morris or any
two of them before dividing them & that my
daughters Frances W. Hope, Eliza A. D. Lumpkin
and Sarah H. Spindle shall then have given to
them at the appraised value such a part of the
said slaves as shall be equal to one fourth of
the land willed to my son Thomas L. Jones, said
land to be estimated as heretofore directed at
five dollars per acre. 6th. It is my will and
desire that the slaves given to my daughters
shall be held by each of them during their
lives & at their deaths to be equally divided

among their children. If should any one of the
die without child that the slaves given her
shall revert & be equally divided among the
children of my surviving daughters & my son
Thomas L. Jones save that under no circumstance
is David Isbell or his wife Elizabeth to own o'
possess any of my slaves, but shall receive in
money from the other children of my daughter
Frances W. Hope at the division of said slaves
a child's part of their appraised value, such
appraisement to be made by George Fleming, E.
Morris & Charles Morris or any two of them and
that under no circumstances are the said slave
or any part of them to be subject for the debt
or liable to the control of the husbands of my
said daughters. 7th. It is my will and desire
that none of the slaves given to my daughters
shall be removed from the State of Virginia
until after the final division of them among m
grandchildren under a penalty of forfiture of
all interest in said slaves & should any of my
daughters die leaving a child or children unde
twenty-one years of age, it is my will and
desire that my executor shall take possession
of the slaves allotted to such minors until
they become of age. 8th. It is my will and
desire that my executors shall pay Thomas M.
Jones of Richmond one dollar in full of all
interest directly or indirectly in my estate.
9th. It is my will & desire that the slaves
heretofore received by my children from me & a
in my possession at the time of my death shall
be appraised by George Fleming, E. W. Morris,
& Chas. Morris or any two of them & that my
children shall each retain the same slaves at
their appraised value & after allotting to my
wife the ten slaves she may select & to my
daughters such slaves as would at their apprai
ed value give each of them a slave equal to on
fourth of the land willed to my son Thos. L.
Jones at five dollars per acre, I then direct
that that the remainer of my slaves shall be
equally divided amongst my three daughters & m
son Thos. L. Jones & that each child shall have
one equal share taking into the estimate the
appraised value of the slave heretofore receive
by each of my children from me. 10th. It is m
will & desire that at the death of my wife the
ten slaves willed to her & their increase with
all the rest & residue of my property (except
the land) shall be equally divided among my
three daughters & my son & at the death of my
daughters to be equally divided among their
children & should any of my children die leaving no child it is my will that all the propert
received from me shall revert to my surviving
children & be equally divided among them save
that under no circumstances is David Isbell or
his wife to have or possess any of my slaves
but to receive their proportion in money from
the other children of my daughter Frances W.
Hope at appraised value & under no circumstances are said slaves to be liable for the debts
or subject to the control of the husbands of m

aughters. 11th. I do hereby constitute &
ppoint my son Thos. L. Jones & Wm. Lumpkin
ach of Hanover County executors of this my last
ill & testament revoking all others made by me.
o all of which I have hereunto affixed my hand
seal.   September 4th 1858."

                                        Thomas Jones
enj. Vaughan
oseph E. Leadbetter
. Fleming Hope
has. H. Vaughan.

robated 24 January 1865. Proved by the oaths
f Joseph E. Leadbetter and Chas. Vaughan.

THOMAS JONES, of Hanover. Will dated 4 Sept.
   1858, probated 24 Jan. 1865. Survived by his
idow, Elizabeth, who died prior to 1872, and
y issue:
1. THOMAS L. JONES, Executor of his father's
      Estate.
2. FRANCES W. HOPE, widow.
3. ELIZA A. D. LUMPKIN, dec'd, survived by
      husband, William Lumpkin, and issue:
      1. WILLIAM L. LUMPKIN.
      2. THOMAS J. LUMPKIN.
      3. BETTY FANNY, wife of Samuel M. Baker.
      4. HARRIET K., wife of Robert B. Hundley.
4. SARAH H. SPINDLE, widow.

homas M. Jones, of Richmond, a devisee, said
ot to be a relative.

ANDERSON VS. JONES &C., 1845 (33)

JONES, WILLIAM H., formerly of Hanover County
   died in Henrico prior to 1872. Possessed
   151 1/2 acres in upper end of Hanover, adj.
eorge W. Morris. Circa 1845 had sold to his
on 130 acres adjoining Edmund Wash, George
ason, Charles Mitchell and the Estate of John
. Anderson, dec'd. Wife, Hulda, also deceased
n 1872. Issue:
1. SAMUEL W. JONES, of Louisa County, had
      purchased land from his father, in the
      upper end of Hanover. Deceased in 1872,
      survived by his widow Sarah, who is in
      Henrico in 1872, and by issue:
      1. DEMETRCUS JONES, of Mississippi in
            1872.
      2. JANE ELIZABETH, wife first of a Mr.
            Harris, second of a Mr. Shepherd,
            and lives in Mississippi, 1872.
      3. CORNELIA J., wife of John C. Roane of
            Charles City County, Va., 1872.
      4. SARAH F., wife of Henry Smith of
            Charles City County, Va., 1872.
2. FRANCES ANN, wife of Oscar F. Chisholm of
      Hanover County, 1872.
3. ARIANNA (ELIZABETH), widow of a Mr. Smith
      of Charles City County, Va., 1872.
      (Her name once given as Elizabeth Arana)

4. CHARLES E. JONES, died prior to 1872, sur-
      vived by his widow, Martha S., living in
      Albemarle County, Va., 1872. Issue:
      1. JAMES B. JONES, "living on Captain
            Buck Early's old place in Albemarle
            County, 1872.
      2. ALICE A. JONES.
      3. MARTHA S. JONES.
      4. CORTEZ F. JONES.
      5. ETNA T. JONES.
      The last four are under age of 21 in
      1872, and residents of Albemarle County.

Others mentioned: Francis Page, dec'd, John
Page, Admr. 1845; George A. Jones, Counsel 1846;
Elijah J. Jones; Robert J. Pulliam; George B.
Mason; W. W. Anderson; C. W. Dabney, Commission-
er 1846. H. Southworth, Deputy Clerk of Han-
over County 1873.

KENNEDY'S ADMR. VS. KENNEDY &C., 1858 (33)

Martin Kennedy's Will

KENNEDY, MARTIN. "In the name of God amen.
   I, Martin Kennedy of the County of Hanover
   and State of Virginia do make and ordain
this my - Will and Testament in manner and
form following. Viz.1st. I desire all my just
debts and funeral expenses paid by my Executor
hereinafter named. 2nd. After the payment of
all just debts and funeral expenses I lend all
the rest and residue of my property both real
and personal to my beloved wife Frances Kennedy
during her natural life   to be so far under
the control of my Exor. that no waste is to be
committed on the same. 3rd. At the death of my
said wife Frances Kennedy I give and bequeath
to my two daughters Sarah Kennedy and Frances
Luck the plantation on which I at present
reside containing one hundred and ninety acres
be the same more or less to them and their
heirs forever to be equally divided between
them if they wish a division to be made and if
divided, I desire that my daughter Frances have
the dwelling house, with the understanding that
sd dwelling house is to be a home for my sd
daughter Sarah so long as she may remain single
or unmarried. 4th. My tract of land in Louisa
County containing two hundred and seventy acres
be the same more or less, I give and bequeath
to my two daughters Croshe C. Hall and Jane
Hall and my two Grandsons Wm. M. and Ira E.
Kennedy, they the said William M. and Ira E.
taking one share only in the said Land to them
and their heirs forever. 5th. To my three
Granddaughters Angeline, Isabella and Cassaty,
children of my son Lancelot Kennedy I give and
bequeath ten Dollars each to be raised out of
the sale of my personal property after the
death of my wife, to them and their heirs forever. 6th. The whole of my personal property
to be sold after the death of my wife and the

balance after paying ten Dollars each to my
three granddaughters named in the 5th clause of
this my will, I desire may be equally divided
between my four daughters Viz - Croshe C. Hall,
Jane Hall, Sarah Kennedy and Frances Luck and
my two grandsons William M., and Ira E. Kennedy
they the said William M. and Ira E. taking one
share only of said sale to them and their heirs
forever. 7th. To my two sons Lancelot and Martin Mc. Kennedy I give nothing having given to
my two grandsons William M. and Ira E. Kennedy
sons of my said son Lancelot Kennedy a portion
of my Estate, and to my son Martin Mc. Kennedy
a tract of land value five hundred Dollars.
8th. Some doubt exists in my mind whether the
tract of land given by this my to my two daughters Sarah & Frances is not more than equal portion of my Estate and to prevent injustice I
desire that said tract of Land may be valued by
three of my neighbors, one of whom is to be
selected or chosen by each of my Exors and they
are to select a third and the valuation of the
three be final and my said two daughters are to
account for said Valuation to my Estate. I desire that the same course may be persued in
relation to my tract of land in Louisa given to
my two daughters Crashe C. and Jane Hall and my
two grand sons William M. and Ira E. in the 4th
clause of this my will. 9th. If upon a final
Settlement of my Estate my four daughters, Viz-
Croshe C. Hall, Jane Hall, Sarah Kennedy and
Frances Luck and my two Grandsons William M. &
Ira E. Kennedy as one Legatee their respective
portions should amount to five hundred Dollars
each then I desire of the remainder my son Martin Mc. Kennedy have an equal share. 10th. And
Lastly I appoint my two sons in - - Zephemiah
Hall and Robert G. Luck Exors to this my will
hereby revoking all former wills and declaring
this to be the only one. In testimony whereof I
have hereunto set my hand and affixed my seal
this 8th day of February 1838."

                        Martin Kennedy (Seal)
Signed sealed published
& declared as the last will
of the above named Martin Kennedy in the presence of us: William E. Sims, Charles Thompson.

At a Court of Quarterly Session held for Hanover
County at the Courthouse on Tuesday the 26th of
October 1847. This last will and Testament of
Martin Kennedy dec'd was proven by the oaths of
William E. Simms and Charles Thompson the wit-
nesses thereto and is ordered to be recorded.
    Teste, Wm. O. Winston, C. H. C.
    A Copy, Teste, Wm. O. Winston, C.H.C.

MARTIN KENNEDY, of Hanover. Will dated 8 Feb.
1838. Probated 26 October 1847. George W.
Doswell qualified as Administrator with the will
annexed. Survived by his widow, Frances K., who
died in January 1858, between 75 and 80 years
of age, and children and grandchildren:

1. SARAH KENNEDY, widow of Austin Yearmans,
   who she married prior to February 1838.
2. FRANCES ANN, wife of Robert G. Luck. Sol
   her interest in land devised to her by
   her father, to Edward A. Rowzie on 17
   July 1848. Land adjoined land of Willi
   Ashley, dec'd.
2. MARTIN Mc. KENNEDY.
3. LANCELOT KENNEDY, who had sons, devisees
   of their grandfather:
   1. WILLIAM M. KENNEDY.
   2. IRA E. KENNEDY.
4. JANE, wife of William S. Hall.
5. CROSHE C., dec'd, married Zephemiah Hall
   also dec'd. Surviving children:
   1. ALEXANDER F. HALL.
   2. MARTHA, wife of Samuel E. Hall.
   3. CASSIDY, wife of GEORGE M. HALL.
   4. LEXINGTON HALL, under 21 years of a
      in 1858.
   5. IRA HALL, under 21 years of age 185
   6. ZEPHEMIAH CURTIS HALL, under 21 yea
      of age in 1858.

Commissioners appointed to divide or appraise
land: Lancelot Phillips, John S. Smith, Charl
B. Richardson, Charles E. Thompson, Henry R.
Carter. Others mentioned: B. B. Dickinson.

FERRELL & WIFE VS. DOSWELL'S EXOR., 1832 (42

                Pitman Kidd's Will

KIDD, PITMAN. "In the name of God amen. I,
    Pitman Kidd of the County of Hanover bei
    of sound science and memory do make and
ordain this to be my last will and Testament
manner and form as follows. Imprimis. My will
and desire is that my whole Estate be kept together as land as my wife continues a widow
except such things as shall hereafter be mentioned. My will and desire is that my wife
Agnes Kidd shall remain in the house she now
resides in undisturbed and receive annually o
third part of the incomes of my estate except
my mill plantation & that my two daughters
shall receive the other two-thirds of the incomes of my estate and the income of the mill
plantation all so my will and desire is that n
two daughters retain the property I have let
them have on a lone dureing their lives. I le
to my wife's two daughters Susan H. Sharp and
Mary R. Sharp two negro girls Ginney and Nancy
to take in possession at any time they think
proper. I give to my wife all my Household and
Kitchen furniture that she had at the time we
were married also all she has bought, made and
repaired that came by her, and after her decease or marreing any other man I lend to my
wife's two daughters dureing their lives and
give to their children four negroes whose name
are as follows: Dicky, Jacob, Rachael and Mill
together with their increase if Either of the

ould die without issue, I give it to the
her children and if both should die without
sue, my will and desire is Both of their
rts should be equally divided between my
fe's Brother Samuel Richardson and her sister
ry Royester's children in case my wife should
e before myself I give all the household and
tchen furniture I have given her, to her two
ildren. I give to my wife's two daughters
l my wright and title that I have to any part
the rents of Richard Sharp dec'd land after
e decease of my wife. I lend to my two
ughters Sarah B. Watt and Mary C. Jones dure-
g their lives and give to their children all
estate that has not be given nor lent before
be equerly divided betwen them so as for
ch ones Children to have one half if either
my Daughters should die and leave no living
ild my will and desire is that the others
ildren should have the hole of my estate at
e decease of both of my two Daughters if the
nnagers of the estate of Richard Sharp dec'd
ould call on me or my children or Executors
r the things my wife bought at his sail I
all charge board for keeping her children, if
t I shall charge nothing. In case my daugh-
r Mary C. Jones should die before John Jones
o is her husband my will and desire is that
may have the same interest in my estate
ering his life as I have given her and at his
ath for it to go as I have before mentioned
this my last will and testament. My will
d desire is that my daughter Sarah B. Watt
ceive her part of the incomes of my estate as
have devised to herself and make what use
e pleases with it and lastly I appoint Thomas
arke and John Jones, Thomas Accree and my
fe my executors an extx to this my last will
d testament given under my hand and seal this
ird day of november eighteen hundred and six."

                     Pitman Kidd
gned sealed & delivered
 presence of
 Thos Acree
John Acree
Daniel + Tyler
Samuel + Boaze.

t a Court of Monthly Session held for Hanover
ounty at the Courthouse on Wednesday the 25th
f May 1808. This last will and testament of
itman Kidd dec'd was offered for proof by
ohn Jones one of the executors therein named
nd was proved by the oaths of Daniel Tyler and
y the oath Samuel Boaze witnesses thereto and
lso by the oath of the said executor and is
rdered to be recorded.

Teste, William Pollard, C.H.C.
 A Copy,
        Teste,
            Philip B. Winston, C.H.C
No other papers of this suit found)

LUCK &C. VS. PAGE &C., 1866 (28)

KIMBROUGH, BARBARA P., (who was Barbara P.
Blunt) " according to recollection, gave
her daughter Elizabeth P. Page, who died
6 September 1872, 'Point Lookout' 22 3/8 acres
and at her death to be divided equally among
Elizabeth's children, whose names are as follows: "
  1. BARBARA A., died in September 1875, widow
        of William H. Duke, who died in 1864.
        Their issue:
        1. CHARLES HENRY DUKE.
        2. GEORGE W. DUKE.
        3. MARIA L., wife of Andrew Thacker.
        4. BENJAMIN F. (or D.) DUKE.
        5. SUSAN ANN, wife of John Perrin.
        6. MARY JANE, wife of Carter Mallory
        7. FRANCES M., wife of Thomas Mallory.
        8. WILLIAM DUKE.
        9. ALEXANDER DUKE, under 21 years of age
            in 1876.
  2. ELIZABETH K., widow of John N. Mallory in
        1876.
  3. SARAH J., wife of Frederick H. Duke.
  4. MARY F., widow of a Mr. Ammons. She has
        been non compos mentis since circa 1855,
        and lives in Williamsburg, Va.
  5. SUSAN E., wife of William H. Luck.
  6. LUCY E. M., wife of Thomas S. Kelley, and
        lives in Alexander, Va., 1876.
  7. WILLIAM C. PAGE, died 27 December 1869,
        survived by his widow Catherine, who in
        1876 is living in Richmond near the old
        market. Their children are:
        1. MORDECAI T. PAGE.
        2. WILLIAM WARREN PAGE.
        3. MARY ANN, wife of John Kearn(or Hearn)
        4. JOHN PAGE.
        5. ALONZO PAGE.
        6. KATE PAGE.
  8. JOSEPH F. PAGE.
  9. JOHN L. PAGE. "Went to Tennessee 46 years
        ago. Last heard from about 34 years ago."
 10. JAMES N. PAGE. "Went to Mississippi 43
        years ago. From there he went to Arkan-
        sas. Heard from him about 29 years ago."

Others mentioned: Elizabeth P. Kimbrough, Exor.
of James D. Kimbrough of King William County.

KING &C. VS. KING &C., 1860 (51)

KING, JAMES, dec'd of Hanover, a widower at
his death, possessed 273 1/2 acres adjoining Robert S. Jenkins, Nath[l] Acree, Pleasant Slaughter, Est. of Jesse G. Yarbrough, Thos.
M. Green and William M. Wingfield. Issue:
  1. GEORGE W. KING.
  2. LUCY A. KING.
  3. LEMUEL P. KING.
  4. CELIA A., wife of Robert M. McKenzie.
  5. SARAH J. KING, under 21 years of age 1860.
  6. REBECCA W. KING, under 21 years in 1860.

HARRIS &C. VS. KING'S EXORS. &C., 1843 (20)

Henry King's Will

KING, HENRY. "In the name of God Amen. I, Henry King of the State of Virginia, County of Henrico and City of Richmond, do constitute and ordain this my last will and testament. Item 1st. All my just debts I wish my executors to pay punctually out of the Cash, bonds, notes and accounts or personal property which may be on hand at my death. Item 2nd. To my brother William King's children, namely Louisa, Amanda, Albert & Adaline, I give and bequeath one fifth part of my real and personal estate to be equally divided between them, to them and their heirs forever. Item 3rd. To my sister Betsey Ellett, I give and bequeath one-third part of my real and personal estate during her life and at her death to be equally divided between her heirs forever. Item 4th. To my sister Patsey Wyatt I give and bequeath one-half of the balance of my real and personal estate during her life, and at her death to be equally divided between her heirs forever. Item 5. To my sister Anne E. Souther, I give and bequeath the ballance of my real and personal estate during her life (except as she be hereafter mentioned) I give and bequeath out of this legacy one hundred dollars to the Agents of the Bible and Miconary Societys of the City of Richmond: and should my sister Anne E. Souther die without an heir I wish that part of my estate given to her to be equally divided between the heirs of my Sister Patsey Wyatt, my sister Betsey Ellett and the four heirs of my brother William King as named in the second item: but should my sister Anne E. Souther hereafter have an heir or heirs, then I wish that part of my estate so arranged as to make the legacies given to the heirs of my three sisters as nearly equal as possible. Item 6th. To my half sister Sarah Brown I give and bequeath the sum of one dollar to her and her heirs forever. Item 7. Should my friend Mr. Abner Robinson continue in business after my death, I wish him to use any part of my funds (after the payment of my just debts) and after paying himself for his trouble; the amount so used and the profits arising from the business I wish paid over to my executors, which they will dispose of as directed heretofore, and should he continue in business five years I wish him to take the profits of the last year as a compensation for his services. Item 8th. Should it not be practical to divide my real estate between the legatees without selling the same, I wish my executors to hold the real estate for ten years from this date before a sale shall be forced: without in their better judgment they should think it will be to the interest of the legatees to sell, and in that case they will select the most favorable time to make the sale, and use their judgment also on the terms, and after advertising the time place and

terms they will sell the same to best advantage and the rents together with the proceeds of sale they will dispose of as directed heretofore. If unhappily any difficulty should arise between any of the legatees on account of my having said too much or too little on any item or for want of legal knowledge then it is positively my will, in order to prevent law suits, that my executors should select three gentlemen noted for their probaty to say what is the meaning of the testator and their decision shall be as binding as if decided in any court of judication in the United States. And lastly I do hereby constitute and appoint my particular friends Mr. Abner Robinson, Col. Reuben Tankersley, Major Charles P. Goodall and my brother in law Major John Wyatt my executors of this my last will and testament. In witness whereof I have hereunto subscribed my hand and affixed my Seal this nineteenth day of April in the year of our Lord 1822."

Henry King (Seal)

"Memorandum. All acts. which has already or may hereafter originate in my books, or any amt. which I may be liable to pay for my brother William, or either of my sisters: I wish all such sums to be considered part of my estate, and for each one to settle their respective accts out of their special legacies.
April 19 1822."   Henry King (Seal)

At a Court of Hustings held for the City of Richmond at the Courthouse, the 2d day of March 1837.

This writing purporting to be the last will and testament of Henry King late of this City deceased, and a writing purporting to be a codicil to the same, were this day produced to the Court and there being no subscribing witnesses thereto, Isham Puckett and John King were sworn and severally deposed that they were well acquainted with the handwriting of the said Henry King deceased: Whereupon the said writings are ordered to be recorded as the true will and testament and codicil of the said Henry King, deceased. And at a like Court held on the 8th day of May 1837, on the motion of Charles P. Goodall, one of the executors named in the last will and testament of Henry King late of this City deceased - who made oath as required by the act entitled "An Act to amend the Act entitled "An act reducing into one the several acts concerning wills, the distribution of Intestates estates, and the duty of executors and administrators," passed 16 February 1825, and entered into and acknowledged a bond in the penalty of one hundred and fifty thousand dollars conditioned as directed by said act, with Robert Snead, Parke Street, Philip B. Winston, Edmund B. Crenshaw, Nathaniel B. Crenshaw, Peter Winston, William Wingfield, Jr., James McDowell and Robert M. Carver, his securities

who justified as to their sufficiency, the said Robert Snead as to the sum of $10,000, the said Parke Street as to the sum of $25,000, the said Edmund B. Crenshaw as to the sum of $30,000,the said Nathaniel C. Crenshaw as to the sum of $30,000, the said Peter Winston as to the sum of $20,000, the said William Wingfield, Jr., as to the sum of $7,000, the said James McDowell as to the sum of $5,000, and the said Robert M. Carver as to the sum of $5,000 (which was bond was executed as to the said Philip B. Winston by the said Charles P. Goodall, his attorney, appointed by power of attorney, proved in Court by a witness and filed) - Certificate is granted him for obtaining a probat of the said will in due form, liberty being reserved to the other executors in the said will named to join in the said probat, when they shall think fit.
   Teste, Chas. Howard, Clk.
   A Copy, Teste, Chas. Howard, Clk.

HENRY KING, died in the City of Richmond with will dated 19 April 1822, Codicil dated the same, and probated in the Hustings Court of Richmond 2 March 1837. Mentions a half sister Sarah Brown, and other sisters, a brother, and heirs:

WILLIAM KING, a brother, whose four children were legatees of their uncle Henry King, deceased:
1. LOUISA, widow of a Mr. Thacker in 1843.
2. AMANDA W. married Joseph W. Nash of Henrico. She is a widow in 1847.
3. ALBERT P. KING.
4. ADALINE W., deceased in 1843. Estate administered by Ed. B. Crenshaw, Sheriff of Hanover. Survived by her husband Martin P. Hackett, who, in 1846 is in Abbeville District of South Carolina.

BETSEY, a sister, wife of William Ellett, in 1844, of Bowie County, Republic of Texas. Their children:
1. ALFRED H. ELLETT, in 1844, of Madison Co., Alabama.
2. AMBROSE K. ELLETT, living in Hemstead Co., Arkansas 1844-45.
3. JOSEPH W. ELLETT, in 1844, living in Bowie County, Republic of Texas.
4. FRANCES, dec'd in 1843, Edmund B. Crenshaw Sheriff, Hanover County, Va., admr. Survived by her husband, a Mr. Clipton.
5. MARY ANN ELIZABETH, wife of Robert Linsey of County of Bowie, Republic of Texas.
6. SUSAN ANN, wife of Oliver Thompson. In 1845, living in Lauderdale Co., Alabama.
7. HENRY K. ELLETT, of Bowie Co., Republic of Texas. William Ellett, Guardian.
8. JOHN W. ELLETT, in 1844, living in Madison County, Alabama.
In 1844, William M. Burton of Spring Mill, Hemstead Co., Arkansas, deposed as to the children of William and Betsey Ellett.

ANN E., died intestate, a sister, and wife of Simeon Souther. No issue.

PATSEY, a sister, married first a Mr. Harris, by whom she had issue. Married secondly prior 19 April 1822, Major John Wyatt, by whom there is no issue in 1843:
1. HARRIET, wife of Richard W. Wyatt, 1843.
2. BARBARA, widow of H. W. Kelley, and in 1847, wife of Milton King.
3. EVELINA O., dec'd in 1843, survived by her husband, Henley C. Doswell, and issue. (Names of children not stated.)
4. MARTHA ANN HARRIS.

Others mentioned: Edmund Hallam, former Guardian of Nancy, wife of Isaac Hallam, and Elizabeth, wife of James Penderford; John Shore, Commissioner; Robert G. Scott, Attorney.

LANKFORD'S EXOR. VS. LANKFORD'S EXOR. 1838 (24)

LANKFORD, JAMES, deceased in 1824. Sterling Lankford, Executor. Keziah Lankford was the wife of James, who sues by William Littlepage.

LITTLEPAGE & WIFE VS LANKFORD'S EXORS., 1835 (23)

Sterling Lankford's Will

LANKFORD, STERLING. "In the name of God Amen. I, Sterling Lankford of the County of Hanover and State of Virginia being in my perfect mind do declare this to be my last Will and Testament. Item 1st. It is my wish and desire that no sale shall take place of any of my property, it is my wish that my plantation and all my property shall be kept together for twenty years and then that all my property both real and personal shall be equally divided amongst my four children, viz - Hardinia Lankford, Ann Lankford, Harriet Lankford & Sarah Lankford. But should any one of them die without issue, that their part shall return to the surviving ones or to their issues as the case may be. But should it so happen that all four of them should die without issue, then the property to Return to the Lankford family. Item 2nd. It is my wish in keeping my plantation and property together that it shall be for the benefit of my family, and should any one or all four of my daughters above named get married and their husbands should die before the expiration of twenty years that my plantation and house shall be their home. I wish Hector Davis to act as Executor of my estate. As witness my hand and seal the seventeenth day of January in the year of our Lord one thousand eight hundred and twenty-nine."

Sterling Lankford (Seal)

84

Signed and Sealed in the
presence of
    Turner Christian
    John T. Duke
    John + Butler.

At a Court of Quarterly Session continued and
held for Hanover County at the Courthouse on
Friday the 27th of February 1829. This last
will and Testament of Sterling Lankford dec'd
was proved by the oaths of John T. Duke and
John Butler two of the witnesses thereto and is
ordered to be recorded.
    Teste, Philip B. Winston, C.H.C.
    A Copy Teste, Philip B. Winston, Jr.,D.C.H.C.

CONNOR &C. VS. LANKFORD'S EXOR., 1849 (82)

STERLING LANKFORD, of Hanover. Will dated 17
January 1829, probated 27 February 1829. Possessed considerable real and personal property.
Hector Davis, Executor. Survived by his widow,
Maria M. J. who married John C. Littlepage, Jr.,
and by four daughters, who were the grandchildren of Mrs.Burruss, who was alive in 1835.
    1. ANN, wife in 1850 of William G. Conner of
       Mercer County, Kentucky.
    2. HARRIET, in 1835 "age about 12 to 14" and
       wife in 1849 of William Davenport.
    3. SARAH, "aged about 10 in 1835" and wife
       in 1849 of Peter Brickey of Mercer Co.,
       Kentucky.
    4. HARDINIA A. LANKFORD, in Jefferson County,
       1851.

Others mentioned: Hudson M. Wingfield, Francis
Blunt and John J. England, Commissioners in
1835. Depositions in 1835 of: Reuben Timberlake,
Samuel J. Winston, Thomas King, John D. King,
John S. Priddy, Joseph Whitlock, all of Han-
over, and Nathaniel Glenn of Henrico County.

LIPSCOMB VS. LIPSCOMB'S EXOR., 1847 (24)

LIPSCOMB, NATHANIEL C., of Hanover County,
"died with a will." Survived by his widow
Mary B. Lipscomb, an infant granddaughter,
Jane L. Green (N. C. Lipscomb, Jr., Guardian),
and by children:
    1. NATHANIEL C. LIPSCOMB, JR Executor of his
       father's Estate.
    2. MARTHA P., wife of Benjamin Wingfield, in
       1847.
    3. MARIETTA A. McGHEE (perhaps her married
       name)
    4. REBECCA A., wife of Peter W. Grubbs, 1847
    5. FRANCES T., wife of David B. Franklin,1847.

Others mentioned: Harrietta E. Wingfield, pos-
sessed of real and personal property - land adj.
Wm. F. Wickham, 150 acres, where Christopher
Wingfield lately resided,(Deed of Trust to Ros-
Cow Lipscomb) to marry O.M.Wingfield,Chesterfield.

LOWRY VS. SPICER &C., 1849 (24)

LOWRY, MARY C., of Hanover, died intestate in
1849 possessed of 267 acres in upper end
of Hanover, near Terrell's Tavern. Reference is made to a law suit "Lowry & Others vs.
Lowry & Others 1847). Issue:
    1. ALBERT LOWRY.
    2. ELIZABETH, wife of Thomas A. Spicer.
    3. MARY JANE, dec'd, who was wife of a Mr.
       Mahone. Infant children in 1849:
           1. JAMES MAHONE.
           2. JOHN B. MAHONE.
           3. JULIA ANN MAHONE.
    4. WILLIAM R. LOWRY.
    5. SOPHIA LOWRY.
    6. FRANCIS LOWRY.
    7. GASSET LOWRY.
    8. MILDRED LOWRY.
    9. JAMES C. LOWRY.
   10. JAMES LOWRY, under 21 years of age, 1849.

Commissioners: Alfred Duke, Milton M. Brown,
Charles Thompson.

LUMPKIN VS. TOLER & OTHERS, 1832 (23)

John Gardner's Will

GARDNER, JOHN. "In the name of God Amen. I
John Gardner of the County of Hanover
being of sound mind, Do make and ordain
this my Last Will and Testament Revoking all fo
mer Wills by me made. First it is my Will and
desire that all my just debts be paid. Secondly
I Emancipate my negro Child Harriett with a request that she be bound to my Daughter Sarah
Kilby until she arrives to the age of twenty
one years: and I give and bequeath to the said
Harriet to be paid out of my Estate the sum of
five Hundred Dollars: the interest of which I
desire shall be paid to the said Sarah Kilby
for the support and maintenance of the said Har
riet until she arrives to the age of twenty-one
years; and it is my will and desire that my
Executors, out of my Estate, pay to the said
Sarah Kilby one hundred Dollars, in addition to
the Int. before mentioned for her trouble in
taking care of the said Harriett, but should
the said Harriett die before she arrives to the
age of twenty-one years, I give and bequeath
the said five hundred Dollars to my Grand Children, to be equally divided among them, to them
and their Heirs forever. thirdly, I give and
bequeath to my Grand son John G. Wade, to be
raised out of my estate the sum of one thousand
Dollars. But if the said John G. Wade should
claim anything from my estate as administrator
of his fathers John Wade then it is my will and
desire that the said thousand Dollars bequeathed
to him shall be equally divided among all my
Grand Children: forth I lend to my Grand Daugh
ter Frances Mosby, during her natural life the

following slaves, To wit, Sony, Hannah, Robert, Mason and George, and after her death I give and bequeath the said Slaves to her son John Mosby to him and his heirs forever: but if the said John Mosby or Daniel Spotswood Mosby her husband should claim anything from my Estate as Administrator of John Wade Father of the said Frances Mosby, then it is my will and desire that the said Negroes bequeathed to my Grandson the said John Mosby, be equally divided between all my Grandchildren: Fifth, It is my will and desire that the remainder of my Estate Except the perishable property after the payment of the foregoing Legacies be divided into two equal parts, one of which I lend to my Daughter Sarah Kilby In Trust dureing her natural life, to be placed in the hands of her son John G. Wade, and it is my will and desire that the profits arising therefrom shall be for the support of the said Sarah Kilby, and after her death, I give and bequeath the said part, to be equally divided among them, to her the said Sarah Kilby's Children, namely, John G. Wade, Frances Mosby, William Talley and George Washington Talley, to them and their heirs forever. Sixth. the other part of my Estate I lend to my Daughter Patsy Lumkin during her natural life, and after her death, I give and bequeath the said part, to be equally divided among them, to her children, namely, Virginia Tyler, William Lumkin, Mary Lumkin, Frances Lumkin and Martha Lumkin, to them and their heirs forever. Seventh. It is my Will and desire, that all of my perishable property be sold and the money arising there-from Together with all the money I may have and all debts, dues and demands, either by acct. note, bond, or otherwise, Collected and be laid out in bank stock and the Int. arising thereon, drawn and paid to the aforesaid Sarah Kilby and Patsey Lumkin, equally, annually for the bene-fit of the aforesaid Sarah Kilby and Patsey Lum-kin during their lives and after the death of the said Sarah Kilby I give and bequeath one half of the moneys thus in bank, to the Chil-dren of the said Sarah Kilby, and after the death of the said Patsey Lumkin I give and be-queath to her children the other half to them and their heirs forever. Lastly I constitute and appoint John G. Wade and James Pitmond Tyler Executors of this my last Will and Testa-ment. In witness whereof I have hereunto set my hand and affixed my seal this 14th day of October in the year of our Lord one thousand eight hundred and twenty fore.

John Gardner (Seal)

Signed, sealed and
acknowledged in the presence of
George Toombs.
Martha hughes
Pleasant Vae
John Kilby
Pleasant D. Wooddy
John Toombs.

At a Court of Monthly Session held for Hanover County at the Courthouse on Wednesday the 22d of June 1825. This last Will and Testament of John Gardner dec'd was offered for proof by James P. Tyler one of the Executors therein named and was proved by the Oaths of George Toombs, John Kilby and John Toombs witnesses thereto and also by the Oath of the said Execu-tor and is ordered to be recorded.
    Teste, William Pollard, C.H.C.
    A Copy, Teste, Tho Pollard, D.C.H.C.

JOHN GARDNER, of Hanover. Will dated 14 Oct. 1824, probated 22 June 1825. James P. Tyler qualified as Executor. Testator was survived by two daughters:
1. SARAH KILBY. Not involved in these suits. Our knowledge of her acquired entirely from her father's will. She had been the wife of John Wade, dec'd, of whom her father was Administrator, by whom she had issue. It will be noticed that two of her children were named Talley. The names of her children in 1824 were:
   1. JOHN G. WADE.
   2. FRANCES (nee Wade) in 1824, wife of Daniel Spotswood Mosby, when she had issue, a son:
      1. JOHN MOSBY.

   3. WILLIAM TALLEY.
   4. GEORGE WASHINGTON TALLEY.

2. PATSEY, dec'd, had been the Administrator of her husband Robert Lumpkin, who died prior to 1832 possessed of a considerable Estate. Wm. H. G. Lumpkin is her Admin-istrator in 1832. Issue:
   1. VIRGINIA, married prior to 1825, James P. Tyler, who was Executor of John Gardner's Estate.
   2. MARY, dec'd in 1832, her husband Thomas Micure, Administrator. She left an infant child who is also deceased.
   3. FRANCES, wife of Dabney M. Miller.
   4. MARTHA LUMPKIN, under age in 1832 and unmarried.
   5. WILLIAM H. G. LUMPKIN. His mother's Administrator.

Others mentioned: James Lyons, Jr., Attorney at Law 1832; Commissioners in 1832: Laney Jones, Sr., Edwin Shelton, John Haw, Benjamin Pollard, and John Jones.

WINN'S LEGATEE'S VS. WINN'S ADMR., 1877 (24)

Archilles Lumpkin's Will

LUMPKIN, ARCHILLES. "I, Archilles Lumpkin of the County of Hanover do make this my last will and testament in manner and form fol-lowing, Viz - I give $10,500.00 Ten Thousand

five Hundred Dollars to my Daughter Julia A.
Crane. I give my Gole watch to Julia A. Crane
all of my negroes to be sold at public auction
for cash and the money and proceeds of said
negroes to be equally divided between my two
children John G. Lumpkin and Julia A. Crane. I
hereby constitute and appoint my son John G.
Lumpkin and my Daughter Julia A Crane Executors
of this my last will &c this will is in my own
hand right Whereof I have hereunto set my hand
and Seal this 24th day of December 1855. I
require no Securitys of my Executors.

(Two copies)   Archilles Lumpkin (Seal)

At a Court of Monthly Session held for Hanover
County at the Courthouse on Tuesday the 24 of
May 1859. These two papers writings purporting
to be the last will and testament of Archilles
Lumpkin deceased were offered for proof by John
G. Lumpkin one of the Executors therein named
and there being no subscribing witnesses to the
said will Nathan B. Clarke and William Priddy
were sworn and examined who declare that they
are well acquainted with the handwriting of the
said A.L. that they have examined the said
papers and verily believe that same to have
been wholly written and Subscribed by the said
A. L. whereupon it is ordered that the said
papers be recorded as the last will and testament of A. L. deceased.
        Wm. O. Winston, C.H.C.
    A Copy, Teste, Wm. O. Winston, C.H.C.

ARCHILLES LUMPKIN, of Hanover. Will dated 24
December 1855. Probated 24 May 1859. Survived by two children:
  1. JOHN G. LUMPKIN.
  2. JULIA A CRANE. On 12 September 1859,
     recorded in Hustings Court of the City
     of Richmond, also in the County Court of
     Hanover, made a marriage agreement with
     James B. Winston.

[This suit, instituted in 1877, continues too
late to be included in this volume.]

RICHARDSON VS. LYON'S EXOR & OTHERS, 1839 (34)

                John Lyons' Will

LYONS, JOHN. "In the name of God amen, I, John
Lyons of the County of Hanover and State
of Virginia do constitute and ordain this
my last will in manner following. Confiding in
the mercy of the Superior being who has permitted me to exist and dispensed so many blessings
on me I feel no terrors or apprehensions of the
eternal tortures which have become predominant
impressions of the present times and in my belief derogate from the highest attributes of
the God whom we worship. I give to my beloved
wife who has sufficient property of her own but

at inconvenient distance, all my estate for
her maintenance and the support of my children
and appoint her my Executrix and Guardian of
my children but she is to give no security
except her own bond. I give her my house and
lot in Richmond in fee simple and my furniture
of every description. I give to my son all my
lands upon condition that he pays to his
mother annually one-third of the proceeds of
the farm called the Fork and furnishes her
with wood if it should become necessary. If my
daughter marries I wish she should have one-
third of the negroes and if any - - - negroe
misbehaves I authorize my wife to sell them my
just debts will be paid. In witness to this
my last will written wholly with my own hand.
I hereunto set my name."
                        John Lyons
                        April 10 1817

"The Codicil to the last Will of John Lyons
written wholly with his own hand. I desire my
son Peter may be allowed to qualify as my
executor at whatsoever age he may be at the
time of my death & give to him all my estate
except what I have in my will given to his
mother, upon this condition that he shall when
she shall require it convey to her five hundred acres of the fork land in fee simple and
shall secure to his sister the house and lot
in Richmond free from incumbrance . I desire
that no person be permitted to remove or in-
spect any papers in the house unless my son or
his mother shall be present. If it should happen which may God prevent that my children
should die without issue, I give my estate to
my wife, and as I have no relations in want,
and none who have a right to expect anything
from me I desire she may dispose of it to the
most beneficial purposes."
                        John Lyons

At a Court of Monthly Session held for Hanover
County at the Courthouse on Wednesday the 26th
of May 1819. This writing purporting to be
the last will and Testament of John Lyons dec'd
& a codicil thereto annexed was offered for
proof by Ann of C. Lyons the executrix in the
said will named and it appearing to the Court
by the oaths of three witnesses that the said
Will and codicil were wholly written and signed
by the deceased, and the same being also proved
by the oath of the said Executrix the Court do
order the same to be recorded as the last will
and Testament of the said deceased. There being no dates to the said Codicil the Court
upon reference to a letter proved to be written
by the testator bearing date on the 13th of
February 1819 are satisfied that the said
Codicil was written after the date of the said
will.
    Teste, William Pollard, C.H.C.
    A Copy, Teste, Wm. O. Winston, D.C.H.C.
[There was an earlier but similar will]

Peter Lyons' Will

LYONS, PETER. "In the name of God amen, I, Peter Lyons of the County of Hanover (but now in Richmond) do make this my last will and Testament in manner and form following, to wit -After the payment of my just debts I give to my sister all my estate both real and personal provided she does not marry Mr. William Pryor, but if she does so, I give my farm called Studley to S. A. Roane daughter of my friend W. H. Roane, forever and the rest of my estate of whatsoever kind it may be, both real and personal, I wish to be equally·divided between my friends Doctor L. W. Chamberlayne and George P. Crump except my negroe slaves Edmund and old Judy and I wish them set free, so far as the Law will permit, and I also wish old Judy supported out of my estate. I appoint my friend P. B. Winston of Hanover County, executor to this my last will and Testament. Witness my hand and seal this 20th day of January in the year 1837.

Peter Lyons (Seal)

At a Court of Monthly session held for Hanover County at the Courthouse on Tuesday the 28th of November 1837. This writing purporting to be the last will and Testament of Peter Lyons, dec'd was offered for proof by Philip B. Winston the executor therein named and Wm. Brockenbrough, Ezekiel T. Talley and Laney Jones being sworn declare that they are well acquainted with the handwriting of the said Peter Lyons dec'd, that they have examined the said writing and verily believe the same to have been wholly written and subscribed by him. Whereupon it is ordered that the said writing be recorded as the last will and Testament of the said Peter Lyons, dec'd.
    Teste, Philip B. Winston, C.H.C.
    A Copy, Teste, Wm. O. Winston, D.C.H.C.

JOHN LYONS, of Hanover. Will dated 10 April 1817, probated 26 May 1819. Possessed considerable estate including 55 slaves. Survived by his widow, his Executrix, Ann of Cleves Lyons, who died prior to 1839 (Geo. P. Crump, Admr.) and two children:
1. PETER LYONS, of Hanover County, and City of Richmond. Will dated 20 January 1837, probated in Hanover 28 November 1837. No issue.
2. ANN ELIZA CARTER, married between 20 Jan., 1837, and 1839, Robert P. Richardson.

Others mentioned: Gustavus A. Myers in 1839; John Shore, Commissioner. Inventory of the personal Estate of Peter Lyons, deceased, in 1838, by William Winston Jones, Ezekiel L. Talley, John Haw, and William T. H. Pollard.

This suit concerned only Peter Lyon's Estate.

MINOR'S GUARDIAN VS. MINOR, 1866 (26)

Lucius H. Minor's Will

MINOR, LUCIUS H., "I, Lucius H. Minor do constitute this my will written in my own handwriting hereby revoking all wills which I have heretofore made. I desire that my body may be decently interred without pomp or any more than necessary expenses. I give to my much beloved wife Catherine F. Minor all my estate of every kind during her life with power to dispose it among my children in such portions and at such times as she may think necessary and proper for the well being of our children. I also give her full power to dispose of any of my estate which she may think necessary for the purpose of paying my debts, or the comfort of her self and our children. Should my wife think proper to form a second marriage she will cease to have a will of her own, and of consequence will cease to have the power to act for our children as I am sure she wishes to do. I therefore, in that event, revoke the devise in her favor, and will that she shall have no part of my estate whatsoever, after the second marriage. I constitute and appoint my wife Catherine F. Minor sole executrix of this my will, and guardian of my children, but should she marry as before named I then revoke this clause of my will and appoint my brother Dr. Lewis W. Minor executor of my will and guardian of my children. Signed this twelfth day of November eighteen hundred and forty seven."

L. H. Minor

"Since the above will was written it has pleased God to take from us my beloved wife and a dear child. I therefore appoint my son C. R. C. Minor Executor of this my will. If my said son should from any cause not act as executor, I hereby appoint my son C. N. B. Minor for that purpose and if he should be under age at the time of my death I request my kinsman and friend John B. Minor of the University of Va. to act as my Executor until my said son C. N. B. Minor shall reach the legal age. I do not wish that either of the above mentioned Executors shall be required to give security. I will also that the above mentioned Executor shall act as Guardian of my children & not give security in either capacity. I do not wish it to be supposed that I make this change from any want of confidence in my brother "Lewis" but because he is a Naval Officer & must be often aboard for years at a time."
(Signed) L. H. Minor.
December 9th 1859.

"I especially request that my coffin shall not be bought in town, but that it be made at home by a carpenter hired by the day."
December 9th 1859 (Signed) L. H. Minor.

"Note. See Codicil on a separate paper which I have not time to copy just now."

"On the 23rd of October 1859 It pleased God to take from me my darling boy "John" so that I have now only 7 children. I will that my whole property of every description be divided into <u>eight</u> equal parts of which my daughter "Fanny" shall take <u>two</u> parts and the other six children shall take <u>one</u> part each."

                     (Signed) L. H. Minor.

Aug. 3, 1862.

August 4th 1863:

    "By the will of my Brother John (the paper admitted to probat in the Clerk's Office of Fredericksburg a month or two after my brother's death, which I do not believe to be his last will for I think that his last will was buried with his body in the breast pocket of his coat) he bequeathed to me - in trust for my children - one-third part of all his property of every kind - but authorized me to divide his property among my children in such manner and proportion as I think fit. Therefore I will that the whole of the said property of my brother John shall be divided into eight equal parts of which my daughter "Fanny" shall take two parts and the other six children shall take one part each.   I do make this provision with the respect to my daughter Fanny because her health is & has been very feeble through life and I wish to secure her the means of comfort at least.   Moreover I know that she will promptly render aid to any one of her brothers and sisters who may stand in need of assistance, and that to the extent of her ability.   If my daughter Fanny should think proper to contract marriage the objects for which the above provisions with respect to her may be frustrated. Therefore in the event of her marriage I will that all my property of every kind - including the property bequeathed to me in trust by my brother John - shall be equally divided among my seven children. If a later will of my brother John making different provisions should be found, I will that the above provisions with respect to my daughter Fanny and my other children, shall stand as above written."

                     (Signed) L. H. Minor.

[No endorsement of probate]

LUCIUS H. MINOR, of Hanover. Will dated 12 Nov. 1847. Codicils dated 9 Dec. 1859, Aug. 3, 1862, and Aug. 4, 1863. No endorsement of probate. Died 25 Oct. 1863. Estate included tract called "Edgewood" containing between 900 and 1000 acres. His wife, Catherine F. died after 12 Nov. 1847 and before 9 Dec. 1859. Testator mentions his kinsman John B. Minor of University of Virginia; brother Dr. Lewis W. Minor, a Naval Officer, and brother John Minor, dec'd. whose will was recorded in Fredericksburg circa

August 1863. Also mentioned in the Codicil of August 3, 1862, the death of his son John Minor, as being on 23 October 1859. The surviving children in 1866, were:
1. FANNY B. MINOR.
2. CHARLES L. C. MINOR, Guardian of the following brothers and sisters - infants:
3. C. N. B. MINOR.
4. LUCY L. MINOR.
5. THOMASIA M. MINOR.
6. ROBERT B. MINOR.
7. MARY W. MINOR.

Commissioners: R. F. Berkeley, W. L. Carpenter William Nelson, Edmund Berkeley, and Wm. O. Winston.

MANN'S EXOR. VS. KING, 1834 (26)

MANN, JAMES, of Hanover County, "died with a will in 1815." He possessed 95 acres of land adjoining Charles Toler, William Bowles, Hezekiah Ford and Daniel Burton. William and Benjamin Mann were directed to sell the Testator's land, and Benjamin became the purchaser, and in turn, sold to Thomas Cauthorn of the City of Richmond. On 15 July 1817, Cauthorn being in debt to the said Benjamin Mann, conveyed this land in trust to John Mann and Fleming Brown of Hanover County. The witnesses being: John D. G. Brown, William Shepperson and William I. Cauthorn. Testator was survived by his widow. In 1834 his heirs, who are not otherwise designated, were:
WILLIAM MANN.
BENJAMIN MANN.
AUSTIN PARKER & FANNY, his wife, formerly Mann.
JAMES MANN.
ELIZABETH MUNDAY, formerly Mann,
MARY GILMER, and her children:
   1. GEORGE GILMER.
   2. WILLIAM GILMER.
   3. MILLEY GILMER.
THOMPSON MANN.
ELIZABETH, formerly Mann, wife of Martin.
JUDITH, formerly Mann, wife of Moore.
WILLIAM MANN.
GEORGE MANN.
SARAH MANN.
ELIZABETH MANN.
JUDITH MANN.
GEORGE MANN.
WILLIAM MANN.
SALLY MANN
These heirs of James Mann were plaintiffs, and William King, Sr., and Philip B. Winston, Clerk of Hanover, were defendants. It would appear that most of the papers in this suit are lost. William King died intestate during this suit, and Philip B. Jones was appointed his Administrator.

Others mentioned: Anthony Street.

MALLORY'S ADMR. VS. KIMBROUGH &C., 1832 (26)

MALLORY, WILLIAM, of Hanover County, died intestate circa 1832. No mention is made of his Estate, or of his wife. He had two daughters:
1. [   ] a daughter married a Mr. James, and has issue.
2. AMANDA, "now deceased, an infant at the death of her father. John Kimbrough, Jr., was appointed her Guardian. George Mason, his Security."

MALLORY & OTHERS VS. MALLORY &C., 1857 (18)

MALLORY, WILLIAM C., of Hanover County, died intestate, siezed of 216 acres of land. Survived by his widow, Catherine L., who died 1 September 1857, and children:
1. SALLY C. MALLORY.
2. ELIZA R., wife of Richard P. Mallory in 1857.
3. WILLIAM W. MALLORY.
4. CHARLES L. (or S.) MALLORY.
5. JOHN E. MALLORY.
6. MARY JANE, wife of Peter Tinsley in 1857.
7. JAMES F. MALLORY.
8. LAVINIA C., died 2 August 1856, survived by her husband, John D. Taylor, and children:
    1. JAMES W. TAYLOR.
    2. SARAH L. TAYLOR.
    3. CHASTAIN H. TAYLOR.
    4. CHARLES C. TAYLOR, over 14 and under 21 years of age in 1857.
    5. FRANCES T. TAYLOR, over 14 and under 21 years of age in 1857.
9. PHILIP N. MALLORY, wife is Mrs. Margaret C. in 1857. Under date of 10 September 1849 "Desirous of making provision for wife and children, in Deed of Trust to Charles S. Mallory and William W. Mallory, conveys all the right, title and interest of the said Philip N. Mallory in and to the estate of the late David Crenshaw, and Garland Crenshaw of Henrico county." His children were:
    1. CATHERINE E. MALLORY
    2. RICHARD W. MALLORY.
    3. JOHN B. MALLORY
    4. BILLY C. MALLORY.
    5. CROWDER MALLORY.
    6. SARAH E. MALLORY.

Others mentioned in 1857: R. B. Hendrick, and John H. Blunt.

GOVAN VS. WINGFIELD, 1842 (17)

MACON, COLONEL, of New Kent County, father of Miles Macon of Hanover in 1842. Others mentioned: Peter W. Brown; Dr. Henry Curtis.

McCOOK & OTHERS VS. McCOOK'S ADMR., 1855 (27)

Neal McCook's Will

McCOOK, NEAL. "I, Neal McCook of the County of Hanover and of Virginia do publish and ordain this as my last will and Testament in manner and form following, Viz: Item. My will and desire is that my Executor or Executors herein after named shall at my death sell by publick auction or otherwise the tract of land whereon I now live, and also all my personal estate and out of the proceeds thereof pay all my Just debts & funeral expenses and the ballance to be divided in manner following, To wit - One-third part thereof to my wife Nancy McCook and the remaining two thirds to be divided one-half thereof to my son Neal McCook and one-third part of the remaining ballance to my son Thomas O. McCook, one-third to my son Charles McCook, and one-third to be divided between my Grandsons Benjamin and Andrew Hatton. I do hereby constitute and appoint Charles P. Goodall and William Wingfield, Jr., as Executors of this my last will and testament hereby revoking all others heretofore made by me."

                                    Neal McCook
September 5, 1835.
Teste, William Wingfield, Jr.
    Chas. Childress

At a Court of Monthly Session held for Hanover County at the Courthouse on Tuesday the 27th of March 1838. This last will and Testament of Neal McCook dec'd was proved by the oaths of William Wingfield, Jr., and Charles Childress the witnesses thereto and is ordered to be recorded.
    Teste, Philip B. Winston, C.H.C.
    A Copy, Teste, Wm. O. Winston, C.H.C.

NEAL McCOOK, of Hanover County. Will dated 5 September 1835. Probated by the witnesses on 27 March 1838. Thomas O McCook and James McCook, appointed Administrators. Survived by his wife, Nancy. Their issue, perhaps among others:
1. NEAL McCOOK.
2. THOMAS O. McCOOK.
3. CHARLES McCOOK, dec'd in 1855.
4. [   ] daughter, who married Mr. Hatton, and has issue, perhaps among others:
    1. BENJAMIN HATTON.
    2. ANDREW HATTON.

In 1855, John H. Weldon is Administrator of Benjamin Hatton, who may have been the husband or the Benjamin above. Others mentioned: James McCook, one of the Administrators of Neal McCook; James McDowell, merchant of Richmond, dec'd, survived by his widow, Elizabeth in 1863. Blackwell Hughes, Notary Public, Richmond 1863.

The will of Charlotte A. Wharton is among the papers of this suit. Probably misplaced.

Charlotte A. Wharton's Will

WHARTON, CHARLOTTE A., "In the name of God amen. I, Charlotte A. Wharton being of sound mind & disposing memory do make and constitute this my last will and testament. Item 1st. I request my Extors hereafter named to cause my body to be decently interred. Item 2nd. It is my will that my said Extor (if he can do so) shall pay all my just debts by the hire of my slaves who is hereby authorized to hire them out from year to year untill the said debts are fully paid & sattisfied. Item 3rd. After the payment of my just debts, it is my will that all my slaves be divided in three equal parts and one-third to be held by my sd Extor in trust for & during the life of my brother Dr. Rob[t] H. Wharton & by my said Extor to be hired out for the time aforesaid, the hires to be applied to the better manitenance & support of my said brother's wife & family & at his death to be delivered over to his wife Mrs. S. Wharton for life or in the event of her death to the children of the said Robt. H. Wharton who may have survived her. Item 4th. The other two thirds of my slaves I desire shall be equally divided between my two brothers R. G. Wharton & Charles D. Wharton each to retain his one third of said slaves during the term of his natural life & in the event of my said two brothers each leaving issue living at the time of their deaths, then the portions of my slaves given to each to descend to their issue but should either or boath die without issue living at the time of their deaths then it is my will the part of such brother or brothers dying without issue, shall be equally divided amongst those who may be the lawful representatives of my other brother or brothers. Item 5th, I have a beaureau & Looking Glass now at my brothers R. H. Whartons which I hereby give in trust to my said Exor to hold for the benefit of my brother's wife Mrs. S. Wharton. Item 6th. I hereby constitute & appoint Wm. Beverley Dabney Exor of this my last will & testament hereby requesting the County Court of Goochland not to require him to give security as I have full confidence in him. In testimony whereof I have hereunto affixed my hand & Seal this 1st day of April 1840."

Charlotte A. Wharton (Seal)

Signed sealed &
delivered in the
presence of
    J. B. Ferguson.
    Jno. S. Fleming.

Proved in Goochland County, 15 February 1841 by oaths of James B. Ferguson and John S. Fleming.

Wm. Miller, C.G.C.
    A Copy,
        Teste,
            Na W. Miller, Clk.

WINSTON'S GDN. &C. VS. McGEE & OTHERS, 1859 (83)

McGEE, EDWARD H., of Hanover. Will probated 28 October 1845 (No copy in the papers of this suit. He was survived by his widow, Marietta A. McGee, who is deceased in 1880, and by issue:
1. MARY ANN, married William C. Taliaferro, who died in 1880. Their issue:
    1. MARIETTA TALIAFERRO.
    2. HERNDON TALIAFERRO, a minor in 1880.
    3. MELVILLE TALIAFERRO, a minor in 1880.
2. MARIA LOUISA, wife of P. P. Winston. Their issue in 1880:
    1. EDWARD H. WINSTON.
    2. LOUIS PHILLIPS WINSTON.
    3. MARY W. WINSTON, a minor over 14 in 1880.
    4. ELIZABETH W. WINSTON, under 14 years of age in 1880.
    5. JOHN G. WINSTON, under 14 in 1880.
    6. WESLEY M. WINSTON, of legal age 1880.

3. LOUIS C. McGEE.
4. WESLEY McGEE, died circa 1880 unmarried
5. JAMES A. McGEE.
6. NATHANIEL C. McGEE,
7. FRANCIS M. McGEE.
8. EDWARD F. McGEE, died circa 1880 unmarried

Those familiar with Edward H. McGee's land were: S. N. Davis, Peter W. Grubbs, D. B. Franklin, and N. C. Lipscomb.

McGHEE & OTHERS VS. TAYLOR, 1836 (26)

McGHEE, WILLIAM M., of Hanover, died prior to 1836, survived by his widow Eliza H., who is also deceased, intestate. Under date of 5 February 1828, Edward Valentine and John J. Taylor "having purchased sundry articles for the benefit of Mrs. Eliza H. McGhee, wife of William McGhee . . . and at her death to be disposed of as she may think proper." The Trustee, Fran[s] G. Taylor, also of Hanover. Her children, of whom the Guardian in 1836, was Edmund M. Anderson:
1. ELEONORA McGHEE.
2. MARY E. McGHEE.

WHITLOCK VS. WINGFIELD, 1847 (11)

ALLEN, WILLIAM, Admr. of Thomas Boaze, dec'd, vs Edward Melton, Exor. of Thomas Melton, dec'd, and others. Thomas Melton, dec'd, Absolum Melton, dec'd, Wm. T. H. Pollard, admr. vs. Franci Page, late Sheriff, Admr. of Reuben Melton, dec'd, vs. Allen McGregor and Sarah his wife & Charles Martin and Elizabeth his wife.

[This paper found among those of the suit referred to. Irrevelent.]

ANTHONY VS. LAND, 1867 (1)

MELTON, EDMUND, deceased of Hanover County. Survived by infant children: William T. Melton, Sarah E. Melton, and Martha E. Melton, of whom Thomas J. Melton is Guardian. Others concerned: Martha E. Kern, a married woman, Joseph T. Adams, E. T. Kern and Joseph T. Priddy.

CLARKE & OTHERS VS. MICHIE'S ADMR. &C., 1843 (12)

William Watson Michie's Will

MICHIE, WILLIAM WATSON. "Aware of the Casualties of human life and the uncertainty of its duration, I William Watson Michie make and indite with my own hand this my last Will & Testament. I give and bequeath to my Daughter Cornelia Michie during her natural life all of my Estate Real and Personal except the part herein after otherwise provided subject however to the following limitations. I wish the revenue and profits appropriated to her support and education, or so much thereof as shall be sufficient for a liberal support and as good an extensive Education as the Estate can afford, and if there be a surplus I wish it invested in Bank Stock, government or Real security as the situation of the times may suggest to my Executors. I will - direct - that my negroes Dick and Robin, the last now in Louisa County inherited from my Grandfather's Michie's Estate should be sold by my Executor, and also a tract of Land containing two hundred and thirty two acres and a half, adjoining the Plantation of Joseph C. Wingfield and others lying in the Junction of the Roads leading from Richmond to Hanover Courthouse, the one by the Brook and the other by the Mechanicsville Turnpike, and likewise two small contiguous parcels lying on Totopotomoy Creek purchased of Frederick Bowe, adjoining the Land of Albert Bowe, Wilson B. Clarke and others, containing together thirty-two and a half acres the above named Land and negroes or any part of them to be sold by my Executors as soon after my death as they shall deem advisable. My tract of Land called the Glebe I wish leased out and also my Land in Louisa County, lying in the Green Spring neighborhood for such terms as my Executor that deem best, with proper restrictions and obligations towards improvements. The tract whereon I reside I wish cultivated by a few hands and an Overseer under the direction of the Executor and the women and children kept together thereon, except such of the women without encumbrance as can be hired out to a manifest and much greater advantage. The rest of the negroes above sufficent to cultivate the plantation to advantage I wish hired out by my Executor in Hanover, Henrico or the City of Richmond and restricted not to work on River plantations, canals or Rail-

roads. The renting or leasing and hiring out to continue until my Daughter attains the age of twenty-one or marries, at that time, should it ever come, whichever takes place first, it shall be discretionary with her to occupy which tract of Land soever she pleases, and to employ at home such servants as she may choose, and enjoy the rents and profits of the rest which I wish continued hired out and rented as before, the money to be paid into her own hand and employed and used by her alone - whether covert or single. At her death I give and bequeath the said property to her children equally to be divided amongst them, if any there be, children or other descendants, I mean, the Grandchildren taking the share of their deceased parent, if there be none, I will and devise that all the negroes be free and forever liberated from bondage and hired out or bound to trade as may be suitable in the direction of my Executors, until a fund may be accumulated sufficient to carry them to some more hospitable and equal clime where they may enjoy the common rights of citizenship. And that the Land be sold and the proceeds invested in Bank Stock or Government stock as my Executors deem best: and the interest or dividends or other profits applied first to the support, maintenance and clothothing of my servants Indianna, America, and Lydia and their children which they now have or may have at the time of my death. Secondly, any surplus to be applied to the education of such children, or themselves if they desire it, at the North wherever my Executors may think best, and thirdly any left beyond and the charges for the Executional duties to be laid out in the same stock for an accumulating fund. I will and devise them supported as long as they shall or all of them live, and when Joseph a son of America and Martha Susan the Daughter of Indiana attain severally the ages of twenty one I wish them to have the use of the profits above the support of the rest during their life, and if either of them dies the other to have the like profits and the share of the deceased, if the deceased should leave no children, if one of them leave children, or children reputed theirs, the children shall have the free simple in the stock of that other, provided that one leave no children so if the part which shall accrue on the death of any of the above named women shall be dead and the children Joseph and Martha Susan dead without children, or leaving no reputed children, acknowledged children, then I will and devise all the funds to accumulate by laying out the profits in new stock until that stock be sufficient to endow a Professorship of Civil and International Law and Rhetorick and Belles letters at the University of Virginia with a salary equal to that of a Judge of the General Court at the time of endowment, and of the equal amount of the highest professional Salary at the University whichsoever shall be most, the salary of the Professor of that of the

Judge of the General Court. Then shall the Trusteeship of my Executors who are hereby appointed Trustees to carry into effect each and every of the duties or Trusts directed in my Will terminate, and the visitors of the University appointed perpetual Trustees to carry into effect by appointing the professor and subsequently to direct the payment of the salary and Manage the fund with peremptory directions never to reduce the Principal, nor apply to the profits to any other purpose than that above appointed. It is my Will and desire that my servant maids Indiana, America and Lydia and their children which they now have or any of them may have at the time of my death shall be immediately free and emancipated and never hired out by my Executors but shall be suffered to remain or reside whereever they choose, and be allowed and paid by my Executors thirty Dollars a year each, the children the same for their maintenance, the same to be paid to them in Mrs. Sarah Branch's presence if convenient, if not to her, and her receipt for the same in both cases shall be a sufficient voucher. I desire Mrs. Sarah Branch to act as Mistress and protectress, as also my Executors as protector of the said emancipated slaves so long as they remain in the State of Virginia. As soon as Martha Susan attains the age of eight years I wish her and Joseph both sent to the North to be educated as respectably as the funds at that time shall admit. The same rents, profits and dividends over and above the amount expense for educating and boarding, clothing &c. of my Daughter in the best stile as directed above. I wish her to have the best Education to be acquired in the State of Virginia but I desire and direct Joseph and Martha Susan to have the best in the Northern States, which the surplus funds will justify, and if they are sufficient the very best and most extensive. I would prefer that the maid servants herein liberated should live at Mrs. Branch's if she consents thereto and learn the different species of house work which might be useful to them and contribute something towards their support - just so long however and no longer than Mrs. Branch might be willing and they each and all satisfied. I do not intend in the least to abridge the full and perfect freedom bequeathed them by this will. If Mrs. Branch is unwilling to act for them, and they cannot remain here consistently with the Laws of Virginia, I desire my Executors to pay their expenses of moving and send them to another State and provided sufficiently for their support and settlement. There is also a small lot or tract belonging to David Michie and W. M. Michie called Self's old field, which I empower my Executors to sell and apply the proceeds as the rest of my Estate. I wish them to use their discretion as to the fittest time for the Sale of this as well as the rest of the Land directed and authorized to be sold. To this my last will and

Testament contained in this sheet and another written entirely with my own hand and sealed with my seal, and at the foot of every page whereof my name is signed for greater security and identification, I make constitute and appoint Philip B. Winston and Benjamin Wingfield my Executors and Trustees to carry into effect the provisions and directions thereof. I direct them to apply the proceeds of the sale of the Lands and the personal perishable property after paying my just debts and the proper charges to the purchase of Bank Stock or Government Stock or put it out on Real security as they may think best, and if the State of the funds for the payment of debts do not require it, after the Sale of the Lands, and the perishable property. I do not desire Dick to be sold but hired out with the rest of the Slaves so directed, and be subject to the limitations and conditions of the rest, and to be thereafter free on the same contingency that it was directed should liberate the others, or the main body of my slaves. John Lastly of the County of Louisa who owns Robin's wife may purchase him if he desires at appraised value. Signed, sealed and executed by me this 10th day of September one thousand eight hundred and thirty seven."

Wm. Watson Michie.

At a Court of Quarterly Session held for Hanover County at the Courthouse on Tuesday the 26th of April 1842. This writing purporting to be the last will and Testament of William W. Michie, dec'd was produced in Court for probat and there being no subscribing witnesses thereto, Thomas Perrin and Park Perrin were sworn who declare they are well acquainted with the handwriting of the said William W. Michie, dec'd, that they have examined the said Writing and verily believe the same to have been wholly written and subscribed by him. Whereupon it is Ordered that the said writing be Recorded as the last will and Testament of the said William W. Michie, dec'd.

Teste, Philip B. Winston, C.H.C.
A Copy, Teste, Wm. O. Winston, D.C.H.C.

In Hanover County Court September 27th, 1842: On the motion of Philip H. Jones and James P. Hopkins a certificate is granted them for obtaining letters of administration with the Will annexed of the estate of William W. Michie, dec'd, they having taken the oath of Administration with the Will annexed, and the said Philip H. Jones with Charles S. Jones and Gabriel Jones his securities who justified as to their sufficiency and the said James P. Hopkins with William Michie & Charles H. Hopkins his securities who justified as to their sufficiency, entered into and acknowledged two several bonds according to Law which bonds are ordered to be recorded.
A Copy Teste, Philip B. Winston, C.H.C.

WILLIAM WATSON MICHIE, of Hanover. Will dated 10 September 1837, probated 26 April 1842. Philip B. Winston and Benjamin Wingfield, the Executors in his will relinquished their right, and Philip H. Jones and James P. Hopkins were appointed Administrators with the will annexed. Testator much in debt. Survived by his daughter Cornelia V., of whom Philip B. Winston was appointed Guardian. In 1843 she was under legal age and living in Chesterfield County. Sometime prior to 5 October 1849 she was the wife of Robert B. Watkins and in 1873 they were living in Gordonsville with "their several children whose names and number are unknown."

Others mentioned: David Michie, dec'd of Albemarle County, who devised his property to his wife for life, then to her legal heirs. She and Hardin Massie were designated Executrix and Executor of his will, who declined to qualify and George Carr was appointed Administrator. John D. G. Brown, Surveyor, Hanover, 1851; R. H. Cardwell, Attorney 1881; Wilson B. Clarke who was deceased prior to 11 March 1877; Richard H. Coleman and W. S. Barton, Judges; Jonathan T. Cowherd leased Wm. Watson Michie's slaves. He had been the personal representative of P. H. Jones, and died in Louisa County prior to January 1873; Charles W. Dabney 1849; James P. Hopkins was dec'd 12 March 1853; James A. Harwood, former Sheriff of Hanover; Chapman Johnson, Rector, The University of Virginia; P. H. Jones, dec'd 17 March 1860. Gabriel Jones succeeded Jonathan T. Cowherd as his personal representative, and later acted as Executor. Gabriel Jones was deceased 27 April 1880, when the Estate of P. H. Jones was committed to W. W. Waller, Sheriff of Spotsylvania County; Ro. M. Kent, and Linden Kent of "Kent & Neale, Attorneys at law, Alexandria, Va., 1873; J. M. McKenzie; William Josiah Leake, Master Commissioner: Henry W. Maury, Commissioner 1874; Nathaniel Mills, Justice of Louisa County 1849; John Priddy who purchased for William Priddy land of Wm. W. Michie's Estate; John F. Cross also a purchaser of land; George W. Richardson, Attorney; B. W. Talley, leased slaves; Archibald B. Timberlake leased slaves of Michie's Estate, died prior to 7 May 1872, W. W. Timberlake, Executor; Charles Thompson, Commissioner; Francis T. & Thomas W. West purchased 40 acres of the Estate's land; Joseph C. Wingfield, in 1843, living in Richmond, Va.

MICHIE VS. BOWLES, SHERIFF &C., 1837 (26)

MICHIE, JAMES F., of Louisa County, "long since married Mary Ann Tinsley, ward of John Wingfield of Hanover, about sixteen years ago, and after said marriage."
Others mentioned: Anderson Bowles, Sheriff, dec'd, Abraham P. and Jessie T. Bowles, Exors; William F. Michie; William W. Michie.

PRICE & OTHERS VS. MILLS' ADMR., 1832 (28)

Charles Mills' Will

MILLS, CHARLES. "In the name of God amen. I, Charles Mills, Ser of the County of Hanover and State of Virginia do make this my last Will and Testament, revoking all others. First it is my will that all my just debts be paid also my funeral expenses. Secondly I give unto my daughter Polly Holloway all the remainder of my land lying in Louisa County supposed to be one hundred acres, to her & the heirs of her body lawfully begotten forever. Thirdly I lend to my beloved wife Sarah Mills all my estate both real and personal dureing her natural life. Fourthly I give unto my son Charles Mills the land upon which I reside containing one hundred and twenty-six and a half acres: I also give unto my son Charles Mills one hundred dollars to him and his heirs lawfully begotten, forever. Fifthly - After the death of my wife it is my will that all my estate (except that already disposed of above) to be equally divided amongst my surviving children & my two Granddaughters (to wit) my sons Charles Mills, Robert Mills, Polly Holloway my Daughter, Wade Mills, Nathaniel Mills, Jackson Mills and my two grand daughters Elizabeth Weigeser and Susan Woodfin upon the following terms (to wit) That my son Wade Mills pay unto my Executors for the benefit of my Estate the sum of one hundred and eight pounds twelve shillings, and my son Jackson Mills pay Fifty-three pounds eleven Shillings for the benefit of my estate and my son Robert Mills pay the sum of thirty pounds eighteen shillings for the benefit of my Estate. It is my will that if any thing remains over and above one hundred & seven pounds six shillings which my grandson Charles M. Mills has already had of me, that it shall be equally Divided between my Grand Daughters Elizabeth Weigeser and Susan Woodfin them three making one legatee and if any of my legatees die without lawful Children it is my will that their proportion of my Estate shall be equally Divided amongst the survivors, and in every case shall descend to the Lawful heirs of their bodies. And Lastly I appoint my sons Charles Mills, Robert Mills and Wade Mills my Executors to this my last will and testament. Given under my hand and seal this 6th day of February one thousand eight hundred and twenty seven."

In presence of
Charles Swift
John M. Moody
Samuel Pleasants

Charles his ✝ Mills(Seal)
mark

At a Court of Quarterly session Continued and held for Hanover County at the Courthouse on Thursday the 23rd October 1828. This last will and Testament of Charles Mills, Senr., deceased was proved by the Oaths of Charles Swift and

Samuel Pleasants two of the witnesses thereto and is ordered to be recorded.

Teste, Philip B. Winston, C.H.C.

A Copy, Teste, Philip B. Winston, C.H.C.

CHARLES MILLS, Sr., of Hanover. Will dated 6 February 1827, probated 23 October 1828. Survived by his widow, Sarah, who died early in 1831, intestate, possessed of a life estate in twelve slaves. Issue:
1. CHARLES MILLS, JR.
2. ROBERT MILLS.
3. POLLY, wife of Jacob Holloway.
4. WADE MILLS.
5. NATHANIEL MILLS.
6. JACKSON MILLS.
7. JOHN MILLS, deceased. Died before his father, leaving issue:
    1. CHARLES M. MILLS.
    2. ELIZABETH, wife of Jacob Weiseger of Richmond, Va. in 1833.
    3. SUSAN, wife of George Woodfin of Richmond, Va., in 1833.

Others mentioned: Josiah Mills a witness in 1828; Major Baughan 1833; James Higgason 1828; William L. Stanley 1833; Michael Stanley; Charles Thompson, Jr. 1832; Pleasant J. Tiller 1833; Felix Winston 1832; Jesse Winn late Sheriff of Hanover 1832.

MILLS & OTHERS VS. WISDOW & OTHERS, 1867 (69)

MILLS, JOHN N., dec'd of Hanover County. Died intestate in 1840 possessed of 500 acres of land near Totopotomoi Creek. Survived by his widow, Elizabeth W., and issue:
1. JOHN T. MILLS.
2. CHARLES H. MILLS.
3. MARY J., wife of Nathaniel H. Talley.
4. WILLIAM N. MILLS.
5. ELIZABETH C., widow of a Mr. Sweeney.
6. NANCY W., died in 1858, wife of Samuel White. Issue:
    1. MARY F. WHITE, died without issue.
    2. JOHN M. WHITE, a minor.
    3. INDIANA M., wife of John Miscoe.
    4. ELIZABETH S., dec'd, who was wife of Minor Wisdom. Surviving issue:
        1. WILLIAM WISDOM.

BROWN'S COMMITTEE VS BROWN'S EXORS., 1853 (4)

Milton M. Brown's Will

BROWN, MILTON M. "I, Milton M. Brown of the County of Hanover being of perfect mind and memory do make this my Last will in the following manner, viz - Item 1st. I wish my executors hereinafter named to pay my Just debts out of the moneys in hand and due to me now and at the time of my death. 2nd. I desire that my executors inclose the space at the burying ground at Hollowing Creek left for my wife and her two sisters by the side of my daughter Jane A. Brown with a good post and railing and that a slab of stone be placed at the head and feet of the grave of my daughter and one on the top of a brick wall around the grave with a suitable inscription. 3rd. I wish to be buried at the old family burying ground where I now live, and that my executors have the same slabs of stone and a wall around my grave as that directed for my daughter with a like suitable inscription. 4th. I lend to my sister Emily Mitchell widow of Charles C. Mitchell all my Estate both real and personal during her widowhood and at her death or marriage I give the same to her children by the said Charles C. Mitchell to them and their heirs forever. 5th. It is my wish and desire that my sister shall at any time after any of her children arrive at the age of twenty-one may advance to them any portion of the property loaned to her in the 4th clause of this my last will that she may think proper, provided it does not exceed their full share of my Estate and it is my earnest request and desire that my Sister and her children treat the slaves hereby loaned and given to them in the most humane manner so as to induce them to be true and faithful servants during life. 5th. I give to Pamelia Hall twelve dollars annually during her single life, provided she maintain her integrity because of her faithful services to my wife after her return from the Western Asylum at Staunton. 6th. I wish and desire that Patsey Hall the wife of Zackiah Hall and her children be permitted to live on my plantation with the use of a house, garden spot and fire wood during the life of the said Patsey. 7th. I wish and desire that my wife Elizabeth be supported out of my estate in such manner as her situation requires and that she be well taken care of. 8th. I hereby appoint Wm. Hatch and George W. Parrish, Executors to this my Last will and desire that no security be required of them and for their services as such I wish them to receive two and a half percent on the appraised value of my real and personal Estate. Witness my hand and seal this 1st day of October 1852."

                                    M. M. Brown (Seal)
Signed sealed, published
and released as the last will of Milton M. Brown
in presence of
    J. D. G. Brown
    Pleasant Yearmans
    John M. Thomas.

At a Court of Quarterly Session held for Hanover County at the Courthouse on Tuesday the 26th of October 1852. This Last will and Testament of M. M. Brown dec'd was proved by the oaths of Pleasant Yeamans and John W. Thomas.

    Teste, Wm. O. Winston, C.H.C. (Copy by same)

BROWN'S COMMITTEE VS. BROWN'S EXORS., 1853 (4)
MITCHELL VS. MITCHELL, 1872 (27)

Charles C. Mitchell's Will

MITCHELL, CHARLES C. "In the name of God, Amen. I, Charles C. Mitchell of the County of Hanover being diseased in body but of sound mind & disparing recovery (for which I thank God) & calling to mind the uncertainty of human life & being desirous to dispose of all such earthly estate as it has pleased God to bless me with. I give & bequeath the same in name following, that is to say. Item 1st. I will that all my just debts & funeral expenses be first paid by my Executrix hereinafter named. Item 2nd. I lend to my beloved wife Emily A. Mitchell so long as she remains my widow the land whereon I now live together with all my personal estate except such as I give to my children at the time of their marriage or become twenty-one years old. Item 3rd. I give to my daughter Nancy Jane Mitchell at such time as she may marry or become of age the following slaves - Moses & Violet with their future increase & should either of the above named slaves die before posession is given, I will that one equally valuable be selected from the remainder of my servants not herein after disposed of & substituted for it. I give also one bed and furniture to my said daughter Nancy. Item 4th. I give to my Daughter Mary D. Mitchell the following slaves at such time as she may marry or become of age, namely Ben & Louisa with the future increase thereof & should either of said slaves die before posession is given to my daughter Mary I will that one equally valuable be selected from my servants not herein disposed of & substituted for it. I give also to my daughter Mary one bed & furniture. Item 5th. I give to my son John G. Mitchell the following slaves Lewis & Ellen with their future increase & should either of said slaves die before my son John is of lawful age or takes possession I will that one equally valuable be selected from the remainder of my servants not herein after disposed of & substituted for it. I also will my son John one bed & furniture. Item 6th. I give to my daughter Sarah E. Mitchell when she marries or becomes of age the following slaves namely William & Frances with their increase & should either of the said slaves die before possession is given I will that one equally valuable be selected from the remainder of my slaves & substituted for it. I also will my daughter Sarah one bed and furniture. Item 7th. I give to my daughter Lucy C. Mitchell when she marries or becomes of age the following slaves namely James & Sarah with their future increase & should either of them die I will that one equally valuable be selected from the remainder of my slaves & substituted for it provided it dies before possession is given. I also give my daughter Lucy one bed & furniture. Item 8th. I will that should my wife have any other child by me it shall have equally with my other children in all my property real and personal. Item 9th. I will that should the death of any of the above named slaves render it necessary to substitute others from my estate my beloved wife & Robert Coleman of Hanover one or both of them shall make such selection as they may think just and equitable. Item 10th. I will that all my children shall live upon my land with their mother free of board until they marry or become of age & that they have a liberal education. Item 11th. I will that should any of my children die without legal heirs of the body that all the property willed to them revert to my surviving children & be equally divided amongst them. Item 12. I will that should my beloved wife Emily find it necessary to sell the one hundred and fifteen acres of land adjoining her brother Milton M. Brown for the purpose of debts or the education of our children or for the purpose of purchasing land else where she shall be at liberty to do so. Item 13th. I will that at the death of my wife all my lands be equally divided amongst my children. Item 14th. I will that two or more disinterested judicious persons shall be selected by my wife to value the property willed to each child when posession is given. Item 15th I will that all the residue of my property not herein disposed of shall at the death of my wife be equally divided amongst all my children & should any of them die without lawful heirs of the body their proportions to revert to the survivors & to be equally divided amongst them. Item 16th. I will that Milly on account of her faithfulness shall be at liberty to go with her daughter Louise in the division of my slaves if she wishes it. Item 17th. I will that there be no appraisement or sale of my property after my death & that my beloved wife Emily be appointed my Executrix without being required to give any security whatever. In witness whereof I have hereunto set my hand & affixed my seal this 2nd June 1842."

Charles C. Mitchell
Signed sealed & declared   (Seal)
by Charles C. Mitchell as
& for his last will and testament in the presence & hearing of us who at the request & in his presence have subscribed our names as witnesses: Geo. Fleming

M. M. Brown
George B. Mason
Charles L. Colley

"Postscript:
I also will that my son John shall assist his mother in the management of my estate & as soon as he is old enough to qualify as my executor without being held to security.

Charles C. Mitchell."
Wit.: M.M.Brown, George R. Mason, Chas. L.Colley
(No endorsement of probat)

MILTON M. BROWN, of Hanover. Will dated 1 Oct. 1852, probated 26 Oct. 1852. Appointed Wm. Hatch and George W. Parrish, Executors. Personal Estate appraised at $33,484.27. Only daughter Jane A. died prior to the date of his will. Survived by his widow, Elizabeth Brown, who was related to Garland Walton. Milton M. Brown had sisters, perhaps among others:

EMILY, widow in 1852, of Charles C. Mitchell.

[   ] a sister, wife of Pleasant Yeamans in 1853. He is Committee of Elizabeth Brown, the widow of Milton M. Brown.

CHARLES C. MITCHELL, of Hanover. Will dated 2 January 1842, died in 1851, will probated in 1852. Survived by his widow, Emily A., who was a sister of Milton M. Brown. Issue:
1. NANCY JANE MITCHELL.
2. MARY D. (POLLY), married John B. Jones, and both died prior to 1872, leaving an infant daughter, their only issue:
   1. EMILY JONES.
3. JOHN G. MITCHELL, married Miss Chisholm, and both are deceased in 1872, leaving issue two infant children:
   1. ALMA V. MITCHELL.
   2. CHARLES E. MITCHELL.
4. SARAH E., wife of John M. Thomas.
5. LUCY C. MITCHELL, died under age and unmarried.
6. CHARLES M. B. MITCHELL, born after the death of his father, married Plannie Ferrell.

MONTAGUE & OTHERS VS. JANEY'S EXOR., 1837 (25)
   MONTAGUE VS. GRESHAM, CIRCA 1839, (26)

MONTAGUE, SAMUEL, of Essex County, died circa 1810, intestate. Possessed a large personal estate and a farm called "Jones." George Haskins was first appointed Administrator, later succeeded by Joseph Janey, and in 1834, Washington H. Purkins was Administrator. The intestate was survived by three daughters, all in 1811, under 21 years of age:
1. LUCY ELIZABETH, born circa 1800, married in 1816, William W. Garrett, and died in 1817, leaving issue one child. William Wright was appointed her Administrator. In 1839, Robert L. Garrett was the Administrator. William W. Garrett left the State in 1818 and never returned. He is deceased in 1837, and Erastus T. Montague is his Adminsitrator. The name of their child is not stated.
2. CATHERINE YATES, married in 1818 George Haskins, and died in 1826, survived by her husband, her Administrator, and by three children, whose names are not stated. George Haskins (also called Hoskins) was alive on 21 June 1839.

3. AMELIA STANNARD, married in 1820, James Allen who died in 1826. She survived and was not twenty-one years of age in 1827 when she married Erastus T. Montague.

In an Indenture of 21 June 1811, of which James Montague and Elizabeth his wife were parties of the first part, and Joseph Janey, Admr. of Samuel Montague, dec'd was party of the second part, and the three infant children of Samuel Montague, dec'd, parties of the third part, it is stated that William Jones "by his last will, recorded in Essex County, devised, after the death of his mother, Mrs. Elizabeth Jones, the tract of land whereon the said William Jones did live - a part thereof to Samuel Montague, and 600 acres - further part to John F. Montague. That the said John F. Montague died in the lifetime of the said Mrs. Elizabeth Jones, and his part of the land descended to his brothers:
   WILLIAM MONTAGUE.
   SAMUEL MONTAGUE, and
   JAMES MONTAGUE, as his only heirs subject to the life estate of the said Elizabeth Jones - and she is now dead and Samuel Montague took possession, as the same has never been divided between the said John F., Samuel and James."

JANEY, JOSEPH, of Essex County, Executor of Samuel Montague, dec'd, was extensively engaged in the mercantile business circa 1810. He suffered considerably during the years between 1810 and 1815 by destruction of his property by the British. Died prior to 1837, survived by his widow Adelaide, and perhaps children. Thomas Gresham of King & Queen County was his Executor. In 1841 Gresham is dec'd and Wm. Dew is his Executor. "Edward M Wade of Henrico attorney in fact for Claude Janey and Simon Mory de Bullie, and Mrs. Mary Janey, his wife."

Others mentioned: George W. Banks, Sheriff of Essex County in 1810, removed to Tappahannock in 1811, and in February 1835 a resident of York County, Va.; Edward Ward and James Webb of Essex County, 1809.

[The Bill covering this suit is missing. Papers include many depositions relative to Joseph Janey, merchant, of which are too numerous to be included in this compilation]

Depositions: 19 July 1839 of John Edmondson and others at Clerk's Office of Mercer County, Ky., in town of Harrodsburg

23 July 1839, deposition of Mrs. Elizabeth Montague and others, at the house of Samuel Hodsin, in the town of Elizabeth, and the County of Harden, in the State of Kentucky.

No further information concerning the above Mrs. Elizabeth Montague, or of the second husband of Amelia S., Erastus T. Montague.

SMITH &C. VS. HARDY, 1853 (39)

Eliza J. Hardy's Will

HARDY, ELIZA J. "In the name of God amen. I, Eliza J. Hardy, consort of James G. Hardy of Barren County and State of Kentucky, being in a low state of body but of sound mind and memory & knowing that life is uncertain & death is certain do hereby direct what it hath pleased God to bless me with of this world's goods; do hereby appoint and direct the disposition of the same, in manner & form following - 1st. I give to my two youngest children, viz - Thomas & Martha Ann Hardy one cow to each and to Martha Ann my Loom, large iron pot and pot rack, one feather bed & furniture and Bedstead and my wearing apparel half of my bed clothing. I also wish and direct that a Skillet & oven be one of them to Martha A. & the other to Thomas. I also give to my son Thomas a new feather bed - and whereas I have a note of $125.00 on Israel Cox I hereby direct that the same be divided between my son Thomas and Martha A. equally - and whereas I have a reversionary claim of property by the will of Mary Jennings dec'd of Virginia which is now in the hands of Mary Houston formerly Mary Yancey the whole of which I hereby give to my two youngest children to wit Thomas and Martha A. to be equally divided between them. Also I expect there is or will be something devised to me from my Father's estate, if so I hereby give the same to my aforesaid two youngest children Thomas and Martha A. equally between them - and whereas my first children to wit Cornelia Walton and Maria Walton, Frances L. and John B. Smith have heretofore received their full portions is the reason of my not devising anything to them. Signed & sealed the 23rd of Dec. 1845."

her
Eliza J. E. + Hardy (Seal)
mark

Teste:
  K. Jamison
  S. P. Taylor
  Robert S. Jarvis

Barren County, Kentucky, April Term 1846.
    The foregoing writing purporting to be the last will and testament of Eliza J. Hardy dec'd was produced in Court and proven in due form of law by the oath of Kendrick Jamison and Samuel P. Taylor witnesses thereto whereupon the same was ordered to be recorded as the true last will of said Eliza J. Hardy, dec'd.

ELIZA J. HARDY, of Barren County, Kentucky. Will dated 23 December 1845. Probated in April 1846. She was a daughter of Francis Muncus, dec'd, and his wife Mary of Hanover County, Virginia. Eliza married first William Smith by whom she had issue in 1833:
1. JOHN B. SMITH.
2. FRANCIS L. SMITH.

3. MARIA, wife of William A. Walton.
4. CORNELIA, wife of George H. Walton.

Eliza J. married secondly James G. Hardy in Barren County, Kentucky. Their marriage agreement dated 10 October 1833. He granted to her the tract of land whereon he lived, bounded by the lands of Isham Hardy, Wilcoxen, and others, with the understanding that the said land is to revert to his children at the death of the parties. She granted to him for their joint use as long as they lived the tract of land on which she now lives, and her undivided interest in five slaves - the said land and slaves to revert to her children, Cornelia, Mariah, Francis and John, at the death of the parties.
The issue of James G. Hardy and his wife Eliza:
1. THOMAS J. HARDY, a minor, non-resident of Virginia, 1853.
2. MARTHA ANN HARDY, a minor, non-resident of Virginia 1853.

MUNCUS, FRANCIS, of Hanover County, died circa 1845, possessed of considerable estate, including over 600 acres of land. He was survived by his widow, Mary. Issue:
1. JOHN M. MUNCUS.
2. LAVENIA C., wife of Taliaferro Davis.
3. MARIA, wife of John Cosby.
4. ELLEN F. MUNCUS.
5. ELIZA J., wife of James G. Hardy.
6. RUFUS B. MUNCUS.
7. MARY E. MUNCUS.
8. [   ] daughter, dec'd, who married Mr. Duncan, and left issue:
    1. ROBERT ALEXANDER DUNCAN.
    2. MARY ANN DUNCAN, under age of 21 in 1845, John D. G. Brown, Guardian.
9. JUDITH A. E., married George W. Stockdell.

Commissioners to divide land: Edwin Snead, C. P. Goodall, Nathaniel Cross, and Walter Crenshaw.

MUTTER VS. GOVAN, 1840 (26)

MUTTER, JOHN, of Hanover County, on 27 Sep. 1839, purchased of Edward Govan, 362 acres of land called Powhite, bounded by Powhite Creek, Wooddy's branch, Boatswain's Swamp, and by lands of Watt and Parsons, and Chickahominy Swamp, surveyed by Thomas M. Ladd. Consideration $5,672.50. The Govans, in 1834, appears to have possessed a tract of land called "Blyths" which Edward Govan, and James and Archibald Govan, Executors of James Govan deceased are concerned with William Trueheart and Henry Curtis. James Govan is called of King & Queen Co., and William H. Curtis is his attorney in fact. John Mutter was appointed attorney in fact 1839 of Miles Macon, Edwin Burton, Jr., witness.

Others mentioned: Nathaniel Ellyson, Henry Eubank in 1836, and William B. Sydnor in 1840.

NELSON VS. NELSON, 1836 (28)

Francis Nelson's Will

NELSON, FRANCIS. "I, Francis Nelson of Mount Air in the County of Hanover, by the blessing of Almighty God being in good health and of sound and disposing mind, do make, ordain and constitute this as my last will and Testament. Imprimis. It is my will and desire that my whole estate, both real and personal shall be kept together during the life of my dear wife Lucy, to be to her use during the period for the support and maintenance of herself, and such of my children as shall continue to live with her as long as she lives, to be supplied to them as she chooses, during her continuance with her. Item. It is my will and desire that after the death of my said wife, all my estate of every sort and kind shall be equally divided amongst all my children living at the death of my said wife and the representatives of such as may be dead taking per stirpes only and in all cases, where I have given property to any of my children or to the husbands of such of my daughters as have been married that those who may thus have received portions, shall be charged with the full value of the property thus advanced and shall in no case be entitled to a part of the Estate remaining at my wife's death, except when the property thus advanced, shall fall short in value of a childs part of the residue of the Estate at my said wife's death, in which case the child thus receiving too small a portion, or the representatives of such as may be dead having been similarily situated shall be made equal to each of my other children in the division that is to say, it is my will and desire to make an equal division of all my property, held at my death and of what I have heretofore held, amongst all my children during my life, it is my will and desire that if what I have so given to any child, be equal to a childs part, of the Estate left at my wife's death, that in such case, the child thus receiving such portion, shall have no more - but in case what has been given to any child shall not be equal to a childs portion of the Estate left at my wife's death, then such child so receiving less shall be made equal to my other children in the division & Just and equal distribution of the property. I have sold to my son William, Grace the daughter of Betty, Robert the son of Suckey, and Isaac and Peter the sons of Rachael. I have sold to my son Philip, Billy and Henry Mead the sons of Betty, Sucky the daughter of Esther and Susan the daughter of Jennetta. These are not to be considered as portions advanced to William and Phillip. But they have received them, having paid for them a just equivalnt. It is my will and desire that my daughters Maria, Sally, Betsy and Fanny shall each have a maid to be chosen by themselves, at the death of their mother. But these maids must form a portion of my estate & be valued to them. I have advanced to my son Thomas two hundred and twenty-one acres of Land and two negro boys. I have advanced to my son in Law John Page three negro boys and one negro girl. I have advanced to my son in Law Mann Page two negro girls and one man. I have received from him a horse of the value of one hundred Dollars for which credit must be allowed. To my son Mann I have advanced one thousand Dollars and a negro girl & boy. These articles I desire may be charged to them respectively at their just value: Further it is my desire that my Executors herein named shall have the direction & management of such portions of my property as in the division of the Estate after my wife's death may be allotted to the sons of my daughter Judith to be held by them my said Executors in Trust for my said Grandsons, until they respectively arrive to the age of 21 years, and in case of the death of either of my said Grandsons under 21 years of age it is my will and desire that the survivor of them shall have the whole of what they may be jointly entitled to under this will and in case of the death of both my said Grandchildren under 21 years of age it is my will and desire that the portions to which they would have been entitled at 21 years of age shall revert to my other children and form a part of the Common Stock of property, for equal distribution amongst my children according to the intent and meaning of this my will. I hereby constitute my dear wife Lucy and my brothers Philip and Hugh the Executors of this my will and desire that no appraisement may be required and that no security shall be demanded of my Executors on qualifying as such to this my last will and Testament, Signed sealed & Executed as & for my last will and Testament this 19th day of february in the year 1830 in the presence of the subscribing witnesses, who signed in my presence & in the presence of each other."

Witnesses who subscribed,   Francis Nelson
   Carter Berkeley
   Robert C. Berkeley
   Carter N. Berkeley.

At a Court of Monthly Session held for Hanover County at the Courthouse on Tuesday the 24th of December 1833. This last will and Testament of Francis Nelson, dec'd was offered for proof by Lucy Nelson the Executrix therein named and was proved by the oath of Carter Berkeley a witness thereto. And at a Court of Quarterly session held for the said County at the Courthouse on Tuesday the 27th of October 1835, the said will was further proved by the oath of Robert C. Berkeley another witness thereto and is ordered to be recorded.

Teste, Philip B. Winston, C.H.C.
A Copy, Teste, Philip B. Winston, C.H.C.

FRANCIS NELSON, of "Mont Air" Hanover County. Will dated 19 February 1830. Probated 24 December 1833. Executors were his brothers Philip and Hugh Nelson. Possessed a considerable Estate including 706 acres of land valued at $4,000. Survived by his widow Lucy, who died prior to 1836. Children who survived her:
1. THOMAS L. NELSON.
2. MARIA, wife of John Redmond.
3. MANN P. NELSON.
4. SARAH P. NELSON.
5. WILLIAM NELSON.
6. PHILIP NELSON.
7. FRANCIS NELSON.
8. ELIZABETH M. NELSON.
9. FANNY B. NELSON.
10. HUGH NELSON.

In addition to these there were two daughters, one of whom married Mann Page and the other who married John Page, and both died prior to their father. It is not shown in the will or in the suit which of these daughters married the Pages, respectively.
11. JANE, died before her father, married a Mr. Page, and left five children, infants in 1836:
    1. ROBERT F. PAGE.
    2. EDWIN PAGE.
    3. JUDITH C. PAGE.
    4. LUCY PAGE.
    5. THOMAS MANN PAGE.
12. JUDITH, died before her father, married a Mr. Page called "Jr." and left two children who were under age of 21 in 1836:
    1. FRANK PAGE.
    2. POWHATAN P. PAGE.

Others mentioned: William Dabney who "has long known Mont Air the Estate of Philip Nelson, having lived in the neighborhood for many years;" Ira S. Bowles, and J. D. Andrews, witnesses in 1838.

NELSON &C. VS. NELSON, 1863 (28)
NEWTON'S ADMR. VS. EDWARDS &C., 1869 (88)

NELSON, DR. WILLIAM R., of "Gould Hill" Hanover County, died intestate in August 1862. He possessed a considerable Estate of real and personal property. Dr. E. S. Talley qualified as Administrator on 28 September 1863 and gave bond in the amount of $85,000. His Securities being William B. Newton, William Gibson, Richard Burnett, Ralph R. Horne, William E. Norment, Gilson Via, John Haw, William S. R. Brockenbrough, Edmund D. Waid, and George William Pollard. "Gould Hill" consisted of 810 1/4 acres was sold to John P. Ballard at $74.00 per acre, or $59,958.50, and another tract of 22 3/4 acres was sold to George W. Elliott at $50.00 per acre, or $1,137.50. The slaves, of which there were 20 were sold to John P. Tyler and George W.

Elliott. Dr. Nelson left no children, father or mother, and his next of kin and heirs at law were his sisters and brothers or their heirs:

MARY MINGE NELSON, a sister, married Mann Page, and had an only surviving child, a son:
1. CHARLES PAGE, dec'd, who had an only child, a daughter:
    1. MARY M. P., married William B. Newton of "Mahixen" an estate of 400 acres on Pamunkey River, near Hanover Town ferry. He died intestate in 1863. She is alive in 1869, when her children are:
        1. WILLOUGHBY NEWTON, a minor.
        2. LUCY NEWTON.
        3. CATHERINE B. (KATE) NEWTON.

DR. WILLIAM ARMISTEAD NELSON, dec'd in 1863, a brother.

SUSAN M., a sister, widow in 1863 of a Mr. Burwell of Clarke County, Virginia.

SARAH C., a sister, deceased in 1863, married first Charles Page, whom she survived with issue: Married secondly Mr. Atkinson, dec'd.
1. CAROLINE N., widow in 1863, of John Camm Pollard, deceased.
2. NORBORN T. PAGE.
3. WILLIAM A. PAGE, who had issue in 1863, four children, all under 21 years of age:
    1. MARY CARTER PAGE.
    2. ROBERT PAGE.
    3. ANN PAGE.
    4. WILLIAM PAGE
4. BETTY BURWELL, dec'd, married a Mr. Wellford, and had only issue, a daughter:
    1. BETTY BURWELL, married a Mr. Page and had only issue, a daughter:
        1. SALLY, wife of the Rev. Joseph M. Atkinson, of Raleigh, N.C., in 1863.

HUGH NELSON, a brother, deceased in 1863, who left issue:
1. SALLY NELSON.
2. LUCY NELSON.
3. FANNY, wife of Charles Carter.
4. MARY NELSON.
5. HUGH NELSON.
6. WILLIAM R. NELSON, under 21 years of age.

NORBORN T. NELSON, a brother, deceased, of the State of Tennessee, who left issue:
1. LUCY C., married Henry W. Robinson of New Orleans, Louisiana.
2. THOMAS NELSON, dec'd, who had a daughter:
    1. MARY, dec'd, who married a Mr. Robinson of New Orleans, leaving issue:
        1. EMMA ROBINSON, of New Orleans.
3. CATHERINE, wife of a Mr. Collier, and living in Tennessee.

4. BLANCHE NELSON.
5. WILLIAM NELSON.
6. CHARLES THOMAS NELSON, deceased in 1863,
   leaving unknown descendants in Louisiana

FANNY, a sister, deceased, married Spotswood
Wellford, deceased in 1863, leaving issue:
1. DR. WILLIAM R. WELLFORD.
2. MARY C., wife of George F. Carmichael.
3. JANE WELLFORD, dec'd, married James P.
   Corbin, and left issue:
   1. RICHARD CORBIN.
   2. S. W. CORBIN.
   3. FANNY N., wife of William H. Dickin-
      son, in 1863.
   4. KATE C. CORBIN.
   5. JAMES P. CORBIN, Jr., a minor 1863.

NUCKOLS & OTHERS VS. NUCKOLS & OTHERS, 1869 (28)

William W. Nuckols' Will

NUCKOLS, WILLIAM W. "In the name of God
amen. I, Wm. W. Nuckols of the County of
Hanover being of sound mind, memory, do
make this as my last will and testament in
writing hereby revoking all former wills made
by me. 1st. I hereby devise and bequeath to my
wife Harriet C. Nuckols my whole estate both
real and personal during her life to be used
managed and enjoyed in such manner as in her
judgment would best promote her welfare and
interest and that of her children and at the
death of my said wife it is my wish and desire
that my estate shall be equally divided among
all my children. I hereby authorize and empower
my said wife at such times as she may think
proper, taking an account of thereof, to make
advancements to any of my said children, as she
may think proper, and that said advancements be
accounted for by such of my children as shall
receive the same, After the death of my said
wife in the final distribution of my estate. I
hereby appoint my wife Harriett C. Nuckols the
sole Executrix of this my last will and testament and request that she may be permitted to
qualify as such without being required to give
security. Witness my hand and seal this
day of 1860."
                        Wm. W. Nuckols (Seal)

In Hanover County Court Clerk's office, December 31st 1872. This will with a copy of the
order setting up and establishing the same was
this day delivered to me, and is admitted to
record.
   Teste, John R. Taylor, C.C.

WILLIAM W. NUCKOLS, of Hanover. Will dated
in 1860, probated in 1864. Survived by his
widow, Harriet C., who qualified as Executrix.
Issue as of 1869:
1. MARY E. NUCKOLS.

2. ROBERT S. NUCKOLS.
3. ARCHER B. NUCKOLS.
4. ANN M., wife of Thomas Q. Powers.
5. LAURA NUCKOLS, under 21 years of age.
6. IDA P. NUCKOLS, under 21 years of age.

SUTTON VS. OLIVER, 1842 (39)
SUTTON VS. OLIVER. 1847 (38)

David Oliver's Will

OLIVER, DAVID. "In the name of God, amen,
I, David Oliver of the County of Hanover
do make this my last Will and Testament
hereby revoking all other wills by me heretofore made. 1st. I assign my soul to its creator
in humble hope of its future happiness, as in
the disposal of a being infinately good. 2nd. I
will and desire that my body be decently buried
at a spot I have pointed out in the rear of my
garden and that it my grave be enclosed by a
brick wall of sufficient height and thickness,
having in the clear of the enclosure atleast
ten feet of width by sixteen feet in length,
the bricks to be of prime quality and the work
to be done in the best manner. 3rd. I will that
my just debts be paid. 4th. I will that my beloved wife Elizabeth have a loan to her uninterrupted use and benefit so long as she remains
my widow the tract of Land on which I at present reside with its appurtenances, including
the mill on it and whatever property appertains
to it; all my household and Kitchen furniture
and plantation utensils, my carriage and harness, all my stocks of horses, cattle, sheep
and hogs, all my liquors, meat, grain and forage, and all my crops which may be at my death
and the following named slaves, to wit, Mima,
Joe and wife, Rose, Sylvia and her children,
Livinia, Harry, Lewis, Grace, Winston, Sam,
Betsy, Biddy, Nancy, Agness, Matt & his wife
Sophia and their children Isam, George, Charles,
Reuben and little Joe, with the increase of the
females of the said slaves from and after this
time. 5th. I will that in case my wife does
not marry, that she be priviledged to express
by her last will and Testament to which of my
children and grandchildren, the fourteen slaves
hereinbefore first named, with the increase of
the females of them from and after this time
shall pass and as she may thus express herself
by her said last Will and Testament duly signed
and sealed, I will to her or them in whose
favor she may thus express herself, and to his,
her or their heirs and assignes forever. 6th. I
will that should my wife marry, that all the
bequests herein before made in her favor, at
her marriage cease, determine and that thence
forth she receive no benefit or advantage therefrom. 7th. I will that should my wife marry,
that she then have of my Estate three thousand
Dollars to be paid to her by my Executors hereinafter named, and that out of the Estate that

I shall herein after bequeath to my sons in Law Mr. James Sutton and Doct.ʳ Stephen Sutton to be paid to her, three-fifths out of what I leave to James Sutton and the remaining two-fifths out of what I leave to Stephen Sutton. 8th I will that in any event, my wife have all the specie which may be in the house at my death which specie I give to her, her heirs and assigns forever. 9th. I will that my daughter Polly Sutton wife of Mr. James Sutton have on loan to her uninterrupted use & benefit during her life, my negroes John, Milly, Nancy and Maria now in the possession of her husband, together with the increase of the females of them, from & after this time, also my negro lad (blacksmith) William also from and after the marriage or death of my wife the land and mill which I have lent to my wife and the slaves lent to my wife whose names follow, to wit: Matt and his wife Sophia and their son Isam, George, Charles, Reuben and little Joe, with the increase of Sophia from and after this time; and at the death of my said daughter Polly, I give the said land, mill and slaves with their increase to be equally divided amongst the children of my said daughter living at the time of her death, to them respectively, and their heirs forever. 10th. I will that my daughter Eliza Sutton wife of Doct.ʳ Stephen Sutton have a loan to her uninterrupted use & benefit during her life, my negros Ned and Judy now in the possession of her husband together with the increase of Judy from and after this time, also my negroes whose names immediately follow, to wit Taylor, Ranson, Sally, Mary, Minerva, Martha, Milley, Randall, Julia, big Isaac, Dick, Pleasant, Aggy, Jim, Caroline, Mahala, Louisa, Fleming and Cynthia with the increase of the females of them from and after this time; also at the death of my said daughter Eliza I give the said slaves and increase to be equally divided amongst the children of my said daughter living at the time of her death, to them respectively & their heirs forever. 11th. It is my will that my Executors lay out three hundred Dollars in the purchase of a negro girl which I give & bequeath to my granddaughter Eliza Sutton to her and her heirs forever. 12th I give and bequeath my negro boy Richard son of Rose to my grandson David Sutton, to him and his heirs forever. 13th. I give and bequeath my negro boy little Isaac to my grandson Armistead Sutton to him & his heirs forever. 14th I give & bequeath to my son in Law Mr. James Sutton all the money he may owe me at the time of my death, also one thousand Dollars to be raised out of any part of my Estate not specially disposed of. 15th. I give and bequeath to my son in Law Doct.ʳ Stephen Sutton all the money he may owe me at the time of my death. 16th. It is my will that all my Estate not hereinbefore disposed of, be equally divided between my sons in Law, Mr. James Sutton & Doct.ʳ Stephen Sutton which I give to them and their heirs for-

ever. Lastly I constitute and appoint Park Street, Stephen Sutton and Philip B. Winston, Executors of this my last Will and Testament. In Testimony whereof I have hereunto set my hand and affixed my seal the eate 8 day of August one thousand eight hundred and twenty-two."

                              David Oliver (Seal)
Signed sealed, published
& declared by the Testator
to be his last Will & Testament in the presence
of us: Thos. Pollard
    Wm. C, Winston
    F. Winston.

"I make this Codicil to this my will - Item. I lent to my wife during her life or widowhood, Big Isaac (one of the nergoes by the tenth clause in my will) loaned to my daughter Eliza Sutton, and upon the death or marriage of my said wife, it is my desire that the said negro pass in same manner as expressed in the said Will. Item - it is my will that the fourteen first named negroes in my said will upon the death or marriage of my said wife be equally divided between my two daughters Mary Sutton and Eliza Sutton, instead of being at the disposal of my wife as expressed in the fourth clause of my said will. Witness my hand and seal the 30th day of Sept. 1822."

                              David Oliver (Seal)
Signed Sealed & acknowledged
in presence of us -
    Philip B. Winston
    Thos Pollard

At a Court of Quarterly Session held for Hanover County at the Courthouse on Wednesday the 23d of October 1822. This Last Will and Testament of David Oliver dec'd and the Codicil thereon endorsed were offered to proof by Stephen Sutton and Philip B. Winston, two of the Executors in the said Will named, and were proved the said will by the oaths of Thomas Pollard and F. Winston and the said Codicil by the oaths of Philip B. Winston and Thomas Pollard witnesses thereto, and the said will and Codicil were also proved by the oath of the Executors and are ordered to be recorded.
    Teste, William Pollard, C.H.C.
    A Copy, Teste, Wm. O. Winston, C.H.C.

DAVID OLIVER, of Hanover. Will dated 30 Sept. 1822, probated 23 October 1822. Appointed Philip B. Winston, Park Street and Stephen Sutton, Executors. Street never qualified and in 1847 is deceased. Winston and Sutton qualified. Sutton died intestate and his widow Eliza, his Administrator. Oliver left a considerable estate. His funeral·sermon was by Parson J. H. Turner for which his Estate paid $20.00. Richard Kersey of the City of Richmond made the bricks for the grave wall, the number required being 7083, length 24 feet, breadth 21 1/2 feet, and height 4 feet, 4 inches. Among his possessions were several shares of Virginia Bank Stock which was sold to Robert & Temple Gwaltmey of Richmond, on 5 November 1845, at $105.00. per share. He was survived by his widow Elizabeth M., who lived in the home of her son-in-Law James Sutton. At her death she devised 800 to 1000 acres of land, a mill, and 40 slaves. Their issue were two daughters and these had issue, among others, mentioned in David Oliver's will: Eliza Sutton, David Sutton and Armistead Sutton, whose mother or mother's name is not stated.

1. MARY (POLLY), married prior to 30 September 1822, James Sutton.
2. ELIZABETH M. (ELIZA) married prior to 30 September 1822, Dr. Stephen Sutton. He died intestate in 1840. Had purchased since 30 September 1822 of James Lyons and his father "Mangohick" a plantation in King William County which the said Lyons inherited from his grandfather, of which James' father had a life interest. Elizabeth M. Sutton on 10 January 1854 was in King William County. She had issue, perhaps among others, a son,
   1. PULASKI SUTTON.

Others mentioned: William Sutton who lived with James T. Sutton for several years; Richard Anderson, President Branch Bank of United States in Richmond; John C. Brock, Constable Hanover in 1828; Edward T. Morris, Attorney; Richard H. Napier; John S. Priddy; Samuel C. Scott and Francis W. Scott, law partners circa 1834-26; Thomas L. Scott, Justice of Caroline County and Executor of Samuel C. Scott, 1855; William M. Turner Sheriff and Ro. J. King, Deputy Sheriff of King William County. Isaac Leadbetter, Constable, Hanover, 1833. Wm. H. Lyons, Notary Public of Richmond, Va.

PAGE VS. PENDLETON &C., 1850 (32)

PAGE, FRANCIS, of Hanover County, died 4th November 1849, possessed of tract of land called "Rug Swamp" of 1192 acres on New Found River. Survived by his widow Susan Page, who died intestate 8 January 1850. Children:
1. ANGOLETT E., wife of William N. Pendleton.
2. FRANCES B., wife of Philip N. Meade.
3. THOMAS L. PAGE.
4. ANN ROSALIE PAGE.
5. FRANCIS M. PAGE.
6. JOHN PAGE.

Commissioners: John Page and William Nelson. Others mentioned: George Fleming, Thomas Nelson, Thomas Hardin, Charles Thompson, Cleverua S. Chisholm; Catherine Turner, widow of Claiborne Turner in 1869, who was in the employ of Major John Page during the late war.

SAUNDERS VS. VAUGHAN, 1841 (36)

PARSONS, SAMUEL, deceased, of Hanover Co. John A. Pilcher, Executor. Survived by his widow, Elizabeth M. Parsons. On 20 April 1838, Parsons and wife and Samuel S. Saunders of the City of Richmond, purchased of Henry Leadbetter and Mary T., his wife, for the consideration of $3,000, two tracts of land containing 702 1/2 acres as surveyed by Lemuel Crew, "being the same tracts conveyed to the said Henry Leadbetter by R. K. Ambler" as follows: 605 acres called the "Cottage" adjoining the lands of Nathaniel C. Crenshaw, Samuel Lambert, Edmund Gilmon, B. Anthony, John Harris and others; and 97 1/2 acres on the east side of "road leading to Crew's Mill" bounded by the said Nathaniel C. Crenshaw, William Stone and others. On 25 August 1841, Parsons and wife, and Samuel S. Saunders and Eliza S., his wife, conveyed the same tracts to Peter Massie.

PARSLEY VS. PARSLEY & OTHERS, 1854 (31)

William Parsley's Will

PARSLEY, WILLIAM. "In the name of God of God amen. I, William Parsley, of the County of Hanover, being of sound and perfect mind and memory but knowing that it is allotted to all persons to die and feeling a wish to dispose of such Estate as it has pleased God to bless me with do make and ordain this my last will and Testament. It is my will and desire that all my Just debts and funeral Expenses be paid. I lend to my loving wife Molly Parsley all my Estate both real and personal during her natural life and widowhood and at the death or intermarriage of my said wife It is my wish that all my Estate both real and personal be valued and to be equally divided between my five children in manner and form following to wit: I lend to my daughter Molly B. Alexander wife of William Alexander the one-fifth part of my Estate dureing her life and at her death the said Estate to be equally divided among all her children. I give to my two sons William Parsley and Joseph Parsley and to them and their heirs forever all my land to be equally divided between them and in the division of said which ever of my sons should have the Mansion house he is to let the other have the use of one room in said house until he can have reasonable time to build on his own land. I give to my son John P. Parsley to him & his heirs forever as much of my personal Estate as will make him equal in value with William or Joseph Parsley in the land given them. And I give to my daughter Martha Parsley and to her and her heirs forever as much of my personal Estate as will make her equal in value with William or Joseph Parsley in the land given them. I give all the remainder or residue of my Estate after the lone of the before mentioned one-fifth of the whole of my Estate to my daughter Molly Alexander and at her death to be equally divided among all her children. I give the remainder to be equally divided between my four children Martha Parsley, John P. Parsley, William Parsley, and Joseph Parsley herein before mentioned to them and their heirs forever. And it is my wish that this my last will be construed liberally and according to my intention and meaning. And Lastly I do constitute and appoint my son John P. Parsley my Executor to this my last will and testament. In witness whereof I have hereunto set my hand and seal this 17th day of December one thousand eight hundred and thirty-one."

                        William Parsley (Seal)
Signed sealed & delivered
by Wm. Parsley to be his last will and Testament in the presence of Wm. H. Peace, Robert Johnson, Michel Daniel.

At a Court of Monthly Session held for Hanover County at the Courthouse on Tuesday the 24th of May 1836. This last will and testament of William Parsley, dec'd was proved by the oaths of Robert Johnson and Michel Daniel witnesses thereto and is ordered to be recorded.
    Teste, Philip B. Winston, C.H.C.
    A Copy, Teste, Wm. O. Winston, C.H.C.
                    Mar 23d 1853

WILLIAM PARSLEY, of Hanover. Will dated 17 December1831, probated 24 May 1836. Appointed son John P. Parsley, Executor. Survived by his widow Molley, who died prior to 1854, and five children:
    1. WILLIAM PARSLEY.
    2. JOSEPH PARSLEY.
    3. JOHN P. PARSLEY.
    4. MARY, wife of WILLIAM Alexander, and
        have issue in 1854:
        1. MARTHA JANE, wife of Spotswood Liggon.
        2. WILLIAM J. ALEXANDER.
        3. JAMES M. ALEXANDER, a minor.
    5. MARTHA, wife of John Via, of Henrico Co.,
        in 1854.

Others mentioned: Edward W. Allen, Surveyor of New Kent County; Thomas M. Ladd, Surveyor of the City of Richmond; Benjamin B. Pleasants of Rockville, Surveyor of Hanover County in 1855, and as such since June 1852; William Pleasants, sometime Surveyor of Hanover County.

    PRICE VS. PETTERSON'S ADMR. & OTHERS, 1836 (30)
    PATTERSON VS. PAGE, 1845 (32)

            James Patterson's Will

PATTERSON, JAMES. "In the name of God amen. I, James Patterson of the County of Hanover being of infirm body but of sound mind and disposing memory and wishing to dispose of my property in a manner that seems to me most proper do hereby make and ordain this my last will and Testament - revoking all others: in manner and form following. Imprimis. My will and desire is that my just debts and funeral expenses be first paid. Item 2nd. I lend unto my wife Sarah Patterson all my property of every description both real and personal during her widowhood but should she marry it is my will that she shall be thirded - agreeably to law and the balance of my property or the two-thirds be equally divided among my surviving children and their lawful heirs except Susanna Holloway and Sally King to each of whom I will five shillings. Item 3rd. It is also my will that at the death of my wife above named, should she marry, the property lent to her as above, be equally divided among my surviving children and their lawful heirs, except as before excepted, and also it is my will that should she die before marriage that all property lent to her be divided as aforesaid with the exception aforesaid. Item. It is my will that my son Joseph Patterson have a negro boy named Peter at valuation to go towards discharging the debt I owe him to take sd boy when sd son wishes. Item 5th. I leave my friend H. J. Anderson Exor of this my last will and testament. In testimony whereof I hereunto set my hand and seal this 3rd day of April 1826."

                        James Patterson (Seal)
Witnesses:
    Ann M. Taylor
    Ann (+) Haskins
    Richard Arnall
    Henri Cressor
    John D. Taylor

"Know all persons whom it may concern that I, James Patterson do hereby make and constitute and add the following Codicil to the above my last will and testament in words as follows:

            Codicil

1st. It is my will and desire that my executor sell all my land and negroes above specified upon such credit as he shall think proper, nothing being construed to effect the widow's right and title during her widowhood or before marriage as above expressed. 2nd. It is my will that there shall be an equal division of my Estate or the money arising therefrom among all my children or heirs of their bodies respectively but what would fall to my daughters Susanna Holloway and Sally King shall be reserved by my Executor and distributed equally to the heirs of their bodies respectively for the benefit of their education and a receipt of any instructor or teacher shall be proper voucher for my Executor - not wishing to exclude the heirs of their body from a benefit of my Estate as done in the above will, but should either of them die without heir or heirs the money that would have fallen to either or both shall revert to my surviving children and their lawful heirs agrreeably to Law. Nothing in this Codicil shall be construed to effect the loan of my Estate to my wife during her widowhood or untill she shall have married as before expressed in the will. As witness my hand and seal this 9th day of April 1826."

                                        James Patterson (Seal)
Witness:
    George Hoskins
    Rich^d (+) Davis
    John D. Taylor

At a Court of Monthly Session held for Hanover County at the Courthouse on Wednesday the 28th of June 1826. This last Will and Testament of James Patteson dec'd was proved by the oath of Henri Cressor one of the witnesses thereto and at a Court of Quarterly Session held for the said County at the Courthouse on Wednesday the 26th of July then next following the said will was further proved by the oath of John D. Taylor another witness thereto and the Codicil there-under written was also proved by the oaths of Richard Davis and John D. Taylor two of the witnesses thereto which will and Codicil are ordered to be recorded.
    Teste, William Pollard, C.H.C.
    A Copy, Teste, Wm. O. Winston, D.C.H.C.

JAMES PATTERSON, of Hanover. Will dated 3 April 1826, Codicil 9 April 1826, Probated 28 June 1826. Harod J. Anderson, Executor. Estate included 260 acres of land and seven slaves. Survived by his widow, Sarah, who died 14 Dec. 1844. Francis Page, Sheriff, Administrator. George Doswell, Deputy. Issue, probably among others:
    1. SUSANNA, wife of a Mr. Holloway.
    2. SALLY, wife of a Mr. King.
    3. JOSEPH PATTERSON, in 1845 a resident of Goochland, living 30 miles from Hanover Courthouse.

Others mentioned: Thomas Taylor, Justice of the Peace, Goochland County.

PRICE VS. PATTERSON'S ADMR. & OTHERS, 1836 (3)

PATTERSON, HENRY, of Hanover County "died many years ago, intestate and unmarried." His heirs being his sisters and brothers, seven in number:

JAMES PATTERSON, dec'd, who was a brother. Anderson Bowles, Sheriff of Hanover, Admr.

SAMUEL PATTERSON, dec'd, a brother, of Caroline County, survived by his widow, Nancy, who was Nancy Mills, his Administrator. Robert K. Evans of Caroline, in 1845, her attorney.

Issue of Samuel, dec'd and Nancy Patterson:
    1. ALBERT PATTERSON.
    2. ELIZABETH, wife of John Spicer.
    3. MARY PATTERSON, inft, John Hackett, Gdn.
    4. ANN PATTERSON,   "   "   "   "
    5. SARAH PATTERSON. "   "   "   "

NANCY, dec'd, a sister, who was wife of Henry Arnall, her Administrator in 1849.

BETSY, a sister, who married a Mr. Hubbard.

JOSEPH PATTERSON, a brother.

EDMUND PATTERSON, a brother.

MARY, a sister, married a Mr. Williams, and has issue:
    1. SARAH, wife of Edward Lowry.
    2. SAMUEL WILLIAMS, who is married and has an only child in 1836:
        1. ANDREW S. WILLIAMS.

                SLAUGHTER VS. ANDERSON, 1837 (39)

PEACE, WILLIAM H., deceased of Hanover Co., He was survived by, perhaps among others, three infant children, of whom Robert Anderson and Richard G. Smith were associated:
    1. WILLIAM H. PEACE.
    2. EDMUND W. PEACE.
    3. ELIZABETH PEACE.

Others mentioned: William Slaughter, a free man of color.

                PEACE'S GDN. VS. PEACE'S HEIRS, 1838 (30)

PEACE, WILLIAM, deceased, of Hanover County. Possessed two tracts of land in Hanover containing 140 and 23 acres respectively. No mention of wife. Survived by children:
    1. WILLIAM W. PEACE.
    2. MARY S. PEACE.
    3. FANNY W. PEACE.
    4. CAROLINE L. PEACE.
All infants in 1838, John P. Parsley their Guardian. In 1842, Powhatan B. Moore, Guardian.

Depositions in 1838 of: Watt W. Tyler, George Barker and George W. Barker.

                PERKINS VS. HARFIELD, 1866 (32)

PERKINS, JOHN, late of Hanover County, "died some years since." He possessed 120 1/2 acres, subject of this suit. Survived by his widow Martha, who has since died, and by six children:
    1. URIAH PERKINS.
    2. JOSIAH PERKINS.

3. ZACHARIAH PERKINS.
4. SARAH T., wife of William Harfield.
5. JOHN T. PERKINS, a minor in 1866.
6. WILLIAM PERKINS, deceased, survived by his
      widow, LUCY C.,(who has since married
      Reuben Southworth.) Issue of Perkins:
      1. EMMA PERKINS, 12 years of age in
            1866, Chas. S. Mallory, Guardian.

Others mentioned: Benjamin Southward, Reuben
Southward (note spelling) J. H. Blunt, and W. W.
Mallory.

PERRIN VS. PERRIN'S EXOR. &C., 1836 (31)
PERRIN VS. CARTER COMR., 1840 (32)

PERRIN, ELIZABETH, of Hanover County, in
1840, appears in this suit to be a married
woman, though her husband's name is not
mentioned, and to have been the mother of:
1. ELIZABETH PERRIN, called "Jr."
2. POLLY PERRIN.
3. THOMAS PERRIN.
4. JOHN PERRIN, deceased, who in partnership
      with Francis Blunt, had owned a Grist and
      Saw Mill in Hanover.
5. PARK PERRIN, who it is said had married
      in March 1833.

6. NANCY PERRIN.

PERRIN, ISAAC, of Hanover County, deceased
in 1830. Nathaniel Tinsley (dec'd in 1836
Jeremiah S. B. Tinsley, Executor) and
Isaac Perrin, Executors. His legatees in 1830:
1. VAIDEN PERRIN.
2. THOMAS PERRIN, Administrator of Samuel
      Perrin.
3. JOHN PERRIN.
4. HENRY PERRIN.
5. JOSEPH PERRIN.
6. ISAAC PERRIN.
7. CATHERINE, dec'd, who married Mr. Davis,
      and who has children, whose names are
      not stated.

Others mentioned: Lyddall Bowles, H. Davis,
Thomas Eubank; Henry S. Carter and James Lyons,
Commissioners; John Haw, John Hitchcock, John D.
King. Thomas Tinsley

PHILLIPS & WIFE VS. FONTAINE, 1867 (60)

PHILLIPS, WILLIAM, and Ellen M. (died 15
February 1886) on 4 January 1842, executed
a Deed of Trust to Edmund Fontaine of Hanover and John O. Harris of Louisa, for the benefit of their present children, and any others
which they may have. The land conveyed consisted
of 60 acres, at Beaverdam Depot, on C&O. Ry.,
adjoining George M. Hall's Estate. Issue, as of
1867:

1. ELLEN C., wife of a Mr. Farmer.
2. JAMES H. PHILLIPS.
3. CHARLES W. PHILLIPS.
4. JOHN L. PHILLIPS, deceased.
5. RICHARD T. PHILLIPS, born after 4 January
      1842, died without issue, 3 October 1889.
6. ADA M. PHILLIPS, died unmarried.
7. MARY A., born after 4 January 1842, wife
      of a Mr. Hall.
8. WALTER L. PHILLIPS, born after 4 January
      1842.
9. JOSEPH F. PHILLIPS, born after 4 January
      1842.
10. MARGARET E., wife of a Mr. Yeamans
11. ELIZABETH FRANCES, wife of Westley P. Hunt-
      ley.
The last six of these children were born after
4 January 1842.

William Phillips, the father of these children
was indebted to Lancelot Phillips in the sum of
$800.00. In 1867 "Lancelot Phillips has been
dead for many years, and his son John W. Phillips is his Administrator." Also in 1867 it is
stated "Edmund Fontaine and J. O. Harris has
been dead for many years."

PICOT DE BOISFEILLET VS. PICOT DE BOISFEILLET,
1853, (90)

PICOT, MICHEL de BOISFEILLET, formerly of
France, died in Hanover County, in September 1851, intestate. William Gouldin of
City of Richmond, Va., Administrator. Survived
by his widow, Josephine Picot de Boisfeillet,
who was living in New York in 1853, and by issue:
1. JOSEPHINE PICOT de BOISFEILLET, the young-
      er of New York.
2. ALFRED PICOT de BOISFEILLET.
3. LEONIA PICOT de BOISFEILLET.
4. MICHEL PICOT de BOISFEILLET.
5. LOUISE, wife of Armand Hemery de Goascar-
      adec, of France.
6. YOLAND PICOT de BOISFEILLET, died in Han-
      over County, unmarried in October 1851.
7. ADELE PICOT de BOISFEILLET, a minor, resi-
      dent of New York in 1853.
8. HENRY PICOT de BOISFEILLET, a minor, resi-
      dent of New York in 1853.
9. JOSEPH PICOT de BOISFEILLET, a minor,
      resident of New York in 1853.

POITEAUX'S WIFE VS. GRANTLAND'S EXOR., 1834 (30)

Samuel Grantland's Will

GRANTLAND, SAMUEL. "In the name of God,
Amen. I, Samuel Grantland of the County
of Hanover do make and ordain this my
last Will and Testament. It is my will and desire - That my estate shall not be appraised;
That all my estate be kept together subject to

the management and control of my beloved wife
during her life or until our granddaughter Frances G. Talley shall be married, for the support
and maintenance of my wife and granddaughter.
That should my said Granddaughter marry during
the life of my wife - Then my wife shall retain
my land, and the balance of my estate is to be
equally divided between my wife and granddaughter. The one-half of which estate that is divided, together with my land , it is my will
shall be managed and controlled by my wife for
her own benefit during her life. And the other
half of my estate thus divided I give to my said
granddaughter and the heirs of her body forever.
That the division (if to be made) shall be made
by three respectable Gentlemen of the neighborhood, to be indifferently chosen and without an
order of court. That my wife shall be allowed
by her last will and testament in writing to
give to whomsoever she may choose, not more
than four of my negroes, and for the whole of
the negroes she may thus give, not to be worth
in the aggregate more than one thousand Dollars
- and should she make such gift, or any part
thereof, by her last will and Testament in
writing in such case, I do confirm the will she
may thus make. And at the death of my wife, I
give all my lands, and all such estate as she
may possess in virtue of this my will, and all
and any other estate which I have power to give,
to my aforesaid granddaughter Frances G. Talley
and to the heirs of her body forever. But the
preceeding bequest in favor of my said granddaughter shall be subject to the following restrictions, that is to say - To the provisions
of my wife's will aforesaid should she make one
in writing, and should my said granddaughter
depart this life before she is married, in such
case, the estate which I have intended for her
as aforesaid, shall be divided into two equal
parts; one of which parts to go to my nearest
of kin and the other part to go to my wife's nearest of kin to be divided amongst my own kin;
and my wife's kin respectively, agreeably to
the law making distribution of intestates estates. It is further my will and desire - That my
executors hereinafter named, deliver to my
relation Miss Lucy McDougle my feather bed, the
tick of which is now with a bolster and pillows
but which has no other furniture, which bed
bolster and pillows I give to her, Her heirs and
assigns. And it is further my will and desire
that my Executors buy as a Gift from me and deliver to my relations, the said Lucy McDougle
and her sister Elizabeth McDougle children of
Richard McDougle each a small 'negro girl, to
cost (each negro girl) about $150.00; which I
give to my said relations Lucy and Elizabeth
McDougle each one negro girl to be thus purchased, Lucy having choice, to her the said
Lucy and Elizabeth respectively, and to her
heirs forever. I do hereby appoint my executors
hereinafter named, testamentary guardians of my
granddaughter Frances G. Talley. And lastly I

do appoint my beloved wife and my friend Col⁰
Parke Street executrix and Executor, of this my
last will and Testament hereby revoking all
wills by me heretofore made, And I direct, that
my said executors shall not give security for
the Executorship. In Testimony whereof I the
said Samuel Grantland have hereunder set my
hand and seal this 20th day of July 1824."

                    Samuel Grantland (Seal)
Signed sealed published
& declared by Samuel Grantland
to be his last Will and Testament in the presence of: Wm. Davenport, Thomas Nixon, Henry
Street.

At a Court of Monthly Session held for Hanover
County at the Courthouse on Wednesday the 25th
of August 1824. This last Will and Testament
of Samuel Grantland dec'd was offered for proof
by Parke Street the Executor therein named,
and was proved by the oaths of William Davenport, Thomas Nixon and Henry Street the witnesses thereto and also by the oath of the said
executor and is ordered to be recorded.
     Teste, William Pollard, C.H.C.
     A Copy, Teste, Philip B. Winston, C.H.C.

CAPTAIN SAMUEL GRANTLAND, of Hanover. Will
     dated 20 July 1824, probated 25 August 1824.
Parke Street qualified as Executor. In his will
mention is made of a relative, Richard McDougle
who has daughters, Lucy and Elizabeth, unmarried in 1824. Survived by his widow, whose name
is not stated. They had issue, an only child,
a daughter, dec'd, who married Billy T. Talley:
   1. [   ] daughter, dec'd, married Billy
      T. Talley, merchant of Hanover Town who
      was deceased in 1820. They had an only
      child, a daughter:
      1. FRANCES G., who lived with her grand-
         parents after the death of her father
         and mother. On 1 February 1826, in
         accordance with arrangements made by
         her grandfather's Executor, Parke
         Street, she became an intimate of the
         family of Mr. Nicholas Mills of the
         City of Richmond, from whose home she
         attended school with Mr. Nicholas'
         daughter, and where she continued to
         live until her marriage with Charles
         W. Poiteaux early in the year 1829

Others mentioned: Robert Anderson, John Beale,
Wm. Cunningham, Dr. Henry Curtis "a practising
physician of high repute for many years in the
neighborhood of Hanover Town;" Dr. Wm. R. Nelson who was a resident of Hanover Town 1820;
Dr. Ezekiel S. Talley; George W. Dixon; John H.
Earnest who acted as cryor at Capt. Grantland's
sale; Francis Harris who has a wife, also daughter named Ann; B. L. Johnson; Hezekiah Mantlo
lived with Capt. Grantland at the time of his
death; George W. Robinson; Poiteaux Robinson.

BALL VS. POLLARD'S EXOR. & OTHERS, 1868 (40)

POLLARD, MRS. CAROLINE N., dec'd of New Kent County, Virginia. Left a will recorded in that county. Possessed a plantation called "Roxbury" of 600 acres on Chickahominy River. she devised "all her estate to her two sons." Issue mentioned:
1. JAMES POLLARD, of Hanover County.
2. THOMAS A. POLLARD, of Augusta County, Va.
3. [   ] daughter, wife of Thomas Ballard of Hanover.

Others mentioned: Elijah Ball of New Kent Co.

HUNDLEY'S ADMR. VS LYONS' ADMR. & OTHERS, 1830(18)

William Pollard's Will

POLLARD, WILLIAM. "In the name of God Amen. I give to my beloved wife the following named nine negroes, to wit: Dorcas, Cooper, Jacob, Wilson, Sally, Fleming, Henry, Lewis, Armistead & Elizabeth with the future increase of the females to her and her Heirs forever. I give to my Grand Daughter Susanna Darracott the children of Delphia now in the possession of her father, to her and her Heirs forever; but on his condition that in the case of her death under age and not theretofore married, then the same shall go to her sister Mary to her and her Heirs forever. I lend to my wife all the rest of my Estate both real and personal during her life and in widowhood, subject to the limitations, restrictions and incumbrances herein after mentioned, that is to say first to the payment of my debts then to the liberal education of my son George William and to his maintenance until he shall become entitled to share in my Estate. When my son comes to the age of twenty-one years or his lawful issue I give him one-half of what shall remain of the Estate lent to my wife both real and personal to him and his Heirs forever. On the death or marriage of my wife I give to my said son all the residue of the real estate lent to my wife and as many more of my negroes as shall make with the one-half already given him his number thirty-three in all, and I also give to my said son the residue of my personal estate, all which I give to him and his Heirs forever. If my wife should die or marry before my son comes to the age of twenty-one years, or his lawful issue, then part of my estate provided for him, to wit, all my real estate, thirty-three negroes, and all the residue of my personal estate shall go to him immediately, to him and his Heirs forever. But if my son should die under the age of twenty-one years and without lawful issue the said estate given him is to go to my Daughters Darracott and Sheppard to hold during their respective lives and then to their children forever. My Executrix and Executor are at liberty to sell any of my negroes (should it be necessary

to accomplish the objects herein before mentioned) which are loaned to my wife after which shall have been done, and my Estate finally settled should there then remain more than the thirty-three which I have given to my son, I give the surplus of the said negroes, that is to say all over the thirty-three aforesaid, (of which there are at this time fifteen) besides those given to my wife, to my two daughters aforementioned, to hold the same during their respective lives and thereafter to their children forever. I desire that my wife may act as Guardian of my son and take the advice of my much respected friend the Revd. Jesse H. Turner in respect to his education. My debts being inconsiderable and my Executrix and Executor being principally interested in my estate I desire that neither of them be required to give security nor to have my estate appraised. I appoint my wife Executrix and should my son come to age of twenty-one years I appoint him my Executor. The foregoing is my will, written wholly with my own hand and signed by me this 7th day of April 1830."

William Pollard (Seal)

"The provision made for my wife in the aforegoing will is in stead of Dower."

William Pollard.

At a Court of Quarterly Session held for Hanover County at the Courthouse on Wednesday the 22d of February 1832. This writing purporting to be the last will and testament of William Pollard dec'd was offered for proof by Elizabeth P. Pollard the executrix in the said writing named: and Park Street and Philip B. Winston being sworn and examined (there being no subscribing witnesses to the said writing) declare that they are well acquainted with the handwriting of the said deceased, that they have examined the said writing and the memorandum thereunder written and verily believe that the same, together with the signatures thereto were wholly written by the said William Pollard dec'd whereupon the same are ordered to be recorded as the last will and testament of the said William Pollard, dec'd.
  Teste, Philip B. Winston, C.H.C.
  A Copy, Teste, Wm. O. Winston, C.H.C.

WILLIAM POLLARD, of Hanover. Will dated 7 April 1830, probated 22 February 1832. Survived by his widow, Elizabeth P., Executrix. He and David Oliver had been security for Dr. James Lyons. Our only knowledge of his issue is from his will:
  1. [   ] daughter, wife of Mr. Darracott.
  2. [   ] daughter, wife of Mr. Sheppard.
  3. GEORGE WILLIAM POLLARD, a minor in 1830.

HUNDLEY, WILLIAM, dec'd in 1830. Jane Hundley, Administratrix, B. F. Michie, her counsel. She died prior to 20 August 1845. William T. H.

Pollard, in 1847, Admr. de bonis non of William
Hundley's Estate. Hundley had purchased land of
Judge Peter Lyons.

LYONS, JUDGE PETER, of Hanover. Said to have
left a will. James Lyons, Executor. Judge
Lyons had a sister, Ann Eliza, in 1830, wife
of Dr. Robert P. Richardson. Judge Lyons had
issue, perhaps among others:
  1. DR. JAMES LYONS, wife in 1829 was Sarah S.
     He died circa 1845, James Underwood,
     Administrator. In 1847 William B. Crit-
     tenden was Admr. de bonis non. (Also was
     Executor of his wife Eliza C. Crittenden
     on 20 August 1845. Issue of Dr. Lyons,
     probably among others:
     1. JAMES LYONS, JR., of Richmond, Va.
     2. [   ] daughter, wife of Mr. Green.
  2. JOHN LYONS.

Judge Peter Lyons, in 1830, had a grandson,
Peter Lyons.

UNDERWOOD, JAMES, of Hanover County, died
prior to 22 March 1847. Francis Blunt, Sheriff, Admr. Underwood had been Administrator of
Dr. James Lyons.

Others mentioned: William Cunningham; Peter V.
Daniel, Esq., counsel for Jane Hundley; G. N.
Johnson, counsel; David Oliver, who had been
one of the Securities for Dr. James Lyons, in
1830 is deceased and Stephen Sutton and Philip
B. Winston, Executors; Stephen Sutton, died
prior to 12 December 1842, intestate, Eliza
Sutton, Administrator; Thomas Green, counsel.

        POLLARD'S ADMR. VS. POLLARD &C., 1864 (32)

            William T. H. Pollard's Will

POLLARD, WILLIAM T. H. "I hereby make and
constitute this as my last will and testament. 1st. It is my will that my Executor hereinafter named proceed to collect all the debts
due me as soon as it can be done. 2nd. It is
my will that my Exor. Sell upon Such terms as
may seem best all my intrust in the Grist & saw
mills owned by Jas. D. Winston and myself (my
interest being one moiety) (unless the said Winston will consent to carry on the meal & Timber
business as at present) the proceeds of such
sale, together with the debts due my Estate, I
wish applied to the payment of my debts. Should
the said Winston consent to carry on the meal &
timber business as at present, then in that
event, I wish the business to be carried on as
at present. If the debts due my estate and the
proceeds of the sale of my interest in the
above named mills in the event they be sold
proved insufficient to discharge the debts due
from my estate, it is my will that my Exor.
Sell my Stock in the Richmond and Petersburg

Rail Road or such of my perishable property as
can best be Spared. So as Completely to discharge and pay off my debts. 3rd. It is my will
that my estate that shall remain after the payment of my debts be kept together for the support of my wife and children and the education
of my children, during the widowhood of my
wife. 4th. Should my wife marry it is in that
event my will that my Estate be equally divided among my wife & children. The portion falling to my wife to be used by her during her
life & at her death to be equally divided
among my children which I give to them & their
heirs forever. And the portion falling to my
children I give to them and their heirs forever
5th. It is my will that should either of my
children marry or attain the age of twenty-one
years during the widowhood of my wife, she may
in her own discretion make advancements from my
estate to such child or children. Such advance
ments to be brought into hotchpot on a final
division of my Estate among my children. 6th.
It is my will that at the death of my wife my
estate be equally divided among all my children
7th. Should my wife not marry and die before
my children are educated my will is and I hum-
bly make it as a last request to my sister Mrs.
C. E. Overton (which I know she will take pleas
ure in complying with) that she take care of
and watch over my children. I wish them to live
with her. 8th. Lastly I appoint Wm. O. Winston
my Executor. Witness my hand & seal this 4" day
of January 1853."
                          Wm. T. H. Pollard

"Codicil - Should my Exor. think it to the
interest of my children after the death of my
wife to keep my estate together it is my will
that it be kept together for their mutual benefit till the eldest surviving arrive to the age
of twenty-one years or till some one of them
marry when the said child so arriving to the
age of twenty-one years or marrying may require
a division. Witness my hand & seal the 4" day
of January 1853."
                          Wm. T. H. Pollard

"Codicil - Made 27th June 1853. Upon reflection
I have concluded to adopt the suggestion of my
wife & leave the property which I have given to
my children in trust for their benefit. I there
fore wish & it is my will that the property
devised to my children by this my last will &
testament be held in trust for their benefit by
my relation & friend Benjᵃ Pollard to be kept
together and managed as directed in previous
part of this my wills."
                          Wm. T. H. Pollard

"1854, Jany. 27. Further Codicil. Should Dr. Wm.
H. Howard of Texas buy Land in that State for
me with funds I have remitted him my will is
that my Exor sell the same when it shall appear
to be to the best interest of my Estate to do s

"I do not wish my negroes under the age of 14 to be hired out unless it be such as go with their mothers and I do not wish any of them put on public works except with the approbation of my wife."

Wm. T. H. Pollard
22 May 1854

At a Court of Quarterly Session held for Hanover County at the Courthouse on Tuesday the 22nd of July 1856. This last will and Testament of William T. H. Pollard deceased and the Codicils thereafter written were offered for proof by William O. Winston the Executor in said will named, there being no subscribing witnesses to the said will or Codicils and George W. Doswell and George W. Richardson being sworn and examined declare that they are well acquainted with the handwriting of the said William T. H. Pollard, deceased, that they verily believe the same to have been wholly written and subscribed by the said William T. H. Pollard deceased. Thereupon the Court doth order the said will and Codicils to be recorded as the last will and Testament of the said William T. H. Pollard.

Teste, Wm. O. Winston, C.H.C.
A Copy, Teste, R. O. Doswell, D.C.H.C.

WILLIAM T. H. POLLARD, of Hanover. Will dated 4 January 1853. Codicils 4 January 1853, 27 June 1853, 27 January 1854, 22 May 1854. Proated 22 July 1856. Appointed William O. Winston Executor. In 1864 William Winston Jones was Administrator de bonis non. Testator mentioned a sister Mrs. C. E. Overton. Survived by his widow, Susan C. Pollard. Issue:

1. MOLLIE T., wife of Thomas H. Kinney.
2. ELIZABETH A. B. POLLARD.
3. WILLIAM O. POLLARD, a minor in 1864.
4. ALICE B., wife of Carter S. Anderson.
5. MARIA L. P. POLLARD, a minor in 1864.
6. JOSEPHINE J. POLLARD, a minor in 1864.
7. BENJAMIN POLLARD.

These names are not, perhaps, in order of birth.

CHRISTIAN'S TRUSTEE VS. PRYOR & OTHERS, 1857 (81)

William S. Pryor's Will

PRYOR, WILLIAM S. "I, Wm. S. Pryor of the County of Hanover make my will in the manner following. Item - 1st. It is my desire that my Executor proceed with as little delay as possible to pay all my debts never taking advantage of the Law in any case and it is my wish that no legal barrier should be used to prevent the payment of just debts. Item - 2nd. It is my desire that my daughters Ellen & Susan be sent to Richmond to School till she arrives to the age of sixteen and to be taught music together with the usual branches of an English education. 3d Item. It is my desire that my daughter Susan be sent to Richmond to school

till she arrives to the age of fifteen. 4th Item. It is my wish that my dear little helpless orphan children John and Thomas Henry be sent to school as long as my Executor may think it necessary & to be taught the Languages if their capacity will justify it. 5th Item. It is my wish that my estate be equally divided between my children when they marry or become of age. 6th. Item. It is my wish if my Daughter Ellen is taught Music that my Executor shall give her when she leaves School a Piano Forte and cost to be deducted from her portion of my estate this however is to be left to her own choice and should she not wish to have the Piano Forte in that event she is to share equally with my other children. 7th Item. It is probable that almost the whole of my estate will be in money it is my desire that my Executor take my daughters portion and hold it in Trust and vest it in Stock for their benefit paying the interest to them. 8th Item. It is my desire that in the event of any my children dying before they become of age or should not leave lawful issue of their body the portion left to the one so dying shall be equally divided between the survivors. 9th. And Lastly It is my desire to be interred by the side of my dear wife Joanna W. Pryor and that my Executor procure a neat marble slab to be placed over each of our graves and also over the grave of my dear Horacess with such inscriptions as may deem proper. I appoint my affectionate son Wm. W. Pryor Executor of this my last will and Testament this 19 day of January 1835."

W. S. Pryor

"Codicil to my will dated 19" Jany. 1835 (towit) Having purchased a Piano Forte for my daughter Ellen it is my wish that the cost of said Piano to wit thirty dollars shall be deducted for her portion of my estate & that amount be equally divided among the rest of my children. 19 Jan. 1836."

W. S. Pryor

At a Court of Monthly Session held for Hanover County at the Courthouse on Tuesday 24 March 1840. This last will and testament of William S. Pryor, dec'd. was proved by oaths of Philip B. Winston and Wm. O. Winston, as to the deceased's handwriting.

WILLIAM S. PRYOR, of Hanover. Will dated 19 January 1835, Codicil 19 January 1835. Probated 24 March 1840. Appointed son William W. Pryor, Executor, who dying before his father, William T. H. Pollard was appointed Administrator and Guardian of the infant children, until his death in 1856. Will mentions deceased wife Joanna W., and son Horace. Issue as of 1857:

1. BENJAMAN P. PRYOR, married "B.F." - only initials being stated.
2. JOHN PRYOR.

3. SUSAN B., wife of Charles Patterson of
   Buckingham County, Va., in 1853.
4. MARTHA ELLEN, wife of James D. Christian,
   Clerk of Hanover County in 1857. On 24
   February 1852, the heirs of John B.
   Green, dec'd, for consideration of $575.
   00, conveyed 130 acres to Wm. T. H. Pollard, Trustee for Martha Ellen, wife of
   James D. Christian. Green's heirs were:
   1. George Green, 2. Thomas N. Green and
   Jane his wife, 3. John D. Thomas and
   Frances A. J., his wife, and 4 Martha E.
   Green. James D. Christian and Martha E.,
   had issue in 1857:
   1. SUSAN T.(or C.) wife of Benjamin E.
      Smith, Jr.
   2. JOANNA P., wife of Ambrose W. Binns.
   3. ELLEN D., wife of John M. Rudd.
   4. CATHERINE C. (KATE O.), wife of War-
      ner L. Fleming.
   5. WILLIAM P. CHRISTIAN.
   6. VIRGINIA CHRISTIAN.
   7. HORACE CHRISTIAN.
   8. ELIZABETH A. (LIZZIE) CHRISTIAN.
   9. PERCY CHURCHILL CHRISTIAN.
   10. JAMES D. CHRISTIAN, JR.
5. WILLIAM W. PRYOR, appointed by his father
   Executor, but died. Does not appear to
   have left issue.
6. THOMAS HENRY PRYOR, mentioned in will only.
Others mentioned: William Pollard, late of Hanover, for many years owned a water grist mill
on Crump's Creek, which adjoined lands of Laney
Jones, dec'd. After death of Pollard land passed to his son, George William Pollard; Edwin
Shelton 1857; Benjamin E. Smith, Jr. 1860.

PRICE'S EXORS. VS. ANDREWS & OTHER, 1839 (33)

Thomas Price's Will

PRICE, THOMAS. "In the name of God. I, Thomas Price of the County of Hanover do make
& ordain this my last Will & Testament revoking all other Wills heretofore made. I give
to my wife Elizabeth T. Price for and during
her natural life all my lands on the east side
of the Road leading from Fork Church to the
road called Stanley's Road and all my Lands on
the North Side of the road leading from the
Newfound Mills to Scotch Town with all the buildings and improvements to the said Lands appertaining and also one lot of land adjoining the
Fork Church now occupied by Mordecai Page with
appurtenances - and the following slaves: Shop,
Henry, Fleming's Peter, Louisa, Yellow John,
Miller Joe, Shoe Maker Joe, Martin, Hanna, Waller, Caty, Homes, Randolph, Martha daughter of
Shop, Harry, Mirna, Daphne and child Patty and
Clarissa with the increase of the females after
the date hereof and the following perishable
property To wit all Merchandise which may be in
my store at the time of my death, my carriage

and horses, four other work horses or mules,
twenty head of cattle, twenty head of sheep,
thirty head of hogs and all household and kitch
en furniture used at my residence at the time
of my decease or such part of it as she may
choose, my said wife having the privilege of
selecting the horses and stock given her from
such as I may be possessed of at the time of
death. I also give to my said wife one year's
provisions of corn, Bacon, pork, flour, et al
the said provisions if I shall die on the first
day of March, on the said first day of March
next ensuing otherwise on the first day of January next ensuing my decease. And after the
decease of my said wife I give all the property
devised or bequeathed to her to & unto my two
executors hereinafter named the survivor of
them his heirs or assigns, for and during the
natural life of my son James W. Price - In trus
nevertheless to permit my said son to have the
possession and take the profits thereon during
his natural life to his own proper use and behoof, but not to allow said property or any
part thereof to be in any wise subject to the
contract or disposition of my said son.   And
after the death of my said son to settle the
said property real and personal upon any child
or children lawfully begotten of my said son
living at the time of his death (and the representatives of such as may be dead leaving such
if any there be, in portions according to the
Law of Virginia in fee simple - and in default
of such children or representatives said
property to go with the residue of my estate
and to be disposed of as hereafter directed. I
also give to my said son one horse, Saddle and
Bridle of the value of one hundred and fifty
dollars. And I moreover give to my said Executors the survivivor and his assigns the sum of
five thousand dollars to bear Interest from the
day of my death for and during the natural life
of my son James W. in trust to pay the Interest
thereof Sem-annually to my said son for his own
proper use during his said life and thereafter
to be disposed of in the said manner as directe
in relation to the other property devised or
bequeathed for the benefit of my said son). I
give to my son Lucien B. Price one negro boy
named Braxton and one negro man named Walker. :
also release my said son from all demands I may
have against him on open account or specially
upon condition that he shall execute a similar
release to my estate. I give to my said son .
the two tracts of land I severally purchased of
Carter B. Page and the Trustees of Samuel Gist
lying before Hanover Courthouse and adjoining
the lands of Andrew Stevenson, Benjamin Wingfield, William Carter and others with all the
buildings & improvements thereunto appertaining, to him and his heirs. But if my said son
should depart this life leaving no children
living at the time of his death then it is my
will that said lands and all other property
which may come or fall to my said son under

his will should be and remain to my two executors hereinafter named the survivor of them his
heirs and assigns in Trust for the residuary
purposes hereinafter mentioned. I give to my
son Thadius Price one negro boy named Leonard &
one horse saddle and Bridle of the value of one
hundred and fifty dollars. I also give to my
two Executors hereafter named for and during the
natural life of my said son the sum of five
thousand Dollars to bear interest from the day
of my death. In trust to lay the said sum out
at interest to the best advantage and to pay
the Interest semi-annually as well before the
investment thereof as after to or for the use
and benefit of my said son during his natural
life and after his death In trust to dispose of
the same according to the limitations directed
with regard to the sum of money hereinbefore
bequeathed for the benefit of my son James W.
give to my Grandson Thomas P. Temple the tract
of land called Richardsons & Birds lying on
Beaver Creek and between the two roads, the one
leading from Newfound Mills to Negrofoot with
all and singular the appertenances to him and
his heirs forever subject nevertheless to the
limitations herein before prescribed for the
land devised to my son Lucien B. Price. I also
bequeath to my said Grandson one-fifth part of
all my slaves not herein specifically bequeathed
subject to like limitations, but all upon the
express condition that he relinquish to and for
the benefit of his sisters all interest whatso-
ver in the estate of his late father and
mother. I give to my daughter Camilla Price
one negro Girl and the sum of Ten thousand Dollars. And to my daughter Mary Randolph Price
one negro girl named Julianna and the like sum
of Ten thousand Dollars. And I do direct that
the said slaves and money and all slaves money
or other property herein devised or bequeathed
immediately to my said daughters shall be and
remain in the hands of my Executor hereafter
named, the survivor, his heirs or assigns. In
trust to permit them severally to take the
profits and to have the benefit thereof during
their natural lives to their sole and separate
se not subject to the control and free from
the control or disposition of any husband or
husbands they may severally marry - And at their
several decease to settle the same on their
child or children severally according to the Law
of Virginia in fee simple. And if either of
them shall depart this life leaving no child
living at the time of her death or issue of such
as may have died. Then to pay and deliver the
same over to the residuary purposes hereinafter
provided for. And I appoint my Executors or the
survivor Guardians or Guardian for my said daugh-
ers. I give and devise all the rest and residue of my estate real and personal & all remainer or remainders which may result from the
limitations of this my will to and unto my two
executors hereafter named the survivor his heirs
or assigns. In trust as to the said real estate

to sell and convert the same into money at the
earliest day and upon such terms as may be most
advisable - And the whole of said property the
personal forthwith and the real as early as may
be to divide in five portions. One-fifth portion whereof I give to my son Lucien B. Price
subject nevertheless to like limitations as are
subscribed for the real estate heretofore devised to him. One other portion each to my said
daughters Camilla and Mary R. Price subject as
to their portions of the residue which may be
left at my death to the conditions and limitations heretofore prescribed for their portions,
and as to any portions of the aforesaid resul-
ting remainders in fee simple. One other portion I give and bequeath to be divided between
my Granddaughters Barbara O. and Elizabeth Thilman. But upon the express condition nevertheless that if at any time their mother should
be in a state of poverty and destitution they
shall pay to her in equal Portions the annual
sum of one hundred and fifty Dollars during her
said necessity - And if they or either of them
shall fail to do so then the said portions to
be entirely forfeited & go to my Executors for
the residuary Trust herein provided for - said
payments to be made by my Granddaughters to my
said Executors to Survivor or his assigns upon
their or his demand and to be for the sole use
and benefit of their said Mother - And one
other fifth part (except as to the one-fifth
of my slaves left at the time of death not
specifically bequeathed which I have already
bequeathed to my grandson Thomas P. Temple and
which are nevertheless designed to form part of
said dividend) I give to be equally divided
between my Granddaughters Maria Louisa, Ella
and Eugenia Temple the portions nevertheless
assigned to my Granddaughters Barbara O. &
Elizabeth Thilman & to my Granddaughters Maria
Louisa, Eugenia & Ella Temple to be charged
with the sum of four thousand dollars each for
advances severally made heretofore to their
parents. And it is my will that all property
which may fall to my said Granddaughters shall
be and remain in the hands of my Executors,
their survivor, or his assigns in Trust to
appropriate the incomes of the same for their
benefit severally until they shall severally
arrive at full age or marry - And upon their
or either of their so arriving at the full age
or marrying to deliver and pay over her several
portions to her for her own use & behoof. - And
if the said Barbara O. or Elizabeth shall either
of them depart this life within the age of
twenty-one years and unmarried to pay the whole
to the Survivor of them and if they both so die
then the whole to the residuary purposes herein
provided for. And if either of my said Granddaughters Maria Louisa, Ella or Eugenia shall
so die then the whole continually to the survivors, and if they shall all so die then over
in like manner. And I hereby release to the
estate of my late son in Law John S. Temple all

demands whatsoever which I may have upon the
same. Upon condition that my Grandchildren,
children of the said John S. shall release my
estate from all and every demand arising from
contract or otherwise - Not intending to release or give up any balance which may be due
me as Trustee or administrator of said Temple
and his wife - children. And in as much as I
am desirous of preventing any litigation or controversy arising under or upon this my Will I
do direct that if any such difference should
occur the parties interested in the same should
faithfully submit the said controversy to two
intelligent and disinterested free holders of
the neighborhood, one to be selected by the person or persons interested on the one side and
the other to be selected by the person or persons interested of the other side, or their
umpire and if any person or persons so as aforesaid interested shall fail in good faith & in a
reasonable time to agree to said reference & to
appoint or join in appointing said reference as
aforesaid or shall not submit to or any abide
the award & arbitration, so as aforesaid made,
he she or they so failing, shall immediately
forfeit & loose all devises portions or bequests
to them made or for their benefit in this my
Will the same to result if my said Executors
general Trustees, for the residuary purposes
hereinbefore expressed. Finally I constitute
and appoint my son Lucien B. Price and my
nephew Charles William Dabney Executors of this
my last will & testament. In Testimony of all
which I have signed sealed & published this my
last will and Testament this 28th day of June
one thousand eight hundred & thirty-four. "

                         Thos Price (Seal)
Signed sealed & published in presence of us & by
us subscribed in the presence of the Testator
at his request:
      Benj Pollard
      Wm. O. Winston
      B. L. Winston

"Codicil I hereby revoke the bequest of **five**
thousand Dollars to trustees for the benefit of
my son James W. Price and direct that the same
shall go with the general residue of my estate.
Signed sealed and published as a Codicil to my
last will and Testament this 5th Feb. 1838"

                         Thos Price (Seal)

"Codicil 2d. The bequest in this my last will to
my son James I hereby In consequence of his
intemperate extravagent habits and I give the
whole of the bequest made my said son to Lucien
B. Price under the same limitations & restrictions that my son James would have held said
legacy having the most implicit confidence in
my said son Lucien's magnaminity and generosity
dont entertain a doubt that he will bestow
liberally to James if he conducts himself pru-

dently. I further more constitute and appoint
Benjamin Pollard as my Exor in place of Charles
W. Dabney. As witness my hand & seal this 4th
July 1838."
                         Thos Price (Seal)

At a Court of Monthly Session held for Hanover
County at the Courthouse on Tuesday the 27th of
November 1838. This last will and Testament of
Thomas Price, dec'd, and the Codicils thereafte
written and annexed were offered for proof by
Lucien B. Price one of the Executors in the
will named and Benjamin Pollard, Jr., called in
the last of the said Codicils Benjamin Pollard,
also an Executor in the last Codicil named and
the said will was proved by the oaths of Willia
O. Winston and B. L. Winston witnesses thereto
and Thomas R. Price and Charles W. Dabney being
sworn declare that they are well acquainted wit
the handwriting of the said Thomas Price, that
they have examined the said Codicils and verily
believe the same to have been wholly written an
subscribed by him. Whereupon the said will and
Codicils are ordered to be recorded.
      Test, Philip B. Winston, C.H.C.
      A Copy, Teste, Wm. O. Winston, C.H.C.

THOMAS PRICE, of Hanover. Will dated 28 June
1834. Codicils 5 Feb. 1838, 4 July 1838. Pro
bated 27 November 1838. He was generally known
as Captain Thomas Price, Jr. of "Newfound Mills
His plantation called "Dundee." In his lifetime
had obtained a decree in the Superior Court of
Law and Chancery of Goochland County against
his son-in-law, John D. Andrews, in the amount
of $942.73. Since this suit of Hanover is not
one involving the Testator's Estate, we do not
have a complete list of his children:
  1. JAMES W. PRICE.
  2. LUCIEN B. PRICE.
  3. THADIUS PRICE.
  4. [   ] dec'd, married John S. Temple,
     also dec'd in 1834, leaving issue:
     1. MARIA LOUISA TEMPLE.
     2. ELLA TEMPLE.
     3. EUGENIA TEMPLE.
  5. [   ] daughter, married Mr. Thilman;
     He appears to be dec'd in 1834, leaving
     issue: (She removed to Texas prior 1839)
     1. BARBARA O. THILMAN, removed to Texas
     2. ELIZABETH THILMAN. removed to Texas.
  6. CAMILLA PRICE.
  7. MARY RANDOLPH PRICE.
  8. EUGENIA, wife of John D. Andrews, who at
     one time operated the Tavern at Hanover
     Courthouse, which he conveyed to Francis
     Nelson. Andrews entered into a partner-
     ship agreement with a Mr. Wilson and
     another party of Baltimore for the opera-
     tion of a mercantile business in the
     town of Houston, Texas. Andrews was ther
     in 1837, and his wife was to follow by
     boat in October 1838. Later they returne
     to Virginia. He had brothers: Lewis An-

drews of Orange County, and William H. Andrews of Spotsylvania County, Va., also a brother Samuel Andrews who acted as his Agent whilst in Texas. In 1839, John D. Andrews and Eugenia, his wife, had issue, a son:
1. JAMES ANDREWS.

Joseph F. Price of Hanover, brother of Capt. Thos. Price, Jr.

Others mentioned: Richard Archer, Teller, Bank of Virginia 1839; Ira S. Bowles; William B. Dabney, Teller, Bank of Virginia 1839; John S. Fleming, Attorney 1834, Goochland County; Dr. John P. Harrison; John Hoskins 1839; Peyton R. Johnson; George B. Mason 1839; Cary Nelson; Major Powers of Goochland; Wesley Saunders; Francis G. Taylor, at home of William D. Taylor at Taylorsville, deposition.

PRIDDY'S EXOR VS. PRIDDY, 1834 (31)

Thomas Priddy's Will

PRIDDY, THOMAS. "In the name of God Amen. I, Thomas Priddy of the City of Richmond and state of Virginia being of sound memory but aware of the uncertainty of this life do make and ordain this my last Will and Testament, revoking all others that may have been made by me. Item. I give my soul to the Almighty God, from whom it was received, with the hope that it may enjoy eternal happiness in his presence. Item 2d. I request my executor (hereinafter named) will first pay all funeral expenses &c and then all my just debts, which are very triffling after paying sisters Jane and Catherine their a/c p. my book. Item 3. I give and bequeath to Miss Susan Thomas my house and lot in the City of Richmond, in the valley on I Street, with all the improvements thereon, to herself forever, in fee, and also I give to the said Susan Thomas, the sum of six hundred dollars in cash, to be raised immediately by collection or otherwise, to be paid the first that comes to hand. I also give my bed & furniture & steads - indeed every description of furniture in the room (ex cepting my two writing desks, mahogany, and my books. Item 4. I give and bequeath unto Susan Thomas' son William Henry, born 30th December 1829, all the remainder of my estate real and personal to him forever, to be invested in some safe fund that will bring an interest. I desire that he may be sent to some good school as early as necessary. Then my executor will apply in part or the whole of the interest as may be necessary for his the sd Wm Henry's board and schooling . After receiving his education it is my desire that he be bound to some good trade or business to his own liking. After he is bound out it is my desire that he may be furnished with a part of the

interest as pocket money, the balance to be invested in some Stock carrying interest, until he the sd Wm. Henry shall arrive at the age of twenty years; then my executor will please consider him free, and hand him whatever he may have in his hands bequeathed to the said Wm. Henry. Keep my watch for Wm. Henry. I request that my old friend Philip B. Winston of Hanover County will act as my executor; and I give and bequeath him my two mahogany writing desks; and I most earnestly desire that my executor will (if agreeable to him) he will take the boy & manage his affairs for him until he arrives at the age of twenty one years; if he would be so kind as to take this boy himself, or put him out in good hands to bring him up properly. Should Susan Thomas and Wm. Henry, both or either of them die before Wm. Henry becomes of age then I desire that it may go to the survivor of them; should both die, then, I wish it equally divided amongst my brothers & sisters children (excepting brother Robert's they are to have nothing). In testimony of this my last will and testament, I have hereunto set my hand and seal this 8th July 1831."

Tho Priddy (Seal)

At a Court of Hustings, held for the City of Richmond, at the Courthouse, the 27th day of January 1832: The last will and testament of Thomas Priddy dec'd was produced in Court and there be no subscribing witnesses thereto, Nath[l] Glenn was sworn and William I. Clark affirmed, and severally deposed that they were well acquainted with the handwriting of the said deceased, and verily believe that the said will and the name thereto subscribed, are wholly written by the said Thomas Priddy's own hand whereupon the said will is ordered to be recorded. And on the motion of Philip B. Winston the executor therein named who made oath and entered into bond, as required by the Act passed the 16 February 1825, with Charles P. Goodall, Nathaniel C. Crenshaw and Jesse Winn his securities, in the penalty of forty thousand dollars conditioned as required by the said Act, the said Goodall justified on oath as to $8,000, the said Crenshaw on affirmation as to $24,000, and the said Winn affirmation as to $8,000. Certificate is granted him for obtaining a probat of the said will in due form.
Teste, Th. C. Howard, Clk.
A Copy, Teste, Th. C. Howard, Clk.

THOMAS PRIDDY, of Hanover and the City of Richmond, Va. Will dated 8 July 1831. Probated by Philip B. Winston, Executor, 27 Jan. 1832. This suit involves a Deed of Trust executed by John L. Priddy and Sally his wife of Hanover, dated 11 June 1827, covering 74 1/2 acres of land four miles from Hanover Courthouse. The said John L. Priddy being indebted to Thos. Priddy. No further mention of legatees in the suit.

JNO. C. PULLIAM VS. PULLIAM, 1832 (31)

PULLIAM, JOHN C., of Hanover County, married Elizabeth W. Cocke (deceased in 1832) a daughter of the late Benjamin Cocke, Jr., and his wife Elizabeth. Cocke died intestate, possessed of a considerable estate, including 394 acres of land in Fluvanna County which was allotted to John C. Pulliam for life. He and Elizabeth W., his wife, had issue:
1. MARTHA W. PULLIAM.
2. ELIZABETH JANE PULLIAM.

PULLIAM &C. VS. PULLIAM'S ADMR.&C., 1853 (31)

Stephen T. Pulliam's Will (Abstract)

PULLIAM, STEPHEN T. "I, Stephen T. Pulliam of the County of Hanover do hereby make, publish and declare the following writing as and for my last will and testament hereby revoking all other and former wills by me made. Item 1st. My will and desire is that all my just debts be paid by my executors hereinafter named. 2d. I have in my possession three slaves named John, Elizabeth & Nancy, children of a woman named Franky Kinney formerly of the estate of John Richardson dec'd that I purchased some years past as a sale of the slaves of the said John Richardson dec'd made by Commissioners at Hanover Courthouse, feeling a great attachment for the said slaves John, Elizabeth and Nancy and being determined that they shall never serve any other person as slaves: I do hereby emancipate and set free my said three slaves John, Elizabeth and Nancy children of the said Franky Kinney and do moreover declare in pursuance of the Act of the General Assembly of the Commonwealth of Virginia passed the 2d of March 1819 entitled "An Act reducing into one the several Acts covering slaves, free negroes and mulattoes" the said John, Elizabeth & Nancy being mulatto slaves shall from and after the day of my death be entirely and fully discharged from the performance of any contract entered into (by me or any other person) during their servitude and that the said John, Elizabeth and Nancy shall each enjoy as full freedom as if they had been particularly named and freed by the said Act of the General Assembly. 3d. I do hereby give and devise to each of my said slaves, John, Elizabeth and Nancy emancipated and set free by me in the second item in this my will above specified the sum of two thousand dollars each to them and their heirs or the survivor or survivors of him, her or them, if either of them shall die without lawful issue. 4th. I do hereby request and direct my executors as soon as convenient after my death and particularly within the time limited by law for their remaining within this Commonwealth after their right of freedom accrues to remove them to the City of Philadelphia and on their arrival in the City of Philadelphia pay to them six thousand dollars, that is to say, two thousand dollars to each of them, or in proportion as the case may be, if either of them be dead without leaving lawful issue, but if either one or more of them be dead leaving lawful issue, then the issue of such one or more of them that may be dead, to be entitled and shall receive the proportion of the said six thousand dollars that the parent of such issue would have been entitled to if living, and to enable my said executors to pay the said six thousand dollars together with the expenses attending the removal of the said John Elizabeth and Nancy, I do hereby direct them to use any money remaining after the payment of my debts that I may be possessed of or may be due to me at my death, and if necessary to sell any portion of my other estate that in their discretion they may deem best to raise the deficiency that may be required to raise the sum of six thousand dollars and the additional sum necessary to defray the expenses of removal aforesaid." In the event of his marriage : "which is contemplated" makes provision for her and any children born to them. Should he not marry, then the residue of his estate "in trust to my friends Nathaniel Crenshaw, Joseph J. Pleasants and Walter Crew, and their successors to keep the remainder of the slaves on the lands he owns or may be entitled to, to cultivate etc. for the benefit of the said slaves "it being my wish and desire that my said trustees shall extend to my said slaves all the indulgence and privilege consistent with the character and relation of human masters and obedient servants, that can be extended to them without a violation of the laws of Virginia." Should they become "so numerous they cannot make a reasonable support on my land . . . trustees, if they deem it best for my slaves, that they shall be removed from the Commonwealth, then full power and authority is hereby given and granted to my said Trustees . . . to sell all my lands hereinbefore devised in trust . . . to manumit, emancipate and set free all my said slaves, and their increase, then living, and put them under the control of the Colonization Society to be removed to Africa or any other place under the supervision of said society, and then to deliver to the said slaves the proceeds of the sale of my said lands after deducting therefrom all necessary expenses attending the execution of this item of my will for their joint use & support." 10th. All the rest and residue of my estate not disposed of by this my will I give and devise to be equally divided between my brother and sister George Washington Pulliam & Nancy M. Mitchell, to them & their heirs forever. Lastly I do hereby appoint my friends Nathaniel Crenshaw, Joseph J. Pleasants & Walter Crew executors of this my last will & testament & having full confidence in them I do hereby direct that they shall not give any security for executing this my will.

In testimony whereof I do hereby declare the foregoing to be my last will & testament & affix my hand & seal this 3d day of September in the year 1847. "

S. T. Pulliam (Seal)

Signed, sealed & acknowledged by Stephen T. Pulliam as & for his last will & testament in our presence & we being requested by him to witness it as his last will & Testament.

   Benj. Anderson
   Richard L. Wade
   Aug. K. Bowles
   Jesse T. Bowles
   Jos. K. Bowles

At a Court of Monthly Session held for Hanover County at the Courthouse on Tuesday the 28th of January 1851. This last will and testament of Stephen T. Pulliam dec'd was proved by the oaths of Aug. K. Bowles and Jos. K. Bowles witnesses thereto and is ordered to be recorded.

Teste, Wm. O. Winston, C.H.C.
A Copy, Teste, Wm. O. Winston, C.H.C.

STEPHEN T. PULLIA M, of Hanover. Will dated 3 September 1847. Probated 28 January 1851. He appointed Nathaniel Crenshaw, Joseph J. Pleasants and Walter Crew, Executors. None qualified. Charles W. Dabney and George Doswell qualified as Administrators with the will annexed. Pulliam never married, and died without lawful legal issue. His next of kin being his brothers and sisters:
   1. GEORGE WASHINGTON PULLIAM, a brother, who lived with Stephen T. Pulliam at the time of the latter's death. George W. Pulliam came to Stephen's house "from the West." Aged about 60, in 1852.
   2. FRANCES W., wife of a Mr. Armstrong.(sister)
   3. WILLIAM W. PULLIAM, a brother.
   4. NANCY M. wife of a Mr. Mitchell.
Stephen T. Pulliam possessed two small tracts of land and some slaves. He was engaged in the merchandising business. The emancipated slaves John Pulliam, Elizabeth Pulliam and Nancy Pulliam - the last two infants in 1852 - were then residents of Philadelphia, where they had been located in accordance with Stephen T. Pulliam's will.

Others mentioned: Creditors of Pulliam - Ellen Lindsay, Extx of William Lindsay , dec'd; Wm. O. Winston, Committee of Simeon Souther, Edwin Turner, assignee of Eleanor Brooks, Maria Fleming, Peter Guerrant, Leroy D. Toler, George Turner, Valentine, Breeden & Co., Matthews & Timberlake, John S. Fleming, Price O. T. Armstrong. Witnesses: William Wiltshire 1852; Thomas M. Woodson 1852.

FROM OLD WILL BOOK, PAGE 79

ROANE, WILLIAM H., dec'd. daughter Sarah A. L., orphan. James Lyons appointed Gdn. 12 Apr.1847

RAGLAND'S ADMR. VS. RAGLAND & OTHERS, 1833 (36)

Gideon Ragland's Will

RAGLAND, GIDEON. "In the name of God amen. I, Gideon Ragland of Hanover County and Parish of Saint Paul being sick and a very low state of Health and small hopes of recovery - do make and ordain this to be my last will and testament Revoking all other wills heretofore made by me. In the first place I recommend my soul unto the hands of Almighty god who gave it me, and my body to the Earth to be buried in a christian like manner by my Executors hereafter mentioned. In the first place I give and bequeath to my son John Ragland a tract of land lying on Stoney Run containing one hundred and fifty-five acres be the same more or less known by the name of Gilcrest's tract on the conditions as follows that is to say, if he continues in the shaking way that he now is in to the age of twenty-one years, and should be adjudged not capable of getting his living, but if he should die before he comes of age or without an heir lawfully begotten of his body then my desire is that it should be sold and the money equally divided among my other surviving children. I lend to my beloved wife (Mary Ragland) during her life or widowhood the Land whereon I now live, also the land in Stoney Run untill my son John Ragland becomes of age, likewise all my negroes, stock of all kinds, Household and Kitchen furniture, plantation utensils, for the benefit of bringing up and Schooling my children dureing her life or widowhood also she shall not rent the Lands nor hire out the negroes, nor waste the Estate in any manner whatsoever, and at her death or marriage, my Estate of Land, negroes (and their increase) stock of all kind, Household and Kitchen furniture, plantation utensils should be equally divided between Abner Ragland, James Ragland, Betsey Ragland, Nancy Ragland, Polley Ragland, John Ragland, Reuben Ragland and to my young son not Baptized and in case any of my children should die before he or she becomes of age, or has a lawful heir then to be equally divided among the survivors. I appoint my son Abner Ragland and John Cross, Executors to this my last will and Testament. As witness my hand and seal this twenty-fourth day of July one thousand seven hundred and ninety-five."

Gideon Ragland, (Seal)

Signed sealed and proclaimed in presence of
   John Martin
   George Davis
   Henritty (+) Davis
   Lucy (+) Davis

At a Court held for Hanover County at the Courthouse on Thursday the 1st of October 1795. This last will and Testament of Gideon Ragland,

dec'd, was offered for proof and was proved by the oath of John Martin, George Davis and Lucy Davis, three of the subscribing witnesses thereto and is ordered to be recorded.
    Teste, William Pollard, C.H.C.
    A Copy, Teste, Philip B. Winston, C.H.C.

GIDEON RAGLAND, of Hanover. Will dated 24 July 1795. Probated 1 October 1795. Appointed John Cross and his son Abner Ragland, Executors. Apparently neither qualified. Henry Pollard was appointed Administrator de bonis non. The widow Mary Ragland also had qualified as Administrator. Testator possessed 300 acres of land and 19 slaves. Survived by his widow, Mary, dec'd in 1833, and by children; stated to have been 8 in number, but only 7 are named:

1. BETSEY, dec'd in 1833, survived by her husband, Henry Pollard of near Montpelier, Hanover, and six children:
  1. WILLIAM R. POLLARD.
  2. HENRY S. E. POLLARD.
  3. ELLA, wife of John Tiller.
  4. REUBEN P. POLLARD, a minor in 1833.
  5. HEZEKIAH G. POLLARD, a minor in 1833.
  6. JAMES M. POLLARD, a minor in 1833.
2. ABNER RAGLAND, dec'd in 1833, survived by his widow, Nancy Ragland, a resident in 1833, of Putnam County, Ga., and by seven children:
  1. REUBEN RAGLAND, of Putnam Co., Ga.
  2. RICHARD RAGLAND, of Putnam Co., Ga.
  3. POLLY, wife of Nelson C. Elliott, of Putnam Co., Ga.
  4. WILLIAM RAGLAND, of Monroe County, Ga., in 1836 appoints William B. Right of Pittsylvania County, Va., "lawful attorney for my interest in my late father Abner Ragland, late of Jones County, Va." ?
  5. EDWARD RAGLAND, a minor in 1836 and living in Monroe County, Ga.
  6. JOHN RAGLAND, a minor in 1839, and living in Pike County, Ga.
  7. NANCY RAGLAND, in 1833, of Putnam Co., Georgia.
3. JAMES RAGLAND.
4. NANCY, widow of John Brooks in 1833.
5. MARY (POLLY), widow of Charles Jarvis in 1833. The following appear to be her daughters, but not definitely mentioned as such:
  1. ANN M. JARVIS.
  2. ELIZA JARVIS.
6. REUBEN RAGLAND, of Powhatan County, in 1833 Subletts, post office. 1836, Flat Rock, Powhatan County.
7. JOHN RAGLAND.

Others mentioned: John A. Lancaster of Richmond.

    Note: In the will of Gideon Ragland, mention is made of unbaptized son. Probably dec'd.

LANKFORD'S EXOR. VS. BOWE'S EXOR., 1840 (24)
STARKE &C. VS. RAGLAND'S ADMR. &C. 1841 (39)

Pettus Ragland's Will

RAGLAND, PETTUS. "In the name of God amen. I, Pettus Ragland of the County of Hanover; calling to mind the mortality of my body, and knowing that it is appointed for all men once to die, do make & ordain this my last will & testament that is to say principally, & first of all, I give and recommend my Soul unto the hands of almighty God that gave it, and my body I recommend to the earth, to be buried in a decent Christian buriel at the discretion of my Executors, and as touching my worldly estate, wherewith it has pleased God to bless me in this life, after paying all my just debts, I give devise and dispose of the same in the following manner and form i.e. To my daughter Jane Chick I give one negro girl named Riah now in her possession with her present & future increase, & a boy by the name of Peter to her & her heirs forever. Secondly, I give to my son John Ragland & his heirs forever one negro man, named Harry now in his possession. Thirdly I give to my son William Ragland and his heirs forever one negro man named James whom my Son has Sold. Further, I give to my Son Evan Ragland & his heirs forever one negro boy named Arthur Said Slave was by him Sold. Fifthly I give and devise to my son Pettus Ragland and his heirs forever a tract of land in Halifax County on which he is now in possession containing by estimation three hundred & six acres, together with a negro man named Randolph, now in his possession, as his and their property forever. Sixthly I give to my daughter Sarah Rice and her heirs forever one negro girl named Criss now in her possession with her present and future increase together with a negro girl named Sukey and her increase, as her & their property forever. Seventhly I give to my daughter Martha Ragland and her heirs forever one negro girl named Milley now in her possession with her present & future increase, a negro boy named Harry, all that part of my land lying on the north side of the north branch adjoining David Hanes and Oliver Cross, tho not including another piece of land I have adjoining David Hanes and John King on the Same Side of the said branch but that only which is herein particularily specified, a bay mare and fold formerly the property of Richard Priddy, one feather bed & furniture and ten pounds as her and their property forever. Eighthly. I give to my daughter Elizabeth Right now dead & her heirs forever one negro boy named Peter which boy was in her possession before her death and to the children of the said Elizabeth I give one negro girl named Rhina to them & their heirs forever. Ninthly I give to my daughter Ann Starkes children (to wit John, Elizabeth and Wyatt seventy two pounds being the price of a slave I gave the said Ann which with her and Joseph Starke her husband's consent, I sold for the above Sum to be paid them out of my estate,)- lent my wife. Tenthly I lend to my daughter Ann Starke one hundred acres land to be laid off of the plantation known by the name of Hixes so as to include the plantation during her life, and a negro girl named Scillar all of which at her death to be equally divided amongst her children i.e. John, Elizabeth and Wyatt, and one feather bed and furniture to her & her heirs forever also I give to my son Fendall Ragland and his heirs forever the residue of my land reserving to my well beloved wife Elizabeth Ragland one-third part of the said Land Should my said son think proper I alot the same to her and at her death I give unto my said son the said land so laid off to my wife together with the aforementioned residue as also a negro boy named Skelton & a feather bed & furniture as his & their property forever. And I lend to my beloved wife Elizabeth Ragland during her natural life or widowhood the remainder of my estate be it of what kind or nature soever and at her death or marriage to be equally divided amongst my children and such as may be dead for their children to receive their fathers or mothers part as the case may be in the same manner as their father or mother would have received provided they were living at the time of my death. But lastly and finally I constitute and appoint my three sons John, William and Fendall Ragland Executors to this my last will and Testament disallowing revoking & disannulling all & every other former testament, wills legacies and Executors by me in any wise made hereby ratifying & confirming this & no other to be my last will & testament. In witness whereof I have hereunto affixed my hand & seal this first day of December Anno domini eighteen hundred & six." presence of

     Pettus Ragland (Seal)

Signed Sealed Acknowledged
& delivered in presence of
 Nath¹ Tinsley
 A. Ragland
 Nathan Hanes
 John Nowell

At a Court of Monthly Session held for Hanover County at the Courthouse on Wednesday the 28th of January 1807. This last will and testament of Pettus Ragland dec'd was offered for proof by John Ragland one of the Executors therein named, and was proved by the oaths of Nathaniel Tinsley, A. Ragland and John Nowell, Witnesses thereto: and also by the oath of the said Executor & is ordered to be recorded.

Teste, William Pollard, C.H.C.

A Copy,

   Teste, William Pollard, C.H.C.

PETTUS RAGLAND, of Hanover. Will dated 1 Dec. 1806. Probated 28 January 1807. Appointed sons John, William and Fendall Ragland, Executors. Only John qualified. His Securities were Fendall Ragland, Absolom Ragland, John Bowe, Reuben Martin, and Nathaniel Bowe. Personal Estate included seven slaves, and was appraised in 1807 by Shelton Ragland, Sterling Lankford and James Lankford, value 712.12.0 Lbs. Survived by his widow, Elizabeth, and issue:

1. JANE, wife of a Mr. Chick.
2. JOHN RAGLAND, Executor.
3. WILLIAM RAGLAND.
4. EVAN RAGLAND.
5. PETTUS RAGLAND, who was devised a tract of land in Halifax County, (Va.?)
6. SARAH, wife of a Mr. Rice.
7. MARTHA RAGLAND.
8. ELIZABETH WRIGHT, dec'd, wife of a Mr. Wright. She had issue in 1840 three sons:
 1. WILLIAM WRIGHT, of Goochland, who assigned his interest in the Ragland Estate to John England.
 2. [ ] a brother.
 3. [ ] a brother.
9. ANN, wife of Joseph Starke, who had issue:
 1. JOHN P. STARKE, a grandson of Pettus Ragland, assigned in 1813 his interest in Estate (excepting the land sold to John King) to Sterling Lankford. The witnesses to this conveyance were John L. England and Samuel (+) Butler.
 2. ELIZABETH ANN STARKE.
 3. WYATT STARKE, "out of the state 20 years or more and not heard from."
10. FENDALL RAGLAND, died prior to 1840.

Others mentioned: Anderson Bowles, died with a will. Executors: Abraham P. and Jesse T. Bowles. Anderson Bowles had three sons; John Bowe,dec'd, William Bowe, Executor; Nathaniel Bowe, dec'd, Nathaniel Bowe, a son, Executor; William Davis 1795; Peter Deacon 1795; Hector Davis, Attorney and Executor in 1813 of Sterling Lankford,dec'd; Joseph Hix; N. C. Lipscomb 1816; Absolom Ragland, deceased in 1840; William Tinsley 1816; William M. Thomas, who keeps a Tavern in 1840.

RAGLAND &C. VS CHICK &C., 1854 (33)

CHICK, PETTUS W., of Hanover County, died circa 22 March 1854. Will dated 11 March 1854, probated 25 April 1854. William Bagby of Louisa County, Executor. His heirs were his brothers and sisters, of whom the following are concerned in this suit:

JOHN R. CHICK, a brother, who has issue perhaps among others:
 1. ANN SELDEN, wife of John Shelton Ragland of Richmond, Va.. in 1854.
PATSEY, a sister, wife of a Mr. Jones and has

probably among others:
1. ROBERT J. JONES.

DAVIS S. CHICK, a brother, who is married and living in Henrico County in 1854, and has a son, perhaps among others:
1. WILLIAM J. CHICK, of Richmond, Va. 1854.

Others mentioned in 1854: John E. Kelley, Samuel B. Ragland, and Powhatan L. Woodson in 1854 in Richmond.

RICHARDSON'S ADMR. VS. RICHARDSON
& OTHERS, 1832 (34)
PULLIAM VS. SCOTT & OTHERS, 1832 (28)
KENNON VS. RICHARDSON, 1836 (22)

RICHARDSON, JOHN. "Hanover County, July 30th 1825. On the 28th Inst. in the last illness of the late John Richardson of this County, the said Richardson apparently directing his discourse to George Fleming, Esq. and myself said that it was his wish that all those who were interested in his estate should contribute their proportions to make up the sum of one thousand Dollars for an illegitimate daughter called Jane, but added this gift is on condition that she lives not with her mother - for if this girl Jane lives with her mother I give her nothing - this was at a time when Mrs. Peter Wade and Mrs. Robt Pulliam the said Richardson's near relations were present. Given under my hand the day & date above."
Sandy L. Mayo.

At a Court of Monthly Session held for Hanover County at the Courthouse on Wednesday the 24th of August 1825. This writing purporting to be the nuncupative last will and Testament of John Richardson, dec'd was produced in Court and was proved by the oath of Sandy L. Mayo the witness thereto. And at a Court of like session held for the said County at the Courthouse on Monday the 28th of September then next following The said writing was further proved by the oath of George Fleming and is ordered to be recorded.
Teste, William Pollard
A Copy, Teste, Philip B. Winston, C.H.C.

JOHN RICHARDSON, of Hanover. Nuncupative will of 28 July 1825, probated 24 August 1825. Witnesses Sandy L. Mayo and George Fleming, Esq. None of his kin applied for administration, the Court appointed Francis W. Scott. In 1828 his certificate was revoked, and the Estate committed to Jesse Winn, High Sheriff. Left a considerable estate, including 417 acres of land (not subject to a nuncupative will) and between 30 and 40 slaves. Francis W. Scott hired some of the slaves to Stephen T. Pulliam who rehired to John Bowles, now dec'd 1832, to work on the James River Canal. Richardson was survived by his widow Judith who died in North Carolina on

12 June 1840. On 8 December 1837, Wm. Kennon of Caswell County, N. C. (Peter Wade, witness) certified that he lives about six or seven miles from Mrs. Judith Richardson, widow of John Richardson, late of Hanover County, and verily believes she is now in better health than she was before she left Virginia. She left no issue by Richardson. His illegitimate daughter:

JANE HOOPER, after the death of John Richardson "made her home in the family of David Richardson, and in the home of his mother and brother-in-law, until she married Charles B. Richardson." All of Louisa County.

John Richardson's only heirs at law were his seven sisters, and their children and grandchildren:

SALLY (PEGGY), a sister, died before John Richardson, married Beverley Glenn, who removed to North Carolina, and had issue, a son:
1. GEORGE GLENN, on 10 December 1836, living in Person County, North Carolina.

URSULA, a sister, married first, John Perkins who died prior to 1825, leaving four children
1. PLEASANT PERKINS, died unmarried prior to 1832.
2. LUCY PERKINS, married first Cornelius Grant, dec'd, who left issue:
    1. JOHN T. GRANT, died unmarried prior to 1832.
  Married secondly, Richard Cate, and had issue four children:
    2. MARTHA, dec'd in 1836, married Mordecai Hammonds, and had only issue:
        1. THOMAS HAMMONDS.
    3. SARAH P. CATE, of Person County, North Carolina, 1837.
    4. ISAIAH CATE, of Person Co., N.C. 1837
    5. URSULA, married a Mr. Wisdom. Living in Person County, N. C. in 1837.
3. DICE, dec'd, married Archibald Coleman, who survives in 1832, with one child:
    1. PLEASANT P. COLEMAN, of the State of Georgia.
4. SALLY PERKINS, died prior to 1825.
Ursula married secondly William Kennon who is also called William Cannon (signs his name both ways) of Yanceyville, Caswell County, North Carolina in 1836, when on 23 Sept., he conveyed to Anderson Bowles, as attorney in fact for his two sons, Richard R. Cannon and John Cannon, "all the right title, etc. in the lands belonging to their Uncle John Richardson in Hanover, also what are entitled to from the widow's dower - the said Cannon having purchased the life interest of the widow of the said John Richardson and all her dower in the said lands." Witness, J. D. Andrews.
(Signed)　William Cannon.

On 25 October 1836, David G. Mason and Hannah his wife, formerly Hannah Mayo, being a child of Robert Mayo, dec'd, of Chester District, South Carolina, whose wife was formerly Margaret Richardson, now dec'd, appoints Wm. Kennon of Caswell County North Carolina, their lawful attorney to recover all money, etc. due them from the Estate of John Richardson, dec'd, or may be due them at the death of Judith, wife of John Richardson, dec'd.

"8 December 1837 - Received of And. Bowles full satisfaction for all money due Josiah Cates, Sally P. Cates & Urly Wisdom from Est. of Jno. Richardson dec'd of Hanover Co. - due from sale of Decedants landed estate, I have sold to And Bowles - all that part to which Pleasant Coleman now of Georgia is entitled Supposed to be 1/27th, he being the grandson of Usly Kennon, formerly Ursely Richardson."

Wit.   William Kennon
   A. N. Lambert
   Peter Wade
   N. H. Wash

In 1839, Anderson Bowles was assignee of David G. Mason and Sarah, his wife, William T. Dandridge and Nancy, his wife, John Kennon and Richard Kennon, Isaiah Kate, and Ursula Wisdom.

"Know all men, that we, Isaiah Cates, Sarah Cates and Ursula Wisdom of County of Person, North Carolina, appts Wm. Cannon of Caswell Co., N. C. attorney for us to receive money due us as three heirs at law of John Richardson, dec'd of Hanover Co., Va."

William Kennon (or Cannon) and his wife, Ursula Richardson-Perkins, dec'd, had issue:
   1. RICHARD K. KENNON.
   2. JOHN KENNON

LIZABETH (BETTY), married John Mayo, and removed to North Carolina, where both died prior to 1832, leaving issue:
1. RICHARDSON MAYO, in 1828, living in Butts County, Ga.
2. THOMPSON MAYO, of Fairfield District, S.C.
3. JOHN MAYO, in 1829, of Perry Co., Alabama.
4. SARAH, wife of a Mr. Beam, and living in Fairfield District of South Carolina.
5. MOURNING, wife of John Floyd, of Butts County, Georgia.
6. NANCY, wife of Osborn Mayo.
7. ELIZABETH MAYO, dec'd.
8. HANNAH MAYO, dec'd.

ARGARET (PEGGY) also a sister, married Robert Mayo, both deceased in 1832, leaving issue:
1. JANE, dec'd, married William Hatcher.
2. SARAH, wife of John Coleman of Chester Dist.

South Carolina. (Robert Coleman was an heir of John Richardson, but not identified).
3. JAMES MAYO, of Chester District, S. C.
4. RICHARD MAYO, of Fairfield Dist., S.C.
5. JOHN MAYO, of Chester Dist., S. C.
6. ROBERT MAYO, of Chester Dist., S. C.
7. HANNAH, wife of David G. Mason.
8. MARY, wife of Lott Chitwood, of Chester Dist., S. C.

JANE, a sister, married Joseph Mayo, and both are dec'd, leaving issue of 9 children:
1. MARTHA MOURNING, wife of a Mr. Bradshaw.
2. JAMES G. (or E.) MAYO.
3. JOSEPH T. MAYO.
4. MARY MAYO.
5. NANCY MAYO. (may have married Dandridge)
6. JULIUS R. (or B.) MAYO.
7. SANDY L. MAYO.
8. DICE MAYO.
9. JANE MAYO
John W. Mayo is mentioned in connection with these heirs, and would thus appear to have been a son, but it is stated there were only 9 children. He is not otherwise identified.

HANNAH, a sister, married Thomas Whitlock, and died prior to 1832, survived by her husband and one child:
1. PATSEY, wife of Stephen Williams of Fluvanna County. The name is also given as Stevens Williams of Louisa County. Sold their interest in the Richardson Estate to Stephen T. Pulliam in 1841.

MOURNING, a sister, married William Pulliam, and died prior to 1832, survived by him and four children:
1. ROBERT J. PULLIAM.
2. THOMPSON W. PULLIAM.
3. SALLY, wife of Peter Wade in 1825
4. NANCY, wife of William T. Dandridge:
   "11 Feb. 1835, William T. Dandridge and Nancy his wife, late Nancy Pulliam of County of Henry, State of Virginia . . . sells to Anderson Bowles of Hanover . . their interest in the Lands of John Richardson, dec'd."

Others mentioned:
Elizabeth Lunsford of Person County, N. C., on 25 Nov. 1836 "appoints her son Alexander Lunsford of same County & State lawful attorney in the matter of Jno. Richardson's Estate." George Glenn and wife Elizabeth. On 10 Dec. 1836, George Glinn in his own right of Person County, N. C., and Alexander Lunsford of said State & County, acting under power of attorney for his mother, Elizabeth Lunsford, sells to Anderson Bowles their interest in lands of John Richardson, dec'd - lying on Turkey Creek, bounded by Anderson Bowles, and others, tract containing 416 acres." Elizabeth probably a

daughter of Sally and Beverley Glenn.
Nancy Attkinson certified that she lived with
Judith Richardson nearly five years. She judged
on 23 March 1838, that Judith's age 62 or 63
years. States that Judith was married about 22
years ago last February and "she then said she
was 40 or 41." Susan L. Lambert lived with
Judith Richardson "upwards of a year." and
stated on 22 March 1838 that Judith's age was
63 years. Archibald Attkisson; Anderson Bowles,
dec'd prior 1845; Chas. K. Bowles, commissioner
1835; Jesse Bowles 1832; Richard Key Bowles;
Thomas Carter, Commissioner 1835; John Cocke of
Goochland County 1835; William Glenn and Wm. P.
Hopkins, Appraisers 1835; Warner L. Guy, Jus-
tice of the Pea ce of Caroline 1834; Michael R.
Jones; Philip B. Jones; Archibald W. Lambert;
Hancock Lee, Teller, Farmers Bank, 1842; Thos.
Loyall, of Louisa County, Auctioneer; Reuben
Nuckols, Commissioner 1835; Ro. S. Payne, Teller
Farmers Bank 1858; Shandy Perkins, merchant of
Hanover; Thomas W. Pulliam; Augustus Rowley;
Francis W. Scott of Caroline Co. 1834; James
Wash; N. A. Wash 1841; Isham R. Woodson.

Samuel Rountree, in letter dated 13 August
1846, at Sparta, Buchanan County, Mo.,says:
"I am one of the heirs of John Anderson. I
married a daughter of Dudley Richardson of
Hanover County, and he married Betsey M.
Anderson, a daughter of John Anderson which
makes me one of the legal heirs of Anderson's Estate. Also my wife is a sister of
Dudley Richardson of Fluvanna County."
[This letter, among the papers of this suit,
pertains to John Anderson's Estate, page 3.]

RICHARDSON'S ADMX. VS. WINSTON &C., 1838 (36)

RICHARDSON, JOHN H., deceased of Hanover
County. Left a will, but no copy in the
papers of this suit. Sally Richardson, was
the Executrix.

Others mentioned: William S. Richardson, John B.
Richardson, Samuel J. Winston, John Seabrook,
Anderson Bowles, Sheriff, Philip B. Jones,
Deputy Sheriff, Hanover 1835.

RICHARDSON VS. RICHARDSON'S EXOR.
& OTHERS, 1857 (33)

RICHARDSON, WILLIAM, "long since dead". Survived by his widow Harriet, late of the
City of Richmond, now (1857) of the City
of New York, #143 Second Avenue. She was a daughter of the late Edmund Hallam, and his wife,
Mary Hallam of Richmond. Issue as of 1857:
1. MARY D. RICHARDSON, of New York State.
2. SUSAN B., wife of William R. Donaghe of
   New York City.
3. GEORGE N. RICHARDSON, of Staten Island,
   New York.

4. JOHN H. RICHARDSON, of Berrien County,
   Michigan.
5. D. WALKER RICHARDSON, of New Haven County,
   Connecticut.
6. EDWARD H. RICHARDSON, of Siskiyou County,
   California.
7. WILLIAM D. RICHARDSON, dec'd, left issue
   in the State of Minnesota.

HALLAM, EDWARD, late of Richmond, Virginia,
died sometime prior to December 1831, when
an agreement, recorded in the Hustings Court of
that City, under date 8 December 1831, executed
by his widow, Mary Hallam, Harriet Richardson,
formerly Hallam, and Mary Hallam, residuary
legatees and devisees of the said Edward Hallam
dec'd, conveyed to Abner Robertson and Henry
King, creditors of the said Hallam, certain
property, in consideration whereof they agreed
to pay to Charles William Dabney of Hanover Co.,
Trustee, $7,500. The interest of said sum to be
enjoyed by Mrs. Mary Hallam during her life and
at her death the principal sum to be enjoyed by
her two daughters, the said Mary Hallam the
younger and Harriet Richardson. The widow, Mrs.
Mary Hallam died in August 1835, survived by
her two daughters:
1. MARY D., wife of William L. King of New
   York.
2. HARRIET, widow of William Richardson, late
   of the City of Richmond.

In 1857 she made application to the Courts
to permit a change in the Trustee. As has
been seen, Charles William Dabney of "Ald-
ingham" Montpelier, Hanover County, whom
she calls "Cousin" was the present Trustee.
In her application she stated that with
her daughter and two youngest sons went to
reside permanently in the City of New York
and all of her children have long since
removed from Virginia on account of the
greater opportunities for lucrative employ-
ment for her sons and for the purpose of
enjoying the society and protection of her
sister, Mrs. King and her husband, she has
considered it her duty, as it has been her
inclination to make this change - and that
the result has justified her doing so up
to this time. Her family are near or with
her; in circumstances of mutual comfort;
and owing to the liberal assistance of Mr.
and Mrs. King she and her family are enjoying many more advantages, that the income
from this Trust fund could possibly obtain
for her in her native state.

The Court appointed John Milner Vickers of
New York, Trustee, in place of Charles Wm.
Dabney, Esq. of Hanover.

RICHARDSON VS. AUSTIN, 1832 (36)

RICHARDSON, JOHN ALLEN, of Hanover County, on 1 January 1822, leased of William Smith Austin, for a period of five years, a certain piece of low or swamp land being a part of the land on which the said Austin now lives - near the Canal, Chickahominy Swamp. The witness being William H. Earnest. On 1 January 1824, the said Austin conveyed to William S. Richardson, for consideration of $600.00 the same piece of land under contract to his brother, John Allen Richardson. Witness, Thomas M. Ladd. It appears that a large portion of this land was owned by Major Edmund Christian of Henrico, and that Austin had no title.

Others mentioned: Alexander Frazier 1832; John D. Andrew's Tavern at Hanover Courthouse 1833; Thomas Austin; John W. Brockenbrough, Attorney; Thomas Gardner, Justice of the Peace, Louisa County, 1832; Solomon Jenkins worked for Wm. S. Richardson 1828-29; James Lyons, Attorney; John B. Shelton, Justice of the Peace, Louisa 1832; John W. Sheppard, Overseer for Wm. S. Richardson; Henry G. Street 1833; Edward Sydnor in Richmond 1833; George W. Trueheart; John O. Trueheart in Louisa County; Thomas J. Trueheart of Henrico 1833; William T. Trueheart.

EARNEST VS. MACON &C., 1839 (55)

ROBINS, THOMAS, deceased, late of Gloucester County, Virginia. One of his children, who was entitled to a 1/7th or 1/8th part of his Estate, was a daughter, Elizabeth, widow of Richard Garrett, dec'd, and now the wife of William H. W. Luke.

ROYSTER & OTHERS VS. COCKE & OTHERS, 1846 (35)
PURCELL VS. COCKE'S EXOR., 1861 (20)
HOPKINS VS. COCKE & OTHERs,1867 (19)

ROYSTER, WILLIAM, of Hanover County, died many years prior to 1846. On 1 May 1808, he conveyed in trust to John Michie of Goochland County, for the benefit of his wife, Mary Royster, 200 acres on the Byrd Creek in Goochland County, being a part of the land on which her father Samuel Richardson lived at the time of his death, and her inheritance of a "third". Previously, on 29 November 1804, she had sold to her brother Samuel Richardson other land in Goochland. The witnesses to this deed were Thomas Attkinson, Charles May, John W. Royster and John Clarke. Samuel Richardson, Sr., father of Samuel Richardson, Jr., and Mary Royster had died intestate. William Royster at the time of his death possessed by survey 330 1/2 acres which were divided by commissioners to his children and heirs. His widow then deceased.

1. SARAH H. (SUSANNAH), married Richardson Woodson, and both are deceased in 1846 leaving issue: (Allotted 461/2 acres)
   1. MARY R. WOODSON, in Henrico Co. 1846.
   2. CAROLINE M., wife of Christopher Holland, living in Henrico Co. 1846.
   3. FRANCES R., wife of James Gates. living in Petersburg, Va., 1846, though she appears not to have been married at that time.
   4. JOHN W. WOODSON, of Henrico 1846.
   5. SAMUEL A. WOODSON, of Rockbridge Co., in 1846.
   6. HARRIET E. WOODSON, in Henrico Co., in 1846.
   7. SUSAN H, wife of James M. Green of Henrico County, 1846.
2. ALEXANDER H. ROYSTER, removed from the State and not heard from for over seven years, in 1846.
3. JOHN W. ROYSTER. Allotted 80 1/2 acres of his father's land
4. MARY A. ROYSTER, allotted 27 acres of her father's land.
5. SAMUEL R. ROYSTER, allotted 130 acres of his father's land.
6. FRANCES A., married prior to 1846, Thomas Cocke of near Rockville, Hanover County. He died in 1867. She was allotted 46 1/2 acres of her father's land. Her will, dated 28 August 1857, was probated 24 November 1857:

Frances A. Cocke's Will

"In the name of God amen. I, Frances A. Cocke of the City of Richmond being weak in body, but of sound and disposing mind and memory do make this to be my last will and Testament (that is to say) I desire that my body may be buried at the direction of my Executor hereinafter named and I direct that all my estate both real and personal be sold and the proceeds thereof together with all my interest in my mother's estate after paying all my just debts be loaned out and the interest on the same be paid semiannually to my daughter Mary E. Purcell as long as she lives. If my said daughter Mary E. Purcell shall die leaving an heir or heirs of her body then and in that case I direct that all my said Estate be given to such heir or heirs, but if she shall die leaving no heir or heirs of her body, then I further direct that the aforesaid estate be equally divided and given to my nieces Mary Woodson, Susan Green, Frances Gates, and Caroline Holland and their heirs forever. Finally I constitute and appoint William N. Waldrop my Executor to this my last will and Testament. Given under my hand and seal this twenty-eighth day of August, one thousand eight hundred and forty-seven."

                              Frances A. Cocke (Seal)
Teste: A.J. Waldrop, Geo. Kelly, Wm.N. Waldrop.

At a Court of Monthly Session held for Hanover County at the Courthouse on Tuesday the 24th of November 1857. This paper writing, purporting to be the last will and Testament of Frances A. Cocke deceased was this day propounded for probat by William N. Waldrop the Executor in the said will named, Whereupon came John Purcell and Mary E. his wife who opposed the probat of the said will, and thereupon the probat of the said will is continued until the next Court. And at a Court of like Session held for the said County at the Courthouse on Tuesday the 22nd day of December then next following the said will was proved by the oaths of William N. Waldrop and George Kelley two of the witnesses thereto and is ordered to be recorded.

Teste, Wm. O. Winston, C.H.C.
A Copy, Teste, Wm. O. Winston, C.H.C.

Frances A., and her husband, Thomas Cocke deceased, had an only issue:

1. MARY E., wife in 1857 of John Purcell, a mechanic. Their issue in 1861, one child:
    1. JAMES P. PURCELL, aged six in 1861.

Others mentioned: Commissioners to divide land in 1867: Chas. K. Bowles, Nathl H. Wash, Wm. R. Irby; Surveyor: Joseph J. Pleasants; Attorney for Thomas Cocke: Chastain White; Depositions 1847: Jesse T. Bowles at his Tan Yard; Ira S. Bowles, Joseph K. Bowles; Wm. P. Hopkins, at his Shop, who purchased Cocke's interest in the Royster lands; Patrick J. Isbell,; Constantine Moore; John F. Parrish; George M. Powers; and Edward Vaughan, Sheriff of Hanover 1867.

KELLAM VS. SCHERER, 1858 (22)

SCHERER, SAMUEL, of Hanover County, died circa 1812, possessed of 485 acres of land which was divided by order of Court between his five children then living. Each of them were assigned 97 acres, which included the dower of their mother:

1. NICHOLAS SCHERER.
2. SAMUEL SCHERER, died intestate, without issue.
3. ANN SCHERER.
4. GEORGE N. SCHERER, who has five children:
    1. SAMUEL SCHERER. His interest "near Atlee Station on Virginia Central Railway," which he sold to Nathaniel B. Clarke.
    2. FRANCES E., wife of a Mr. Kellam, and has an only daughter:
        1. ESTELIA F. KELLAM, under 21 years of age. Her uncle, Edwin E. Kellam, Guardian, in 1858. On 25 April 1871, she married at Baltimore, Md., Edward W. Anderson of Northumberland Co.

N. A. Sturdivant, dec'd had been a special commissioner.
    3. CHARLOTTE A., wife of Mr. Benson.
    4. MARY H., wife of T. B. Jarvis.
    5. GEORGE N. SCHERER.
5. SARAH SCHERER, deceased.

SIMS' ADMRS. VS. SIMS & OTHERS, 1836 (38)

David Sims' Will

SIMS, DAVID. "In the name of God amen. I, David Sims of the County of Hanover & Parish of St. Martin's being weake in body, but of sound & disposing mind and memory, do make and ordain this my last Will and Testament in manner and form following (viz) Imprimis. I will that all my just debts be paid. Item - I lend to my beloved wife during her life all my real and personal Estate. My will and desire is that after the death of my wife all my estate be sold by my executor and equally divided among all my children giving to my two Grandchildren Metilda Quarles Terrell & Jane Terrell their mothers part of my estate. And I do ordain constitute and appoint my son John Sims my sole executor to this my last will and testament. In witness whereof I have hereunto set my hand and affixed my seal this sixteenth day of January one thousand eight hundred and seventeen."

David Sims (Seal)

Sealed & acknowledged in the presence of us:
    Snelson Anthony
    James Martin

At a Court of Quarterly Session held for Hanover County at the Courthouse on Wednesday the 22nd of October 1817. This last Will and Testament of David Sims dec'd was offered to proof by John Sims the Executor therein named and was proved by oath of Snelson Anthony one of the witnesses thereto, and also by the affirmation of the said Executor and is ordered to be recorded.

Teste, William Pollard, C.H.C.
A Copy, Teste, Benj Pollard, Jr., D.C.H.C.

DAVID SIMS, of Hanover. Will dated 16 January 1817, probated 22 October 1817. Appointed his son John, Executor. George S. Netherland was appointed Administrator de bonis non. He was survived by his widow, who is not named, and who is deceased in 1836. Their issue:

1. JOHN SIMS, of Kentucky.
2. GARLAND SIMS, of Kentucky.
3. ELIZABETH SIMS, of Kentucky.
4. WILLIAM B. SIMS, died intestate, unmarried. Charles Thompson, Jr., Admr.
5. FRANCES MATILDA, wife of Thomas Goodman.
6. DAVID SIMS, died intestate. Samuel Luck, Administrator. Issue:
    1. WILLIAM SIMS, a minor in 1836.

2. LUCY SIMS, a minor in 1836.
7. REBECCA, married Benjamin Grubbs, whom she
   survived, but is now deceased, leaving
   one child. Charles. Thompson, Admr.
   1. MARY, wife of Henry Baker.
8. [   ] a daughter, deceased, who married a Mr. Terrell, and left two children:
   1. MATILDA QUARLES TERRELL.
   2. JANE TERRELL.

SIMS VS. TERRELL'S EXOR. &C., 1842 (38)
SIMS VS. THOMPSON'S EXORS., 1843 (39)
   THOMPSON VS. SIMS, 1859, (38)
   THOMPSON VS. SIMS, 1859, (45)

SIMS, WILLIAM, of Hanover County died prior
to 1833. Possessed land and slaves which he
left to his widow Margaret (Peggy) Sims for
life, then to sons. She died, testate, circa
4 October 1849. The dower slaves were sold 21
December 1833 to Nathaniel Thompson of Louisa
County for $1,200.00. Two sons mentioned:
1. GARLAND L. SIMS, and his wife, Paulina S.,
   on 26 August 1840 sold a tract of land
   in Louisa County to Michael Jones for
   $290.00. On 2 January 1841, he executed
   a Deed of Trust to George S. Netherland
   covering tract of land "left by William
   Sims to Margaret Sims for life, on which
   the said Margaret resides, and the rever-
   sion the said Garland L. Sims holds in
   the said land and negroes left the said
   Margaret by the said William." This conveyance was for the benefit of the said
   Garland L. Sims' creditors: James A.
   Chewning, Larkin B. Hancock (a debt due
   William Hatch) Charles Thompson, William
   Hancock, George S. Netherland, Thomas T.
   Duke, William A. Wash for which John M.
   Moody is Security to John L. Sims and
   that he and Garland L. Sims and the said
   George S. Netherland is security for
   Nathaniel Thompson a debt due William
   Nelson of Louisa, &c."
2. PATRICK H. SIMS. On 21 December 1833 "Pat-
   rick H. Sims of Hanover and Garland L.
   Sims of Hanover . . . to Nathaniel Thomp-
   son of Louisa, for consideration of
   $1,200.00, dower slaves now in the posses-
   sion of Peggy Sims, mother of the said
   Patrick and Garland." His will was dated
   15 October 1824, and probated 25 November 1834:

Patrick H. Sims' Will

"In the name of God amen. I, Patrick H. Sims of
Louisa County, do make and ordain this my last
will and testament in manner and form following:
Imprimis 1st. I give and beequeath unto my beloved wife Hardenia one negro boy name Juba to
her & her heirs forever. Imps. 2nd. I also give

to my beloved wife Hardenia as a return for her
affectionate regard fifty dollars to be paid by
my Executor hereinafter mentioned out of any
sale of my estate twelve months after my decease.
Imps. 3d. The balance and residue of my estate
of every kind soever (my just debts being first
paid) I give to my beloved mother during her
natural life, and after her decease, I give the
same to my beloved brother Garland L. Sims. But
in case he the said Garland L. Sims should die
without lawful heir or heirs, I give the said
estate to my Cousins Frances McCawley and Margaret Thompson children of Nath[l] Thompson, jr. to
them and their heirs forever. I do hereby constitute and appoint Nath[l] Thompson, jr. my
Executor of this my last will & testament. In
Testimony whereof I have hereunto set my hand
and seal this the 15th day of October one thous-
and eight hundred and twenty-four".

                  Patrick H. Sims (Seal)
Witness:
   Tarleton Pleasants
   Henry I. Hall.
   Pleasant Yeamans
   George W. Lively

At a Court of Monthly Session held for Hanover
County at the Courthouse on Tuesday the 25th of
November 1834. This last will and Testament of
Patrick H. Sims dec'd was proved by the oath of
Pleasant Yeamans a witness thereto.
   Teste, Philip B. Winston, C. H. C.
At a Court of Monthly Session held for Hanover
County at the Courthouse on Tuesday the 23d of
December 1834. This last will and Testament of
Patrick H. Sims dec'd was further proved by the
oath of Tarleton Pleasants another witness
thereto and is ordered to be recorded.
   Teste, Philip B. Winston, C.H.C.
   A Copy, Teste, Philip B. Winston, D.C.H.C.

Others mentioned: Wm. H. Anderson, merchant,
1834-'37; Cleveras S. Chisholm, deposed at
Oscar F. Chisholm's store in Hanover, on 19
July 1844, that he resided in the family of
Margaret Sims for sometime; Christopher Good-
man rented lands of Margaret Sims; W. Hatch,
merchant 4 March 1844; Samuel R. Jones; Elisha
Melton's Tavern at Louisa Courthouse; William A.
Netherland, Administrator in 1846 of George S.
Netherland; Charles Terrell, deceased in 1842,
Nicholas Terrell, Executor; Timothy Terrell
1842; Smith B. Thomas; Charles Thompson, Jr.,
assignee of Charles Thompson, Sr.; Philip M.
Thompson.

GLINN &C. VS. GLINN'S ADMR. &C., 1857 (81)

Cealey Smith's Will

SMITH, CEALEY. "In the name of God Amen. I,
Cealey Smith of the County of Hanover & State

of Virginia being weak in Body but of sound and disposing mind and memory, do hereby make my last will and Testament in manner and form following that is to say - 1st. I lend to my daughter Sarah Dabney intermarried with James King one equa l sixth part of my estate during her natural life. I lend to my daughter Mary Roads who intermarried with Jerman R. Glinn one equal sixth part of my estate during her natural life. I lend to my daughter Rebecca Crutchfield who intermarried with Gustavus Jarvis one equal sixth part of my estate during her natural life. I lend to my son William Smith one equal sixth part of my estate during his natural life. I lend to my son James Henry Smith one equal sixth part of my estate during his natural life. I lend to my daughter George Anna Smith one equal sixth part of my estate during her natural life. Now if either of my children herein before named shall die leaving an heir or heirs of their Body to such heir or heirs if there be more than one I give that portion of my estate hereinbefore loaned to them and their heirs forever, but if either of my before named children shall die leaving no heirs of their Body then in that case the portion of my estate herein loaned to such child or children shall pass to all my surviving children in equal proportions to be held by them during their life or lives and at their deaths to their heirs in fee simple. I also give to my son James Henry Smith and my daughter George Anna Smith each a Bed and furniture and each one a cow to make them equal with the rest of my Children to whom I have heretofore given a Bead and Cow each. And lastly I appoint my son William Smith and James King my Executors. In witness whereof I have hereunto set my hand and seal this 9th day of March 1839."

                            her
            Cealey   +   Smith (Seal)
                            mark
Witnesses:
    Hudson M. Wingfield
    Jesse G. Yarbrough
    Nathaniel Acree.

At a Court of Monthly Session held for Hanover at the Courthouse on Tuesday the 26" of Nov. 1839. This last will and testament of Cealey Smith dec'd was proved by the oaths of Hudson M. Wingfield, Jesse G. Yarbrough and Nathaniel Acree the witnesses thereto and ordered to be recorded.
    Teste, Philip B. Winston.
    A Copy, Teste, R. O. Doswell, D.C.H.C.

CEALEY SMITH, of Hanover County. Will dated 9 March 1839, probated 26 November 1839. She appointed son William Smith and son-in-law James King, Executors. William Smith qualified. No mention is made of the name of her husband, nor of what her estate consisted, other than land. The Commissioners appointed to divide the same: Hudson M. Wingfield, Thomas H. Goddin, and James

F. Hoffman. Issue:
  1. WILLIAM SMITH, Executor of his mother's Estate.
  2. JAMES HENRY SMITH.
  3. REBECCA CRUTCHFIELD, wife of Gustavus Jarvis.
  4. SARAH DABNEY, wife of James King.
  5. GEORGE ANNA SMITH, daughter.
  6. MARY ROADS, first wife of German (Jerman) R. Glinn. She died 21 August 1841, survived by four children:
      1. WILLIAM R. GLINN, born in 1834.
      2. PETER D. GLINN, born in 1836.
      3. GERMAN R. GLINN, of age in 1866.
      4. ARAMINTA, married under age, prior to 1866, Simon T. Walton.
     German R. Glinn, (Sr.) widower, died in August 1856, survived by his widow, Lucy G., and in addition to the above four children by his first, wife, two others by his second wife:
  5. FRANCES (or Francis) A. E. GLINN
  6. JOHN H. GLINN.

German R. Glinn's Will
(Abstract)

GLINN, GERMAN R., of Hanover County. Will dated 17 November 1855. Probated 28 October 1856. Witnesses: Samuel Davis, Wm. H. B. Campbell, and William H. Timberlake. Executors: Widow, Lucy G. Glinn and brother Peter D. Glinn. Mention is made of his brother Nathaniel Glinn's Estate "of which my interest around $500.00." Requests that his Estate not to be disturbed until son John H. Glinn arrives at the age of twenty-one." Bequests to children: William R., Peter D., Araminta, German R., Francis A. E., and John H. Glinn.

LIGON VS. WM. C. SMITH, 1858 (23)

Richard G. Smith's Will

SMITH, RICHARD G. "In the name of God amen. I, Richard G. Smith of Eastern View, Hanover County being possessed of all my mental faculties, but of feeble health do make and publish this to be my last will and testament, hereby revoking all others. First. I desire that all my just debts shall be paid in the most judicious way that my executors can adopt. Secondly; I bequeath and devise to my son Lewis Oliver the sum of fifteen hundred or that amount of Slaves property. And I bequeath and devise to my youngest daughter Margaret Farley the sum of twenty-five hundred dollars or that amount in negro property exclusive in each case of Lewis Oliver and Margaret Farley of equal Slaves with my other children in the rest and residue of all my estate of every kind. Their being young without the benefit of education which the rest of my children have had the opportunity of acquiring is the reason & motive of making the difference in their favour. Thirdly - I give and bequeath to my youngest daughter Margaret Farley before mentioned as an additional legacy the negro girl Patty, the daughter of Caroline (a house woman.) Fourthly. I give bequeath and devise all the rest and residue of my estate both real and personal, land Stocks of all Kind of horses cattle Sheep, and hogs, Negroes, house hold and Kitchen furniture to be equally divided among all my children, to wit: William C., Richard G., Mary Elizabeth, Ann C., Lewis Oliver and Margaret Farley. Fifthly. There is attached to my estate whereon I reside known and called Eastern View on the western side of the Yard, Seven or eight acres or more of the land of the Bloomsberry estate which was inherited by my late wife from her father the late William Cunningham and which will be inherited at my death by my children from the deceased mother , the said Seven eight or more acres included in the enclosure of the yard of my residence Eastern View and is separate from Bloomsberry Tract by the public road as it now runs on the same. My barns, Stables and many other houses are situated. Now it is my will and determination that the same (to wit the 7, 8 or more acres Spoken of & above described shall continue as they are connected as they are to my Estate called (Eastern View) therefore should any one of my Children or more than one raise any objection to the arrangement and Seek in any way to Separate the said Seven, eight or more acres from the Eastern View estate as they would otherwise have a right to do then it is my will and express Command that such Child or Children Seeking & endeavoring to serve the shall forfeit & pay to the rest of my children out of the property I have herein devised to such Child or Children three times the value of the said Seven eight or more acres. Lastly. I herein appoint my Son William C. Smith the Executor of this my last will and Testament. Witness my Signature this the 21st day of December in the year 1853."

                    Richd G. Smith.
In presence of
   J. H. Earnest
   P. H? Clopton
   R. M. Johnson

At a Court of Quarterly Session held for Hanover County at the Courthouse on Tuesday the 28" of February 1854. This last will and testament of Richard G. Smith, dec'd, was proved by the oaths of J. H. Earnest and P. H. Clopton witnesses thereto and is ordered to be recorded.

   Teste,
        Wm. O. Winston, C. H. C.

   A Copy,
        Teste,
             Wm. O. Winston, C. H. C.

RICHARD G. SMITH, of "Eastern View" Hanover. Will dated 21 December 1853, probated 28 February 1854. Son, William C. Smith, Executor, with whom he was partner in the mercantile business under the style of "Wm. C. Smith & Co." He survived his wife who was a daughter of the late William Cunningham of "Bloomsberry." Issue:
   1. WILLIAM C. SMITH.
   2. RICHARD G. SMITH.
   3. MARY ELIZABETH, wife in 1858, of George G. Boyd.
   4. ANN C. SMITH, who is not mentioned in the suit.
   5. LEWIS OLIVER SMITH, a minor in 1858.
   6. MARGARET FARLEY SMITH, a minor in 1858.

Others mentioned: Commissioners: John Beale, Cornelius H. Dabney, George W. Bassett, John W. Tomlin, and John H. Earnest. James A. Harwood, Sheriff of Hanover. Samuel Putney, W. K. Watts and Stephen Putney, merchants and partners, trading under the style of "Putney, Watts & Putney," successors to Samuel Putney and W. K. Watts, trading as "Putney & Watts."

SNEAD VS. SNEADS, 1855 (39)

Edwin Snead's Will

SNEAD, EDWIN. "In the name of God amen. I, Edwin Snead of the County of Hanover do make this my last will & Testament hereby revoking and making void all former will by me at any time heretofore made. In the first place I wish all my just_to be paid. Secondly. I lend to my wife Jane W. Snead all my estate both real and personal as long as she remains my widow for her use and behoof, and for the support and education of my children. In the event of my widow's marriage again it is my wish that my property both real and personal be disposed of as though I had died intestate. At the death of my wife, I wish all my Estate both real and personal to be equally divided among my children. I do hereby appoint my wife Jane W. Snead my Executrix of this my last will & Testament. In witness whereof I have hereunto set my hand and seal this 5th day of September in the year of our Lord eighteen hundred and forty-two. "

                         Edwin Snead (Seal)
Signed, sealed & delivered
in the presence of us
   Charles C. Tinsley
   Wm. M. Carter
   G. N. Clough.

At a Court of Quarterly Session held for Hanover County at the Courthouse on Tuesday the 27 Oct. 1846. This last will and Testament of Edwin Snead dec'd was proved by the oaths of Charles C. Tinsley & G. N. Clough witnesses thereto and is ordered to be recorded.

EDWIN SNEAD, of Hanover. Will dated 5 September 1842, probated 27 October 1846. Wife, Jane W. Snead, Executrix. Issue:
1. CHARLES F. SNEAD, wife, Susan E., on 24 September 1856. No issue at that time.
2. SUSANNA W. SNEAD, a minor in 1855.
3. ANN C. SNEAD, a minor in 1855.
4. ALBERT J. SNEAD, a minor in 1855.
5. PHILIP B. SNEAD, a minor in 1855.

Others mentioned: Creditors of Charles F. Snead: William P. Stone, Richard A Thornton, Lucius A. Cauthorne, and Charles R. Montgomery. Charles W. Dabney, Commissioner; Marian M. Gary purchased land; Walter C. Shelton; Wm. L. White.

SPILLER &C. VS. SORRELL &C., 1859 (58)

James Spears' Will

SPEARS, JAMES. "I, James Spears of Buckingham County and State of Virginia do hereby constitute and make this my last will and testament in the manner and form followeth: That is to say after all my just debts are paid I give to my daughter Polly Spiller three hundred and fifty acres of land lying in the County of Buckingham, Two hundred acres a part thereof is lying on the waters of David Creek and was granted to James Fendley by patent bearing date on the 20" day of September 1745 and joining the lines of the said Polly Spiller (the land which I have heretofore conveyed to her by a deed in fee simple) the lines of David Kyle and others lying on the north side of Spears Mountain, and one hundred and fifty acres thereof was granted to John Spears by patent bearing date the 27th of June 1764 and lies on the top, and on the east side of said Spears Mountain and joining the lines of said David Kyle & others. Also I give to my daughter Polly Spiller twenty-five negroes & all their increase that is to say &c. [names are given] to the said Polly Spiller her heirs, executors, administrators, and assigns forever. Secondly. I give to George Spiller (the husband of Polly Spiller) one negro man named Robin to him and his heirs, executors, administrators and assigns forever. Thirdly. I give to my daughter Sarah Jones twelve negroes, that is to say, [names are given] to her the said Sarah Jones her heirs, executors, administrators and assigns forever. Fourthly. I give to my daughter Elizabeth Sorrell ten negroes, that is to say [names are given] during her natural life, and if she the said Elizabeth Sorrell should die without issue of her body it is my will and desire that the above named slaves together with their increase shall be equally divided between my two daughters Polly Spiller and Sarah Jones, to them and their heirs forever. But in case the said Elizabeth Sorrell should have a legal heir or heirs, the issue of her body, then and in that case it is my will and desire that the above mentioned

slaves at the death of the said Elizabeth Sorrell shall go to her legal heirs, executors, administrators or assigns forever. Fifthly. I give to my grandson James M. Spiller Forty acres of land lying on James River which was granted to James Spears by patent bearing date on the 13th day of October 1795 and joining the lines of William Walton and Thomas S. McCleland, also one negro man by the name of Billy to him the said James M. Spiller, his heirs, executors, administrators and assigns forever. Sixthly. I give to my grandson George A. Spiller one negro boy of the name of Nicholas to him and his heirs forever. Seventhly. I give to my granddaughter Sarah Ann Spiller one negro girl by the name of Isabella to her and her heirs, executors, administrators and assigns forever. Eighthly. I give to my granddaughter Sarah Frances Jones one negro girl by the name of Cyrene to her and her heirs, executors, administrators and assigns forever. Ninthly. I give to my daughter Polly Spiller one walnut Desk, one Walnut Table, one walnut cupboard to her and her heirs, executors administrators and assigns forever, and all the residue of my estate of negroes, stock of every description, Plantation utensils and household and kitchen furniture it is my will and desire shall be equally divided among my three above mentioned daughters, that is to say Polly Spiller, Elizabeth Sorrell and Sarah Jones to them and their heirs, executors, administrators and assigns forever. It is also my will and desire that the elderly slaves belonging to me which are not already devised, shall be indulged to choose and go to which of the aforesaid legatees they wish to go to, by such legatee paying a reasonable price for the same. And lastly I do hereby appoint my friends John Harris and George Spiller executors to this my last will & testament and it is my will and desire that they shall not be required to give any security for their faithful performance as executors to this my last will and Testament. In witness whereof I have hereunto set my hand and seal this 24th day of August in the year of our Lord one thousand eight hundred and twenty-nine."

James Spears (Seal)

Signed, published & declared by James Spears as & for his last will and Testament in the presence of us, who at his request & in his presence have subscribed our names as witnesses: Richard Clarke, Wilson Hix, John H. Davidson, James Farriss, John R. Megginson.

"Aug. 20, 1831. A negro man called Joe Burton I have this day sold to James Spiller and have made him a bill of sale for him. He is one mentioned in the foregoing will. It is now my will and desire that one of the negroes in the foregoing will mentioned named Peter after my death I bequeath to my daughter Elizabeth Sorrell and her heirs forever. And lastly I appoint Richard

Clarke and James Farris my executors in this my
last will & devise."

James Spears

Witnesses:
  Silas P. Vawter
  Wilson Hix
  John Johnson, Jr.

"At a Court heldfor Buckingham County the 13th
day of May 1833. The order and judgment of the
Circuit Superior Court of Law and Chancery for
this County in an appeal. Fielding Jones and
Reuben Sorrell appellants and Polly Spiller
Appellee was this day produced in Court in pursuance. Whereof it is ordered that this writing
and codicil annexed be established and recorded
as the last will and testament of James Spears
deceased. Richard Clarke and James Farriss the
surviving executors named in the said will having refused to take on themselves the burthen
of the execution thereof, on motion of James M.
Spiller who made oath of the said will and
entered into bond with security as the law required, letters of administration are granted
to him of the estate of James Spears deceased
with the said will annexed in due form."
  Teste, R. Eldridge, C.
  A Copy, Teste, R. Eldridge, C.B.C.

JAMES SPEARS, of Buckingham County. Will dated
24 August 1829, Codicil 20 August 1831, probated 13 May 1833. He nominated as Executors,
Richard Clarke and James Farriss, who denounced
the office. James M. Spiller, a grandson, was
appointed Administrator. Survived by three
daughters:
1. MARY (POLLY) SPEARS, married George Spiller, both deceased in 1859, survived by
   issue:
   1. JAMES M. SPILLER.
   2. SAMUEL F. SPILLER.
   3. PRESTON H. SPILLER.
   4. GEORGE S (or A.) SPILLER, deceased in
      1859, survived by three children
      whose names are unknown.
   5. SARAH ANN, married a Mr. Bocock, and
      in 1859, both are deceased, survived
      by two infant children:
      1. JOHN F. BOCOCK.
      2. A. B. BOCOCK.
2. ELIZABETH, died 19 January 1862, married
   Reuben Sorrell, formerly of Hanover, but
   of Orange County in 1859, in which year
   it was stated that she was 63 years of
   age and that they had been married 25
   years. No children.
3. SARAH, married Fielding M. Jones, and both
   are deceased in 1859, leaving issue:
   1. [   ] a daughter, who married
      James W. Watts.
   2. WILLIE ANN JONES.
   3. FRANCES (SARAH FRANCES), married a Mr.
      Watkins, and both are deceased in

1859, without issue.

Others mentioned: Col. Thomas M. Bondurant, of
Buckingham, a former member of the General As-
sembly, and in 1859, principal owner of the
Richmond Whig, newspaper. "Reputed to be worth
One Hundred Thousand Dollars." George N.Clough,
deceased, who dealt in slaves. John D. G.Brown
Admr. Mrs. Clough, his widow, married B. T.
Stanley; John W. Ellington; James W. Flowers;
John W. Lindsay; John E. Page; A. B. Ragan.

PARSLEY'S ADMR. &C. VS. GAINES' ADMR.
& OTHERS, 1875 (20)

Fanny Spindle's Will

SPINDLE, FANNY. "In the name of God amen. I,
Fanny Spindle do make and ordain this my last
Will and Testament in manner and form following, to wit. I first will and devise that all
my just_and funeral expenses be paid_my Exor
here in after named. 2ndly I give and bequeath
to my granddaughter Sally Garlock Gaines when
she attains the age of eighteen years or shall
marry, my negroes Rebecca and Cook and Six hundred dollars provided my daughter Jane she be
disposed that she shall receive this legacy at
that time, should she not be thus disposed I
wish her to retain the said Legacy so_as she
lives and at her death, I then give the same to
my said Granddaughter Sally G. Gains to her and
her heirs forever. All the rest and residue of
my both real and personal_I lend to my beloved
daughter Jane E. Gains for and during her natural life and at her death I give the same to
all her children who may survive her and to the
survivors of such as may have died before her
to them and their heirs forever. Lastly I nominate and appoint my son in law Dr. Wm. F. Gains
my exor of this my last will and testament. In
Testimony whereof I have set my hand and affixed my _al this 28th day of Dec. 1833."

Fanny Spindle (Seal)
Signed sealed published and declared by the testratrix as and for her last Will and testament
in the presence of us who in her presence and
at her request have subscribed our names as
witnesses: Richard Rouzie, Mordecai L. Spindle,
Barba Spindle.

At a Court of Quarterly Session begun and held
for Essex County at the Courthouse in Tappahannock on the 20th day of March 1837. This last
Will and Testament of Fanny Spindle dec'd being
brought into Court and offered for proof by
William F. Gaines the nominated Executor therein
was proved by the oaths of Richard Rouzie and
Barba Spindle, two of the Subscribing witnesses
to the same and ordered to be recorded. Whereupon on motion of the said Wm. F. Gaines a Cer-

tificate was granted him in order to his obtaining probat of the said Will and Testament in
due form of Law, he having first taken the oath
in such case required by Law and entered into a
bond payable to the Sitting Justices in the penalty of Twenty thousand dollars with Wm. M.
Gary and Lawrence Roane his securities which
said bond being conditioned as the Law directs
was acknowledged by the obligors and also ordered to be recorded.

    Teste, James Roy Micou, Jr., Clk.
    A Copy, Teste, James Roy Micou, Clk.

FANNY SPINDLE, of Essex County. Will dated 28
December 1833, Probated 20 March 1837. She
was survived by a daughter, Jane E., wife of
Dr. William F. Gaines, her Executor, and these
two had a daughter, probably among others,
Sally G. Gaines, mentioned in the Test atrix's
will. This suit is a civil one concerning a
debt of Dr. William F. Gaines.

                FROM OLD WILL BOOK, PAGE 85

        Mary B. Stevens' Will (Abstract)

STEVENS, MARY B., of Hanover. Will dated 6
April 1848. Probated 5 October 1848. Nominated son-in-law Edward W. Kimbrough, and
friends Williamson Talley and John D. G. Brown,
Executors. Witnesses: John S. Brown and Carter
M. Kimbrough. Issue:
  1. LEWIS STEVENS.
  2. LUCY STEVENS.
  3. JUDITH, wife of Edward W. Kimbrough.
  4. ROBERT STEVENS, dec'd, who left children.
  5. HORACE STEVENS, who is married and has
     issue.
  6. POLLY WINSTON, dec'd, who married a Mr.
     Winston, and left issue.
  7. RICHARD STEVENS, who is married and has
     issue.

                STANLEY VS. STANLEY, 1868 (22)

STANLEY, FRANCES, of Hanover County, died in
1848 with a will which was destroyed by
fire 3 April 1865, and no copy remains. She
left her real estate consisting of 80 acres to
her nephews Gideon Stanley and Thomas J. Stanley, and her personal property to two brothers,
Thomas Stanley and Abram Stanley. Other heirs
at-law sue for interest in her estate. These
parties, whose various relationships are not
stated:
  John Stanley.
  Mildred M., wife of Jacob K. Strong.
  Susan, wife of William M. Strong.
  Sarah A., wife of John F. Duke.
  Martha M., wife of Samuel R. Wingfield.
  Frances E. Stanley
The children of Lucy Tiller, dec'd, who was wife

of Robert Tiller:
  Edith A., wife of John Yarbrough.
  Roberta, wife of Franklin Davis.
  Martha Tiller.
  Lemuel S. Tiller.
  Elwood Tiller.
  J. Eubank Tiller.
  Washington Tiller.
  Lee Tiller.
  John Tiller.
The children of Judith Wingfield, dec'd,:
  Samuel W. Wingfield.
  Martha E., wife of Westley Gilman.
  Ella Wingfield.
  Edward Wingfield.
  Gideon Wingfield.

  Sarah, wife of Gideon Stanley.
  Jonathan Stanley, a non-resident of Virginia.
  Joshua Stanley, a non-resident of Virginia.
  Hulday, wife of a Mr. Crew, a non-resident of
    Virginia.
  Edith Stanley.
  Nancy, wife of a Mr. Callahan, a non-resident
    of Virginia.

  Thomas Stanley, a brother of Frances, and
  Abram Stanley, dec'd, survived by wife, Sarah.
    He was another brother.

Others mentioned: Henley C. Doswell who testified that he wrote Frances Stanley's will.

        STARKE'S ADMR. VS. DUKE & OTHERS, 1832 (38)

STARKE, JOHN, of Hanover County, deceased. His
administrator was Joseph Starke.

DUKE, JOHN T., of Hanover County, has a son,
Edwin Duke.

Others mentioned: William B. Green; Bowling
Starke; Richard O. Haskins.

        CENTRAL BANK OF ALABAMA VS. WM. E. STARKE
                    & OTHERS, 1861 (56)

STARKE, WILLIAM E., a resident of the State
of Louisiana, was in debt to Central Bank
of Alabama in the amount of $34,000, and
the interest on $16,000 a part thereof, from 3
April 1860. Judgment obtained in May 1860 in
the District Court of New Orleans. Starke had
interests in three race horses, "Planet",
"Exchequer," and "Fanny Washington" in possession of Thomas Doswell of Hanover County, Va.,
and Thomas D. Doswell of the City of Richmond,
who owned the remaining interests. The Doswells
were in debt to Starke.

STREET VS. STREET &C., 1831 (37)
STREET VS. STREET &C., 1835 (36)
WRIGHT VS. STREET, 1839 (48)
STREET'S EXORS. VS. GOODALL &C., 1846 (39)

John Street's Will

STREET, JOHN. "I, John Street of St. Paul's
Parish in the County of Hanover being advanced in years but of sound mind, Thanks to
Almighty God for the same. Calling to mind the
uncertainty of life do make, ordain and constitute this writing as my last will and Testament
revoking all other wills by me heretofore made,
in manner and form following to wit. My will is
that my body be decently buried by my beloved
in the family burying ground and that the form
used at the interment and burial may be according to the form of the Church of England; which
I have examined in my prayer book and recommend
to my children, grandchildren and acquaintances
and wish them to recommend it as I have done,
if they profess the name of Jesus. As to my
worldly possessions, which it hath pleased God
to give me. I do dispose of them in the following manner - I give to my son William Street my
young negro man named Jemmey to him and his
heirs forever. I give to my son Parke Street my
negro man Cesar to him and his heirs forever. I
give to my daughter Hannah Brown wife of Captn.
William Brown my young negro woman Nanny & her
young child Violet and their future increase,
to her and her heirs forever; and the feather
Bed & furniture heretofore given & delivered
her, is not to be considered in her share or
portion of my estate. I give to my son George
Street my negro boy Fleming to him and his heirs
forever. I give to my daughter Sally Street my
young negro woman Mary with her future increase
to her and her Heirs forever, also one feather
bed and furniture which bed and furniture is
not to be considered in her share or portion of
my estate. I give to my son Anthony Street my
negro boy Garland to him and his heirs forever.
And whereas my said son Park Street hath put
the young negro man Cesar given to him to the
blacksmiths trade by which it is reasonable to
suppose that he will become more valuable than
without a trade, and it being reasonable in the
valuation of my estate, that the said negro
Cesar should be valued to my said son Parke at
a higher price than if not possessed of such
trade. It is also therefore my will that if any
of my said children shall make the negroes thus
bequeathed to them, by given them trades or
otherwise more valuable than they would be if
only bred up in the ordinary way that these
extraordinary advantages shall not be taken into
the valuation of such negroes, but that they
shall be valued as if they possessed no such
advantages. And as to the residue or remainder
of my estate both real and personal, it is my
will That my Executors hereafter named dispose
of it as they may think most advantageous to my
legatees, with the reserve only, that if they
do sell it at public auction and a majority of
the legatees should think twelve months credit
most to their general advantage, that in such
case it shall not be sold for a shorter credit,
and the amount of such sales, after paying all
my just debts and making generous compensation
to such of my Executors as act for their trouble
to be divided between my said six children in
such manner as to allot to each including the
negro or negroes herein before given him or her
an equal part or portion.   And whereas a considerable part of the estate of which I am now
seized & possessed is held by me as heir at Law
to my son John Street, Jr., dec'd being Lands
in the State of Virginia & in other states of
the Union, and the estate of my said dec'd son
being in an unsettled state & it being therefore uncertain how it will close, that is,
whether his personal estate will be sufficient
to discharge all his just debts or not - It is
my will & desire that if his personal estate
should not be sufficient to discharge his debts
that so much of the real estate of which I am
possessed as his heir at Law as will be sufficient fully to discharge his debts, even if it
takes the whole of it, be sold by my Executors
as they may think best & applied by them to the
discharge of his said debts. But should the
estate Heired by me as aforesaid, not be sufficient to discharge the debts of my said son
John, in that case this clause is by no means
to be construed to subject the estate possessed
by me independent of such Heirship to the payment of the said debts. It is my wish that my
old negro woman Betty after my death (should
she survive me) Live with either of my said
Children that she may desire - and that during
her life she shall not be allowed to suffer for
want of competant or reasonable sustenance. But
when her services is not fully sufficient to
compensate for such sustenance that then she be
allowed it from my estate. And lastly I do
appoint my dutiful and well beloved sons William,
Parke, George, and Anthony Street, Executors to
this my last will and testament. In witness
thereof I have hereunto set my hand & seal this
. . . day of April 1800."

John Street (Seal)

At a Court of Monthly Session held for Hanover
County at the Courthouse on Wednesday the 18th
of March 1801. This last will and testament of
John Street deceased was offered to proof by
William Street, Park Street, George Street, &
Anthony Street Executors therein named, and the
said Will having no subscribing witnesses thereto, three of the Sitting members of the Court
were sworn & examined & thereupon declared that
the signature of John Street subscribed at the
foot of the said will was from their acquaintance with the handwriting of the said John
Street to their belief written with the proper

hand of the said John Street, the same is thereupon ordered to be recorded.
    Teste, William Pollard, C.H.C.
    A Copy, Teste, Philip B. Winston, C.H.C.

JOHN STREET, of Hanover. Will dated in April
1800, probated 18 March 1801. His four surviving sons qualified as Executors. Some of his
lands were sold on 25 October 1824, as follows:
    Half of a lot in the City of Richmond, Va.,
    sold to William J. Morris for $3,000.
    200 acres of Military Land on Eagle Creek,
    Adams County, Ohio, sold to Richard H.
    Whitlock of Richmond, Va., for $200.00
    One moiety of 1280 acres of Military Land
    granted to Charles Lewis and John Street,
    Jr., in the State of Kentucky, on north
    side of Tennessee River, sold to George
    Street for $256.00.
He survived his wife, who is not mentioned.
Their issue:
    1. JOHN STREET, JR., "Had acted as Deputy
       under William Johnson, Sheriff of Han-
       over County, 1795 and 1796, and died
       sometime toward the last of January 1797."
       He and Charles Lewis had 1280 acres of
       Military Land in Kentucky, on the north
       side of Tennessee River. His interest in
       this land was inherited by his father,
       and subsequently sold on 25 October 1824
       to George Street. He died unmarried.
    2. WILLIAM STREET, died intestate circa 1840.
       William D. Wren, Sergeant of City of
       Richmond, Va., Administrator.
    3. PARKE STREET, died prior to 12 May 1842
       with a will. Charles P. Goodall, Execu-
       tor. On 27 October 1805 he and General
       Thomas White made an agreement, in which
       it was stated that White expected to
       succeed John Thompson as Sheriff, and
       the agreement was that White would "farm"
       to Street his term of sheriffalty and
       all the fees of office and emoluments
       arising therefrom: "Should the commission
       issue that is anticipated, appointing
       White to the office of Sheriff, the said
       White and Street are mutually to bring
       forward three friends to become security
       for the said White's due performance of
       his office as Sheriff of said County (Han-
       over). The said White is to qualify as
       Sheriff and is to allow said Street &
       such other proper persons as the said
       Street may wish, to qualify as his deputy
       sheriffs. Whereupon Street is to give
       White as Sheriff, sufficient security to
       indemnify him as usual for High Sheriffs,
       to be indemnifyed for and on account of
       the Conduct of the said Street & such
       other persons as may at his request be
       allowed to qualify as deputy sheriffs
       during the term of Sheriffalty. Should
       Street wish any person to qualify that
       does not meet with White's approbation,

or should White wish to dismiss from office said deputy sheriffs, contrary to
the wish of Street, Nathaniel Pope and
John Bowe, Esq., or an umpire of their
choosing or the survivor of them, are to
determine the propriety of such deputies.
Street to have sole power, directing &
conducting, of the Sheriffalty, except
what the law requires to be done or executed by the High Sheriff in person. In consideration of the sheriffalty farmed to
him as aforesaid, is to pay to White the
sum of Four hundred pounds for two years."
This document was witnessed by J. White.
On 27 August 1806, Thomas White gave a
receipt to Parke Street for 133.6.8 Lbs.,
which was witnessed by Peter Foster. A
receipt for the final payment was witnessed by Clement White. Gen. Thomas
White had qualified as High Sheriff on
27 August 1806. His deputies being Parke
Street, Anthony Street, and Charles P.
Goodall, and as such served for the two
years. Col. Park Goodall, (the father of
Charles P. Goodall, and of Mrs. Parke
Street, and of the lady who subsequently
became the wife of Anthony Street) was
appointed High Sheriff to succeed General
White, and Charles P. Goodall, Anthony
Street, and John P. Wilkinson appointed
his deputies. Parke Street did not qualify, his wife being in very delicate
health during the summer of 1808, took
her to Virginia Springs, and in his ab-
sence, Parke Goodall having qualified. He
served for two years, during which the
partnership as to the benefit of office
continued. His term expired in October
1810. On 20 June 1811, Park Goodall and
Mary, his wife, executed a Deed of Trust
on 300 acres in Caroline County to Wilson
Quarles; and 1000 acres "whereon Park
Goodall now resides in Hanover County, 18
miles from the City of Richmond, on both
sides of road leading from Richmond to
Louisa Courthouse, and ten slaves, to
Samuel Grantland. Witnesses: Joseph M.
Sheppard, Stephen Anderson and Martha Hall
Trevilian. Goodall had been indebted to
Park Street from 26 June 1811, with int-
erest, on 943.0.0. Lbs; to Anthony Street
on 15.12.0 and interest from 26 June 1811;
to Charles P. Goodall 12.16.4 1/2 with
interest from 26 June 1811; and to Jane M.
Goodall on 233.6.3. with interest from 16
July 1812.
Park Street died during one of these law
suits. His will is not included. Only two
of his children are definitely named:
    1. CHARLES STREET.
    2. SAMUEL STREET.
In a letter dated "Santee" or "Sautee" 29
January 1823 he mentions son Charles. Also
mentions Mary Riseley, perhaps a daughter.

4. HANNAH, married prior to April 1800, Capt. William Brown. (Not residents of Hanover)
5. GEORGE STREET. Merchant of Hanover circa 1800-'10, trading sometime under the style "Street & Wilkerson" and as "George Street & Brothers Company." On 25 Oct. 1824, purchased of his father's Estate Kentucky lands formerly owned by John Street, Jr., dec'd. Also had purchased lands in Ohio. Removed circa 15 November 1824 to Trigg County, near Hopkinsville, Kentucky where he was residing on 18 May 1829, and where he later died intestate. He may have been the Major George Street mentioned in these suits.
6. SALLY, married prior to 1834, John Seward.
7. ANTHONY STREET. Will dated 20 July 1842, probated 22 October 1844. Wm. T. H. Pollard and Philip B. Winston qualified as Executors. He had served as Deputy Sheriff to General Thomas White and Colonel Park Goodall, and married the latter's daughter, whose name is not stated. On 28 January 1823, he wrote to his brother Park Street, dating his letter from "Neck Farm" , in which he mentions sister "Eliza" and "James". He owned land in Hanover and Louisa Counties. His issue was:
1. CHARLES H. STREET.
2. PARK GOODALL STREET, deceased in 1846. Rebecca A Street, of Henrico County in 1846, Administrator.
3. PATSEY STREET, probably deceased in 1842.

Anthony Street's Will

STREET, ANTHONY. "In the name of God amen. I, Anthony Street of the County of Hanover and State of Virginia being of sound mind do make & ordain this my last will and Testament. First. It is my will & desire that all my just creditors shall be first paid. Secondly. It is my will and desire that all my Landed Estate shall be advertised and sold at Public Auction at Hanover Courthouse at the first day of a Court on the following terms, to wit: One-fourth of the Sales payable in three years from the date of sale, and all to carry interest from the day of sale until paid. Bond with approved security & also a Deed in Trust upon the said property is to be required of the purchaser. Thirdly. My will and desire is that my son Park G. Street shall be allowed to take at appraised value my silver watch, my old large print Bible containing my family Register and any other books and any of my counterpanes that he may prefer, all which articles are to be charged to him the portion of my Estate hereinafter mentioned with the interests and profits from which the said Park is to receive and use under the restrictions hereinafter mentioned - also that my son Charles H. Street shall be allowed to take at

appraised value my shaving implements, my shirt and sleeve buttons, my small bible that has his name written in it and any other of my books that his brother does not take and any of my counterpins that his brother does not take, all which articles are to be charged to him the portion of my Estate herein after mentioned Interest and profits from which said portion he is to receive & enjoy under the restrictions herein after mentioned. Fourthly. My will and desire is that my executors hereinafter named shall privately dispose of my old woman Caty and my old woman Lucy commonly called Lucinda privately and to persons that they believe will treat them with care and humanity that persons of their time of life should be treated. Fifthly. My will and desire is that my other slaves and all my perishable estate be advertised & sold at Public auction on one year's credit, to carry interest from the day of sale until paid for all sums above twenty dollars and under. Bond with approved Security to be required from purchasers. Sixthly. When the nett amount of my said Estate is assertained, including any articles that my said Sons have taken at the appraised value respectively, my will & desire is that my said son Park G. Street Shall receive, possess & use the interest & profits upon half of my said Estate, the articles that he takes at valuation included, to support himself & his family & to educate his children during his life, but it is not my will that the said interest and propits shall be sold in anyway, or be to pay his debts and liabilities, and when he dies I give the principal to his children to be equally divided among them according to Law and I give to each an_ separately and to his or her heirs and assigns forever. Also it is my will and desire that my son Charles H. Street Shall receive possess and use the interest and profits of the other half of my said estate during his life, to support himself and his family when he has one and to educate his children if he has any lawfully begotten, but it is not my will that the said Interest and profits shall be sold in any way or be subject to pay his debts and liabilities and at his death I give the principal to his children to be equally divided among them according to Law: what I give to each one Separately and to his or to her heirs and assigns forever. But if my said son Charles H. Street dies single or if he is married when he dies, and he leaves no children as aforesaid, but leaves his widow pregnant and she is delivered of a child that lives to be one year old, in that case I give that child the said principal to him or to her, his or her heirs & assigns forever. If my said son Charles H. Street leaves no children and no widow when he dies, it is my will and desire that my said son Park G. Street shall receive possess and use the interest and profits arising upon or from the principal that his brother did receive and use during life, during the life of the said Parke G. Street to support himself & his family and to educate his children. But it is not my will that the said interest and profits shall be sold in any way, or be subject or be applied to pay his debts and liabilities and at his death I give to his children the said principal to be equally divided among them which I give each one, and to his or to her heirs and assigns forever. Seventhly. I appoint Mr. Philip B. Winston, Mr. Jesse Winn, Mr. Wm. O. Winston, Mr. William Thomas Henry Pollard and my two sons Park G. Street and Charles H. Street Executors to this my last will and Testament. Witness my hand & seal this 20th day of July 1842."

                                    A. Street
Witnesses:
   G. W. Bassett
   Edwin Snead
   Richd G. Smith
   William Payne

At a Court of Quarterly Session held for Hanover County at the Courthouse on Tuesday the 22^d of October 1844. This Last will and Testament of Anthony Street, dec'd, was proved by the oath of Edwin Snead a witness thereto and at a Court of like Session continued & held for the Said county at the Courthouse on Wednesday the 23^d of October 1844 the said Will was further proved by the oath of George W. Bassett another Witness thereto and is ordered to be recorded.
   Teste, Philip B. Winston, C.H.C.
   A Copy, Teste, Wm. O. Winston, C.H.C.

Others mentioned: Robert Anderson 1838; Robert K. Blackwell 1835; Nathaniel Burnett 1838; Wm. Cunningham 1835; Dr. Henry Curtis 1819; Samuel Grantland "a monied man"; N. S. Green, Deputy Sheriff 1840; William Grubbs 1838; William H. Howard, Commissioner 1846; William A. Jones 1838; Archibald Lambert, Constable 1840; Dr. James Lyons 1801; James G. Pettus 1835; John Robinson, Commissioner of the late Chancery Court of the District of Richmond; Dr. Charles P. Street 1838; Barrett White 1835; Robert White 1835; Joseph Whitlock 1838; Wm. Wingfield, Sheriff 1840;

WRIGHT VS. STREET, 1839 (48)

LITTLEPAGE, JAMES, of Hanover County, circa 1800, possessed a tract of land containing 125 acres in the lower end of the County near Pole Green Meeting House. This land descended to his only heir:
   1. JOHN CARTER LITTLEPAGE, who, with his wife, Maria M. J., indebted to Park Street, on 16 April 1835, conveyed in Trust to Richd G. Smith and John H. Earnest, for the benefit of Park Street, a tract of land containing 125 acres on which the said

J.C. lives, near Polegreen Meeting House, in the lower end of the County, bounded by the lands of Nathaniel Whitlock's Estate, Isaac Oliver's Estate, John Jones' Estate, and others.

WHITLOCK, JAMES, of Hanover County, on 13th December 1838, deposed that his land was about a quarter of a mile from Littlepage's, near Pole Green Meeting House. That James Littlepage, father of John Carter Littlepage the younger, about 30 to 40 years ago resided on this land. That John Carter Littlepage, the younger, occupied the land until he removed to Kentucky a few years ago. That James Littlepage has no other descendants except John Carter Littlepage, the younger, of Kentucky.

WRIGHT, THOMAS, of Hanover County, whose wife was a sister of Richard Burnett claims the right to occupy the farm under a lease and refused to vacate the premises.

James Littlepage's Will

"In the name of God amen. I, James Littlepage of the Parish of St. Paul and County of Hanover do make and ordain this my last Will and Testament in the manner and form following: I give and bequeath unto my uncle John Carter Littlepage all the estate that I am entitled to under the will of my father James Littlepage, of every nature and kind whatsoever to him my said uncle and his heirs forever. I also give and bequeath unto my said uncle all the rest of my estate of every nature & kind whatsoever to him and his heirs forever. I do hereby constitute and appoint him my said uncle John Carter Littlepage, Executor of this my last will and Testament desiring that he shall not give security of his qualifying as such to the same. In witness whereof I have hereunto put my hand and affixed my seal this fifth day of April in the year of our lord one thousand eight hundred & sixteen."

                                    J. Littlepage
Signed, sealed, published
and declared in the presence of
   Isaac Oliver
   M. L. Whitlock

At a Court of Quarterly Session held for Hanover County at the Courthouse on Wednesday the 22^d of Oct. 1817. This Last Will and Testament of James Littlepage dec'd was offered for proof by John C. Littlepage the Executor therein named and was proved by the oath of Isaac Oliver one of the Witnesses thereto and also by the oath of the said Executor and is ordered to be recorded.
   Teste, William Pollard.
   A Copy,
                Teste, Philip B. Winston, C. H. C.

STRONG'S EXOR. VS. CAMERON &C., 1853 (39)

Judith Strong's Will

STRONG, JUDITH. "I, Judith Strong of the County of Hanover being far advanced in life and desiring to set my house in order both for time and eternity do make and ordain this my last will and testament in manner & form as followeth. I lend unto my sister Jane Strong all my slaves and all the interest that I have or may have at the time of my death in any slaves during her natural life, and at her death it is my will that my executors hereinafter named shall place Rhoda in some family amongst my relatives or others where she shall be well taken care of, and as far as may be enjoy the proceeds of her labour. It is my will that the rest of my slaves and such as may be alloted to me out of my interest in any slaves that I now have or may have at the time of my death shall be hired out by my Exors hereinafter named to raise a fund for the purpose of removing them to some free state or Government where they may enjoy their liberty. When a sufficient fund has been raised to pay the expense of their removal my Exors shall then select at their discretion what they may consider the most advantageous place for their settlement being in some free state or government, and send them and their increase to it and provide for them in the best way they can out of any surplus which may remain unexpended of their hires. All the remainder of my property I lend to my sister Jane Strong, my niece Emily Camron and her daughter Louisa K. Jones and to the survivor of them during their natural lives and at their deaths I give said property both real and personal to the children of Louisa K. Jones to be equally divided between them or their heirs, if any of them should have died leaving children each of such child's children to receive one share. Lastly I constitute and appoint my friends John J. Jones & Andrew McDowell Executors of this my last will & testament dated this 13th day of August 1851."

Witnessed by   her
  Nath[l] C. Crenshaw   Judith + Strong
  Eliza H. Crenshaw   mark

At a Court of Quarterly Session held for Hanover County at the Courthouse on Tuesday the 27th of April 1852. This last will and Testament of Judith Strong dec'd was proved by the affirmation of Nathaniel C. Crenshaw and Eliza H. Crenshaw the witnesses thereto and is ordered to be recorded.

Teste, Wm. O. Winston, C.H.C.

A Copy,
     Teste, O. M. Winston, D.C.H.C.

Jane Strong's Will

STRONG, JANE. "I, Jane Strong of the County of Hanover being weak in body but of sound mind and memory do make this my last will and Testament as follows: 1st. I give and bequeath to my grand niece Louisa B. Jones negro woman China and her children to her and the heirs of her body forever. 2d. I give to my niece Emily Cameron my negro man Charles to her and the heirs of her body forever. 3d. I give and bequeath to my five nieces Mary Strong, Sarah Strong, Lucy Ann Stanley, the wife of Jesse Stanley, Judith Butler the wife of Clayton C. Butler, and Mary Gammon, slaves Rhoda, George, Esther and Betty to be equally divided among them, but it is my will and desire that the old woman Rhoda shall be well taken care of by them and that the said slaves shall not be sold out of the family for a division but request and require that some of the distributees may buy them to effect the said division. 4th. I give to my niece Emily Cameron and her daughter Louisa B. Jones my part of the land on which I live to them and the heirs of their bodies forever. 5th. I give to my five nieces named in the third clause of this my last will, all my interest in the household and kitchen furniture, plantation utensils, stock of every kind and crops on hand at the time of my death. 6th. And Lastly I appoint my friend John J. Jones Executor of this my last will and wish no security to be required of him and it is my desire too that no inventory or appraisement be made. In Testimony whereof I do hereunto set my hand and seal this 24th day of April in the year 1852."

Signed, sealed, published   her
& declared to be the last   Jane + Strong
will of Jane Strong in the   mark
presence of
  J. D. G. Brown
  Thad[s] C. Brown

At a Court of Quarterly Session held for Hanover County at the Courthouse on Tuesday the 26th of April 1853. This last will and Testament of Jane Strong dec'd was proved by the oath of Thad[s] C. Brown a witness thereto and at a Court of Monthly Session held for the said County at the Courthouse on Tuesday the 24th of June then next following, The said will was further proved by the oath of J. D. G. Brown the other witness thereto and is ordered to be recorded.

    Teste, Wm. O. Winston, C.H.C.
    A Copy, Teste, O. M. Winston, D.C.H.C.

JUDITH AND JANE STRONG, of Hanover, sisters, left a considerable estate. Both died unmarried, Jane on 17 April 1853. John J. Jones and Jacob K. Strong, Special Commissioners.

THOMPSON VS. STANLEY, 1837 (44)

STANLEY, JOSHUA, of Hanover County, died many years ago, possessed of an estate which included 200 acres. The purpose of this suit was to effect a division of this land. The commissioners appointed for this purpose were: James Higgason, John M. Moody, Thomas Swift, Samuel R. Jones and Garland L. Sims. His issue:

1. STRANGEMAN STANLEY, died intestate prior to 1837, survived by his widow Martha, and by five children:
   1. ELIZABETH, wife in 1837 of Wm. Sims.
   2. SARAH STANLEY.
   3. EDMUND STANLEY.
   4. MILTON STANLEY, a minor in 1837.
   5. PRISCILLA STANLEY, a minor in 1837.
2. CELIA, wife in 1837, of Timothy Hall.
3. THOMAS STANLEY, died intestate prior to 1837, survived by his widow Rebecca and by four children:
   1. MATILDA STANLEY.
   2. MARY STANLEY, a minor in 1837.
   3. ARCHIBALD STANLEY, a minor in 1837.
   4. JAMES STANLEY, a minor in 1837.
4. WILLIAM M. STANLEY, and Elizabeth, his wife, had sold their interest in the land to Charles Thompson.
5. POLLY STANLEY, wife of William Stanley in 1837. They had sold their interest in the land to Charles A. Stanley and Nancy his wife, who conveyed in Trust to P. H. Price to secure a debt due Thomas Price, Jr., and by P. H. Price sold, and was bought by Nathaniel R. Stanley and Polly his wife.
6. AMY or AMEDIAH STANLEY.

Others mentioned: Clevears P. Chisholm; George S. Netherland; Charles Swift; Ralph H. Terrell; Charles Thompson, Jr.

TAYLOR VS. TAYLOR, 1858 (58)
TAYLOR VS. TAYLOR, 1867 (72)
TAYLOR VS. EUBANK, 1867 (48)

TAYLOR, WILLIAM D., of Hanover County, married twice - the names of his wives are not given in these suits - and had issue by both. Several tracts of land were conveyed at various times for the benefit of his children and grandchildren:

23 January 1832: H. I. Anderson and Matilda his wife, conveyed to Francis G. Taylor, as Trustee, for the benefit of the children of William D. Taylor, tract of land called the "Eggleston" tract, 300 acres, adjoining James Patterson, dec'd, Wm. Y. DeJarnatte, dec'd, Henry Arnold, and the Taylorsville Tract - not far from Taylor's Mill pond.

1835: John Hackett of Caroline County, con-

veyed to Edmund Winston, Trustee for children and heirs of William D. Taylor, of Hanover County, 126 1/2 acres on road leading from John D. Andrew's Tavern to Hanover Courthouse, adjoining James Patterson and Thomas J. Mallory. Consideration $452.75.

29 March 1836: John B. Green and Eliza his wife conveyed to Garland B. Taylor, Trustee, for benefit of the children of William D. Taylor, 234 acres adjoining Hector Davis, Jack King, and others. Consideration $1,000.

8 March 1856: Thomas King conveyed to Edmund L. Taylor, Fanny B. Taylor, Hardenia M. Pearce, James M. Taylor, John R. Taylor and George K. Taylor, children and grandchildren of William D. Taylor, dec'd, 84 acres which adjoined Edmund Winston, the said children and grandchildren of William D. Taylor, Jack King, and on the road leading from Goodall's to Hanover Courthouse. Consideration $554.00.

Issue of William D. Taylor by his first marriage:
1. GARLAND B. TAYLOR, died intestate. His father, Administrator. Had purchased land of Wm. O. Winston, Commissioner in the suit "Berkeley's Admrs. vs. Eubank &c." Resided on a tract of 150 acres near the town of Ashland. Survived by his widow, Angelina F., and by one daughter:
   1. FANNY B. TAYLOR, over 14 years of age in 1858. Died in 1861.
2. EDMUND L. TAYLOR, wife, Sarah A. in 1858, and residents of Culpeper County, Va.
3. FRANCES A. TAYLOR.
4. HARDENIA M., wife of James Pearce in 1858, and residents of Richmond, Va.
5. WILLIAM J. TAYLOR, died intestate prior to 1858, survived by his widow, Miriam N., and by four children:
   1. ISABEL BURNLEY TAYLOR, over 14 years of age in 1858. Married prior to 1867, George McKnight.
   2. FANNY J., over 14 years of age in 1858, married prior to 1867, Samuel H. Boykin.
   3. CLARENCE E. TAYLOR, over 14 years of age in 1858, died prior to 1873.
   4. FRANKLIN J. TAYLOR, under 14 years of age in 1858.
6. JANE M., (apparently a child of the first marriage) wife of Thomas Garland of Albemarle County in 1858. Deceased in 1867 without issue.
Issue of William D. Taylor by second marriage:
7. JAMES M. TAYLOR, wife, Isabel D.
8. JOHN R. TAYLOR, wife, Sallie E.
9. GEORGE K. TAYLOR, wife, Rebecca L.

EUBANK, THOMAS, SR., of Hanover County, prior to 1842 conveyed a certain tract of land to his children. In 1842, Robert C. Berkeley, representative of Carter Berkeley, Testator, sued these children to set aside the said deed. William D. Taylor, Administrator of Garland B. Taylor, dec'd, also sued Eubanks to protect title to the tract of land Garland B. Taylor had purchased of Wm. O. Winston, Commissioner in the suit "Berkeley's Admr. vs. Eubank &c." The children of Thomas Eubank, Sr.:
1. THOMAS EUBANK, (Jr.)
2. JULIA ANN EUBANK, living in Richmond 1867.
3. REUBEN B. EUBANK.
4. GEORGE W. EUBANK, none-resident of Virginia in 1867.
5. JOHN N. EUBANK, none-resident of Virginia in 1867.
6. JAMES P. EUBANK, died intestate prior to 1867, survived by his widow Catherine and three infant children of Richmond, Va. in 1867. Robert M. Doswell assigned as their Guardian in this suit:
   1. CHAPMAN EUBANK, a minor.
   2. WILLIAM EUBANK, a minor.
   3. ROBERT EUBANK, a minor.
7. PETER EUBANK, resident of Washington, D.C. in 1867.
8. SARAH, wife in 1842 of Elias Lowry.
9. ROYAL H. EUBANK, resident of Washington, D. C. in 1867.

TAYLOR VS. TAYLOR, 1841 (43)

TAYLOR, RICHARD, of Hanover County, died intestate prior to 1841. He possessed 386 acres on Pamunkey River, 20 miles north of Richmond, Va., adjoining the lands of William Carter, Ira S. Bowles, and others. He was survived by his widow, Elizabeth, who has since died, and by four children:
1. JOHN R. TAYLOR.
2. RICHARD S. TAYLOR, deceased in 1841, survived by his widow, Eleanor, and issue:
   1. ROBERT TAYLOR.
   2. MARY H. TAYLOR.
   3. FRANCIS E. TAYLOR
   4. BENJAMIN T. TAYLOR, a minor in 1841.
   5. JOSEPH TAYLOR, a minor in 1841.
   6. ANN MARIA TAYLOR, a minor in 1841.
   7. RICHARD S. TAYLOR, a minor in 1841.
   8. JOHN WILLIAM TAYLOR, a minor in 1841.
   9. EVELYN P. TAYLOR, a minor in 1841.
3. MARY, deceased in 1841, survived by husband, Robert A. Payne, and two infant children:
   1. RICHARD T. PAYNE, a minor in 1841.
   2. MARGARET PAYNE, a minor in 1841.
4. ANN, deceased in 1841, survived by husband Josiah W. Holt, and five children:
   1. ELIZABETH B., wife of Lewis W. Robinson, in 1841.
   2. MARY, wife of McKenzie Robertson 1841

3. HENRIETTA R. HOLT.
4. JOSEPH W. HOLT, a minor in 1841.
5. ANN T. HOLT, a minor in 1841.

Others mentioned: W. H. Gwathmey, Bickerton L. Winston, Lucien B. Price.

DIETRICK &C. VS. TAYLOR'S TRUSTEES &C., 1856 (32)

Nancy Rountree's Will

ROUNTREE, NANCY. "I, Nancy Rountree of the County of Hanover and State of Virginia do hereby make this my last will and testament in manner & form following, viz: 1st. I wish all my just debts to be paid. 2nd. I then will and leave in trust to R. G. Parrish all my property both real and personal and all money or claims that may be due me from whatever source for the benefit and use of my daughter Mary Ann Taylor during her natural life and after her death I give the same to be equally distributed among her children. In testimony whereof I have hereunto set my hand and affixed my seal this the eleventh day of April 1850."

                    Nancy Rountree (Seal)
Teste:
   Ann M. Toler
   John C. Saunders
   John R. Saunders.

At a Court of Monthly Session held for Hanover County at the Courthouse on Tuesday the 27th of January 1852. This Last will and Testament of Nancy Rowntree dec'd was proved by the oaths of John C. Saunders and John R. Saunders witnesses thereto & is ordered to be recorded.
   Teste, Wm. O. Winston, C.H.C.
   A Copy, Teste, R. O. Doswell, D.C.H.C.

NANCY ROUNTREE, of Hanover. Will dated 11 April 1850, probated 27 January 1852. Died circa 1 January 1852. She appointed R. G. Parrish her Trustee, who did not qualify. George W. Doswell, Sub. Trustee. She devised her property to her daughter:
1. MARY ANN, wife of Robert R. Taylor, who died after 1856, survived by seven infant children:
   1. JOHN T. D. TAYLOR.
   2. ROBERT J. TAYLOR.
   3. CHARLES A. TAYLOR.
   4. BENJAMIN F. TAYLOR.
   5. ANN JUDSON TAYLOR.
   6. MARGARET FRANCES TAYLOR.
   7. NANCY ELIZABETH TAYLOR.

Others mentioned: Wm. A. Dietrick and Wm. A. Dietrick, Jr., merchants and partners, trading as Wm. A. Dietrick & Son.; C. P. Woodson employ-'ed by Dietrick, Woodson & Co., Cole Hill, Va.

TAYLOR VS. TAYLOR, 1867 (48)

TAYLOR, JOHN J., of Hanover County, died with a will (which was destroyed) in 1858. George W. Doswell, his son-in-law, Executor. Survived by his widow, Mrs. Lavinia Taylor, and six children:
1. EDMUND TAYLOR.
2. THOMAS F. TAYLOR, aged 31 in 1867.
3. CHARLES TAYLOR.
4. LUCY TAYLOR.
5. ELIZABETH, wife of George W. Doswell.
6. FRANCES, wife of J. B. Brown.

WINSTON VS. HARRIS &C., 1863 (24)
MILLS &C. VS. WINSTON'S EXORS. &C., 1874 (16)

Frances G. Taliaferro's Will

TALIAFERRO, FRANCES G. "I, Frances G. Taliaferro, being of sound mind do hereby make my last will and Testament in manner and form following, that is to say: 1st. I desire my funeral expenses and my just _ paid. 2nd. It is my wish that no public sale of my slaves be made to effect a division thereof at any rates they are not to be sold to traders. 3rd. Some small articles of my household furniture I shall divide amongst some of my relatives, a memorandum of which will be found enclosed in this will stating the articles & to whom they belong which I desire my executors strictly adhere to. 4th. I give to Dr. R. W. Fox in trust for Corinth Church in King William County one hundred Dollars to be applied as the Elders of that Church may think best for their interest. 5th. I wish all the balance of my estate of every kind to be divided in four equal parts or shares, one part or share I give to my brother William O. Harris children and their heirs forever. One other part I loan to my sister Mary G. Cosby and at her death or marriage the share allotted to her I give to her children and their heirs forever. I give another part to John T. Harris in trust for the benefit of Dianna A. Beadles & her children and the children of Frances E. Mills dec'd which share or part I desire shall be equally divided into two parts or Shares one of which I wish Dianna A. Beadles to have in trust as aforesaid during her life and after her death I give the same to her children & their heirs forever. I desire that the other portion bequeathed in Trust to the children of Frances E. Mills dec'd as they become of age that they shall have their portion of the same & that the income of the Share allotted in Trust to Dianna A. Beadles & the children of Frances E. Mills shall be paid annually. 6th. The remaining Share or part being the 4th I loan to my brother John G. Harris during his natural life and at his death I wish the Share or part allotted to him to be divided, that is to say in the following manner to wit: In three

equal parts one which I give to the children of of my brother William O. Harris, one other part to the children of my sister Mary G. Cosby and their heirs forever, and the remaining third part I give in Trust to John T. Harris for the benefit of Dianna A. Beadles & her children and the children of Frances E. Mills to be held and applied to in the same way as that bequeathed to them in the 5th Item of this will. Lastly, I appoint my friend William O. Winston and my nephew George W. Cosby my Executors to this my last will and testament revoking all other or former will made by me. In witness whereof I have hereunto Set my hand and affixed my Seal this 2nd day of May in the year of our Lord one thousand Eight hundred and forty-nine."

                                    Frances G. Taliaferro (Seal)
Witness:
    Mary Jane Williamson
    Dabney Williamson

At a Court of Monthly Session held for Hanover County atthe Courthouse on Tuesday the 26th of June 1860. This last will and testament of Frances G. Taliaferro deceased was proved by the oaths of Mary Jane Williamson and Dabney Williamson the witnesses thereto and is ordered to be recorded.
    Teste, Wm. O. Winston, C.H.C.
    A Copy, Teste, R. O. Doswell, C.H.C.

FRANCES G. TALIAFERRO, of Hanover. Will dated 2 May 1849, probated 26 June 1860. George W. Cosby and William O. Winston (now dec'd) qualified as Executors. No mention is made of her husband. She devised her property to brothers and sisters, and their children:

JOHN G. HARRIS, a brother, died without issue in 1873. Roy Temple was his representative.

WILLIAM O. HARRIS, a brother, who had issue:
1. OWEN R. HARRIS.
2. WILLIAM O. HARRIS, of Nashville, Tenn., in 1863.
3. TEMPLE OVERTON HARRIS, of Nashville, Tenn., in 1863.
4. DENNIS B. HARRIS, of Nashville, Tenn., in 1863.
5. ELLEN, widow in 1873, of William Joseph Cragwell. (also called Craghall)
6. FREDERICK B. HARRIS, of Nashville, Tenn., in 1863.
7. BENJAMIN B. HARRIS, died without issue prior to 1863.
8. THOMAS H. HARRIS, died prior to 2 May 1849, survived by his widow Elizabeth F. (Betty) and two infant children in 1863 and 1874, living in Charlotte, N. C.:
    1. KATE H. HARRIS, a minor.
    2. LUCY R. HARRIS, a minor.
9. CAROLINE E., wife of C. L. Garrett in 1874.
10. FANNIE E. HARRIS, who is non compos mentis.

11. LUCY A., wife in 1874, of Napoleon B. Kean, of Goochland County.
12. KATE, married A. J. Johnson, who survived her, but is now, 1874, deceased, and their children are not known. They were residents of Charlotte County, Va.

MARY G., a sister, widow of a Mr. Cosby, died prior to 1874. J. A. Wingfield, Sheriff of Hanover County, her personal representative. She had issue:
1. WILLIAM H. COSBY, of Albemarle County in 1863. Thos. F. Michie, assignee.
2. JOHN W. COSBY, a resident of Richmond, Va., in 1863, died prior to 1874.
3. BENJAMIN FRANKLIN COSBY, of Petersburg, Va., in 1863.
4. GEORGE W. COSBY.
5. JAMES J. COSBY, of Richmond, Va., in 1863.
6. MELVINA D., married John G. Cooke of Stafford County, Va., and died intestate prior to 1863, survived by her husband and eight infant children of whom he is Guardian:
   1. PHILIP ST. GEORGE COOKE.
   2. MARY G. COOKE.
   3. ELIZABETH COOKE.
   4. SALLY B. COOKE.
   5. JOHN G. COOKE.
   6. WILLIAM H. COOKE.
   7. GEORGE W. COOKE.
   8. LETTIE COOKE.
7. ELIZABETH F., widow of Andrew F. Beadles.

DIANNA BEADLES, a legatee of Frances G. Taliaferro, not stated to be a sister, alive in 1874, when her children are:
1. JAMES E. BEADLES, of Hanover County.
2. JOHN W. BEADLES, Tunstall P.O., New Kent.
3. SUSAN E. BEADLES,   "   "
4. ANDREW J. BEADLES,   "   "
5. ROBERTA ANN, a minor in 1863, married prior to 1874, M. D. L. Runkle, and are residents of Greene County, Va.

FRANCES E., a sister of Frances G. Taliaferro, married John Mills, and died prior to Mrs. Taliaferro. In 1863, John Mills was a resident of Goochland County, and their children were:
1. NATHANIEL MILLS.
2. LUCY F. MILLS.
3. WILLIAM H. MILLS.
4. JAMES L. MILLS.
5. ANNIE E. MILLS.
6. M. J. MILLS

JOHN T. HARRIS, Trustee, a resident of New Kent County in 1863. Mentioned in Mrs. Taliaferro's will.

Others mentioned: Joseph F. Priddy, who was assigned as Guardian of the infants Lucy R., & Cate H. Harris, and Roberta Beadles.

WINSTON, WILLIAM O., of Hanover. Will dated 12 March 1862, probated 25 March 1862. Re-recorded 23 July 1867. Bickerton L. Winston and R. O. Doswell, Executors. Requests brother Bickerton L. Winston to act for his infant children. Survived by his widow, Sarah, and by issue, not in order perhaps of their births:
1. PHILIP B. WINSTON, non-resident of Virginia in 1873.
2. FENDALL G. WINSTON.
3. BETTY, wife in 1874, of Thomas L. Rosser, formerly of Albemarle County, now non-residents of Virginia.
4. SALLY M., wife in 1874, of Edmund P. Winston.
5. WILLIAM O. WINSTON, a minor in 1874.
6. BICKERTON L. WINSTON, JR., a minor in 1874.
7. FANNY WINSTON, a minor in 1874.

TALIAFERRO &C. VS. OLIVER, 1845 (43)
TALIAFERRO &C. VS. TALIAFERRO'S
TRUSTEE, 1849 (43)

TALIAFERRO, WILLIAM A., of Hanover County, married Mary A. S., a daughter of Isaac Oliver who died many years prior to 1845, intestate, leaving a widow, Ann A., and several children. In the division of his real estate, Mary A. S. Taliaferro was allotted 283 1/4 acres being a part of the Spring Grove tract, adjoining William Patman and Samuel Davis and near Wynnes Meeting House. In 1845 the Taliaferros have one living child, under two years of age:
1. JAMES EDMUND TALIAFERRO.

Others mentioned: "Mrs. Fletcher, one of the beneficiaries of an unused fund of Cason Hall's Estate, is dead"- 1853; James A. Oliver, dec'd in 1848; William B. Sydnor "next friend of Mary A. S. Taliaferro" in suit of 1849; Archibald B. Timberlake; William W. Timberlake; James B. Todd, of Caroline County.

GREEN VS. PHILLIPS' TRUSTEE, 1843 (17)
PHILLIPS VS. WADE, 1848 (32)
OLD WILL BOOK, PAGE 82

TALLEY, DIBDRAL, of Hanover County, died with a will prior to 1843. Estate included tract of land called "Black Harry" which it is said he devised to a grandson, Robert H. Phillips. His issue, probably among others:
1. JUDITH, married Thomas Phillips who died prior to December 1840, by whom she had issue, probably among others:
   1. ROBERT H. PHILLIPS, a minor, Robert Wade, Guardian. His securities: John Pate (dec'd in 1848, Maria W. Pate, Admr.); Bentley Wicker, Richard Burnett, and Wm. H. Macon. In 1843, Fleming Green was Security for

Fountain O. Holt, convey to George W. Trice and Judith, his wife, as Trustees for Robert Phillips the tract "Black Harry."

2. DIBDAL T. PHILLIPS. Will dated 19 July 1845, probated 12 April 1848, by Robert Wade, Executor, and by Spotswood Liggon, and Robert H.Phillips "next of kin." Witnesses were: Billy W. Talley, Edmund W. Allen and David Wood. Legatees were his brother, Robert H. Phillips; friends Spotswood Liggon and Robert Wade. (This will is to be found in the old will book, page 82, and carries the notation: "Overruled by Court of Appeals - see Order Book of October 1849.")

Judith, after the death of Thomas Phillips, married George W. Trice, a resident of King & Queen County in 1844.

Others mentioned: Captain William Henry Curtis 1843; Fleming Green, dec'd, John D. Thomas, Admr. with the will annexed; John B. Green; Richard G. Smith.

TALLEY'S ADMR. VS. TALLEY &C., 1849 (58)

Henry Talley's Will

TALLEY, HENRY. "In the name of God amen. I, Henry Talley being of sound mind and discretion do declare this to be my last will and testament. In the first place I desire that all my just debts to be paid, after which I wish my wife Sally Epps to receive independent of her other rights one hundred Dollars being the amount given her by her uncle. The rest of my property including money and effects of every kind I desire to be kept together and used by my Executor in the manner he may consider most advantageous for my wife and children. Should my wife marry again I wish her to receive of my estate whatever the law of the State allows Should a child of mine be born of her after my death I wish such child to share alike in my property throughout. I give to my executor full power to dispose of any land that I may hereafter come into possession and invest the proceeds of such sale in the way he may think best for the benefit of my wife and children. I desire my wife to be furnished with a full suit of mourning apparel without separate charge thereof to her, by my executor. I leave my brother George W. Talley the executor of this my last will and testament. Given under my hand and seal this 15th day of February eighteen hundred and forty-two."

Teste,   Henry Talley (Seal)
    Ro. Johnston
    Albert M. Akin, Henry Cox.

Probated in Henrico County, 7 March 1842 by the witnesses. George W. Talley qualified as Executor, with Ezekiel S. Talley, Security, in the sum of $2,500.

HENRY TALLEY. Will dated 15 February 1842, probated in Henrico County 7 March 1842. His brother, George W. Talley of King & Queen Co., qualified as Executor. Testator had land in Hanover County, adjoining John Pate, Charles R. Hughes, and others, and which was purchased by Hughes. He was survived by his widow, Sally Epps Talley, and three infant children, of whom Bentley Wicker was Guardian:
1. SALLY EPPS TALLEY, a minor in 1849.
2. ROBERT TALLEY, a minor in 1849.
3. MARTHA TALLEY, a minor in 1849.

TERRELL & WIFE VS. DOSWELL'S EXORS., 1832 (42)
TERRELL &C VS. TERRELL &C., 1852 (84)
TERRELL &C. VS. TERRELL, 1868 (86)
TERRELL'S EXOR. VS. TERRELL'S AGENT, 1875 (81)

TERRELL, JOSEPH Z., JR., and wife Martha, on 31 March 1843 executed a Deed of Trust to Nicholas Terrell, Trustee (dec'd in 1852,) Charles P. Higgason, Substitute Trustee 1852, Charles Terrell and John T. Longan, Securities, on the following properties: 849 acres where Joseph Z. Terrell now lives, adjoining Lancelot Phillips, Joseph F. Price and others; 164 1/2 acres adjoining John Terrell; another tract adjoining John Wyatt and others; and one other tract in Ballard County, Kentucky, conveyed to said Joseph Z. by deed from Jonathan W. Terrell, containing 720 acres; also Joseph Z. Terrell's interest in 500 acres on which Elizabeth N. Gillum now lives, adjoining Milton M. Brown, Nicholas Terrell and others; and 20 slaves; and the balance of the interest in the Estate of his father, Charles Terrell, dec'd, -- for the benefit of the children of the said Joseph Z and wife Martha Terrell and children:
1. CHARLES TERRELL, of age in 1852, dec'd in 1868, survived by his widow, Emeline J. Terrell, Executrix.
2. MARY G., of age in 1852, married Franklin L. Weathers, and died prior to 1874.
3. ANN L., between 14 and 21 years of age in 1852, wife in 1868 of Wm. P. Yeamans.
4. BARBARA O., between 14 and 21 years of age in 1852, wife in 1868 of Benjamin F. Johnson.
5. MARTHA T., between 14 and 21 years of age in 1852, wife in 1868 of James H. Snead, and deceased in 1875.
6. JOHN H. TERRELL, between 14 and 21 years of age in 1852.
7. JOSEPH Z. TERRELL, Jr., under 14 years of age in 1852.
8. WILLIAM D. TERRELL, under 14 years of age in 1852.
9. NICHOLAS TERRELL, under 14 years of age

HANOVER COUNTY CHANCERY WILLS AND NOTES

139

in 1852.
10. GEORGE W. TERRELL, under 14 years of age
    in 1852, died under 21 years of age.
11. BENJAMIN F. TERRELL, under 14 years of age
    in 1852, died under 21 years of age.
12. JAMES A. TERRELL, under 14 years of age in
    1852, died under 21 years of age.

ICHOLAS TERRELL, Trustee for Joseph Z. Terrell,
married prior to March 1834, Maria B., widow
of Benjamin Franklin Doswell who lived at
Newfound Mills, and died with a will in 1828,
John T. Anderson and brother Henley C. Dos-
well, Executors. Henley C. Doswell's wife was
Evelina. He and his brother were sons of
Thomas Doswell.

thers mentioned: Caroline County Justices of
he Peace in 1828: Booth Brown and Lewis George;
n 1832: Richard Buckner, Jr., Alexander Chap-
an, William Harrison, Jr., and John P. Miller.
elix Winston, Deputy Sheriff for Laney Jones,
igh Sheriff, Hanover County, 1831; Major Byrd
eorge.

FROM OLD WILL BOOK, PAGE 64

ERRELL, JONATHAN W., of Hanover County, on
7 April 1841, appointed Guardian of the or-
hans of John Terrell, dec'd.:
1. LUCY E. TERRELL.
2. MARY M. TERRELL.

HACKER VS. NELSON'S ADMR., SCOTT &C., 1858 (48)

THACKER, JAMES, of Hanover, deceased in
1858, executed a Deed of Trust dated 9 Feb.
1843, to his friend and neighbor, Dr. Ed-
ard L. Nelson, for 23 1/2 acres. He had issue,
robably among others:
1. WILLIAM A. THACKER, whose wife, in 1858
   is Mahala J. Thacker. He had an Aunt,
   Nancy Hanes.

NELSON, DR. EDWARD L., of Beaverdam, Hanover
County, removed to Henrico County after Feb-
uary 1855, where he died with a will. He left
roperty to Parmelia Thomas and Mary Ann Scott
nd Roberta, Edward L., and Alice Scott, minors
n 1858, and mulattos.

thers mentioned: William L. Mallory and Curtis
. Moore.

HOMAS & WIFE VS BROWN & WINN'S ADMR., 1852 (45)

THACKER, NELSON, of Hanover, died intestate
prior to 1852. Peter W. Brown, Sheriff of
Hanover County, Admr. (John J. Winn, dec'd
as his brother-in-law) The Intestate was survi-
ed by his widow, Hulda Thacker and by three

children:
1. SARAH ANN, married first John J. Heath;
   married secondly, James Thomas, her
   husband in 1858.
2. ELI W. THACKER, a minor, Peter W. Brown,
   Guardian, in 1858.
3. JOHN N. THACKER, a minor, Peter W. Brown,
   Guardian, in 1858.

THILMAN'S ADMX. VS THILMAN'S TRUSTEE, 1836 (44)

THILMAN, JOHN, deceased, owned land in Caroline County, on which John Thornton lived
from 1793 to 1805. He had issue, probably
among others, a son,
1. JOHN THILMAN, Jr., died circa 1811, survived by his widow Jane S., wife shortly
   afterward of Thomas Hickman, Admr. of
   Thilman. In 1812 Hickman is deceased and
   Mrs. Jane S. Hickman, Admr. de bonis non
   of Thilman. Soon afterwards she married
   Henry Hill of "Mt. Gideon", who in 1840,
   has a son, perhaps among others, Garleik
   Hill.

THILMAN, PAUL, (relationship to above not
stated) in circa 1796 his wife was Barbara
Overton Thilman. He died in the summer of 1802,
Paul Woolfolk, Exor. She survived and married a
Mr. Jones, and died in August 1812, Philip B.
Winston, Executor. They had two sons:
1. WILLIAM H. THILMAN, born in 1798.
2. PAUL THILMAN, JR., born in 1800, and died
   early in the Summer of 1817. Philip B.
   Winston had been his Guardian. In 1836
   Benjamin Pollard was Trustee for his Estate, and was sued by John Thilman
   through his attorney, Peyton Randolph.
   Owned the Hanover Courthouse Tavern which
   he rented in 1813 for a term of three
   years to John Thornton, Jr. Also owned
   "stud horse Samplighter and Dungannon, the
   Diomed." [Note: Some of these references
   would appear to pertain to Paul Thilman,
   Sr., who is also sometime styled "Jr."].

"To Mr. Benjamin Pollard:
   Paul Thilman the son of Paul & Barbara
   Overton Thilman, died early in the summer
   of 1817. He was about two years younger
   than his brother Wm. H. Thilman, who came
   of age in the Summer of 1819, consequent-
   ly he was born 1798. This from my account
   as gdn of Paul.
                    Philip B. Winston
                    12 June 1840
   I think it probable my Sister Alice or
   brother Wm can say with more certainty
   than I when P.T. was born. P.B.W."

Others mentioned: Hardin Burnley; Wm. Clarke, Sr.
Deputy Sheriff Hanover 1803; Augustine Davis;
Holdenby Dixon owned land at Hanover Courthouse

circa 1813; Jeremiah Rawlings of Caroline Co., 1808; Henry Robinson; John Thornton, Sr.; Anthony Walke; William O. Winston, Sheriff of Hanover County 1803; W. P. Napier 1805.

THOMPSON &C. VS. THOMPSON'S ADMR. &C., 1846 (44)

THOMPSON, CAPTAIN CHARLES, JR., of Hanover died intestate. Was 88 years of age in 1831. In 1836 Charles Thompson,Jr., qualified as Administrator. Securities, Nathaniel Thompson, Charles J. Thompson, Joseph F. Dabney, Thomas Doswell and Philip B. Winston. (He had been one of the Executors of Timothy Goodman, dec'd.) Left a considerable Estate including some twenty slaves. Appraised valued of personal property $16,892.95. Issue:

1. JOHN THOMPSON, died between 1838 and 1846. Elizabeth F. Thompson, Admx.
2. FRANCIS J. THOMPSON.
3. CHARLES THOMPSON, JR., qualified in 1836 as Administrator of his father's Estate.
4. SARAH J., married prior to 1836, Nathaniel Thompson of Louisa, who is dec'd in 1854.
5. GARLAND THOMPSON, dec'd, who was survived by children:
   1. CHARLES J. THOMPSON, of Louisa, 1846.
   2. PHILIP M. THOMPSON, Lawyer of City of Richmond.
   3. WILLIAM M. THOMPSON.
   4. GEORGE G. THOMPSON.
   5. JULIA THOMPSON, of City of Richmond.
   6. ISABELLA J., wife of Robert M. Sully, sometime of Culpeper County, of the City of Richmond in 1850.

Timothy Goodman's Will

GOODMAN, TIMOTHY. "I, Timothy Goodman of the County of Hanover and State of Virginia taking into consideration the certainty of death but being uncertain when that event may happen, have determined at this time to make my last Will and Testament before sickness of body or the infirmities of age weaken or diminish my understanding or memory, which I do in form & manner following, viz - I desire my Just debts to be paid by my Executors hereafter named, to are but few and to a small amount. I give and devise Elisha Gilliam Crawford at present living in the State of Georgia the eight negroes to wit: Sarah, Fanny, Lucy, Louis, Armistead, Neddy, Jerriah and Dolly to him and his heirs forever. I give and devise to my nephew William Goodman of the State of South Carolina at Vienne the four following negroes to wit Jenny, John, Dorcus and Peter to him and his heirs forever. I give and devise to my nephew Edmund Goodman the three following negroes to wit Mosses, Cressey and Salley to him and his heirs forever. I give and devise to my nephew Zachariah Goodman the two negores following to wit Minor & Delphy

to him and his heirs forever. I give and devise to James Vaughan who lives with Nelson Thompson, Esq. of the County of Louisa one negro named Jesse to him and his heirs forever. I give to my brother William Goodman the tract of land on which I now live, likewise the land called Hinchies together with the four following negroes to wit Nat, Charles, Venus and James for and during his natural life upon this condition and under this restriction that he does not clear any land nor cut down any timber only such as may be necessary for firewood, fencing, to make ploughs, carts &c. I give to my said brother William Goodman as much corn and meat as will be sufficient in the opinion of my Exors for him and his family for one year. If the corn and meat is not on the plantation at the time of my death, then my Exors to purchase it for him . It is my will and desire that the property hereby lent to my brother William for life should at his death be sold, both land and negroes, and the amount of the sales to be equally divided among all his (my said brother William Goodman's children,) the sale to be made on such credit as my Exors may think most to the interest of the children of said brother Willia the amount of which sale I give to them and their heirs forever. I give my brother Charles Goodman one negro woman named Milley with all her future increase from this time to him and his heirs forever. It is my will that my Exec tors purchase as much three per cent stock of the United States as that the interest from the same shall amount to the sum of fifty dollars p. annum: which sum of fifty dollars it is my will and wish that my Executors lay out annually for the use of Joseph Terrell Goodman in such manner as they may deem most proper for his comfort and convenience, the said Joseph Terrell Goodman to have no command or right to the said fifty dollars annually to or . . . for the interest aforesaid, but my said Exors to lay out the same themselves for his use. My said Exors to have said stock transferred to them as my exors and at the death of the said Joseph Terrell Goodman it is my will that the said three per cent. stock be sold and the amount divided among all the Children of my Brother Benjamin Goodman which I give to them & their heirs forever. All the rest and residue of my Estate of what kind and quantity whatsoever I desire may be sold and the amount to be divided as follows: One half to the children of my brother Benjamin Goodman and the other half to the children of my brother William Goodman which I give to them and their heirs forever. In the Last place I constitute and appoint my good friends Charles Thompson, William Walton, Charles Terrell and William Mills, Executors of this my last will and Testament, requesting they would execute the trust thus reposed to them. I have chosen them as my Executors Knowing them to be honest attentive men (and no other description of men would I

ish to appoint) and not wishing in my lifetime
o have services rendered me for nothing, much
ess would I wish it after my death, I have
hought proper as compensation for the trouble
f my Exors of those of them who will oblige me
y acting as such (and I hope they all of them
ct) to give and hereby do give them ten p.
ent on the amount of my Estate that they act
n, or to be more plain, on the value of my
state. I do hereby revoke all wills or testa-
ent heretofore by me made and declare this to
e my last will and Testament. In witness
hereof I have hereunto set my hand and affix
y seal this 6th day of December in the year of
ur lord Christ 1803."
                Timothy Goodman (Seal)
igned, sealed & acknowledged
n our presence, who at the request & in the
resence of the said Timothy Goodman have tested
his his will: Geo. White, Wm. Corley, Sr.,
ohn Thompson, Jno. Waddy, David Bullock.

May 29th 1804. In addition to the Exors within
entioned I now think proper to add Geo. Pattie
f Louisa, and John Thompson son of Chas. Thomp-
on of Hanover. Witness me hand and seal the day
bove."
                Timothy Goodman (Seal)
itness: David Bullock, John Waddy, Geo.White.

Feb. 15th 1805. By way of Codicil to the will
ithin written I will and desire that those of
y slaves that I may leave at my death, who
rom age or other causes should be in the opin-
on of my Exors so infirm as would make it im-
roper in them to deliver the Legatees within
entioned or sold, should by my Exors be sup-
orted during their lives out of my Estate. I
hink I am in duty bound to make provision for
he unfortunate slaves and expect my Exors will
ttend to it. Witness my hand and seal the day
bove."
                Timothy Goodman (Seal)
cknowledged and signed
n presence of David Bullock, John Waddy.

t a Court of Monthly Session held for Hanover
ounty at the Courthouse on Wednesday the 22nd
f May 1805. This last will and Testament of
imothy Goodman deceased and the Codicils there-
o written were offered for proof by Charles
hompson and William Walton, Executors in the
aid will named and the said will was proved by
he oaths of John Waddy and George White wit-
esses thereto and the said second Codicil was
roved by the oath of John Waddy a witness
hereto and the said will and Codicils were also
roved by the oaths of the Executors and are
rdered to be recorded.

Teste, William Pollard, C. H. C.

A Copy,
        Teste, O. M. Winston, D.C.H.C.

TIMOTHY GOODMAN, of Hanover. Will dated 6
December 1803. Codicils: 29 May 1804; 15 February 1805. Probated 22 May 1805. Charles Thompson and William Walton qualified as Executors.
Legatees were brothers William Goodman, and
Benjamin Goodman and children - the latter
living in Newburn District, South Carolina in
1846; Brother Charles Goodman; Nephews: Edmund,
William and Zachariah Goodman; Elisha Gilliam
Crawford of Georgia; Joseph Terrell Goodman,
who was deceased in 1853; and James Vaughan.

WALTON, WILLIAM, of Hanover, one of the
Executors of Timothy Goodman, "died with a
will in 1811" Garland and Nelson Walton, Executors. Both were living in 1853.

Others mentioned: 1854 - Joseph F. Dabney,
dec'd, Administrator: Pichegrue Woolfolk of
Holly Hill, Caroline County, Sheriff; Deputies:
Woodson and Wesley Wright.

THOMPSON & WIFE VS. TYLER & OTHERS, 1859 (48)

THOMPSON, ROGER, of Hanover, "died some
years ago intestate possessed of a small
tract of land near the Junction, adjoining
the land of the heirs of Garland Perkins and
others." This tract consisted of 5 acres. On
27 February 1834, Edmund Lowry and Sarah, his
wife had executed a Deed of Trust to Edmund Winston and Thomas Doswell, Trustees, for the benefit of Mary Thompson and her children. The
intestate was survived by his widow, Mary, who
is also deceased in 1859. Their issue:
  1. JAMES MONTGOMERY THOMPSON, in 1859, wife,
     Margaret E. Thompson.
  2. MELVINA F., wife in 1859, of William N.
     Tyler.
  3. THOMAS D. THOMPSON.
  4. MARY J., wife in 1859, of Joseph H. Young.
  5. ANN ELIZA, dec'd in 1859, survived by her
     husband, Joseph H. Young, who has since
     married Mary J. Thompson, her sister,
     and by two children:
     1. MARY L. YOUNG, over 14 and under 21
        years of age in 1859.
     2. JANE ELIZA YOUNG, under 21 years of
        age in 1859.

Others mentioned: Edward T. Morris, Lawyer; B.
W. Morris; John R. Taylor deposed that Roger
Thompson had two tracts of land, 5 and 2 acres
respectively, which he considered to be worth
$150.00; William W. Mallory also familiar with
tracts.

TURNER VS. DAVIS & OTHERS, 1841 (43)
THORNTON'S EXTX. VS. SMITH & WIFE &C., 1832 (43)
SMITH & WIFE VS. THORNTON'S EXOR &C., 1834 (40)
THORNTON'S EXTX. VS. THORNTON'S EXOR., 1844 (43)
THORNTON'S EXTX. VS. DAVIS' EXOR., 1844 (43)
                [Turn to Next Page]

Countinued from last page.

John Thornton's (Sr.) Will

THORNTON, JOHN, Sr. "In the name of God Amen. I, John Thornton of the County of Hanover do make and ordain this as my last will and Testament revoking all other wills heretofore made by me. Item. I give and bequeath unto my daughter Sarah Hall one negro Girl named Harriet during her natural life, and at her death to her daughter Sarah Hall to her & her heirs forever. I loan to my said daughter Sarah Hall one room in my dwelling house called the shed room with the privilege of firewood and water during her natural life. I also give my said daughter Sarah Hall an annuity of one hundred dollars to be paid annually by my son Anthony Thornton out of the property which I have devised to him in this my will. Item. I give and bequeath unto my daughter Catherine Turner the interest of one thousand dollars to be paid annually by my Executors hereafter to be named and at the death of my said daughter Catherine Turner. It is my will and desire that my Executors do equally divide the said thousand dollars between the three youngest children now in being of my said daughter Catherine Turner and in the event of either of the said three children dying before the death of their mother, then the said Thousand Dollars to be equally divided between the survivors. And it is further my will and desire that my Executors hold in their hands the said thousand dollars until the said children marry or come of age. Item. I give and bequeath unto my daughter Elizabeth Tomkies an annuity of one hundred dollars to be paid by my son John Thornton, Jr., out of the property which I have devised to him in this my will. Item. I give and bequeath unto my son John Thornton, Jr., two hundred and fifty-nine acres of land called and known by the name of Church quarter and adjoining the lands of Thomas Price, jr., & Edmund Taylor, to him and his heirs forever. Item. I give and bequeath unto my son William Thornton the property I have before given him and in the event of my son Anthony Thornton's death without lawful issue, it is my will and desire that my said son William Thornton shall have the tract of land devised in this my will to my son Anthony Thornton called and known by the name of Mill Creek & lying in the County of Hanover. Item. I give and bequeath unto my son Anthony Thornton during his natural life one tract of land called and known by the name of Mill Creek containing one thousand acres to be the same more or less, I also give him the tract of land on which I reside together with the tract called Lawrence's, the tract at the Newfound river bridge, and the tract called Sandidge's making altogether seven hundred and seventy-four acres be the same more or less during his natural life, and in the event of my said son Anthony

Thornton's dying without lawful issue, then it is my will and desire that the tract of land called & known by the name of Mill Creek shoul go to my son William Thornton in fee simple to him and his heirs forever. And it is further m will and desire, in the event of my son Anthon Thornton dying without lawful issue, that the tract of land on which I reside, The tract called Lawrence's, the tract at the Newfound river bridge, and the tract called Sandidge's, all of which tracts of land shall go to my son John Thornton, jr. in fee simple to him and hi heirs forever. Item. I lend unto my Granddaug ter Courtney Davis one negro boy named Washing ton now in the possession of Hector Davis, unt her son John Nicholas Davis arrives at the age of twenty-one years, then it is my will and de sire that the said negro boy Washington should be delivered to the said John Nicholas Davis and I give him to him & his heirs forever. Item. I give and bequeath to my son Anthony Thornton one negro girl named Lucy, daughter o Anna, also all my household and Kitchen furniture to him & his heirs forever. Item. I give and bequeath to my granddaughter Mary Turner one negro girl named Mary, daughter of little Betty, to her & her heirs forever. Item. I give and bequeath to Virginia Turner my granddaughter one negro child named Charlotte, daug ter of Molley, to her and her heirs forever. Item. I give and bequeath unto my granddaughte Sarah T. Tomkies one negro girl named Aggy, daughter of Molley to her & her heirs forever. Item. I give and bequeath to my grandson Josep Tomkies one negro boy David son of Anny to him and his heirs forever. Item. I give and bequeath to my granddaughter Elizabeth Tomkies one negro girl named Lavinia, daughter of Anna to her and her heirs forever. Item. I give and bequeath to my granddaughter Mary Tomkies one negro girl named Nelly daughter of Rachel to her & her heirs forever. Item. I give and bequeath to my grandson Edward Tomkies, one negro boy the son of Rachel her oldest now living, to him and his heirs forever. Item. I give and bequeath to my granddaughter Catherin Tomkies one hundred dollars to be paid to her by my Executors when she marries or comes of lawful age. Item. I give and bequeath to my grandson William Hall one negro boy named Isham son of Anna, to him and his heirs foreve Item. I give and bequeath to my grandsons John Meaux and Richard Meaux, sons of my deceased daughter Ann Meaux one hundred dollars each to be paid by my Executors within twelve months of my death. Item. It is my will and desire that my Executors hereafter to be named do sel on a credit of twelve months my negro man name Bartlett and his wife Mary and all the childre she now has or may hereafter have, together with all my horses and stock of all kinds for the purpose of raising a fund to pay off the legacies left my daughter Catherine Turner and my grandchildren John W. Meaux, Richard Meaux,

d Catherine Tomkies and the overplus to be
ually divided between my sons John Thornton,
., & Anthony Thornton to them and their heirs
rever. Item. I give and bequeath to my sons
hn Thornton, Jr., amd Anthony Thornton all
e remainder of my perishable and personal
tate not heretofore devised or disposed of in
is my last will and Testament to be equally
vided between them, to them and their heirs
rever. And it is my will and desire that my
ns John Thornton, jr., and Anthony Thornton
y out of the personal estate left them, all
just debts and funeral expenses. Lastly, I
point my friends Lewis Berkeley, Hector Davis,
ancis G. Taylor, my Executors to this my last
ll & Testament. In witness whereof I have
rewith set my hand and affixed my seal this
rst day of November one thousand eight hun-
ed and twenty-one."
                    John Thornton (Seal)

gned, sealed & delivered in the presence of:
John J. Taylor
Jos. Patterson
Ira S. Bowles

a Court of Monthly Session held for Hanover
unty at the Courthouse on Wednesday the 23d
January 1822. This last will and testament
John Thornton dec'd was offered to proof by
ctor Davis one of the Executors therein named
d was proved by the oaths of John J. Taylor
d Ira S. Bowles two of the witnesses thereto,
d also by the oath of the Executor, and is
dered to be recorded.
Teste, William Pollard, C.H.C.
A Copy, Teste, Philip B. Winston, C.H.C.

OHN THORNTON, SR.., of Hanover County. Will
dated 1 November 1821, probated 23 January
1822. Hector Davis qualified as Executor with
nd in the amount of $35,000. Securities were
iver T. Cross, John Thornton, Jr., Hugh Davis,
d John B. Green. Some of his children and
andchildren:

1. JOHN THORNTON, JR., called "Captain". He
   dated his will 25 March 1829. Probated
   27 April1829. Widow, Sarah Thornton, his
   Executrix. Their issue:
   1. JOHN S. THORNTON. Living at Taylors-
      ville in 1836, deceased in 1838.
   2. COURTNEY COWLES THORNTON.
   3. THOMAS C. THORNTON, dec'd in 1838.
   4. MELVINA D. THORNTON, dec'd in 1834.
      [written also Melvina D. Thruston.]
   5. HARRIET THORNTON, a minor in 1834.
   6. RICHARD A. THORNTON, a minor in 1834.
      Attended Washington-Henry Academy
      in 1830 and probably other years.
   7. JAMES T. THORNTON, a minor in 1834.

His will is given herewith in its
entirety:

John Thornton's (Jr.) Will

JOHN THORNTON, JR. "In the name of God amen. I,
John Thornton of the County of Hanover being
of sound mind and disposing memory do make and
declare this to be my last will & testament
hereby revoking all others by me heretofore
made. Imprimis. I give and bequeath unto my
wife Sarah Thornton all my estate both real and
personal of every description for and during
her natural life. It is my wish that _wife
should should exercise a sound discretion in
disposing of my property to my children at such
times . . . and in such quantities as she may
think advisable   in the event of my wife's
marying again it is my wish that she she should
only have one third of my estate real and personal and that for her natural life and at her
death the same to be equally divided between
all my children and the Lawful issue of such as
may have died leaving issue. I give and be-
queathe unto my daughters Courtney Cowles Thornton & Harriet Thornton two negro girls Susan
and Martha the same being given to them by my
father in his lifetime. I wish Courtney to
have Susan and Harriet, Martha. I do hereby
constitute and appoint my wife Sarah Thornton
as my Executrix and it is my wish that she
should not be held to any security in the discharge of the same. I wish my wife to act as
guardian of my children and as such it is my
wish likewise that she should not be held to
any security in the discharge of this trust.
I wish my wife in the event of the necessity
for the disposal of any portion of my estate to
pay my debts I wish her to dispose of such property as best can be spared. Signed by me this
twenty fifth of March 1829."
                    John Thornton
H. C. Doswell
Edward Kimbrough

At a Superior Court of Law held for Hanover
County at the Courthouse on Monday the 27th of
April 1829. This Last Will and Testament of
John Thornton dec'd was offered to proof by
Sarah Thornton the Executrix therein named and
was proved by the oaths of H. C. Doswell and
Edward Kimbrough the witnesses thereto and is
ordered to be recorded.
   Teste, Thomas Pollard, C.C.
   A Copy, Teste, Philip B. Winston, C.C.

2. ANTHONY THORNTON, Will dated 21 February
   1822, probated 25 September 1822. Dr.
   Francis G. Taylor, Executor. Devised his
   Estate, of which the personal property
   was appraised at $8,287.00, to his three
   sisters, Sarah Hall, Elizabeth Tomkie,
   and Catherine Turner.

   In 1817 and 1818, his overseer was Edward
   Maynard.

Anthony Thornton's Will

ANTHONY THORNTON. "In the name of God amen. I,
Anthony Thornton of the County of Hanover do
make & ordain this to be my last will and testament revoking all other wills heretofore made
by me. Item. I give and bequeath to my niece
Sarah Hall a negro woman named Caty and her
Children that she now has - or may hereafter
have to her and her heirs forever. Item. It is
my will and desire that my negro girl Lucy,
daughter of Anna be set free. Item. I give and
bequeath to my sisters Sarah Hall, Elizabeth
Tomkie and Catherine Turner after the payment
of my just debts all the remainder and residue
of my estate of all kinds whatsoever to be
equally divided between them to them and their
heirs forever. Lastly, I appoint Fran^S G. Taylor executor to my last will and testament. In
witness whereof I have hereunto set my hand and
affixed my seal this 21st day of February 1822."

                              Anthony Thornton
Acknowledged in the presence of
    Nathan Halloway
    Joseph Tomkies
    Jno. J. Taylor

At a Court of Monthly Session held for Hanover
County at the Courthouse on Wednesday the 25th
of September 1822. This Last will and Testament of Anthony Thornton dec'd was offered to
proof by Francis G. Taylor the executor therein
named, and was proved by the oaths of Joseph
Tomkies & John J. Taylor two of the witnesses
thereto, and also by the oath of the said
Executor and is ordered to be recorded.
    Teste, William Pollard, C.H.C.
    A Copy, Teste, Philip B. Winston, C.H.C.

3. WILLIAM M. THORNTON, of Cumberland County,
   Virginia, 1839.
4. SARAH, wife of a Mr. Hall, prior to 1815.
   Removed with her daughter, Sarah T.
   Smith to Vermont. Mrs. Hall had issue:
   1. SARAH T., married between 1829 and
      1832, Professor Milo W. Smith, head
      teacher in 1830, of Washington-
      Henry Academy of Hanover County.
      Removed prior to 1835 to the town
      of Benson, Rutland County, Vermont.
   2. WILLIAM HALL.
   3. FANNY HALL, died prior to 1818.
5. ANN, deceased in 1821, married a Mr. Meaux,
   and left issue: (Maybe among others)
   1. JOHN W. MEAUX.
   2. RICHARD MEAUX.
6. ELIZABETH, wife in 1821 of a Mr. Tomkies,
   and has issue, probably among others:
   1. SARAH T. TOMKIES.
   2. JOSEPH TOMKIES.
   3. ELIZABETH TOMKIES.
   4. MARY TOMKIES.
   5. CATHERINE TOMKIES.

6. EDWARD TOMKIES.
7. CATHERINE, died in 1835, wife of George
   Turner, who survived and was her Admr.
   They had issue, probably among others:
   1. MARY VIRGINIA TURNER.
   2. SARAH T. TURNER.
   3. ELIZA C. TURNER, of Goochland Co.,
      in 1841.
   4. GEORGE W. TURNER, of Goochland Co.,
   _____   on 17 April 1841 "of age."

COURTNEY, a granddaughter of John Thornton, Sr., in 1821, wife of Hector
Davis, his Executor. Davis died with
will dated 11 June 1852.[no copy] Hi
only issue:
   1. JOHN N. DAVIS, under 21 years of
      age in 1821, mentioned in John
      Thornton's will of 1821. One of
      his father's Executors. Alive
      in 1840.
   2. HECTOR L. DAVIS, died intestate.
      One of his father's Executors.
      Survived by his widow, Martha
      Ellen, his Admx., and by issue:
      1. ULRECA ELMORA DAVIS.
      2. EMUELLA DAVIS.
      3. MARTHA ANN DAVIS.
      4. ELIZABETH DAVIS.
      5. LUCY I. DAVIS.
   Mrs. Courtney Davis' mother is not show

Others mentioned: Appraisers on 28 December
1852 of Hector Davis' Estate: John B. Wood,
Joseph C. England, John L. Priddy, R. A. Thornton; Hugh Davis, dec'd, of Henrico County,
Isaac C. Goddin, Admr. in 1841; Harris Wingfield; Wm. E. Harris, dec'd, Moses Harris, Exo
Robert Parker 1841; Thos. Price, Jr., Deposition 1836; John J. Taylor; Nathan Timberlake
1841; Lemuel Vaughan, Deposition 1836; Edmund
Winston, Deposition 1836; Wm. C. Winston, Deposition 1836; WASHINGTON-HENRY ACADEMY, of Hanover County, Dr. Reuben Meredith, Trustee, Dep
sition: "Mr. Milo W. Smith lived at Washington
Henry Academy in 1830 in capacity of teacher.
The tuition fees from 1827 to 1834 were fixed
at from $15.00 to $25.00 the scholar. The boar
has not usually been fixed but left to the
Teacher and the patrons. The amount of charge
for board and tuition has usually been from
ninety to 100.00."; Jesse G. Yarbrough.

Henry Hill and Jane S., his wife, who was Jane
S. Hickman, Admx. de bonis non of John Thilman

    BURNETT &C. VS. BARKER &C., 1838 (8)

THURMAN, LITTLEBERRY; Hays Murphey and Susan
his wife, who was Susan Thurman, of Hanover
County.

FROM OLD WILL BOOK, PAGE 47

TIMBERLAKE, ARCHIBALD B., of Hanover County was appointed on 27 September 1838, Guardian of his infant children:
1. DAVID A. TIMBERLAKE.
2. JOHN H. TIMBERLAKE.

CLOUGH & OTHERS VS. TIMBERLAKE'S EXOR., 1837 (9)
CLOUGH & OTHERS VS. GENTRY & OTHERS, 1833 (56)

Benjamin Timberlake's Will

TIMBERLAKE, BENJAMIN. "In the name of God Amen. I, Benjamin Timberlake of Hanover County do make my Will as follows to wit, I lend to my wife during her life the land and plantation and appurtenances whereon I life & then the land and plantation and appurtenances which I bought of Hix I also lend to her my negroes Dick, Barnet, Bob, Judy, Frank, Alby, Kate, Liddy, Lily, Louisa, Bowling, Richard and William, my household & kitchen furniture except what is herein after given to my children. My Kitchen furniture - all my stock of every kind & my plantation tools. I desire that my unmarried children remain with my wife until they respectively marry; and be supported, and such of them as require it be educated out of the estate lent my said wife. The property heretofore given to my daughter Lucy Green, to wit Absolom and Sal, a horse and saddle and bed and furniture is hereby confirmed to her forever. The property heretofore given to my daughter Patsey Gentry to wit Matilda and Winny, one hundred dollars and a bed and furniture is hereby confirmed to her forever. I give to my daughter Ann my negroes Kit and Sisley forever. I give to my daughter Mary my negroes Harry and Sharlott forever. I give to my daughter Frances Caroline my negroes Gabriel and Lisa forever. I give to my daughter Harriot my negroes Ransum & Manda forever. I give to my daughter Emmela my negroes George Shadrick & Haley forever. I give to my daughter Eliza Jane my negroes Marshall and Malrina forever. I give to my daughter Hardenia my negroes Lewis and Dilsey forever. I give to each of my daughters: Ann, Mary, Frances Caroline, Harriot, Emmoly, Eliza Jane, and Hardenia a Bed and furniture as they respectively marry or come of age. I also give to my last named daughters one hundred dollars each. I give to my wife all the money that is or may be due me. I also give to my wife my negro woman Jinney forever. My land adjoining Genl. White and others I wish to be sold and the money arising therefrom to be equally divided among all my children. The estate lent my wife except the land I desire at her death may be sold and the money arising therefrom equally divided among all my children. The land and appurtenances lent my wife I desire may be reserved and kept as a home for my daugh-

ters so long as any of them shall be unmarried, if any of them shall be unmarried at my wife's death, and at my wife's death and when all my daughters shall have been married, I desire that the lands and plantation and appurtenances thus lent and reserved to my said wife and children be sold and the money arising therefrom equally divided among all my children. I appoint my wife Extx and Henry D. Gentry Exr of this Will. Witness my hand and Seal this 13th day of Sept. 1816."

Benjn Timberlake (Seal)

Executed in presence of
   Thos. F. Green
   Thos. Oliver
   George R. Smith

At a Court of Quarterly session held for Hanover County at the Courthouse on Wednesday the 25th of October 1820. The last Will & Testament of Benjamin Timberlake dec'd was proved by the oath of Thomas Oliver one of the witnesses thereto. And at a Court of Monthly session held for the said County at the Courthouse on Wednesday the 27th of December next following, the said Will was offered for further proof by Henry D. Gentry the Executor therein named, and was further proved by the oath of Thomas F. Green another of the witnesses thereto and also by the oath of the said Executor and is ordered to be recorded.
   Teste, William Pollard, C.H.C.
   A Copy, Teste, Philip B. Winston, C.H.C.

BENJAMIN TIMBERLAKE, of Hanover. Will dated 13 September 1816, probated 25 October 1820. Henry D. Gentry, son-inlaw, Executor. Possessed a tract of land adjoining Judah King, Fleming Green, Samuel Perrin and Dickey Gilman. Another tract was sold to John S. Dyson, dec'd (Lucien B. Price, Admr.,) adjoining Joseph C. Wingfield, Joseph Hicks' Estate, Peter Jenkins, and surveyed by Hudson M. Wingfield. Testator was survived by his widow, Martha Timberlake, who died in September 1832, intestate, George N. Clough, a son-in-law, Admr. Issue:
1. LUCY, married prior to 1816, dec'd in 1833, Fleming Green, leaving issue:
   1. WILLIAM GREEN, died prior to 1851, Henry Curtis, Sheriff, Admr.
   2. BENJAMIN W. GREEN.
   3. FRANCES ANN, married prior to 1851, John D. Thomas.
   4. JOHN GREEN, died between 1855 and 1858, intestate, John D. Thomas, Admr.
   5. FLEMING GREEN, a minor in 1833.
   6. THOMAS GREEN, a minor in 1833.
   7. ALFRED (also called Albert) GREEN, died in infancy, intestate, and unmarried, prior to 1851.
   8. MARTHA GREEN, a minor in 1833.
   9. GEORGE GREEN, a minor in 1833.

2. PATSEY, wife prior to 1816, of Henry D.
   Gentry, Executor of Benjamin Timberlake's
   Estate. Died between 1855 and 1858.
3. ANN S., married John T. Clough.
4. MARY, wife in 1833, of Washington Jones.
5. FRANCES CAROLINE, wife of George N. Clough,
   who died prior to 1851, John D. G. Brown,
   Administrator.
6. HARRIET, married between 26 July 1836 and
   1851, John J. Palmer.
7. EMILY, dec'd in 1833, unmarried
8. ELIZA JANE (ELIZABETH), unmarried on 26
   July 1836.
9. HARDENIA TIMBERLAKE, died unmarried prior
   to 1833.

Others mentioned: C. L. Mallory, Constable 1851.

TYLER & WIFE VS. WHITLOCK'S ADMR., 1855 (44)

TIMBERLAKE, MRS. LETITIA, of Hanover County
"died sometime since leaving considerable
estate." James F. Huffman "qualified as
her represetative, and Thomas F. Carter and
Hudson M. Wingfield, his Securities." She left
issue who "were legatees of Chapman Timberlake,
dec'd,; and distributees in one-fourth part of
the Estate of Sophia Clarke, dec'd. Benjamin A.
Timberlake, her Administrator." Benjamin A. Timberlake, Sr., was dec'd in 1853. He was uncle
to Mrs. Letitia Timberlake's children:
1. MARY, wife in 1855 of John P. Tyler.
2. JOHN TIMBERLAKE.
3. HENRY TIMBERLAKE.
4. NANCY, wife in 1855, of Josiah Hazlegrove.
5. BENJAMIN F. TIMBERLAKE, called "JR." dec'd,
   Archibald B. Timberlake had been his
   representative. In 1855, William H. Timberlake, Administrator.
6. CHAPMAN TIMBERLAKE.
7. ELIZABETH, widow in 1855, of James N. Whitlock. Ezekiel S. Talley, his representative.

McFARLAND VS. TIMBERLAKE, 1835 (25)
TIMBERLAKE & OTHERS VS. SMITH &C., 1837 (41)

Francis Timberlake's Will

TIMBERLAKE, FRANCIS. "In the name of God
Amen. I, Francis Timberlake of Hanover of
Sound and perfect mind and memory do constitute this writing to be my last will and Testament. Item. I give to my beloved wife Sarah
Timberlake during her natural life the tract of
land whereon I now live and five negroes to wit:
Harry, Robin, Watt, Dorcas and Tamer also three
feather beds and furniture and all the balance
of my furniture except beds to be hereafter mentioned, together with the plantation utensils
of every kind and the crops of every kind that
may be on hand or growing at my decease also my

stock of every kind except one bay mare. Item.
I give and bequeath unto my son Matty Timberlake negro man Ned and one feather bed and furn
iture to him and his heirs forever. I give to
my son Francis Timberlake and his heirs foreve
one negro man Shadrack, one bed and furniture
which he hath already received. Item. I give
and bequeath to my son Reuben Timberlake, and
his heirs forever, one negro man Abram and one
feather bed and furnture . Item. I give and
bequeath to my son Nathan Timberlake and his
heirs forever one negro man, young Cull, and
one feather bed and furniture which he hath
already received. Item. I give & bequeath to m
son Billey Timberlake and his heirs forever on
negro woman Rachel and her futer increase and
sixty pounds in specie to be raised out of my
estate in two years also one feather bed & furn
iture. Item. I give and bequeath to my son
Granville Timberlake & his heirs forever one
negro man Phill and one feather bed & furnitur
Item. I give and bequeath to my son Laney Timberlake and his heirs forever two negro boys
Sawney and Jasper also one feather bed & furniture. Item. I give and bequeath to my son John
B. Timberlake & his heirs forever two negroes
Charles and Winney with her future increase
also one feather bed & furniture. Item. I Give
& bequeath to my daughter Polly Whitlock and
her heirs forever two negroes Aggy and Hannah
with their futer increase also one feather bed
and furniture which she hath already received.
Item. I give and bequeath to my daughter Sally
Ann Sims Timberlake and her heirs forever four
slaves with their futer increase, viz: Jane
and her two children Milly and Sealy and a Girl
named Grace, also one feather bed and furniture
It is my desire that my executors hereafter to.
be named, shall hire out the following slaves,
viz - Roger, Salley & Phillis and apply the
money arising therefrom to the education of my
youngest son and in case any allotment now made
to either of my Children should die before they
are in possession of the same the value of such
loss shall be made up by my executors out of my
estate, the land whereon I now live I leave to
my youngest daughter while unmarried and my
youngest son untille he shall arrive to the age
of twenty one years (as a home) after which
period my wish and desire is that the land I
now live on may be divided into six lots, and
my land in Halifax County into two lots which
said lands I give to my eight sons to be divide
by disintrusted persons. I do appoint my beloved wife Sarah Timberlake Admr my sons Matty,
Francis, Reuben, Nathan and Billey Timberlake,
Executors to this my last will and Testament.
Witness me hand & seal this 14th day of February 1807."

                         Francis Timberlake (Seal)
Signed & sealed in presence of
   John Bowe
   J. W. Ellis
   wm. Tyler

t a Court of Monthly Session held for Hanover
ounty at the Courthouse on Wednesday the 26th
f Sept. 1808. This last will and testament of
rancis Timberlake deceased was offered for
roof by Sarah Timberlake the executrix therein
amed and was proved by the oaths of John Bowe,
. W. Ellis and William Tyler the witnesses
hereto and also by the oath of the Executrix
nd is ordered to be recorded.
      Teste, William Pollard, C.H.C.
      A Copy, Teste, Philip B. Winston, C.H.C.

FRANCIS TIMBERLAKE, of Hanover. Will dated 14
  February 1807, probated 26 September 1808.
Sarah Timberlake, widow, Executrix, died circa
833, in January. Possessed lands in Hanover
nd Halifax Counties. Tract of land in Hanover
ontained 290 acres. Their children:
1. MATTY TIMBERLAKE, died before his father,
     unmarried.
2. FRANCIS TIMBERLAKE, died prior to 1833,
     intestate, survived by his widow Tabitha
     Timberlake (of Richmond, Va. 1836) and
     by four children:
     1. WILLIAM TIMBERLAKE.
     2. BETSEY TIMBERLAKE.
     3. MAJOR (also called John) TIMBERLAKE,
          a minor in 1836.
     4. HENRY TIMBERLAKE, a minor in 1836.
3. REUBEN TIMBERLAKE, of Hanover County in
     1835 and has a son:
     1. REUBEN TIMBERLAKE, JR.
4. NATHAN TIMBERLAKE, wife Mildred in 1836,
     and living in Richmond, Va.
5. WILLIAM (BILLEY) TIMBERLAKE, of Richmond,
     Va. in 1836. Under date 16 September
     1834 "William Timberlake of Hanover"
     conveyed to Granville Timberlake of
     Louisa County for $300,00, "all right,
     title and interest in tract of land in
     Hanover formerly the property of his
     father, the late Francis Timberlake of
     said County, also all interest, etc. in
     tract of land in Halifax County formerly
     the property of his father the said
     Francis, being the undivided part or
     portion devised to said William by the
     said Francis Timberlake." Witnesses:
     John G. McAlister, John J. Snead.
6. GRANVILLE TIMBERLAKE, of Louisa County in
     1834 and 1836. Purchased his brother
     William's interest in their father's
     lands.
7. LANEY TIMBERLAKE, of Richmond, Va., 1836
8. JOHN B. TIMBERLAKE, of Richmond, Va., in
     1836. "Married Martha Finch and they
     have life interest in land by the courte-
     sy of England."
9. POLLY, wife in 1807 of James Whitlock, of
     Hanover County in 1836.
10. SALLY ANN SIMS TIMBERLAKE as given in her
     father's will. In suits she is called
     Sarah, also Elizabeth. Married William
     Simpson of Hanover, who died intestate

in 1832, she survived and died circa 1833,
leaving one child:
1. SARAH ELIZABETH ELLEN SIMPSON, an
     infant in 1836.

Others mentioned: Carter Berkeley, Sheriff of
Hanover 1835; John K. Linn, Sheriff of Halifax
County 1835; George Tranium who deposed in
1837 at the home of Benjamin Hazlegrove in Hanover; John C. Littlepage; James B. Smith.

HUTCHINSON & WIFE VS. TIMBERLAKE &C., 1859 (44)
    JONES VS. TIMBERLAKE & WIFE, 1869 (17)

TIMBERLAKE, REUBEN, JR., of Hanover, died
  intestate in 1845 or '46, possessed of a
  tract of land whereon he resided containing 250 acres on Chickahominy Swamp, ten miles
from the City of Richmond. Value assessed at
$6,000.00. He also possessed some slaves which
were assessed at $2,000.00. Survived by his
widow, Elizabeth Ann Timberlake, who died on
27 January 1859, and by eight children,"of whom
only one is under age." Listing apparently
in order of births:
    1. JACONIA L. TIMBERLAKE, sold his interest
         in his father's land to A. B. Hutchinson.
    2. LEVINA, married prior to 1859, Alexander
         B. Hutchinson.
    3. ANGELINA G., married prior to 1859, Jesse
         S. Martin of Petersburg, Va.
    4. LEBBEUS W. TIMBERLAKE, married circa
         1869, Mary, daughter of James E. Jones
         dec'd of Hanover County.
    5. WILSON H. TIMBERLAKE.
    6. ALPHENS K. TIMBERLAKE.
    7. ELLEN J., wife in 1859, of James H. Mason.
    8. RUBINETTA A. TIMBERLAKE, aged 18 in 1859.

JONES, JAMES E., of Hanover County, deceased in
  1869. Ezekiel S. Talley, Administrator, and
Guardian of the infant children:
    1. ALICE R. JONES.
    2. BETTY JONES.
    3. JOHN JONES.
    4. MARY, wife of Lebbeus W. Timberlake.
    5. WILLIAM W. JONES.
Because of the late date, this suit was not
pursued to its close.

                FROM OLD WILL BOOK, PAGE 65

TINSLEY, CHARLES, of Hanover. Will dated 5
  February 1838, probated 25 January 1842 by
  Turner Christian, and on 23 February 1842
by Polly A. D. Tinsley a free woman of color,
and also by William B. Jones and Peter Tinsley.
The witnesses were: Turner Christian, Thomas
Tinsley and F. P. Harris. Executors: Overton N.
Bumpass and Richardson Glazebrook. After pay-
ment of debts, all estate to Mary A. D. Tinsley
a woman of color, and her heirs.

TINSLEY VS. TINSLEY, 1860 (48)

TINSLEY, THOMAS G., "late of Hanover County, died on or about 13 September 1859." "His will was probated 27 September 1859 and Thomas Tinsley alone qualified as Executor." "He possessed a considerable real and personal estate in Hanover, and an Estate in york County." Survived by his widow, Mrs. Patsey Tinsley, his second wife. Issue of his first marriage:
1. THOMAS TINSLEY.
2. ALEXANDER TINSLEY.
3. SEATON G: TINSLEY.
4. HARRIET B., wife of Jacquelin P. Taliaferro.
Issue of second marriage with Patsey:
5. JAMES GARLAND TINSLEY, in 1860 "under age and quite young." James D. Christian appointed his Guardian.

STARKE VS. JONES, 1846 (57)
YARBROUGH VS. TINSLEY & OTHERS, 1847 (54)
TINSLEY VS. STREET'S EXOR. & OTHERS, 1848 (48)
TINSLEY'S ADMR. VS. STREET'S EXOR. &C., 1848 (48)

TINSLEY, WILLIAM, of Hanover, died prior to 24 July 1809, intestate, possessed of "a large number of slaves and considerable real property." Survived by his widow, Elizabeth, who married a Mr. Harlow, and removed to the State of Tennessee, where she died in 1837. In 1809, Joseph Cross, her attorney in fact, sold the dower slaves to Anthony Street and Laney Jones. William Tinsley had no children at the time of his death, and his heirs at law were sisters and brothers:

LUCY, a sister, married Samuel Cross, survived him, and was deceased in 1848, when Benjamin Hazlegrove was her Administrator.

SARAH, a sister, widow of Richard Starke. Sold her interest in slaves of William Tinsley's Estate to George R. Smith. In 1846, he and Benjamin Hazlegrove were her Administrators.

DAVID TINSLEY, a brother, John L. White his Administrator in 1848.

JOHN B. TINSLEY, a brother, deceased in 1848.

PHILIP TINSLEY, a brother. It is stated that his will was dated 28 March 1793, and that he devised 182 3/4 acres of land to his wife, Judith. Mentioned sons John Burwell Tinsley and William Tinsley and "all my children." Executors were brother William Tinsley and friend Nath[l] Bowe. Witnesses: Thomas Tinsley and David Tinsley. On 22 February 1819, the widow, Judith is called "Judith Caffray, widow of Philip Tinsley, dec'd." Issue:
1. JOHN BURWELL TINSLEY, dec'd in 1849. Wife, Eleanor Tinsley. (Philip M. Tinsley, Admr.)

Their issue:
1. LOUISA V. A., married prior to 1847, a Mr. Tyler.
2. PHILIP M. TINSLEY, in 1863, wife is Sarah.
3. WILLIAM TINSLEY, died in infancy, without issue.
4. FRANCES E., widow of a Mr. Brander, died without issue prior to 1864.
5. NANCY, born after 31 March 1819, married John Cross.
6. MARY JANE TINSLEY, born after 31 March 1819.
7. THOMAS G. TINSLEY, born after 31 March 1819.
8. MARGARET TINSLEY, born after 31 March 1819, married a Mr. Droughton.
9. ELIZABETH (BETTY), born after 31 March 1819.
2. WILLIAM TINSLEY, died in infancy.
3. MARY (PATSEY) wife in 1848 of Obadiah Archer.
4. MARTHA, wife of John P. Kewin of Richmond, Va., in 1838. Both are deceased in 1847.

On 24 December 1838, John P. Kewin and Nancy his wife, James M. Ratcliffe and Isabella his wife, all of the City of Richmond, convey to Jesse G. Yarbrough of Hanover County, for $45.00, their interest in tract of land in Hanover, adjoining lands of the said Jesse Yarbrough, Estate of Peter Lyons', dec'd, Peter Bowles and the Estate of Oliver T. Cross, dec'd, and is the same tract of land on which John B. Tinsley lately dec'd, resided, and formerly the estate of Philip Tinsley from whom the said John P. Kewin and Isabella Ratcliff, who was Isabella Kewin, the only children of Martha Kewin who was one of the children and heirs of the said Philip Tinsley.

It will be noted that she is called Nancy in the above. Issue:
1. JOHN P. KEWIN, wife Mary in 1848.
2. ISABELLA I., wife in 1838 of James M. Ratcliff.
3. MARTHA KEWIN, deceased in 1848.
5. NANCY, married John Henry, who is her Administrator in 1846. He is deceased in 1847. Their issue:
1. WILLIAM HENRY, of Petersburg, Va. in 1847.
2. MARTHA J. HENRY, of Petersburg, Va. in 1847.
3. JANE HENRY, of Richmond, Va. in 1847.
4. SAMUEL HENRY.
5. ROBERT HENRY, died in infancy, without issue.
6. JOHN A. HENRY.

Others mentioned: Oliver T. Cross, dec'd, Polly W. Cross, widow, Land adjoined Yarbrough, Wm. W. Michie, William and Thomas Carter, Peter Bowles and the Estate of John B. Tinsley 1847; Chauncey G. Griswold, Lawyer 1848; James Brown Lane; George R. Smith, dec'd, William Smith of Henrico, Executor 1850; Charles T. Toler deposed in 1849 that he lived within a mile of Anthony Street, dec'd; Jesse G. Yarbrough, dec'd, Ann Yarbrough, Extx., and William N. Yarbrough, Exor. - and James Littlepage, dec'd, whose will is included in one of these suits:

James Littlepage's Will

LITTLEPAGE, JAMES. "I, James Littlepage of Hanover County, viewing the uncertainty of life in all situations and the certainty of death and more particularly in my declining state of health and wishing to dispose of my worldly affairs do make and ordain this my last will and Testament. First I desire that all my just debts be paid. I give to my two sons Lewis Byrd Littlepage and William Chamberlayne Littlepage fifty pounds each over & above the rest of my children to help to raise them. The balance of my Estate of what nature or kind soever I desire may be equally divided amongst my children to wit: Sarah Littlepage, Frances Arnett Littlepage, James Littlepage, John Carter Littlepage, Martha Littlepage, Elizabeth Littlepage, Lewis Byrd Littlepage, and William Chamberlayne Littlepage to whom I give the same amount to them and their heirs forever. I have given to my daughter Sarah Littlepage a maid Jean and to my Daughter Frances Arnett Littlepage a maid named Abby, which they must be charged with and account for in the division of my Estate. I give to my son William Chamberlayne Littlepage a negro boy named Solomon but to be accounted for in like manner. My desire is that my Executors hereafter named will use their discretion as to the sale of my Land. Sh^d they Judge that it will be more beneficial to Keep it for a home for my children till they are raised, they will do so, if not they will sell it on such credit as they or a majority of them shall deem most to the interest of my said children. And the money arising from such sale to be equally divided amongst them. I do constitute and appoint my friends Samuel Overton and Thomas Starke of Hanover County and William Chamberlayne of New Kent County, Executors of this my last Will and Testament, and do request the favour of each of them to act as such. I request the favour of my friend Samuel Overton to be guardian to my son Lewis Byrd Littlepage till he attains the age of twenty one years, and bring him up to such business as he may judge will be most beneficial to him. I request the like favour of my friend Thomas Starke in behalf of my son John Carter Littlepage, and the like favour of my friend William Chamberlayne in behalf of my son William Chamberlayne Littlepage.

I am well aware of the trouble I am imposing on on my friends by the foregoing requests but trust their friendship for me and a helpless number of Orphans will induce them to comply. In testimony of the foregoing I have hereto set my hand and seal this 31st day of October 1803."

                    Ja^s Littlepage (Seal)
Signed, sealed, published
& declared to be his last Will and Testament in our presence & by us subscribed at his request.
    A. Street
    Saml Arnold
    Samuel J. Winston

At a Court of Monthly Session held for Hanover County at the Courthouse on Wednesday the 28th of January 1807. This last Will and Testament of James Littlepage dec'd was proved by the oaths of A. Street and Samuel J. Winston, witnesses thereto and is ordered to be recorded.
    Teste, William Pollard, C.H.C.

At a Court of Monthly Session held for Hanover County at the Courthouse on Wednesday the 25th of Nov. 1807. On motion of Samuel Overton, and William Chamberlayne two of the Executors named in the last Will and Testament of James Littlepage, dec'd, a certificate is granted them for obtaining probat of the said Will they having taken the Oaths of Executors and with the Security, entered into and acknowledged a bond according to law.
    Teste, William Pollard, C.H.C.
    A Copy, Teste, Wm. O. Winston, D.C.H.C.

JAMES LITTLEPAGE, of Hanover. Will dated 31 Oct. 1803. Probated 28 January 1807. Executors, Samuel Overton and William Chamberlayne, qualified 25 November 1807. Survived by infant orphan children:
    1. LEWIS BYRD LITTLEPAGE.
    2. WILLIAM CHAMBERLAYNE LITTLEPAGE.
    3. SARAH LITTLEPAGE.
    4. FRANCES ARNETT LITTLEPAGE.
    5. JAMES LITTLEPAGE.
    6. JOHN CARTER LITTLEPAGE.
    7. MARTHA LITTLEPAGE.
    8. ELIZABETH LITTLEPAGE.

    TOLER VS. TOLER & OTHERS, 1835 (47)
    LUMPKIN VS. POLLARD, Ca. 1840 (23)

Benjamin Toler's Will

TOLER, BENJAMIN. "In the name of God Amen. I, Benjamin Toler of the County of Hanover do make this my last will and Testament. I will that my debts be fully paid and satisfied. I give to my sons Matthew and Henry all my lands in the State of Kentucky to be equally divided between them, to them and their heirs forever. I give to my grandson Benjamin Hooper

one hundred pounds to him and his heirs forever.
I give to my grandson John Jones all the slaves
which I lent to his father Laney Jones, to him
and his heirs forever. I give to my Grandson
Miller W. McCraw one negro girl named Eliza to
her and her heirs forever. All the rest and
residue of my estate both real and personal I
desire to be sold and the money arising therefrom be equally divided among my children Matthew, Henry, Samuel, and Betsey now the wife of
Thomas Hooper or their legal representatives to
them and their heirs forever, provided however
that the share, part or portion which may fall
to my son Samuel be held by my Executors hereafter named and used by them for him at their
discretion. I appoint my sons Matthew and
Henry, Executors and my friend William Pollard
a Trustee to this my last will and testament.
Witness my hand and seal this 4th day of July
1804."

                              Benj^a Toler (Seal)
Published by the Testator as and for his last
will and testament before us:
    Benj^a Pollard
    Bartlett Anderson
    Bathurst Jones

At a Court of Monthly Session held for Hanover
County at the Courthouse on Wednesday the 23d
March 1808. This last will and Testament of
Benjamin Toler, dec'd was offered for proof by
Mathew Toler and Henry Toler, the Executors
therein named and was proved by the oaths of
Bartlett Anderson and Bathurt Jones witnesses
thereto and is ordered to be recorded. And the
said Executors came into Court and relinquished
their right of executorship to the said will
and on the motion of Matthew Toler a certificate
is granted him for obtaining letters of administration with the said will annexed of the
estate of the said Benjamin Toler, dec'd, he
having taken the oath of an administrator with
the will annexed and with Wm. Clarke, John Anderson, Patrick Fowler and Edward Hundley his
securities, entered into and acknowledged a
bond according to law.
    Teste, William Pollard, C.H.C.
    A Copy, Teste, Philip B. Winston, C.H.C.

BENJAMIN TOLER, of Hanover. Will dated 4 July
1804, probated 23 December 1808. Matthew Toler
qualified as Administrator with the will annexed.
Lived at "Woodbury" in Hanover. Possessed land
in Caroline County called "Gooseponds" of 842
acres on which he executed on 24 June 1802 a
Deed of Trust in the amount of 2179.3.0 Lbs.
being the amount of two bonds on which he was
security for Thomas Hooper, due to Wm. Morris,
Sr. Nathaniel Pope, Jr., William Pollard, Ben-
jamin.Brand, and Thomas Pollard, Trustees. At
that time "Gooseponds" "lying in the Counties
of Caroline and King William, adjoining Paul
Woolfolk, William Ellis, William Penn, and William Nelson." This Deed of trust also included

another tract, in Hanover, containing 360 acres
adjoining Matthew Toler, William O. Winston, and
others; together with 36 slaves.

On 30 May 1808, Matthew Toler of Hanover,
Administrator of Benjamin Toler, dec'd,
conveyed to Benjamin Burch of Hanover,
"highest bidder 403.11.5 1/2 Lbs." tract of
land called "David Anderson's Old Store"
containing 365 1/2 acres, adjoining Robert
and James Sharp, William Stanley, dec'd,
Joshua Stanley, dec'd, David Thompson,dec'd,
Joseph Watson and Richard Goodman."Being
the same tract sold by Charles J. McMurdo
under a Deed of Trust to Benjamin Toler."
Witnesses: James Doswell, Austin Corley,
Tarleton Pleasants, John G. Pleasants.

On 30 August 1809, Matthew Toler of "Woodbury", Hanover County, Administrator of
Benjamin Toler, dec'd, conveyed to Thomas
Chrystie of Hanover Town, for $238.00, two
lots, numbers 29 and 30, in Hanover Town,
adjoining Benjamin Oliver, Jr., and those
belonging to the Estate of Nathaniel Anderson, dec'd, being the same which Dr. James
Lyons purchased of Dr. John K. Redd, together with houses, etc.
Witnesses: William Cunningham, Benjn Brand,
William Gardner, Elkanah Talley.

Benjamin Toler's personal estate in Hanover
County was appraised on 22 June 1808 by David
Oliver, William Bowe and Benjamin Timberlake,
at 956.16.0 Lbs. The personal estate in Caro-
line County, at "Goosponds" was appraised by
Philip Taliaferro, John B. Luck and George
Sizer on 10 June 1808, at 1409.16.6 Lbs. The
Accounts Commissioners, Billey Talley, John
Anderson, D. Dickinson, Jr., in 1811, valued
the Estate at 4389.113.7 Lbs.

Thomas N. Walker was appointed Administrator de
bonis non after the death of Matthew Toler,
which occured in 1811.

W. C. Nicholas purchased other lands of the Estate of Benjamin Toler, dec'd.

Benjamin Toler's children and grandchildren:

1. MATTHEW TOLER, Administrator of his father's Estate. Died in 1811. Carter B.
   PAGE qualified as Administrator early in
   1812. Securities: John W. Page and Thos.
   N. Walker. His personal estate in Hanover County was inventoried in 1813 by
   H. Brooke, John Anderson and David Oliver
   at $4,370.63. Personal estate in Caro-
   line County inventoried in 1814 by Philip
   Taliaferro, Joseph Brame, Benjamin
   Hooper, at 1185.10.6 Lbs. He was survived by two children. No mention of wife.

1. ANN, married prior to 1818, Thomas N. Walker, who is dec'd in 1838. Samuel Pleasants, Sheriff of Henrico County, his Administrator. He had been Administrator of Benjamin Toler, dec'd.
2. THOMAS UPTON TOLER, under age in 1818; of Caroline County in 1834, wife Mary C. Toler:

   On 22 October 1834 they convey to Ellis G. Saunders of Caroline, consideration $1,000.00, tract of land "Goose Ponds" of 540 acres, adjoining on northeast by Wesley Saunders, east by Robert B. Taliaferro, south by the Pamunkey River, and on the west by Henry Hill and others.

   On 20 November 1832, Wesley Saunders and Mildred, his wife of Caroline County, convey to Thomas U. Toler of King William County, consideration $200.00, all interest of said Saunders and wife in "Goose Ponds."

   On 16 May 1834, Elizabeth, relict of Thomas Hooper, dec'd, conveys to Thomas U. Toler of Caroline County, consideration $400,00, her interest in the Estate of her father Benjamin Toler, dec'd, lying in Caroline and King William Counties, adjoining George Taylor, Robert B. Taliaferro, Wesley Saunders, Robert Campbell, Henry Hill and others.

2. HENRY TOLER, of "Gold Hill," deceased in July 1808, survived by his widow, who is not named, and by six children, one of whom was born after his death.
   1. MATTHEW TOLER, born in July 1803, dec'd in 1859, Martin M. Lipscomb, Sergeant of the City of Richmond, Admr. He sold his interest in "Gooseponds" to Robert Peatross, Wesley Saunders, and Ellis G. Saunders.
   2. MARY, born in October 1805, wife in 1835, of Patrick Lydane.
   3. JAMES B. TOLER, born in May 1807.
   4. WILLIAM B. TOLER, dec'd in 1859, Martin M. Lipscomb, Sergeant of City of Richmond, Va., Admr.
   5. RICHARD H. TOLER, dec'd in 1858. Martin M. Lipscomb, Sergeant of City of Richmond, Va., Admr. "He was survivied by one child,(who is not named) and by his widow who married a Mr. Evans, dec'd.
   6. HENRY TOLER. born in March 1809, after his father's death, deceased in 1835, survived by his widow Susan who married Martin Derr.
3. SAMUEL TOLER, dec'd in 1835, N. A. Thompson, Sheriff of Hanover County, Admr.

4. ELIZABETH (BETSY), wife in 1804 of Thomas Hooper. On 16 May 1834: "Elizabeth, relict of Thomas Hooper, dec'd, conveyed to Thomas U. Toler her interest in the Estate of her father Benjamin Toler, dec'd. She is deceased in 1838, and A. H. Hutchinson, Late Sheriff of Hanover County, Administrator. She had issue, perhaps among others:
   1. BENJAMIN HOOPER, born prior to 1804 (mentioned in his grandfather's will), deceased in 1835. A. H. Hutchinson, Administrator.
5. [   ] a daughter, married prior to 1804, Laney Jones, and had issue, probably among others:
   1. JOHN JONES, mentioned in his grandfather's will).
6. PEGGY G., married prior to 1804, Miller W. McCraw, who is deceased in 1808. Issue probably among others:
   1. MILLER W. McCRAW, born prior to 1804, (mentioned in his grandfather's will), orphan in 1835.

———

BRAND, BENJAMIN, of the City of Richmond,Va., "died in 1843 possessed of some real estate and considerable personal property in the Commonwealth." His will dated 21 September 1842, probated 9 October 1843. Edward B. Crenshaw, Executor. "The Testator left no children or descendants, nor any father or mother, but left the following brothers and sisters and their descendants:

WILLIAM BRAND, a brother.

JOHN BRAND, a brother, non compos mentis. Powhatan Roberts, Guardian ad litem. Louisa County Court on 8 June 1857 appointed Thomas W. Meriwether, Committee for the Estate of John Brand.

CHILES M. BRAND, a brother.

SARAH, a sister, in 1859, widow of a Mr. Robertson, deceased.

FANNY, a sister, in 1859, wife of David Huckstep.

ELIZA L., a sister, in 1859, widow of Edmund B. Crenshaw, dec'd, "who at the death of her brother Benjamin Brand was the wife of Crenshaw." She was his Administrator, also the Administrator de bonis non of Benjamin Brand. [Crenshaw's named stated as"Edw. and Edmund B."]

ROBERT BRAND, a brother, deceased in 1859. Widow, Amelia Brand, and issue:
1. MATILDA, wife in 1859, of Wm. H. Timberlake.
2. BENJAMIN BRAND.
3. ROBERT BRAND, JR., in 1859, of St. Louis,Mo.

4. AMELIA BRAND, of age in 1846.
5. ELIZA BRAND, of age, and married, in 1848,
   Richard H. Anderson.
6. JOSEPH C. BRAND, of age in 1849.
7. GEORGE C. BRAND, died in 1849, under age.
8. LOUIS R. BRAND, of Saint Louis, Missouri,
   under age in 1849, his brother, Robert
   Brand, Jr., of St. Louis, Guardian.

DAVID R. BRAND, a brother, deceased in 1858,
leaving issue:
1. A NN ELIZA, wife of James M. Williams.
2. BENJAMIN F. BRAND.

GEORGE W. BRAND, a brother, who has issue in
1859:
1. FANNY BRAND.
2. ELIZA, wife of a Mr. Rogers.

JAMES W. BRAND, deceased in 1859, leaving an
only child:
1. MARY, wife of Henry H. Timberlake.

JOHNSON, CHAPMAN, dec'd, had been the Administrator with the will annexed of Carter B.Page,
dec'd. George N. Johnson, Executor. After his
death, William B. Johnson qualified as Executor.
Andrew Johnson was Executor of George N. Johnson, deceased, in 1856.

NICHOLSON, JOHN B., deceased. He was one
of the creditors of Carter B. Page, dec'd.
and beneficiary of a Deed of Trust executed by Page on 20 November 1819. (Reference is
made to a suit in the Circuit Court of the City
of Richmond, Va., 1856, which should shed further light on the heirs of Page and Nicholson)*
In 1856, John B. Nicholson's distributees were:

1/3 to   MARTHA H. NICHOLSON.
1/3 to   MARY, died intestate prior to 1857,
         survived by her husband, John James
         Speed, and one child:
         1. MARTHA CAROLINE, wife in 1856,
              of George Bush.
1/3 to   CAROLINE P., died intestate in 1857,
         married a Mr. Lee, also dec'd,
         leaving five children:
         1. GEORGE W. LEE.
         2. RICHARD H. LEE.
         3. MARY C. L., dec'd in 1858, with-
              out issue, wife of Dr. Henry
              Warne.
         4. JOHN JAMES SPEED LEE.
         5. WILLIAM H. LEE.

PAGE, CARTER B., deceased, on 20 November
1819, had executed a Deed of Trust to John
Gamble and Robert Gwathmey, for the benefit of his creditors, including John B. Nicholson. (Reference is made to a suit in the Circuit Court of the City of Richmond, in 1856*.)

Chapman Johnson qualified as Administrator with
the will annexed of Carter B. Page, dec'd. In
connection with Page, it is stated that:
  CATHERINE PAGE, is deceased, and heirs are
  unknown.
  MARY PAGE, deceased, and heirs are unknown.
It is not stated who these ladies were.

————

SAUNDERS, WESLEY, of Caroline County, died
prior to 1844. Ellis G. Saunders, Administrator. Later, in 1858, Wesley W. Wright,
Sheriff of Caroline, Admr. His wife is mentioned sometime as Mildred. He was survived by his
widow, Sarah Ann Saunders, in 1844, of Henrico
County. (Later wife of Ellis G. Saunders) His
issue:
1. WILLIAM WALLACE SAUNDERS.
2. ROBERT BRUCE SAUNDERS.
3. FRANCES ELLEN SAUNDERS.
4. JOHN WESLEY SAUNDERS.
5. CHRISTOPHER WALTHALL SAUNDERS.
6. GEORGE WAVERLY SAUNDERS.

SAUNDERS, ELLIS G., of Caroline County, dec'd
Francis W. Scott, Administrator in 1858.
Survived by his widow, Sarah Ann Saunders,
(who was widow also of Wesley Saunders, dec'd).
and six children:
1. WILLIAM E. SAUNDERS, in 1858, of King &
     Queen County.
2. ELIZABETH R., wife of Thomas C. McClelland
     of King & Quuen County in 1858.
3. RICHARD W. SAUNDERS, of Ashland, Hanover
     County, 1858.
4. LUCY A. SAUNDERS, infant, and in King &
     Queen County in 1858.
5. MILDRED C. SAUNDERS, infant, and in Caro-
     line County in 1858.
6. MARY, deceased, married a Mr. Evans, and
     left issue, infants in 1858:
     1. CHARLES E. EVANS.
     2. JOHN W. EVANS.

————

STEVENSON, ANDREW, deceased. Owned land in
Albemarle County, Va. He was in South Carolina in 1835. Died intestate, survived by
his widow, Mary Stevenson, who was living circa
1858, in Georgetown, D. C., and two children:
1. JOHN STEVENSON, "long of age" and living
     in Kentucky.
2. MARY S. STEVENSON, aged 6, and living with
     her mother in Georgetown.

————

*Reference is made to a suit in the Circuit
Court of the City of Richmond, 1856:
"Agnes Nicholson, versus Martin M. Lipscomb,
Sergeant of City of Richmond and as such Admr.
of John B. Nicholson and Rebecca Ellzey, dec'd,
John White Page Exor. of Judith R. Page, dec'd,
James E. Heath, Andrew Johnson, Exor. of
George N. Johnson, dec'd, Martha H. Nicholson,

Caroline P. Lee and Mary Speed, distributees of John B. Nicholson, dec'd, John Durham and Mary Durham, his wife."

———

The suit of "Lumpkin Vs. Pollard," Ended File 23 Hanover County:

"William Toler, Henry Toler, Richard Toler, Matthew Toler, James Toler and Patrick Lydane and Mary his wife, who was Mary Toler, Versus:

Thomas U. Toler, Jesse Winn late Sheriff of Hanover, and the Committee of the Estate of Matthew Toler, dec'd; William Clarke, John S. Fleming, Admr. of John Anderson, dec'd; Carter Berkeley late Sheriff of Hanover and Admr. de bonis non of Patrick Fowler, dec'd and Committee of the Estates of Henry Toler, Edward Hundley and Samuel Toler; Thomas N. Walker, Admr de bonis non Benjamin Toler, dec'd; Andrew Stevenson, Benjamin Brand, Chapman Johnson Admr with the will annexed of Carter B. Page, dec'd, John W. Page, Robert Peatross, Westley Saunders, Ellis G. Saunders, Benjamin Pollard, Robert Taliaferro, and Samuel Pleasants, Sheriff of Henrico County and Committee of the Estate of Thomas N. Walker and Elizabeth Hooper, Defts."

———

Others mentioned: Pleasants, slave of Benjamin Brand, dec'd, to whom he made a bequest, frees, and requests that he be sent to Liberia. He refused to go and the Colonization Society would not take him against his wishes; Overton Anderson; John S. Blanton in Caroline County 1836; Robert P. Corbin, Justice of the Peace of Caroline County 1834; Nathaniel C. Crenshaw, Commissioner; John and Leonard Cowley, Securities for Thomas N. Walker; B. F. Dabney, Justice of the Peace, King William County 1835; David Dickinson died in 1835 - was Admr. of Patrick Fowler, dec'd; Charles P. Goodall, Sheriff of Hanover 1845; Elizabeth Hooper and John S. Fleming, Admr. of John Anderson, dec'd, in Goochland County 1835. Fleming was one of the Securities of Matthew Toler; Edward Hundley, dec'd, Ann Hundley, Admx.; Andrew Johnson, Lawyer; George Nicholas Johnson; William Johnson, late Executor of Chapman Johnson, dec'd.; N. H. Massie, Lawyer 1820 and 1859; Rev. William S. Plummer, Presbyterian Minister; Michael B. Poitiaux, Commissioner of Chancery, Richmond, Va.; Conway Robinson, Lawyer; Park Street, Sheriff, Hanover, 1822; Deposition of John Taliaferro and John L. Stevens at store of James and Charles Fleet, near Mangohick Church in King William County 1835; Philip Taliaferro of Gloucester County 1836; Robert Taliaferro of King William County 1836; Thomas Taliaferro, Justice of the Peace, Caroline County 1834; Colonel John Taylor; Deposition of Elizabeth Underwood in Richmond, Va., 1839, who supplies the ages of some of the children of Henry Toler's children.

TUCKER & OTHERS VS. TUCKER & OTHERS, 1860 (46)

TUCKER, JESSE, of Saint Pauls Parish, Hanover County, died prior to 1810, survived by his widow, alive in that year, but is not named, and by three sons:
1. PLEASANT TUCKER, of Hanover, died in the early part of 1860, intestate. Possessed of land and considerable personal estate. Survived by his widow Margaret Tucker. He left no children. He had sold some of his land to William D. Wade. In 1867, Joseph Adams (who purchased the interest of Martha and James Madison) deposed that Pleasant Tucker possessed 270 acres adjoining Thaddeus Higgins, William Wade and others. Pleasant Tuckers heirs were his two brothers:
2. JOHN TUCKER, of Hanover, died circa 1867 with a will, and issue:
    1. MARTHA, wife of James Madison.
    2. VASHTI, married Henry Turner, dec'd. She was living in Richmond, Va. in 1868, when she sold her interest in Pleasant Tucker's Estate to A. R. Courtney.
    3. EMILINE, wife of William E. Goulding.
3. FLEMING TUCKER, died in 1816. He married Tabitha, a daughter of William and Nancy (Bradley) Otey of Charles City County.
    On 6 June 1810, Fleming Tucker and Tabitha his wife of St. Paul's Parish, Hanover County, conveyed to John Tucker, Jr., consideration 22.10.0 Lbs., their interest in the said Fleming's father's Estate, now deceased (Jesse Tucker) one tract of land in Hanover whereon the widow of the said Jesse Tucker now resides, containing 90 acres. Witnesses: Thomas Acree, Richard Hollins, and Otha Tucker.
    Martha F. Hayward of Henrico County, deposed in 1861; "Knew the Tuckers when they first came to Richmond before the War of 1812. My father's name was Elijah Franklin and he lived at Rockett's in Richmond. His wife was Mary Charles and she was raised in James City County and afterwards lived in Charles City County. My age is 74. My father was Inspector of Rocketts Tobacco Warehouse."
    Thomas D. Lipscomb, deposed in 1861: "In the year 1831 or 1832 I was a soldier in the Public Guard under Capt. Bolling. At that time Fleming Tucker enlisted in the Guard and after being there a few months his mother came and took him off, being under age. Her children were: Fleming Tucker, Mary Tucker, Martha Tucker. She was a widow at that time. She was dead in 1840. I was born in 1804. Mrs. Tucker lived on 17th Street in Richmond."

Fleming Tucker and Tabitha, his wife, had issue:

1. MARTHA R., born 19 August 1806, widow in 1860 of a Mr. Franklin of Petersburg, Va.
2. MARY ANN TUCKER, born 30 July 1807, deceased in 1860.
3. LUCY ANN TUCKER, born 12 October 1808, died 6 September 1812.
4. FLEMING TUCKER, born 11 March 1810, of Richmond, Va.
5. MARIA TUCKER, born 11 April 1811, died in September 1813.
6. TABITHA TUCKER, born 10 October 1812, died 2 October 1813.
7. HENRY TUCKER, born 31 December 1815, died 15 March 1818.

OTEY, WILLIAM, of Charles City County, married Miss Nancy Bradley, a sister of Col. John Bradley of Charles City, who died in 1820. (Col. John Bradley was the father of John W. Bradley, born in 1800, and a Justice of the Peace of Charles City in 1860.) William Otey and his wife Nancy, had issue, probably among others:

1. TABITHA, married circa 1805, Fleming Tucker, who died in 1816. She died in 1840 leaving issue. (See under Tucker).
   Deposition of Tabitha Paterson of the City of Richmond, in 1860 at Charles City Courthouse: "Aged 70. Now living in the City of Richmond. Colonel Bradley was Tabitha Otey's uncle. She lived with my sister (Sarah Vaughan) for sometime. From there went to Edward Epp's in Charles City County whose place was called "Grandville." From there she came to my father's William Royall and stayed sometime. She left my father's when her uncle sent her to board in the lower end of the County."
   Mrs. Lucy Kesee deposed in 1860 at Charles City Courthouse that she was a young girl of 16 when Tabitha Otey married Fleming Tucker. Mrs. Kesee stated that her father was John Bousey, who was a cousin of Nancy Bradley who married William Otey.
   Mrs. Eliza Derpuy of Charles City County, deposed in 1860 that herfather was first cousin of Nancy (Bradley) Otey.
2. NANCY, married first a Mr. West. Secondly a Mr. Weymouth, and in 1860 is deceased.

WADE, WILLIAM D., of Hanover County, was deceased on 24 December 1868. He had purchased lands of Pleasant Tucker, adjoining Thaddeus Higgins, and others. Wade died intestate, survived by his widow and four children:

1. WILLIAM THOMAS WADE.
2. EZEKIEL CALVIN WADE.
3. JAMES DELAWARE WADE.
4. MILDRED D. WADE, an infant in 1868.

Others mentioned: Henry G. Cannon, Commissioner. George K. Taylor Deputy Clerk, Hanover County, 1868.

TURNER VS. JONES, 1831 (45)

William Dowles' Will

DOWLES, WILLIAM. "I, William Dowles now of Hanover County, being of sound mind and perfect memory do constitute and make this my last will and testament in manner following to wit. First. Recommending my sole to the Almighty God. Secondly. I give and bequeath forever to my brother Jonathan Cattlett my bridal and saddle and all my wearing apparrel. Thirdly. I give and bequeath forever to my brother Samuel J. Catlett my Gold Watch. Fourthly. I give and bequeath to my Daughter Harriet Dowles one half of all my estate both real and personal but if she should die before she becomes of lawful age or marries then in that case it all goes to my wife Susanna Dowles forever. Fifthly. I give to my beloved wife Susanna Dowles one half of all my estate both real and personal during her natural life and then to go to my daughter Harriet Dowles. But be it remembered that if my daughter Harriet Dowles should before she comes of lawful age or marries - so that my wife Susanna Dowles heirs all my estate then and in that case Susanna Dowles is first to pay my sister Ann Tigners children one thousand Dollars is to be equally divided amongst her the said Ann Tigner's children. And Lastly I do appoint my wife Susanna Dowles and my brother Sam J. Cattlett my whole and sole Exor., they paying to my sister Ann Tigner money sufficient or furnishing her with a good suit of moorning cloths, the whole of the above legicies is given in token for their natural love I have for them after the above legacies is paid and delivered then all my Just debts is also to be paid and then every part to be disposed of agreeable to the true meaning of this my last will. In witness whereof I have hereunto set my hand and seal this ninth day of December one thousand eight hundred and five."

John Kilby   William Dowles
Fanney Tomlinson

At a Court of Monthly Session held for Hanover County at the Courthouse, on Wednesday the 25th Dec. 1805. This last will and testament of William Dowles dec'd was offered for proof by Susanna Dowles the Executrix and Samuel J. Cattlett the Executor therein named and was proved by the oath of John Kilby and Fanny Tomlinson, the witnesses thereto and is ordered to be

recorded."
   Teste, William Pollard, C.H.C.
   A Copy, Teste, Wm. O. Winston, C.H.C.

WILLIAM DOWLES, of Hanover. Will dated 9 December 1805. Probated 25 December 1805. Legacies to his sister Ann Tigner and her children, and to brothers, Jonathan and Samuel J. Cattlett. Wife, Susanna Dowles, Executrix. In 1831 she is 80 years of age and "widow of John Turner, but before her marriage was the widow of William Dowles."
   1. HARRIET DOWLES, in 1831, wife of Patrick H. Clopton.

Others mentioned: Albert S. Jones "expecting to remove from the State of Virginia."

HILL VS. SOUTHALL'S ADMR. &C., 1853 (18)

Thomas Turner's Will

TURNER, THOMAS. "I, Thomas Turner of the County of Hanover being in infirm health but of sound and disposing mind do make this my last will and testament hereby revoking all other wills heretofore made by me. First. I wish my body to be decently interred in a plain and unostentatious manner corresponding with my condition in life. Second. I wish my funeral expenses and all my just debts to be paid as soon after my decease as may be practicable, out of the first monies that shall come to the hands of my executor. Third. I wish that my stock of hogs, horses, sheep and cows &c and my farming implements to be sold by public auction to the highest bidder, upon a reasonable credit for very small sums, after setting apart as much of the stock and implements as may be necessary for the cultivation and maintenance of the farm on which I now live, as to which more particular direction will be hereafter given. Fourth. I give and bequeath to my sister in law Susan C. Turner all my interest in the store lately conducted in Richmond by T. & T. G. Turner after the settlement of the debts due by said firm. Fifth. I give and bequeath to Sarah A. E. Turner the daughter of Susan C. Turner the following negroes and their future increase, Viz - Phil, Joe, Edward, Ann and Eliza. Sixth. I give and bequeath to my executors hereafter named and to any trustee who may by the proper Court be appointed to succeed him my house and lot in the County of Henrico called "Cash Corner" and my house and lot on E or Main Street in the City of Richmond and the sum of Six thousand Dollars for the sole and separate use of the said Sarah A. E. Turner; so that the same shall not in any manner be subject to the debts or contracts of any husband she may have during her natural life, the houses and lots to be rented out in the best manner and the money placed at interest upon a loan or loans to be

secured by lien or liens upon real estate of adequate value to secure completely the repayment of the principal and interest. The rents and interest to be appliedas they accrue, after deducting all proper and reasonable charges and expenses to the maintenance and comfort of the said Sarah - and if the said rents and interest should not be sufficient for that purpose then as much of the principal of the said sum of six thousand dollars as may be necessary may be applied from time to time to the maintenance and comfort of the said Sarah A. E. Turner, upon her written order acknowledged after privy examination before a magistrate, the said order expressing if she then married that the money is not to be applied to any debt, demand or contract of her husband, and in every instance the money, whether rent or principal or interest shall be paid in the proper hand of the said Sarah after she obtains the age of twenty one years and during her infancy to her proper guardian except as much as may be necessary for her pocket money which is to be paid to her. It is also my will and desire and I hereby direct that my executor or the Trustee aforesaid shall have full power to sell the said real estate or any part of it, after the said Sarah shall attain her full age, if she by writing acknowledged as aforesaid shall request and write in the Deed to the purchaser the purchase money to be loaned out and the interest applied in the manner herein before directed. It is further my will and desire that the slaves herein before given (by the fifth clause of this will) to the said Sarah shall be hired out by my executor until the said Sarah attains her full age and the hire applied to her use if necessary, and when she attains her full age the said slaves to be delivered to her for her use during her natural life, and at her death if she dies leaving no child living at her death, the said slaves and all other property and the money herein bequeathed and devised to her shall descend to and be equally divided among her lawful heirs according to the law of descents. But if she leaves a child or children or any descendant of such child or children living at her death, then the said slaves and other property and money, I give and devise to such child or children or their descendants as aforesaid in fee simple. Seventh. I devise my farm and plantation in the County of Hanover, upon which I now reside with a sufficient portion of the stock and farming implements upon it and the following slaves - viz -, Sally, Jinny, Randolph, Lew, Tom & Burwell, their future increase, my two houses and lots in the Town of Manchester in the County of Chesterfield and the sum of four thousand dollars to my executor hereinafter named as the Trustee who may be substituted for him by a proper Court in Trust for the use and benefit of my Nephew Henry M. Turner during his natural life, the farm to be kept up and cultivated for his use and benefit allowing him at all times to use it as his home, and the surplus negroes hired out and the money loaned out at interest to be applied to his maintenance, and if necessary portions of the principal money from time to time - I mean to his discreet and comfortable maintenance of which the Trustee must judge - and at his death if he leaves a child or children or their descendants living, I devise the whole of the said property real and personal to such child or children or their descendants. But if the habits of my said nephew shall become changed, and in the opinion of my executor or the trustee aforesaid, he shall have become at the expiration of five years from my death a discreet and prudent man, safely to be entrusted with the management of his Estate - then the said money and property may be paid and delivered to his, discharged from any limitation or condition hereby imposed upon it. The executor and Trustee shall also have, while the Trust continues, the same power over his real Estate which is given over the Real Estate of Sarah A. E. Turner. Eight. I give and bequeath to James Southerland and Margaret Southerland each the sum of three hundred dollars and to William H. Southerland the sum of five hundred dollars, these are the children of Jane Southerland wife of James Southerland. Ninth. I give and bequeath to my nephew William W. Turner a negro girl named Betsy and Reuben. Tenth. I give and devise to William W. Turner my nephew in Trust for the use of my nephew Thomas G. Turner and his family the following property, Towit: Two little negroes Jane and John and the rest and residue of my Estate which is to be held for the use and maintenance of the said Thomas G. Turner and his family, giving them the interest for that purpose until the said Thomas G. Turner who is now insolvent is released and discharged by the Bankrupt Law or otherwise from his present debts but not to be subject either the principal or interest in any manner to any debt now due or which may be hereafter contracted by the said Thomas G. Turner whilst this trust continues, and when the said Thomas G. is so discharged, then the said property shall be held by the trustee or such other as may be substituted in his stead by a proper Court, during the life of the said Turner (the money being secured by loans or adequate real estate) and the interest applied as aforesaid, and at the death of the said Thomas G. I give and devise the said property to his children who may be then living and the descendants of such as may have died before that time. reserving for his widow the use of one-third while she remains his widow. Lastly, I appoint my nephew Thomas G. Turner the executor of this my last will and testament, and desire that no security may be required of him. In testimony whereof I, the said Thomas Turner have subscribed my name and affixed my seal to this Will which is written on six pages this thirteenth day of April in the year of our Lord one thous-

and eight hundred and forty two."

                              Thomas Turner (Seal)
Signed, sealed and published
by the Testator as his last
Will & Testament in our presence & attested by
us in his presence & in the presence of each
other at his request:
    Miles Macon
    A. Govan
    Geo. W. Livesay

At a Court of Quarterly Session held for Hanover County at the Courthouse on Tuesday the 26th of July 1842. This last will and testament of Thomas Turner deceased was proved by the oaths of A. Govan & Geo. W. Livesay, witnesses thereto & is ordered to be recorded.
    Teste, Philip B. Winston, C. H. C.
    A Copy, Teste, Wm. O. Winston, D.C.H.C.

THOMAS TURNER, of Hanover. Will dated 13 April 1842. Probated 26 July 1842. Appoints nephew, Thomas G. Turner, Executor. Gibson Via, Trustee. He had been a member of the mercantile establishment in Richmond of "T. & T. G. Turner." Legatees were:

SARAH C. TURNER, a sister in law, who in 1842 has a daughter under 21 years of age, unmarried:
    1. SARAH A. E. TURNER, a minor, unmarried in 1842, wife in 1845 of Newton Short formerly of the State of Kentucky. In 1852 they are residents of King William Co., Virginia.

    THOMAS G. TURNER, a nephew, Executor of Thos. Turner's Estate.
    HENRY M. TURNER, a nephew.
    WILLIAM W. TURNER, a nephew.

JANE, wife of JAMES SOUTHERLAND, and their children. Relationship to Testator, if any, not shown:
    1. JAMES SOUTHERLAND.
    2. MARGARET SOUTHERLAND.
    3. WILLIAM H. SOUTHERLAND.

                    ————

GOVAN, JAMES, "the elder" late of Hanover County, died sometime prior to 1846. "By his last will and testament devised that his Executors invest certain portions of his Estate in bank stock and other public stocks for the benefit of his daughters Mary Hill, Margaret Tyler and Elizabeth T. Hill." "His Executors were his three sons, James, Edward and Archibald Govan." No mention of wife. Issue:
    1. JAMES GOVAN, "sole surviving Executor in 1852 of James Govan, dec'd."
    2. EDWARD GOVAN, dec'd in 1852. George W. Richardson, Executor. The deceased together with Ann S. Mutter and Miles

Macon had become bound as Securities for John Mutter (insolvent in 1848) on his qualifications as Executor of George Southall, dec'd of Cumberland Co., Va., of whom Robert Anderson of Williamsburg, Va., in 1853, was Administrator.

"A suit was instituted by Samuel F. Bright and his wife Elianna (he was her Admr. in 1848) versus the Executor, John Mutter and his said Security, in the Superior Court of Law and Chancery for James City County, and City of Williamsburg, to which the said suit all the legatees and devisees, heirs and distributees of the said George Southall were made parties, including the said George W. Southall, Helen M. Southall and Peyton A. Southall, the object being to obtain a settlement of John Mutter's Executors Account."

3. ARCHIBALD GOVAN, died in March 1848. Geo. W. Richardson, Exor. He had executed a Deed of Trust to Wm. John Clarke for the benefit of Elizabeth T. Hill on a tract of land called "Selwind" whereon the said Govan resided, described as being "at the big bridge . . . along the road to Fairfield . . . adjoining Miles Macon . . . along the Swamp . . . bounded on the north by Wm. F. Gaines and the main road leading from Macon's Mill to Richmond, on the south by the waters of Chickahominy and Wm. G. Overton . . . 400 acres together with all his right and interest which the said Govan will be entitled to at the death of Mary Hill, wife of Richard Hill of Henrico, under the will of James Govan, dec'd, in and to the Estate held in trust for the said Mary Hill." Archibald Govan was survived by his widow Lucy Ann, and two sons:
  1. WILLIAM WALLER GOVAN, a minor.
  2. JAMES GOVAN, a minor.
4. MARY HILL, wife of Richard Hill of Henrico.
5. MARGARET, wife of Watt. H. Tyler of Hanover.
6. ELIZABETH T., wife of Edward Hill. Their issue in 1853:
  1. ELIZA G. HILL.
  2. FANNY C. HILL.
  3. EDWARD C. HILL.
  4. ARCHIBALD G. HILL.
  5. JOHN HILL.
  6. MARY G. HILL.
  7. ANN HILL.
  8. WILLIAM M. HILL.

Others mentioned: Judgment creditors of Archibald Govan: Henry Daingerfield, Admr. of John Daingerfield, who died since May 1842; W. W. Battaile, John Battaile, Jr., Byrd Willis Battaile, Jane Battaile; James F. Taylor and Frances his wife, and Henry F. Jones assignee of Edwin Farrar. Edmund Christian died since 1847.

FROM OLD WILL BOOK, PAGE 39

TURNER, WM. W., Will dated 12 Nov. 1836, probated 11 April 1837. "To wife Ann W. during life all Estate including interest in his parent's Estate in possession of John R. Turner of Caroline Co." Issue among others:
1. SARAH W. TURNER.
2. ALONZO C. TURNER.

HANCOCK VS. VAUGHAN, 1868 (19)
Joseph Vaughan's Will

VAUGHAN, JOSEPH. "I, Joseph Vaughan of the County of Hanover and State of Virginia being of sound mind and memory (and I hope in a proper state of mind and feeling) do make and ordain this to be my last will and testament. Viz: I lend to my wife Catherine S. Vaughan, so long as she remains my widow, the profits of my whole estate, both real and personal, for the support of herself and my children and their education, embracing all my lands slaves, bonds due me and money on hand, crops, stocks, tools, household furniture &c. subject to the following conditions, viz - Whenever any of my children become of age or marry they shall receive each five hundred dollars either in money or slaves as may be most suitable or convenient to the parties or advantageous to them or to the estate (as I would myself were I living). And at the death of my wife the remainder of my estate to be equally divided amongst all my children or their bodily heirs. Should my wife marry again I wish a division of my property to be made equally between my wife and children, and my wife to take an equal portion with them (that is, she is to take a child's part) which she may dispose of as she may think proper. And I do constitute and appoint my wife executrix with full power and authority to receive and pay debts and do all necessary and proper acts as I myself would, except it be to dispose of my land and slaves, which is hereby prohibited, and I do not require it of her to give any security for her executrixship, merely giving her individual bond for the faithful compliance with my will and wishes as here pointed out. As there may be some doubts about my will and wishes as above expressed, I will endeavor to explain them. My wife to fill my place and carry on my affairs as I would do myself were I living, as long as she remains my widow. If she marries again, divide the estate and have suitable guardians appointed for the children - all to have an equal amt. of property or money. All made equal and all fare alike, but should any of the negroes become unruly or unprofitable or should the interest of my estate demand or be promoted by selling any of them, do so, and apply the proceeds accordingly as I would do were I living. In testimony whereof I do affix my hand and seal this 28 day of our Lord 1844."   Joseph Vaughan (Seal)

At a Court of Quarterly Session held for Hanover County, at the Courthouse on Tuesday the 23rd of October 1849. This last will and testament of Joseph Vaughan dec'd was offered for proof by Catherine S. Vaughan the Executrix therein named, and there being no subscribing witnesses thereto Bolling Vaughan and Peter W. H. Massie were sworn and examined who declare that they were well acquainted with the handwriting of the said Joseph Vaughan, dec'd, that they verily believe the same to have been wholly written & subscribed by the said Joseph Vaughan dec'd. Whereupon it is ordered to be recorded as the last will and testament of the said Joseph Vaughan, dec'd.

 Teste, Wm. O. Winston, C.H.C.
 A Copy, Teste, R. O. Doswell, D.C.H.C.

"The foregoing is an extract from the printed copy of the Record to the 14th day of February 1856, of a suit depending in the Circuit Court of the City of Richmond between Catherine S. Vaughan widow and executrix of Joseph Vaughan deceased. Benjamin F. Vaughan, John H., George R., Catherine, Duecilla, Luther R., Sallie, William S. and Isaac Newton Vaughan heirs at law and devisees of Joseph Vaughan, deceased, (the last eight of whom were at the time of the institution of this suit infants under the age of twenty-one years and sued by the said Catherine S. Vaughan as their next friend) plaintiffs and Isaac A Goddin, Claiborne R. Mason and James M. Taylor, defendants and called and known by the short title of "Vaughan & Others against Goddin." The said printed copy having been filed in the place of the original papers which were lost or destroyed on the occasion of the Clerk's Office of the said Court by fire in the month of April 1865.

 Teste, Benj^a Pollard, Clerk.
 January 16 1868.

At a Court of Quarterly Session held for Hanover County at the Courthouse on Tuesday the 25th of February 1868. On the motion of Catherine S. Vaughan Executrix of Joseph Vaughan, deceased, who this day produced into Court a copy of the last will and Testament of Joseph Vaughan, deceased. And it appearing to the satisfaction of the Court that the same is a true copy doth order the same to be recorded.

 Teste, R. O. Doswell, C.H.
 A Copy, Teste, R. O. Doswell, C.H.C.

JOSEPH VAUGHAN, of Hanover. Will dated in 1844. Probated 23 October 1849. Possessed considerable estate. Reference is made to a suit in the Circuit Court of the City of Richmond "Vaughan & Others vs. Goddin." The suit in Hanover does not shed further information concerning the heirs. Survived by his wife, Catherine S., Executrix, and by 9 children - the last eight of whom, in 1856, were said to have been under the age of twenty-one years:

1. BENJAMIN F. VAUGHAN.
2. JOSEPH H. VAUGHAN.
3. GEORGE R. VAUGHAN.
4. CATHERINE VAUGHAN.
5. DUECILLA VAUGHAN.
6. LUTHER R. VAUGHAN.
7. SALLIE VAUGHAN.
8. WILLIAM S. VAUGHAN.
9. ISAAC NEWTON VAUGHAN.

WADDILL VS. JORDAN, 1833)50)

JORDAN, JONATHAN, of New Kent County, Virginia, a creditor of Thomas McDougle under a bond dated 20 March 1817 on which John Waddill, James Thompson and Elizabeth Mantlo were Securities. Sometime prior to 1818 Mc Dougle removed to Todd County, Kentucky. Jordan travelled to Kentucky and instituted suit against him in the 7th Circuit Court of the United States for Kentucky District, at Frankfort. Returning to New Kent County in 1817 or 1818, he became intimate with a very poor woman, had three or four children, "and lived with her until his marriage with his present wife in 1822 or 1823." "At this time he bought a small farm and kept house."

DOSWELL VS. ANDERSON, 1877 (36)

Edmund Wash's Will

WASH, EDMUND. "I, Edmund Wash of the County of Hanover, State of Virginia do make and ordain this my last will and testament in manner and form as follows, towit: 1st. I give to my wife Nancy Wash all my estate of every description so long as she may live and no longer. 2d. After the death of my wife I direct my executors hereinafter named to sell all my estate both real and personal except slaves and have the whole of my estate including slaves divided into seven equal shares - one of which share I leave in the hands of my executors to be held by them for the children of my deceased daughter Emily D. Gammon and the income to be used for the schooling and maintenance of the said children until they attain the age of 21 years and as they attain the age of 21 years their ralable portion is to be delivered to them - one other share I leave in the hands of my executors to be held by them for the children of my deceased Son Richard Wash, Lucy Ann Wash widow of the said Richard Wash to have a support from this share as long as she remains his widow and the income to be used (or as much as is necessary for the schooling and maintenance of the said children until they attain the age of 21 years and as the said children attain the age of 21 years their ratable portion is to be delivered to them,)- one other share I bequeath to my son William Wash at his death to his children - one other share I bequeath to my son James C. Wash and at his death to his children. One other share I leave in the hands of my executors to be held by them for my daughter Susan M. Chick and her child or children - the income to be paid annually to the said Susan M. Chick during her life and in the event of her death before child or children attain the age of 21 years I direct my executors to hold the same as aforesaid and use the income for the maintenance & schooling of the said child or children and deliver the share to the said child or children when they attain the age of 21 years. One other share I bequeath to my daughter Sarah A. Walton and at her death to her children. One other share I bequeath to the children of my deceased daughter Ellen V. Wiltshire to be managed by their father William B. Wiltshire until they attain the age of 21 years and then to be delivered to them. In the event of the death of any of my Grandchildren before they attain the age of 21 years their portions shall revert to their brothers and sisters or the children of the deceased if they shall have married and die leaving children. Whatever advances I have made or may hereafter make and have charged to my children is to be accounted for in the division of my estate with interest. Lastly I constitute and appoint James C. Wash and William G. Walton Exors of this my last will and testament. In testimony whereof I have hereunto set my hand and affixed my seal this 8th day of March in the year of our Lord eighteen hundred and fifty eight."

                    Edmund Wash

Signed and acknowledged as his last will & testament by the said Edmund Wash in our joint presence with the request that we would   the same & signed by us in his presence & the presence of each other:
    John R. Dandridge
    William P. Gentry
    William H. Pleasants
    Benjamin F. Wiltshire

At a Court of Quarterly Session held for Hanover County at the Courthouse on Tuesday the 27th day of April 1858. This last will and testament of Edmund Wash, deceased was proved by the oaths of John R. Dandridge and William Gentry witnesses thereto, and is ordered to be recorded.
    Teste, Wm. O. Winston, C.H.C.
    A Copy, Teste, R. O. Doswell, D.C.H.C.

"The foregoing is a true copy of a Certified Copy of the will of Edmund Wash, dec'd, filed in the Chancery Cause of "Wash &c. vs. Wash Exors. &c." pending in Louisa Circuit Court."
Sam¹ H. Pleasants, Clk., Louisa Circuit Court.

EDMUND WASH, of Hanover. Will dated 8 March 1858. Probated 27 April 1858. James C. Wash

and William G. Walton, Executors. Survived by his widow, Nancy Wash, and mentioned issue.
    1. EMILY D., deceased, married a Mr. Grammon, and left issue children who are minors in 1858.
    2. RICHARD WASH, dec'd, survived by his widow Lucy Ann and children.
    3. WILLIAM WASH.
    4. JAMES C. WASH, one of his father's Executors.
    5. SUSAN M., wife of a Mr. Chick in 1858.
    6. SARAH A., wife of a Mr. Walton in 1858.
    7. ELLEN V., dec'd, survived by her husband, William B. Wiltshire and children who are minors in 1858.
This suit is not followed to its conclusion for the reason that it extends to late to be of interest in this volume.

———

ANDERSON, MATTHEW A., of Hanover County, died intestate. Widow, Ellen K. Anderson, Administratrix. Her securities in 1867 were Frederick K. Sims, Mary P. Kimbrough (dec'd in 1877) and Augustus K. Bowles. The widow, Ellen K., died prior to 1877, intestate, and Augustus K. Bowles was appointed her Administrator, and Miss Nicey B. Anderson his Security. Issue of Matthew A. Anderson and Ellen K., his wife:
    1. WILLIAM PEYTON ANDERSON.
    2. GEORGE K. ANDERSON, minor in 1877.
    3. CAROLINE D. ANDERSON, minor in 1877.
    4. MARY S. ANDERSON, minor in 1877.
    5. ELLEN K. ANDERSON, minor in 1877.

———

Others mentioned: William·T. Johnson, Sheriff of Appomattox County, Administrator of N. K. Wash, dec'd; Thomas N. Wash, dec'd, James C. Wash, Executor; Josiah H. Duggins and Virginia E., his wife.

                FROM OLD WILL BOOK, PAGE 28

WATKINS, THOMAS, of Hanover. Will dated 13 June 1835. Witnesses, E. L. Nelson and Isaac Butler. Probated 15 October 1835. Survived by his wife, Elizabeth, and following children:
    1. REBECCA, wife of a Mr. Cobbs.
    2. OVERTON WATKINS.
    3. MILDRED, wife of a Mr. Mallory.
    4. SUSAN WATKINS.
    5. LUCY, wife of a Mr. Robinson.
    6. JAMES WATKINS.
    7. JOHN WATKINS.
    8. WILLIAM WATKINS.
    9. URSULA, wife of a Mr. Jones.
    10. MARTHA, wife of a Mr. Jones.

                FROM OLD WILL BOOK, PAGE 36
BURNLEY, EDWIN, 3 Oct. 1836, Apt'd Guardian of his children, Hardin and Wm. M. Burnley.

WICKER VS. CURTIS & OTHERS, 1844 (48)

WICKER, WILLIAM, of Hanover County died before 26 August 1838, survived by two infant children. William H. Curtis, Guardian, Miles Macon, Thomas G. Clarke and John H. Earnest, Securities:
1. HUBBARD A. WICKER, a minor.
2. MARY E. WICKER, a minor.

WICKHAM VS. WICKHAM, 1846 (51)

WICKHAM, EDMUND F., of Hanover County, deceased. Survived by his wife, Lucy, a daughter of Robert Carter of Shirley who died with a will. Carter was possessed of a large tract of land in Hanover County called "South Wales" consisting of 2000 acres. Lucy died in January 1835 and her husband, Edmund F. Wickham became tenant by courtesy until his death in September 1843. "South Wales" descended to his six children in right of their mother. William Fanning Wickham, uncle of the children, Guardian.
1. WATKINS LEIGH WICKHAM, between 14 and 21 years of age in 1846.
2. DR. WILLIAM F. WICKHAM, JR., dec'd.
3. MARY FANNING WICKHAM, between 14 and 21 years of age in 1846.
4. LUCY CARTER WICKHAM.
5. ROBERT CARTER WICKHAM, dec'd in 1850.
6. JOHN WICKHAM, JR.

Others mentioned: Hill Carter, Commissioner; Pleasant Terrell, Security; Edmund Winston who purchased "South Wales."

FROM OLD WILL BOOK, PAGE 76

WICKHAM, WILLIAM F., of Hanover County, appointed on 1 October 1846, Guardian of the orphans of Edmund F. Wickham, dec'd.:
1. WATKINS L. WICKHAM.
2. WILLIAM F. WICKHAM, JR.
3. MARY F. WICKHAM.
4. LUCY C. WICKHAM.

TYLER VS. TOMB'S ADMR., 1834 (43)

TOMBS, ROBERT, of Hanover County died circa 1815, intestate. James A. Gentry, Administrator. Possessed considerable personal estate. No mention is made of his widow, or of real estate if any. He was survived by three children:
1. KITTY, wife in 1834 of James Tyler of Hanover County.
2. THOMAS D. TOMBS.
3. WILLIAM TOMBS.

Others mentioned: James Hazlegrove, Constable.

BUCKNER VS. YEAMANS, 1872 (60)

Agnes D. Walton's Will

WALTON, AGNES D. "I, Agnes D. Walton of Hanover Co., in the State of Virginia, do make this to be my last will and testament as follows: I lend to my sister Mary Yeamans during her life the whole of my estate both real and personal. At the death of my sister Mary Yeamans I lend to my niece Mary Ann Coats, the wife of Joseph Coats, Jr., during her life the one-third part of my negro property and at the death of my said niece Mary Ann Coats it is my will and desire that the said third part together with the negroes and other property both real and personal of every description which I have loaned to my sister Mary Yeamans shall be equally divided between the children of my nephew Andrew G. Walton and the children of my sister Frances White of the State of South Carolina, that is, the children of Andrew G. Walton shall have the one half and the children of Frances White shall have the other half. I give to my brother in law Pleasant Yeamans my negro boy George and to my friend John A. Netherland I give my negro boy Temple. I also give to Ann Pettus Sims, daughter of Garland L. Sims dec'd my negro girl Louisa Ann and one hundred dollars in Cash at the death of my sister Yeamans. It is also my will and desire that my old negro woman Dorcas and my old man Lewis shall be supported out of my Estate by Executors. In the last place I appoint my brother in law Pleasant Yeamans and my friend John A. Netherland to be executors of this my will. In testimony whereof I have hereunto set my hand and affixed my seal the nineteenth day of November one thousand eight hundred and fifty four, in presence of:"

Witnesses: her
    James Wash, Jr.   Agnes + D. Walton
    Joe Rotenbager   mark
    Frances Yeamans

Probated in Hanover County on Tuesday 27 June 1854.

AGNES D. WALTON, of Hanover. Will dated 19 Nov. 1854. Probated 27 June 1854. Possessed of considerable real and personal estate. In partnership with her brother-in-law Pleasant Yeamans owned a tract called Netherland's; the Goodman tract, and the Walton tract. She devised her property to sisters, a niece, nephew, and to her friend John A. Netherland, and to Ann Pettus Sims, daughter of Garland L. Sims.

MARY, a sister, wife of Pleasant Yeamans. One of the Executors of Miss Agnes D. Walton. He was a son of John B. Yeamans.

MARY ANN, a niece, wife of Joseph Coats, Jr., (mentioned in Miss Walton's will)

ANDREW G. WALTON, a nephew, who has issue in 1872:
1. C. K. WALTON.
2. MILDRED, wife of P. L. Jones.
3. FANNIE E., wife of S. W. Jones.
4. CLARA C., wife of F. W. Wright.
5. MARGARET J., wife of L. L. Jones.
6. [   ] dec'd, who was wife of R. D. Wash, who survives with an infant to whom he is Guardian:
   1. A. M. WASH.

FRANCES, a sister, deceased in 1872, who married a Mr. White. Living in the State of South Carolina since prior to 1854. Her descendants in 1872 are: (Children and grandchildren)
1. A. D. WHITE, wife of a Mr. Wells.
2. WILLIAM WHITE, dec'd, leaving issue:
   1. WILLIAM WHITE, JR.
   2. JANE WHITE.
   3. FANNY WHITE.
   4. FOSTER WHITE.
   5. WALLER WHITE.
   6. SALLY WHITE.
   7. JAMES WHITE.
3. JOSEPH WHITE, dec'd, survived by his widow Julia Ann, and children:
   1. SUSAN WHITE.
   2. MARY (or MANLY) WHITE
   3. ROBERT WHITE.
   4. BETTY WHITE.
   5. JOSEPH WHITE.
   6. THOMAS WHITE.
4. HARRY WHITE, dec'd, survived by his widow Sarah, and children:
   1. FRANCES WHITE.
   2. MARY WHITE.
   3. JAMES WHITE.
5. JOHN WHITE, dec'd, survived by children:
   1. SEGENIA WHITE.
   2. MARY WHITE.
   3. JAMES WHITE.
   4. KITTY WHITE.

Pleasant Yeamans' Will

YEAMANS, PLEASANT. " I, Pleasant Yeamans of the County of Hanover & State of Virginia do make this my last will & Testament in manner and form as follows: Item 1st. I wish all my just debts to be paid out of my estate. Item 2. I give to my wife two hundred dollars for charitable purposes, or to be used in other way she may think proper. Item 3. I wish all my estate both real & personal to remain undivided as long as my wife lives for her benefit & use. Item 4th. I wish my Exor hereafter named to see that my wife has all the necessaries of life so that she may live comfortably the balance of her days. Item 5. I wish the land held in partnership by the Estate of Agnes D. Walton, dec'd & myself Viz the Netherland tract - the Goodman tract and the Walton tract to be divided or sold in a body, as my Exor & the other parties interested may think best. At the death of my wife I wish my interest in the above mentioned tracts to go to my brothers & sisters which I give and bequeath to them & their heirs forever. John B. Yeamans, Nancy Netherland, Elizabeth Netherland if alive, if not to her heirs, Francis Yeamans, Polly Yeamans, to be equally divided between them. Item 5. I wish the tract of land I purchased of M. Q. Terrell & others to be sold after my wife's death and the proceeds to be equally divided between my brothers and sisters mentioned in the 5th clause. Item 7. My interest in the land belonging to the estate of my father John Yeamans dec'd I give and bequeath to my brother John B. Yeamans - the personal portion of the said estate coming to me I wish sold & the proceeds to be equally divided between my brother and sisters excepting my sister Elizabeth Netherland or her heirs which I do not give any portion of sd personal estate. Item 8. I hereby appoint Dr. Charles E. Thompson my Executor. Witness my hand & seal the 19th day of September 1865.

                    Pleasant Yeamans (Seal)
Wit:
  Wm. D. Terrell
  Alex R. Fontain

Probated in Hanover County on Tuesday 27 March 1866.

JOHN YEAMANS, of Hanover County, died sometime prior to 1865, in which year his personal and real estate properties had not been divided. No mention is made of his wife or widow. His issue, probably among others:
1. PLEASANT YEAMANS, of Hanover. Will dated 19 September 1865. Probated 27 March 1866. He died on 7 November 1865, survived by his wife, Mary, nee Walton. He appointed Dr. Charles E. Thompson his Executor, who failed to qualify. Edward Vaughan, Sheriff of Hanover, Administrator. He left no issue. His heirs were his brother and sisters.
2. JOHN B. YEAMANS, aged 76 years in 1872.
3. NANCY, married a Mr. Netherland prior to 1858. A widow in 1872.
4. ELIZABETH, deceased in 1872, married a Mr. Netherland prior to 1858. Her heirs were unknown in 1872 and supposed to be living somewhere in the State of Tennessee.
5. FRANCES YEAMANS, died intestate, without issue.
6. MARY (POLLY) YEAMANS, unmarried in 1872.
7. MARCIA M. YEAMANS, unmarried in 1872. She was not mentioned in her brother's will, but appears in the suit.

Others mentioned: Deposition of William A. Luck, aged 75 years in 1872, and lived near Verdon in 1854, '55 and '56. Lived at Pleasant Yeamans' between 1830 and 1840; Ceaser Phillips who had a son George Phillips who would be 19 years of age in 1872, but not heard from, and thought to be dead; David Woody removed from near Beaverdam in Hanover to Georgia during the winter of 1865. He had been manager for Pleasant Yeamans.

PATTON VS WHITE'S EXOR., 1858 (19)
PETITION OF HARRIET WHITE, 1872 (52)

William White's Will

WHITE, WILLIAM. "I, William White of the County of Hanover do make and ordain this my last will. I lend unto my wife Caty the Land whereon I now live together with all the negroes, stock and other property which I may die possessed of out of which she is to pay my debts and the following legacies, Viz. To my son Richard Baylor four hundred dollars worth of negroes so soon as convenient after my death. To my children Ann Thomas, Millicent, Elizabeth, Allis Lipscomb, Chilcow, Warner, Silas, Eliza each four hundred dollars worth of my negroes as they come of age or marry. At the death of my wife I give the land whereon I now live to my sons - James Thomas, and Edmund to be divided by a line running from the corner near the barn to an in corner stone on Nat Dickinson's line James Thomas to have the part on which the houses stand. ·I give the land which I bought of Fortson to my son Lewis G. White. I give the land which I bought of John Smith in Spotsylvania to my son William. The property left by my wife at her death after paying the above mentioned legacies to be equally divided among all my Children. I appoint sons Richard Baylor, Lewis G., and William White Executors of this my last will. Witness my hand and seal this 20th day of Nov. 1812."

W<u>^m</u> White (Seal)

Acknowledged in presence
of us:
   John B. Anderson
   Nathl Dickinson
   Luke A. Seay
   Elijah Partlow
   Edward T.? Rowzee

At a Court of Monthly Session held for Hanover County at the Courthouse on Wednesday the 23rd day of December 1812. This last will and Testament of William White, dec'd was proved by the oaths of Luke A. Seay and Archer Thomas? witnesses thereto and is ordered to be recorded.
   Teste, William Pollard, C.H.C.
   A Copy, Teste, Wm. O. Winston, C.H.C.

WILLIAM WHITE, of Hanover. Will dated 20 Nov. 1812. Probated 23 December 1812. Survived by his wife Caty, and by thirteen children; of whom eight appear to have been under legal age:

1. RICHARD BAYLOR WHITE. One of the Executors of his father's Estate. He was alive in 1843. In 1872, T. D. Coghill, Sheriff of Caroline County, Administrator with the will annexed.
2. LEWIS G. WHITE. One of his father's Executors. Died in 1820, survived by wife Beckie, dec'd in 1872, leaving issue:
   1. HARRIET A. WHITE.
   2. ALBERT WHITE, non-resident of Virginia in 1872.
   3. WILLIAM LEWIS WHITE, non-resident of Virginia in 1872.
3. WILLIAM WHITE. One of his father's Executors. Alive in in 1864. He and his wife Lucy are deceased in 1872, leaving a son:
   1. WILLIAM WHITE, dec'd in 1872. Maria Ellen White, Executrix. Issue:
      1. ELIZABETH WHITE, a minor.
      2. NANCY E. WHITE, a minor.
      3. CATHERINE B. WHITE, a minor.
4. JAMES THOMAS WHITE, died in 1820, "about a month after Lewis G. White" unmarried.
5. EDMUND T. WHITE, of age in 1812. In 1872 address was Hopkinsville, Davies County, Kentucky.
6. CHILION WHITE, under age in 1812. Alive in 1843, deceased in 1872, and William F. Johnson was his Administrator.
7. WARNER W. WHITE, under age in 1812. In 1843 purchased of his brothers and sisters and their heirs, a tract of land in the upper end of Hanover County on North Anna River, adjoining lands of Joseph F. Price and others. In 1872 he is deceased, survived by his widow, Harriet A. White who is the Petitioner in this Cause, and a son, who is his Administrator:
   1. MALMON WHITE, Administrator of his father's Estate.
8. ANN THOMAS, under age in 1812. Married prior to 1820, Elijah Partlow, and both are deceased in 1872, leaving issue:
   1. E. JOSEPH PARTLOW. Lived in Shelby County, Tennessee for sometime. Returned to Virginia with his brother William circa 1869, and in 1872 they are living together near Chilesburg in Caroline County. They have a cousin William Partlow of Spotsylvania County, Va.
   2. WILLIAM RICHARD PARTLOW. Lived in Shelby County, Tennessee for sometime. In Caroline County, Va., after 1869.
   3. CATHERINE PARTLOW, non-resident of Virginia in 1872.
   4. MARTHA ANN PARTLOW, non-resident of Virginia in 1872.
   5. MARY ELIZABETH PARTLOW, non-resident of Virginia in 1872.
   6. JAMES PARTLOW, non-resident of Virginia in 1872.

9. ELIZABETH (BETSY), under age in 1812, married Thomas Phillips, and both are dec'd
in 1872, leaving issue:
    1. WILLIAM PHILLIPS, non-resident of
    Virginia.
    2. GEORGE PHILLIPS, non-resident of Vir-
    ginia.
    3. JOHN T. PHILLIPS, non-resident of
    Virginia.
    4. MINERVA, married prior to 1864, a Mr.
    Pleasants. Non-resident of Virginia.
10. ELIZA J., under age in 1812, married
Andrew McDowell. She is alive in 1872,
with issue, probably among others:
    1. SILAS L. McDOWELL.
    2. ALICE J. McDOWELL.
    3. OLIN F. McDOWELL.
    4. PAULINE A McDOWELL.
    5. WILLIAM SAULE McDOWELL.
11. ALICE LIPSCOMB WHITE, under age in 1812.
Alive in 1859, and living with her
mother, Mrs. Caty White. In 1872 she is
deceased, was a non-resident, and
Eldridge Cross her Administrator.
12. MILDRED (MILLICENT), under age in 1812.
Her will dated 15 June 1850 was probated
24 September 1850. Re-recorded 27 February 1867: She died unmarried.

Mildred White's Will

"I, Mildred White of the County of Hanover and
State of Virginia being in the perfect possession of my mental faculties, do make this my
last will and testament hereby revoking and cancelling all other papers and writings purporting to be of that character. 1st. I wish all
my just debts to be paid. 2nd. I give and bequeath to my Sister Alice White and her heirs
forever, one hundred and fifty dollars. 3rd. I
give and bequeath to my sister Eliza McDowell
 and her heirs forever two hundred dollars.
4th. Should my nephew William Partlow be living
at my death, it is my will that my executor pay
to him out of my estate the sum of one hundred
dollars, if dead I wish the same equally divided
between the children of my sister Eliza McDowell.
5th. I loan to my brother Warner White during
his life Four hundred and Sixty dollars. At his
death I wish the same to go to his son Mulmore
L. White. 6th. As my Sister Alice White and
myself are securities to a bond executed by my
brother William White to William Hancock for
about three hundred dollars, it is my will I
should said bond not be paid at my death that my
executor hold enough of the sum loaned to my
brother Warner White to pay off and satisfy the
same. 7th. I give and bequeath to my brother
Silas White all the ballance of my estate of
every kind and discription together my reversionary interest in the estate of my father
William White, deceased and every other interest
that may accrue to me. 8th. I hereby appoint
my brother Silas White executor to this my last

will and testament with the wish that the Court
will not require him to give security when he
qualified. In witness whereof I have hereunto
set my hand and affixed my seal the fifteenth
day of June one thousand eight hundred and
fifty."
                                  her
                        Mildred + White (Seal)
                                 will
Witnesses:
  E. A. Rowzie
  John D. Luck
  George M. Hall

At a Court of Monthly Session held for Hanover
County at the Courthouse on Tuesday the 24th of
September 1850. This last will and testament
of Mildred White dec'd was proved by the oaths
of John D. Luck and George M. Hall witnesses
thereto and is ordered to be recorded.
    Teste, Wm. O. Winston, C.H.C.
    A Copy, Teste, Wm. O. Winston, C.H.C.

13. SILAS WHITE, under age in 1812. Will dated
19 October 1864, probated 26 June 1866.
He died unmarried and without issue:

Silas White's Will

"I, Silas White of the County of Hanover and
State of Virginia being in perfect possession of
my mental faculties do make this my last will
and Testament hereby revoking and cancelling all
other papers and writings purporting to be of
the character. 1st. I wish all my just debts to
be paid. 2d. I wish my funeral expenses paid.
3d. I give to my brother William White four hundred dollars. 4th. I give to my sister Eliza J.
McDowell four hundred Dollars. 5th. I give to
my niece Minerva A. Pleasants four hundred Dollars. 6th. I give to my niece Eliza M. Montgomery four hundred Dollars. 7th. I give to my
nephews Joseph Partlow, William Partlow and
Joseph R. White one hundred each. 8th. I give
to Mrs. America Anthony one hundred Dollars.
9th. I give to niece Catherine A. Cross two hundred and fifty Dollars to do as she thinks
proper with. 10th. I give to my nephews and
nieces Silas L. McDowell, Alice J. McDowell,
Olin F. McDowell, Pauline A. McDowell, William
Saule Mc Donall two hundred and fifty Dollars
each. 11th. If the property coming from my
brother Chilion White's estate with all my
other property should be more than a sufficiency
to settle the above legacies the balance of the
property to be equally divided between my
brother & sister, Nephews and Nieces above
named and if there Shall be a deficiency there
Shall be a reduction in the Same proportion.
12th. I have two Yarn & two Cotton Counterpanes
I give to my four nieces Catherine A. Cross,
Eliza M. Montgomery, Alice J. McDowell & Pauine
A. McDowell one each. 13th. The balance of my
property to be Sold publicly and distributed in
proportion as the above. I appoint Silas L.

McDowell and Charles R. Montgomery as Executors of this my last will and Testament."

Silas White (Seal)

Signed, sealed published and declared by the testator Silas White as and for his last will and testament in the presence of us who in his presence at his request and in the presence of each other have hereunto Subscribed our names as Witnesses:
    Sarah A. F. Cross
    Mantell Butler

At a Court of Monthly Session held for Hanover County at the Courthouse on Tuesday the 26th of June 1866. This last will and Testament of Silas White deceased was proved by the oath of Sarah A. F. Cross one of the witnesses thereto. And at a Court of Quarterly Session held for the Said County at the Courthouse on Tuesday the 24th of July 1866, This last will and Testament of Silas White deceased was further proved by the Oath of Mantell Butler the other witness thereto and is ordered to be recorded.
    Teste, R. O. Doswell, C.H.C.
    A Copy, Teste, R. O. Doswell, C.H.C.

The following stated to have been grandchildren of William White and Caty his wife, but whose parents' names are not stated:

    ELIZA M. MONTGOMERY, as mentioned in
        Silas White's Will.

    JOSEPH R. WHITE, mentioned in Silas
        White's will and elsewhere. He made a
        deposition in 1859 in which he stated:
        "The last time I came to Virginia was
        in December 1858. The first time about
        three years ago."

    CATHERINE A. CROSS, as mentioned in
        Silas White's will.

Others mentioned: Fleming J. Hancock of Thornsburg, Spotsylvania County, Va., in 1860, and Nathaniel J. Hancock, Executors in 1859 of William Hancock, deceased.

VIA & OTHERS VS. HIGGINS & WIFE, 1836 (48)

WHITE, JOHN, of Hanover County, "died many years ago, intestate." Possessed of 66 acres of land and a few slaves. Survived by five children, and his widow "who has since married and had a daughter, Rebecca, wife of Foster Higgins." No mention is made of the name of his widow or of her second husband. Children of John White:
1. MARY T., wife of Gilson Via.
2. ELIZABETH, wife of Robert Harwood.
3. SAMUEL WHITE

4. NANCY WHITE, died under age, intestate.
5. PATSEY WHITE, died under age, intestate,

BETHEL & OTHERS VS. HARWOOD & OTHERS, 1859 (56)

WHITE, HUGH L., deceased, of Hanover County, had a sister, Polly, deceased who married a Mr. Hurt, also deceased, and these two had an only child, John Hurt who died intestate in the City of Richmond. John A. Harwood, Sheriff of Hanover, was his Administrator. Hurt's heirs were the children of Hugh L. White, deceased:
1. SARAH A., wife of a Mr. Bethel.
2. MILDRED C., wife of Richard S. Cone.
3. JULIA ANN WHITE.
4. WILLIAM JETER WHITE.

(Reference is made to a Chancery Suit in King William County, 1846, under the short title: "White & Others vs. Crisp & Others.")

Others mentioned: John A. Harwood, late Sheriff of Hanover, who had been Administrator of John Hurt. Harwood's official bond as Sheriff was dated 26 June 1837. The Securities being: N. A. Thompson, John R. Taylor, Billy W. Talley, Thos. W. Talley, George W. Harwood, William C. Smith and G. T. Vest.

FOSTER VS. BURTON, 1877 (56)

Moses White's Will

WHITE, MOSES. "In the name of God amen. I, Moses White of the Parish of St.Paul in the County of Hanover in the State of Virginia being in tolerably good health and of sound mind and disposing mind but considering the uncertainty of life do make and ordain this to be my last will and testament. That is to say. First, I lend to my beloved wife Ann during her natural life the tract of land on which I at present reside, supposed to contain Three hundred and eighty acres, be the same more or less, together with my negro man James and one third of all my other negroes and personal estate over and above the said negro man James in value and I do and give to my said wife in receiving the one third part of my negroes and personal estate, the right to select such of them as she may choose. Secondly. I do give to my son Elisha White my tract of land known by the name of "Amos" supposed to contain three hundred and fifty acres, be the same more or less. This tract was purchased by me in different parcels and is bounded by the lands of John Waddill and others and is the same on which stands the Log Trap Meeting house, to him and his heirs and assigns forever. It is also my wish and desire that at the death of my wife the profits arising from the meadow

attached to the land on which I at present reside should be equally divided between my said
son Elisha and his unmarried sisters for and
during the term of twelve years. Thirdly. having already given to my son James White one
Thousand dollars in the purchase of a tract of
land in New Kent County of Miles C. Tunstall, I
do now give and bequeath to my said son James
White a negro man named John as his full interest in my estate. Fourthly. I lend to my daughter Colly Daverson during her natural life and
give to the lawful begotten heirs of her body
the tract of land which I lately purchased of
Daniel Stewart in Hanover County containing
seventy-five acres be the same more or less and
bounded by the lands of Reynold Parsons, Albert
Ellison and others for which said tract of land
I gave one thousand dollars and moreover if the
gift does not make her equal with each of my
daughters, individually named hereinbefore it
is my will and desire that she and they be made
equal to my said daughters individually. Fifthly. I give to my five _married_ daughters namely,
Ann Burton, Elizabeth F. White, Evelina White,
Mary White and Roxana White at the death of
their mother the tract of land on which I at
present reside, valued at One Thousand dollars
by me, subject however to the contingency before expressed, relating to the meadows, to
them and their heirs forever, but no division
to be claimed of the same during the single
state of either. Sixthly. I give to all my
daughters married or single (with the exception
of my daughter Colley Daverson who has been
provided for above equal interest in the remainder of my estate not heretofore finally disposed of with this provision that my daughter
Ella Jane Parsley is to receive two hundred
dollars more in value for the purpose of equal-
izing the land bequeathed to the others to them
and their heirs forever. Seventhly. I give to
my Grandson Thaddeus Foster when he attains the
years of twenty-one or marries an equal share
with my unmarried daughters in my personal
estate. Lastly I do hereby constitute and appoint my son Elisha White and my son in law
John P. Paisley executors of this my last will
and testament hereby revoking all and every
will heretofore made by me. In witness whereof
I, Moses White have hereunto set my hand and
seal this 11th day of June in the year of our
Lord one Thousand eight hundred and forty-two."

Moses White (Seal)

Signed sealed and delivered by Moses White the
Testator in our presence as his last will and
testament with a request that we would witness
the same which we do by subscribing our names
in his presence:
    James Lane
    John Pate
    Richd G. Smith
    Ezekiel S. Talley

At a Court of Monthly Session held for Hanover
County at the Courthouse on Tuesday the 27th of
Dec. 1842. This last will and testament of
Moses White dec'd was proved by the oaths of
John Pate, Richard G. Smith & Ezekiel S. Talley,
witnesses thereto and is ordered to be recorded.
    Teste, Philip B. Winston, C.H.C.
    A Copy, Teste, Philip B. Winston, C.H.C.

MOSES WHITE, of Hanover. Will dated 11 June
1842, probated 27 December 1842. His property included the estate "Pleasant Green" of 380
acres in Hanover. Survived by his widow, Ann,
and by ten children:
    1. ELISHA WHITE, deceased. Will dated 21 June
       1858, probated 24 January 1860. Died
       unmarried and without issue.

Elisha White's Will

"I, Elisha White of the County of Hanover,State
of Virginia do hereby make and publish this my
last will and testament hereby revoking and
making void any and all former wills made by me
at any time heretofore made and first direct
that my body be decently interred and my funeral expenses be paid as well as any proper debts
that may be due from me out of any money that I
may leave. Secondly, that the remainder of such
money _and its_ due me from any source as soon as
available be invested in State or other profitable stocks the interest thereof I give equally
for life to my named sisters hereafter the devisees for life of the residue of my estate,
the principal or stocks I hereby give in fee to
the remainder parties or party who take the
residue of my estate under this will in fee
after the provision for my named sisters lives
have transferred. Thirdly. I give to my sisters
Elizabeth F. White, Emeline White and Mary White
jointly and severally and the survivor of them
for and during their natural lives or the life
of such Survivor. I lend also every part of my
estate in possession reversions or remainder
not before disposed of both real and personal
consisting of lands, slaves, horses, mules,
plantation stock and implements both in New
Kent and in Hanover County with all else to be
found belonging to me anywhere, and if they or
either of them should leave issue then I give
the same to such issue equally in fee but in
case my said sisters should each depart this
life leaving no offspring then in that event I
give the whole of my estate of what sort or
kind soever to my nephew and niece John White
Davidson & Margaret Ellen Davidson equally
between them as they attain the age of twenty
one years and to their respective heirs forever,
but if either should die under the age of
twenty-one years without leaving offspring then
I give the whole to the survivor in fee. Lastly
I hereby appoint my well beloved sister Elizabeth F. White executrix to this my last will
requesting the court of probate to dispense

with Security for her qualifications herein. In
witness whereof I, Elisha White have to this my
will and testament written on this half sheet
of paper set my hand and seal this 21st of June
1858."

                                    Elisha White (Seal)
Wit-
   Jos. G. Turner
   E. D. Waid
   Ira Barker

At a Court of Monthly Session held for Hanover
County at the Courthouse on Tuesday the 24
January 1860. This last will and testament of
Elisha White deceased was proved by Jos. G. Tur-
ner and E. D. Waid two of the witnesses thereto
and is ordered to be recorded.
   Teste, Wm. O. Winston, C.H.C.
   A Copy, Teste, WM. O. Winston, C.H.C.

 2. JAMES WHITE, deceased. His widow survived
    but now deceased, leaving issue:
    1. SUSAN H. WHITE.
    2. WILLIAM WHITE.
    3. CURTIS WHITE.
    4. SAMUEL S. WHITE.
 3. COLLY W., dec'd, wife of a Mr. Davidson in
    1842. Survived by children:
    1. JOHN WHITE DAVIDSON.
    2. MARGARET E., dec'd in 1858, survived
       by her husband Wingfield S. Lips-
       comb, and infant children of whom
       he is Guardian. Afterward he seems
       to have married Octavia Parsley, a
       cousin of his former wife:
       1. ELLEN W. LIPSCOMB.
       2. ANN F. LIPSCOMB.
       3. THOMAS N. LIPSCOMB.
 4. ELLEN JANE, widow in 1877 of John P. Par-
    sley, dec'd. She had issue, perhaps
    among others:
    1. OCTAVIA, who married W. S. Lipscomb.
 5. SUSAN, dec'd in 1878, widow of a Mr. Foster.
    Her only surviving son:
    1. THADDEUS FOSTER, born prior to 1842.
 6. ROXANNA WHITE, dec'd. She sold her inter-
    est in her father's Estate to Elisha
    White.
 7. EVELIN WHITE, died unmarried after 1858.
 8. ANN, dec'd, married prior to 1842 a Mr.
    Burton and left issue:
    1. WILLIAM BURTON.
    2. MARCUS L. BURTON, who is married and
       has issue:
       1. MARTHA B. BURTON.
 9. ELIZABETH F. WHITE, dec'd. Her will dated
    22 January 1876, was probated 18 October
    1876 by the witnesses: E. W. Allen,
    Spotswood Liggan and Erasmus H. Wright.
10. MARY J. WHITE, dec'd. Her will dated 3
    December 1858, was probated 28 June 1859
    by the witnesses: Spotswood Liggan,
    James E. Burnett and Ira Barker.

The children of Moses White died in the following order: Roxanna, Eveline, Mary J., Elisha,
Ann Burton, James, Elizabeth F., Susan Foster.
At the time of this suit the only survivors
were Mrs. Davidson and Mrs. Parsley.

WHITE & OTHERS VS. WHITE & OTHERS, 1839 (49)

Nathaniel White's Will

WHITE, NATHANIEL. "In the name of God,
Amen. I, Nathaniel White of the County
of Hanover and State of Virginia being
of perfectly sane mind, but laboring under
bodily disease do make and publish this as my
last will and Testament in manner and form following, to wit. I commend my soul to God rely-
ing on the precious promises of the saviour and
in his interposition and my body to be decently
buried. In the disposal of my worldly Goods, it
is my will and desire that all my just debts be
paid. I give and bequeath to my son Josiah
White the horse Tekumsiah. I give to my daughter Catherine Tyler five dollars. I give to my
wife Mildred White two Hundred Dollars to do as
she pleases with. I give Alexander White and
Mildred White children of my dec'd son John
White that portion of my Estate which their
father would have had, that is, one equal share
to be divided between them. In the case of the
death of either before lawful age or marriage,
then his or her portion to go to the survivor,
but in case of the death of both, then to my
surviving children. I give to my son David
White (now living in Mobile) an equal share of
my estate after deducting the amount I have
paid for him since he left me. I give to my
daughter Mary Jarvis one cow and one feather
bed. I give to my son Philman choice of my
horses Flaxen and Nimble, one cow and one feather Bed. I give to my son William one horse,
one cow and one Feather Bed. I give to my daughter Elizabeth one negro girl named Manda, one
Feather Bed and a Loom and Harness. It is my
desire that all my property not specifically
named and bequeathed by me, be kept together,
and that my dear wife have the management and
control of it during her lifetime for the use
of herself and all my children. It is also my
desire that she have the power to dispose of
any part she may at any time deem proper and
that she do with it as she may think best. At
her death however, it is my will and desire
that my Land and all my other property of every
description be equally divided amongst all my
children and my two grandchildren before named.
It is my desire that my wife and my son Josiah
F. White qualify as Executrix and Executor to
this my last will and Testament. In testimony
whereof I have hereunto set my hand and affixed
my seal this 16 day of March 1836."
                                    Nathl White
Signed sealed & delivered in

presence of us:
E. E. Buckner
Robert Wooddy, Senr.
Robert C. C. Wooddy

At a Court of Quarterly Session held for Hanover
County at the Courthouse on Tuesday the 26th of
July 1836. This last will and Testament of
Nathaniel White dec'd was proved by the Oaths
of E. E. Buckner, Robert Wooddy, Sr., Robert C.
C. Wooddy the witnesses thereto and is ordered
to be recorded.
Teste, Philip B. Winston, C.H.C.
A Copy, Teste, Philip B. Winston, C.H.C.

NATHANIEL WHITE, of Hanover. Will dated 16
March 1838, probated 26 July 1836. Widow,
Mildred, Executrix, died circa 1 March 1839.
Joseph F. White, Surviving Executor. Testator
possessed some land and six slaves. Issue:
1. JOSIAH F. (JOSEPH) WHITE, Executor of his
   father's Estate, a resident of Richmond,
   Va. In 1851, Joseph Hooper is his Admr.
2. PHILIP F. (PHILMAN) WHITE, a non-resident
   of Virginia in 1839.
3. WILLIAM WHITE, a resident of Farmville, Va.
   in 1846.
4. DAVID WHITE, a resident of Catawba, Dalons
   County, Alabama. Attached to the Federal
   Court at Mobile. In a letter dated at
   Mobile, Ala., 14 April 1839, he wrote:
   "Am with Cousin David White and all his
   children are here at this time."
5. MARY F., wife in 1836 of a Mr. Jarvis; and
   a non-resident of Virginia. Circa 1847
   she is the wife of John Power and lives
   in Richmond, Va.
6. CATHERINE, dec'd in 1845, married prior to
   1836, Littleton Tyler of Hanover County,
   who survived her.
7. ELIZABETH A. M., dec'd in 1839, survived
   by her husband Henry M. Bowden of James
   City County in 1845.
8. JOHN G. WHITE, dec'd in 1836. Survived by
   infant children:
   1. ALEXANDER A. WHITE.
   2. ELIZABETH MILDRED WHITE, dec'd in
      1851, intestate. John R. Fulford,
      Administrator.

Others mentioned: Dr. H. Curtis, Dr. J. W.
Royster.

WHITE VS. STARKE & OTHERS, 1849 (50)

WHITE, DR. WILLIAM L., of "Spring Grove"
Hanover County, married Elizabeth a
daughter of John Cross also of Hanover
County. Issue in 1849:
1. JOSEPH C. WHITE.
2. WILLIAM L. WHITE, JR.
3. THOMAS F. WHITE.
4. SUSANNA C. WHITE

5. ELIZABETH E. C. WHITE.

Others mentioned: Finch Cross one of the Execu-
tors in 1825 of John Cross; Fleming B. Cross;
Charles W. Dabney; Tinsley Davis; Charles P.
Goodman; Thomas M. White.

DIX &C. VS. WHITLOCK &C., 1843 (11)

David Whitlock's Will

WHITLOCK, DAVID. "In the name of God
Amen. I, David Whitlock of the County
of Hanover & parish of saint Paul,
being of sound mind & memory do make & ordain
this my last Will and Testament in manner and
form following, to wit: It is my will and desire that all my just & lawful debts be paid &
for that purpose I desire that my Executors may
sell a tract of land that I have in the State
of Kentucky which I purchased of Samuel Whitlock & adopt such other methods for the payment
of the same as they think best. Item. I give
and bequeath unto my sons Charles Whitlock,
Turner Richardson Whitlock and David Parish
Whitlock all the land that I am entitled to in
the County of Randolph (State of Virginia) to
be equally divided between them & their heirs
forever. Item. I lend unto my wife Martha
Whitlock the tract of land whereon I now live
during her widowhood and at her death or marriage it is my will and desire that the said
tract of land be equally divided between my two
daughters Rebekah Doran Whitlock and Lucy Ann
Whitlock, to them and their heirs forever, but
in case either of my said daughters should die
under age or unmarried it is my will that the
surviving one have the hole of the said land. I
likewise lend unto my wife Martha Whitlock
during her natural life all the rest of my
estate of every kind & quality whatsoever & at
her death to be divid between my following
children as she shall direct - Charles Whitlock,
Turner Richardson Whitlock, David Parish Whitlock, Rebekah Doran Whitlock & Lucy Ann Whitlock to them and their heirs forever. And lastly
I nominate and appoint my wife Martha Whitlock
and John Allen Richardson executrix and executor to this my last Will and Testament in witness whereof I have hereunto set my hand &
affixt my seal this 28th day of March one thous-
and seven hundred & ninety eight.

David Whitlock (Seal)
Signed sealed & acknowledged
in presence of:
David Gentry
John Lyle
Nath[1] Whitlock

At a Court of Monthly Session held for Hanover
County at the Courthouse on Wednesday the 19th
of September 1798. This last will and Testament

of David Whitlock deceased was proved by the oaths of David Gentry and John Lyle, witnesses thereto and is ordered to be recorded.

Teste, William Pollard, C.H.C.

A Copy, Teste, Philip B. Winston, C.H.C.

Martha Whitlock's Will

"In the name of God amen. I, Martha Whitlock of the County of Hanover do make and ordain this to be my last Will & Testament in the manner and form following. Imprimis. I give and bequeath unto my Daughter Rebecca Whitlock the following slaves, to wit Tom, Abram, Rhoda, Mary, Alice, Rhoda Ann, Little Abel, William, Eliza, Annaka, Sarah, Henry, Pinder, Cyrus and Mildred with the future increase of the females from and after the date hereof, also three feather beds with their furniture and a bay horse called Jack to her and her heirs forever. Item. I give and bequeath unto my daughter Lucy Ann Wingfield the following slaves to wit Watt, Peter, Martha, Natty, Polly, Betsey, Big Hannah, Matilda, Little Hannah and Easter with the future increase of the females of them from the date hereof, also one feather bed and furniture to her and her heirs forever. Item. I give to my Grand Daughter Martha Rebecca Wingfield one negro named Johnson to her and her heirs forever. Item. I give and bequeath unto my Grand Daughter Lucy Ann Barbara Wingfield one negro named Richard to her and her heirs forever. Item. I give and bequeath unto my Grand Daughter Sarah Lewis Wingfield one negro named Robert, to her and her heirs forever. Item. I give and bequeath unto my Grand Daughter Juliet Blair Wingfield one negro named Harriet to her and her heirs forever. Item. I give and bequeath unto my Grandson Henry Clay Wingfield one negro named Nelson to him and his heirs forever. Item. I give and bequeath unto my Grand Daughter Virginia Wingfield one negro named Agness to her and her heirs forever. Item. It is my will and desire that my slave Aggy with her future Increase shall be equally divided among all the children now born or that may be born to my daughter Lucy Ann Wingfield to them and their respective heirs forever. Item. It is my will and desire that my old and faithful servant Abel shall have the privilege of living with any of my Daughters he may prefer. Item. It is my Will and desire that all the residue of my Estate not herein bequeathed including the Halifax Land purchased by my husband David Whitlock, dec'd, of John Garland be equally divided between my two said Daughters Rebecca Doran Whitlock and Lucy Ann Wingfield as they may agree between themselves, to them and their respective heirs forever. Item. My three sons Charles Whitlock, Turner Richardson Whitlock and David Parish Whitlock having departed this life unmarried and without issue is the reason that I have not devised anything to them in

this my last will. Lastly, I constitute and appoint my friend Col. William Trueheart and my son in law Mr. Ralph Wingfield, Executors of this my last will and Testament. In witness whereof I have hereunto set my hand and affixed my seal this 5th day of November 1825."

Martha Whitlock (Seal)

Signed sealed & acknowledged
in the presence of
  Henry Curtis
  Thomas Gardner

"I, Martha Whitlock hereby make this Codicil to be taken as a part and parcel of my last will and Testament, that is to say, I give to my Grandson Henry Clay Wingfield in addition to the bequest herein before made, for his benefit, two negroes, the children of Aggy, to wit, Turner and Daniel the better to enable him to compleat a classical education should other means fail him, to him and his heirs forever. Given under my hand and seal the 22 day of April 1833 as my last Will &c."

her
Martha + Whitlock (Seal)
mark

Signed, sealed & acknowledged
in the presence of
  Henry Curtis

"I also make & ordain this to be a further Codicil to my last Will &c, that is, it is my will and desire that all the Stock, sheep, hogs, and cattle, together with the growing crop, or any that may be on hand at the time of my death be given absolutely and considered belonging to my son in law Ralph Wingfield. Witness my hand & seal this 22d day of April 1833."

her
Martha + Whitlock (Seal)
mark

Signed sealed & acknowledged
in the presence of
  Henry Curtis
  Thomas Gardner

At a Court of Quarterly Session continued and held for Hanover County at the Courthouse on Wednesday the 27th of Feb. 1839. This last will and Testament of Martha Whitlock dec'd and the second Codicil thereafter written were proved by the oaths of Henry Curtis and Thomas Gardner the witnesses thereto. And the first Codicil thereafter written was also proved by the oath of Henry Curtis the witness thereto which will and Codicils are ordered to be recorded.

Teste, Philip B. Winston, C.H.C.

A Copy, Teste, Philip B. Winston, C.H.C.

DAVID WHITLOCK, of Saint Paul's Parish, Hanover. Will dated 28 March 1798, probated 19 September 1798. During his lifetime had purchased of one John Garland lands in Halifax County on Hyco River, which he subsequently sold to Dabney Miller. This land was later devised by Mrs. Martha Whitlock to her two surviving children. A law suit resulted, instituted in the Superior Court of Law and Chancery in Richmond, in which the Court decreed that the tract be divided into four lots "first choice to be cast between Francis Timberlake, Sr., (now dec'd) and Martha Whitlock and John Allen Richardson Executrix and Executor." David Whitlock also possessed lands in Hanover, Randolph County, (now West Virginia) and Kentucky. Survived by his five children and his widow Martha who died with will dated 5 November 1825, two Codicils dated 22 April 1833. Probated 27 February 1839. Their issue:

1. CHARLES WHITLOCK, died without issue between 1798 and 1825.
2. TURNER RICHARDSON WHITLOCK, died without issue between 1798 and 1825.
3. DAVID PARISH WHITLOCK, died without issue between 1798 and 1825.
4. REBECCA DORAN WHITLOCK, unmarried in 1843.
5. LUCY ANN, married prior 1825 Ralph Wingfield. Both are deceased in 1841, leaving issue:
   1. MARTHA REBECCA WINGFIELD.
   2. LUCY ANN BARBARA, married after 1825 William Henry Curtis, and died intestate circa 1855. Alexander B. Hutchinson, Sheriff of Henrico Co., Administrator.
   3. SARAH LEWIS WINGFIELD.
   4. JULIA BLAIR, under 21 years of age in 1841, married circa 1855, Philip R. Norment.
   5. HENRY CLAY WINGFIELD, under 21 years of age in 1841.
   6. VIRGINIA WINGFIELD, under 21 years of age in 1841.

MILLER, DABNEY, died prior to 1804. Had purchased of David Whitlock a tract of land on Hyco or Hico River in Halifax County, containing 400 acres, which was distributed to his seven surviving heirs. The name of his wife was not stated. In the deposition of Mrs. Rebecca Anderson in 1853 of Goochland Co., she stated that she was 73 years of age and that Dabney Miller married her Aunt, survived her, and died in Henrico County many years ago, leaving six daughters and two sons. Mrs. Martha A. Winston deposed on 25 October 1853 that she was connected with the family of Dabney Miller, and that she could add nothing further to the statement of Mrs. Anderson. The issue were:

1. LUCY ANN, married prior to 1805 Thomas Dix. In 1814 living in Henry County, Va.
2. NANCY, married Patrick Fontaine, who is dec'd in 1853. Sold her interest in the Halifax land to Thomas Dix.
3. KITTY, married Samuel R. Cole, dec'd in 1853. Sold her interest to Thomas Dix.

4. SALLY D., married Thomas Shelton. On 25 November 1834, Sally D. Shelton of Louisa County, conveyed to Thomas Dix of Henry County, consideration $100.00, tract of land in Halifax County, 57 1/2 acres being 1/7th part of a tract of 400 acres on Hyco River, purchased by Dabney Miller dec'd who was her father, of David Whitlock. The witnesses were: Nath¹ R. Cole, B. Estes and Walter K. Cole. Sally D. survived her husband and died without issue sometime prior to 1843.
5. ELIZABETH A., married Reuben Alexander, whom she survived. On 28 November 1821, Reuben Alexander and Eliza A., his wife of Cumberland County, Kentucky, conveyed to Thomas Dix their interest in the Halifax land.
6. MARY, married Robert Alexander. On 28 Nov. 1821 she and her husband conveyed her interest in Halifax land to Thomas Dix. At that time they were living in Cumberland County, Kentucky.
7. REBECCA, married William Perkins of Henry County, Va. He survived her and was alive in 1846. They had issue:
   1. SALLY ANN, married Thomas Perkins, and in 1843 were living in Missouri
   2. KITTY, married Robert Taylor and living in Powhatan County, Va., in 1843.
   3. MARY, married Lewis McCormick and in 1843 were living in Pittsylvania County, Va.
   4. WILLIAM PERKINS, Jr., of Henry Co.
   5. JESSE PERKINS, of Goochland County.
   6. MARTHA PERKINS, of Missouri.
8. RICHARD MILLER, and wife Rebecca, of Prince Edward County, Va., on 24 July 1813 conveyed to Thomas Dix 57 acres being the 7th part which is 57 acres, being his share in land which Dabney Miller left in Halifax County to be distributed amongst his children (father of the said Richard) being the same Dabney Miller purchased of Thomas Whitlock dec'd formerly of Hanover.
9. JOHN MILLER, died early, without issue.

WHITLOCK VS. COLLINS & OTHERS, 1872 (80)

WHITLOCK, JAMES N., of Hanover County died in 1855 intestate. Possessed lands adjoining Dr. E. T. Shelton, John Bell Bigger and Mrs. William Tyler. Survived by his widow, Harriet who later married Edward C. Collins, and by two children:

1. MARY MALCENA WHITLOCK.
2. JAMES WHITLOCK, who is under the age of twenty-one in 1872.

GILMAN VS. WINGFIELD, 1867 (17)

WINGFIELD, ALEXANDER, and his wife Charlotte E., of Hanover County, executed a Deed of Trust on land adjoining Charles C. Tinsley, Charles P. Goodall and Benjamin F. Brice, containing 237 1/2 acres, to Charles P. Goodall in trust to secure William E. Saunders payment on a certain bond. This bond was assigned by Saunders to Semple and John Ellett who assigned to Anderson C. Davis.

FROM OLD WILL BOOK, PAGE 71

WINGFIELD, WILLIAM, of Hanover. Will dated 15 January 1843. Witnesses were Walter Crew, C. P. Goodall and Charles C. Tinsley. Proved by the last two named on 7 April 1843. Wife, Mary O. Wingfield. Desires that she educate and maintain "all my younger children." Only child mentioned:
1. PETER WINGFIELD, whom he desires to be educated as a physician.

WINGFIELD VS. CAMPBELL, 1858 (82)

WINGFIELD, HUDSON M., of Hanover County died prior to 1858, intestate. His son Walter L. Wingfield, Administrator. No mention of the widow. Issue:
1. WALTER L. WINGFIELD, Administrator of his father's Estate.
2. WILLIAM M. WINGFIELD.
3. SUSANNA El, wife of Isaac Davenport.
4. MARTHA L,"former wife of William H. B. Campbell." She evidently deceased. Issue:
   1. MARTHA L. W. CAMPBELL, an infant.

WINGFIELD VS. CAMPBELL, 1860 (52)

RAGLAND, SHELTON, of Hanover County, dec'd. He was survived by, perhaps among others, two daughters. No reference is found relative to the widow:
1. ANN B., deceased, married William H. B. Campbell. On 21 June 1838, Benjamin F. Wingfield and Rebecca his wife of Caroline County conveyed to Wm. H. B. Campbell, consideration $100.00, tract of land in Hanover adjoining Thomas Perrin, Claibourn Lipscomb, and others.
2. [   ] a daughter, married a Mr. Wingfield, and had issue:
   1. BENJAMIN F. WINGFIELD, and wife Rebecca A., conveyed land on 21 June 1838 to Wm. H. B. Campbell.
   2. JOSEPH C. WINGFIELD, JR, dec'd, survived by widow Elizabeth, in 1860 a resident of the City of Richmond, Va., and by issue:

1. SALLY L., wife of W. L. Landrum.
2. ANN B., wife of William L. Roach of Richmond, Va.
3. VIRGINIA E., wife of Lucien Q. Landrum, of Richmond, Va.
4. JOSEPH F. WINGFIELD.
5. MARY WINGFIELD.

Others mentioned: Joseph P. H. Campbell of Caroline County, Va.

WINGFIELD VS. WINGFIELD'S ADMR., 1867 (52)

WINGFIELD, ISAAC, deceased of Hanover County. It is said that his will was dated in March and probated in May 1864. No copy among the papers of this suit. He was survived by his widow Annie F. Wingfield. They had no issue. His heirs were his brothers and sisters:

WILLIAM WINGFIELD, a brother.

ALEXANDER WINGFIELD, a brother.

PETER W. WINGFIELD, a brother.

CHARLES E. WINGFIELD, a brother.

JOSEPH T. WINGFIELD, a brother.

INDIANA H., a sister, wife of William J. Carpenter.

MARY, dec'd, who was a sister, married a Mr. Jones and left issue:
1. COLUMBIANNA, wife of John Gary.
2. MOLLY K. JONES.
3. IDA B. JONES.
4. CALLOM B. JONES, JR.

AMANDA H., dec'd, who was a sister, married a Mr. Jones and left issue:
1. WILLIAM JONES.
2. MARY, wife of Lebens Timberlake.
3. ALICE JONES, a minor in 1867.
4. JOHN JONES, a minor in 1867.
5. ELIZABETH JONES, a minor in 1867.

ELIZABETH, dec'd, who was a sister, married a Mr. Jackson, and left issue:
1. EDWARD JACKSON.
2. ELISHA JACKSON.
3. ALEXANDER JACKSON, a minor in 1867.
4. MARY JACKSON, a minor in 1867.
5. ELIZABETH JACKSON, a minor in 1867.

WINGFIELD VS. WINGFIELD, 1837 (56)

Thomas Wingfield's Will

WINGFIELD, THOMAS. "I, Thomas Wingfield of the County of Hanover and State of Virginia, do hereby make my last will and testament in manner and form following, that is to say - Imprimis. I lend to my wife Anne during her life the following property, namely, the tract or parcel of land I purchased of my son Christopher and at her death I bequeath the same to said son Christopher, as his full proportion of all my real estate, to have and to hold the same forever. 2ndly. I also lend to my wife Ann during her life the Farm on which I now live, and at her death I give to my son Joseph One hundred acres of said last mentioned tract of land, the same to be laid off as he the said Joseph shall direct so as to include my dwelling house and other buildings thereunto appertaining; also my orchards & gardens, and he my son Joseph shall be privileged to get fuel and all necessary Timber from any part of the said last named Tract of land, and the residue of said land to be divided as follows: I give Four<u>e</u> fifths of said residue of land in equal proportions to my sons Ralph, John, Charles and Lewis and the other fifth I lend to my son Thomas during his life and at his death I give the same to daughter Jane, to have and to hold the same forever. 3rdly. I further lend to my wife the following negroes during her life, namely Judith, Mary, Hannah and all her increase Nelley and all her increase, Malinda and all her increase, Rhane, Armstead and Simon and at her death, I wish the debts I owe my sons Joseph and Lewis to be paid out of said negroes in any way my executor or executors may think best, and the rest to be equally divided among all my children in the following way. I give to Christopher, Elizabeth, Ralph, Anne, Charles, Jane, Joseph, Lewis & Rebecca their portions to have and to hold the same forever. I lend to my son Thomas during his life, his portion of said negroes, and at his death, I give the same to my acting executor or excutors to them and their heirs forever. I lend to my son John during his life his proportion of said negroes & at his death I give same in equal proportions to his children to have and to hold the same forever. I lend to my daughter Mary during her life her proportion of said negroes and at her death I bequeath the same to my daughter Jane to have and to hold the same forever. 4th. I give to my son Christopher the negro man Caliborne and all other property advanced him as a loan to him and his heirs forever. 5thly. I give to my daughter Elizabeth the negro woman Molley and all her increase, and all other property advanced her as a loan to her and her heirs forever. 6thly. I give to my son Ralph the negro advanced him as a loan to him & his heirs forever. 7thly. I give to my son Thomas the negro man Orlando to him and his heirs forever. 8thly. I give to son John the negro man Jack and all other property advanced to him as a loan to him and his heirs forever. 9thly. I lend to my daughter Mary Sims during her life the following property - namely Aggy and her children, Mary, Tamor, Sarah, Abram, Edmond and Jack and all her future increase except one which I give to my son Joseph as a compensation for his trouble in the management of said negroes. And at her death I bequeath the same to her child Isabella Josephine Lewis Sims provided said child arrive at the age of twenty one years or marry; otherwise I give the said negroes to my son Joseph to him and his heirs forever. 10thly. I give to my daughter Anne Chick the negro woman Nan and <u>Nace Bouncher</u> and all their increase and all other property advanced her as a loan to her and her heirs forever. 11thly. I give to my son Charles the negro man Jim Bouncher and all other property advanced him as a loan to him and his heirs forever. 12thly. I give to my daughter Jane the negro woman Finch and her children Aaron, Ben, and Lewis and all her future increase. I also give her one Cow and Calf, one sow and pigs, one bedstead, bed and furniture, to her and her heirs forever. 13th. I give to my son Joseph the negroes John and Charles also one cow and calf, one sow and pigs, one bedstead, bed and furniture to him and his heirs forever. 14th. I give to my son Lewis the negro Abram, one cow and calf, one sow and pigs, one bedstead, bed and furniture, to him and his heirs forever. 15th. I give to my daughter Rebeccah the negro woman Milley all her increase and all other property advanced her as a loan to her & her heirs forever. 16th. I lend to my wife during her life all my stock of horses, cows, hogs and sheep and (at) her death the same to be equally divided among all my children to have and to hold forever; that is, all my stock of horses, cows, hogs and sheep not hereinbefore disposed of is the intention above. 17th. I lend to my wife during her life all my farming utensils of every description and at her death, I give the same to my son Joseph to him and his heirs forever. I also lend to my wife Anne during her life all my fowls of every kind and at her death I give the same to my daughter Jane. 18th. I further lend to my wife all my household and kitchen furniture, not herein before <u>lend</u> or given, and at her death, I give the same to be equally divided among all my children. I give to my wife all my pork, bacon, corn, wheat and rye and all the property I may not have disposed of. I desire that my daughter Jane and son Joseph live with my wife that may be her Stay and guard while here and that my son Joseph shall have the Control of the whole of estate lent to my wife during her life. My farewell desire is to the Court of my native Cty To whom this instrument may be presented for probat that they Qualify my executors

without security and lastly I do hereby constitute and appoint my son Joseph and my son in
law Benjamin Wingfield executors to this last
will and Testament. In witness whereof I have
hereunto set my hand and affixed my seal the
25th of February 1826."
                    Thomas Wingfield (Seal)
Signed, sealed and delivered
by Thomas Wingfield, Sent. as his last will and
testament in the presence and hearing of us who
at his request & in his presence, subscribed
our names as Witnesses:
    Oscar M. Wingfield
    Nath[l] F. Bowe

At a Court of Monthly Session held for Hanover
County at the Courthouse on Wednesday 24 Nov.
1830. This last will and testament of Thomas
Wingfield dec'd was proved by the oaths of
Nathaniel F. Bowe and Oscar M. Wingfield the
witnesses thereto and is ordered to be recorded.
    Teste, Philip B. Winston, C.H.C.
    A Copy, Teste, Benj[a] Pollard, D.C.H.C.

THOMAS WINGFIELD, of Hanover. Will dated 25
    February 1826, probated 24 November 1830.
Joseph Wingfield qualified as Executor, also of
the widow, Ann who died prior to 1837. Issue:
    1. CHRISTOPHER WINGFIELD, dec'd in 1837,
        survived by his widow, Elizabeth and
        issue:
        1. JOSEPH T. WINGFIELD.
        2. ANN R. WINGFIELD.
        3. BUSHROD W. WINGFIELD.
        4. WILLIS W. WINGFIELD.
        5. GARRET WINGFIELD, a minor in 1837.
        6. PAUL WINGFIELD, dec'd.
        7. FRANCIS WINGFIELD, a minor in 1837.
        8. CHARLES L. WINGFIELD, dec'd in 1837.
        9. HENRIETTA WINGFIELD, a minor in 1837.
    2. JOSEPH WINGFIELD, Executor of his father's
        and mother's Estates.
    3. RALPH WINGFIELD.
    4. JOHN WINGFIELD.
    5. CHARLES WINGFIELD.
    6. LEWIS WINGFIELD.
    7. THOMAS WINGFIELD.
    8. JANE WINGFIELD, by her attorney Hector
        Davis, who represented her in this suit.
    9. ELIZABETH, wife of Francis Wingfield.
    10. ANN, wife of John R. Chick.
    11. REBECCA, wife of Benjamin Wingfield.
    12. MARY, wife of David Sims, who has issue,
        perhaps among others, daughter mentioned in
        the will of Thomas Wingfield:
        1. ISABELLA JOSEPHINE LEWIS SIMS, born
            prior to 1826.

Others mentioned: Joseph S. Wingfield and Joseph C. Wingfield, Commissioners; Roscow Lipscomb.

WINGFIELD'S TRUSTEES VS. WINGFIELD
            & OTHERS, 1884 (6)

WINGFIELD, WILLIAM, of Hanover County
    died intestate. Executor was his son
    Henry J. Wingfield. He married after
1853, Sally J., daughter of Joseph S. Wingfield,
and widow of Thomas Rutherford who it is stated
died with a will recorded 28 June 1853 by his
Executor, John Rutherford of Richmond. Her marriage to Rutherford took place before she was
21 years of age. They had issue, a son:

    THOMAS S. RUTHERFORD.

Issue of her marriage with William Wingfield:
    1. EMMA VIRGINIA WINGFIELD.
    2. HENRY J. WINGFIELD, Administrator of his
        father's Estate.
    3. WILLIE, wife of Benjamin Williams.
    4. BLANCHE WINGFIELD, a minor in 1884.
    5. WILLIAM WINGFIELD, a monor in 1884.
    6. EMMET WINGFIELD, a minor in 1884.
    7. MABEL C. WINGFIELD, a minor in 1884.

Others mentioned: Henry W. Wingfield, Trustee.

GOODALL VS. WINGFIELD, 1844 (17)

WINSTON, ISAAC, of Hanover County died
    intestate sometime prior to 1844. His
    widow, Eliza Ann Winston was appointed
Administrator. They had issue, probably among
others:
    1. ISAAC C. WINSTON, a non-resident of Vir-
        ginia in 1844.
    2. WILLIAM B. WINSTON, a non-resident of
        Virginia in 1844.
    3. THOMAS B. WINSTON, a non-resident of Vir-
        ginia in 1844.
    4. ALFRED WINSTON.

MEREDITH, THOMAS, of New Kent County died
    sometime prior to 1844 intestate. Edward P.
Meredith appointed Administrator. Survived by
his wife Emily and probably children.

others mentioned: Charles P. Goodall, Mary O.
Wingfield. Note: The important papers in this
cause were not found, therefore this digest is
doubtless much abridged.

WOOLFOLK VS. TERRELL &C., 1832 (51)

TERRELL, PLEASANT, of Hanover, married a Mrs.
    Anderson, widow, the mother of:
    1. THOMAS W. ANDERSON.
    2. JOHN T. ANDERSON.

WOOLFOLK, JOSEPH, deceased, had issue, pro-
    bably among others: 1. Wm. H. Woolfolk.

POLLARD &C. VS. WINSTON & OTHERS, 1833 (29)

WINSTON, HENRY R., of Hanover County,
died in 1830. Survived by his widow,
Jane Winston who died with a will since
1833. Thomas Doswell, Admr. with the will annexed. They had issue:
1. SUSAN C., wife in 1833 of William Thomas
   H. Pollard, a nephew of Philip B. Winston.
2. JOANNA E. WINSTON.
3. WILLIAM HENRY WINSTON, a minor in 1833.
4. JAMES D. WINSTON, a minor in 1833.
5. THOMASIA C. WINSTON, a minor in 1833.
6. PHILIP P. WINSTON, a minor in 1833.
7. HENRIETTA R. WINSTON, a minor in 1833.

Others mentioned: Commissioners: Francis Blunt,
Wm. D. Taylor, Harrod J. Anderson, Thomas B.
Cosby, Edmund B. Winston and Thomas Garland.;
James Lyons, Attorney at Law 1833; Col. Park
Street.

GREGORY VS. WINSTON, 1869 (15)

Philip B. Winston's Will

WINSTON, PHILIP B. "In the name of God,
Amen. I, Philip B. Winston of the County
of Hanover, being in the perfect exercise of my understanding do make and ordain
this to be my last will and testament in manner
and form following hereby revoking all wills by
me heretofore made. Imprimis. It is my will
that my son William O. Winston shall have a fee
simple in my Turvey Gun and an old silver table
spoon which were given to me by my father the
late Colonel O. Winston it being the wish of my
father I should so dispose of them. Item. It
is my will that my present wife Jane D. Winston
shall have in fee simple my two curtain bead-
steads, the two feather beds under the beds,
bed curtains and bed furniture used therewith,
two bolsters and four pillows, a Mahogany
bureau, a Mahogany dressing box, a set of walnut drawers, a walnut desk, the portrait of her
father Capt. Thomas Price, the portrait of myself and herself, the gold watch and chain she
now wears, a Mahogany dressing Glass to be
chosen by her out of the furniture which I may
have at the time of my death, two hundred and
fifty barrels of corn, a sufficiency of blade
fodder, all the other long forage on hand, two
thousand five hundred pounds of pork, six barrels of flour, a sufficiency of groceries for
twelve months, eighteen hundred dollars in
money to be paid her immediately after my death
as much of the liquors on hand as she may think
proper, to retain, all the vinegar and vinegar
stands to be delivered to her at the time she
shall take possession of the land loaned her by
this my last will, also my two large Globes and
my large bible and the following slaves and

their increase namely, Lucinday, John Lewis,
Mary Lewis, William, Sarah and her child Lewis,
Thomas, Elizabeth child of Mary Lewis, Jane,
Harriet, Betsy, Silas, Esther, Moses, Sally Ann,
Matilda, Rachael, Venia, Edmund, Aaron, House,
James, Charles, Mary, Louisa Ann, Elizabeth
child of Mary, Martha, Jack, George, Ella and
Susan, also twenty shares of Brook Turnpike
Stock. The said slaves, Brook Turnpike Stock
and thirteen hundred Dollars in Money constituting the fortune which I received with my present wife. Item. It is my will that my present
wife, Jane D. Winston shall have for and during
her widowhood the tract of Land whereon I reside containing by estimation nine hundred and
eighty-two acres which includes the land purchased of Edmund Winston part of the woods
tract for which I have no deed as yet, and the
land I purchased of Callom J. Toler. My carriage and harness, the carriage horses and
therewith at the time of my death, my negro
woman Beck and five other negroes to be selected
by her, four yoke of oxen and yokes, two ox
carts and chains, my wagon and gear for two
mules, two horse carts and gear, eight choice
mules or horses, eight sets plough gear, four
cows and calves, two young steers, and two
heifers not exceeding two years old, one half
my sheep and stock hogs, such of my books as
she may desire to keep, two feather beds, bedstead, two mattresses under the bed and furniture. All my silver plate, my Black Smith's
tools, should she select as one of the slaves
loaned her my Blacksmith, one wheat fan, all my
kitchen furniture, one copper kettle, my carpenter's tools, all my woodware, tinware, earthen-
ware, all my table and tea china   as much of
my glass ware and other household furniture and
plantation utensils as she may think necessary
to her comfort excepting therefrom my desk and
book case and two writing desks and such other
articles of household furniture as are herein
disposed of. But should my said wife prefer it
then it is my will that the carriage horses I
may have at the time of my death be sold and a
pair purchased for her by my Executors. It is
also my will that all the said property mentioned in this Item of my will except the land,
at the death or marriage of my wife be equally
divided in fee simple amongst all my children
and their descendants, allotting to the descendants of a dead child or children the same
portions thereof to which their parent or
parents if living would have been entitled, and
as to the land that the same excepting therefrom the grave yard, at the death or marriage
of my wife be sold by my executors hereinafter
named upon a credit of one, two and three years
the said executors exercising reasonable discretion as to the time of making such sale and
taking bonds with good security to be approved
by them bearing interest from the day of Sale
together with a deed of trust upon the land to
secure the purchase money, and that the

proceeds of the said land be equally divided in fee simple among all my children and their descendants allotting to the descendants of a dead child or children the same portion thereof to which their parent or parents if living would have been entitled. If from the misconduct or any other cause my wife should desire that any of the slaves loaned her by this my will be sold it is my desire that my executors hereinafter named or the survivor of them make sale of the same and invest the proceeds in other negroes or loan out the money as my wife may prefer she having the use of any negroes so purchased or the interest in the money so loaned out subject however to the same limitations and restrictions as are contained in my will in relation to the slaves so loaned to her. Item. It is my will that my estate be kept together until the end of the year after my death unless that event happens on the first of January and if so kept together that my executors have the usual crop wheat sowed in the fall of that year. Item. I give to my son Richard Morris Winston a bed and furniture valued at forty Dollars to be accounted for by him in the division of my estate - also twenty Dollars in lieu of a cow and calf which twenty dollars is not to be accounted for at such division. Item. I give to my daughter Sarah Pendleton Winston a bed and furniture valued at forty Dollars, my Piano forte, cover and stool valued at two hundred and fifty Dollars to be accounted for by her at the division of my estate and twenty Dollars in lieu of a cow and calf which twenty Dollars she is not to account for also my Side Saddle for which she is not to account. Item. In the division of my slaves it is my will that my negro girl Letty be allotted to my daughter Sarah Pendleton Winston as a part of her portion of said slaves. Item. I have conveyed to my daughter Barbara J. Lewis by deed the tract of two hundred and sixty two acres of land in the County of King William purchased by me of William M. Gary for which my said daughter and her heirs are to account at the division of my estate at the price of three thousand Seven hundred and fifty Dollars. Item. If my present wife Jane D. Winston should survive me and renounce the provision made for her by this my will, preferring to have such part of my property as in that event the law would allow her then it is my will that all the above mentioned property as being given to her for life, in fee or during her widowhood or in any other manner in this my last will instead of going to my said present wife shall except the land above mentioned be equally divided in fee simple among all my children and their descendants allotting to the descendants of a dead child or children the same portion thereof to which their parents if living would have been entitled and as to the said land that the same except the Grave Yard be then sold and disposed of upon the same terms, and the proceeds of such sale

to be divided as hereinbefore directed and that all and each of the powers conferred or intended to be conferred upon my said present wife by this my will shall cease and be utterly void and of no effect. Item. It is my desire that out of the rest of my estate not herein before disposed of any debts I may owe shall be paid and that all the residue thereof be equally divided in fee simple among all my children and their descendants allotting to the descendants of a dead child or children the same portion thereof to which their parent or parents if living would have been entitled. Item. It is my will that my executors sell upon such terms and at such time as they may think most judicious, my interest in the Junction property and my still and worm and that the proceeds thereof be equally divided among all my children and their descendants in fee simple, the descendants of a dead child or children taking the same portion thereof to which their parent or parents if living would have been entitled. Item. It is my will and desire that my executor hereinafter named as soon as practicable after my death cause the Grave Yard to be inclosed with Brick not exceeding Eighty feet in length by forty feet in width that they have the right to have the bricks made upon and the wood necessary to burn them out from any part of the land loaned my wife by this my will and that the said grave yard be for the use of my children and their descendants with free ingress and egress to and from the same forever. Item. It is my will and I hereby positively forbid the land loaned my wife by this my will to be cultivated in any other manner than in the relation in which the fields are now cultivated by me. Item. It is my will that any advancements heretofore made or which I may hereafter make to any of my children shall be accounted for by them respectively in the division of my estate without interest an account of which or an acknowledgment in writing of such advancement will be left among my papers except the sum of four hundred and twelve Dollars advanced to each of my children: William O. Winston, Bickerton L. Winston, Philip H. Winston, John R. Winston, Edmund T. Winston, Barbara J. Lewis, Joseph P. Winston and Octavius M. Winston that constituting the amount of my first wife's fortune together with the acquisition of individual industry after our marriage and for which my said children are not to account. Lastly. It is my will that my Son William O. Winston shall act as guardian to my infant children and in their educations shall not be limited to the profits of their estates but in his discretion may appropriate to that object so much of the principal as he may think advisable. It is my will that my sons William O. Winston and Bickerton L. Winston act as Executors of this my last will & Testament. In Witness whereof I have hereunto set my hand and affixed my Seal the 10th day of May 1852." Philip B. Winston (Seal)

Published and declared by the Testator as his
last will & Testament in presence of us:
    Jos. S. Wingfield
    W^mS. C. Wickham
    Edwin Shelton
    J. P. Temple
    John H. Taliaferro

At a Court of Quarterly Session held for Hanover County at the Courthouse on Tuesday the
25th of October 1853. This last will and testament of Philip B. Winston, dec'd, was proved by
the Oaths of Edwin Shelton and John H. Taliaferro, witnesses thereto, and is ordered to be
recorded.
    Teste, Wm. O. Winston, C.H.C.
    A Copy, Teste, Wm. O. Winston, C.H.C.

PHILIP B. WINSTON, of "Popular Springs," Hanover County, a son of the late Col. O. Winston, died on 18 September 1853. His will dated
10 May 1852, was probated on 25 October 1853.
Appointed sons William O., and Bickerton L. Winston, Executors. He left a considerable Estate
which suffered much during the War Between the
States. "Popular Springs," consisted of some
927 acres of land and located near Hanover
Courthouse. He was twice married. The name of
his first wife is not stated. She died early in
the 1830's. Their issue were:
1. WILLIAM O. WINSTON, one of the Executors
   of his father's Estate, died 21 March
   1862. His Executors were Bickerton L.
   Winston and Robert O. Doswell. He had
   been the Guardian of his half brother,
   Richard Morris Winston. He married a
   Miss Gregory, a sister of Dr. Thomas L.
   Gregory.
2. BICKERTON L. WINSTON, one of the Executors
   of his father's Estate. Was married
   twice. His first wife's name is not
   stated, by who he is said to have had
   two children, one of whom was:
   1. MAGGIE WINSTON.

   He married secondly a Miss Bankhead,
   daughter of the late Dr. William Bankhead of Orange County, Va., and sister
   of Mrs. Richard Morris Winston. On 9th
   of March 1869, there was no issue of
   this marriage.
3. PHILIP H. WINSTON, was survived by his
   widow, who after being confined to bed
   for three weeks, died on 21 June 1863.
   Miss S. Carter Berkeley deposed that she
   was living with her uncle Philip H. Winston in 1863.
4. JOHN R. WINSTON, dec'd on 9 March 1869.
5. EDMUND T. WINSTON, in 1869 owned land
   adjoining "Popular Springs" - an Estate
   he has known for forty years. Owns 4000
   acres within six miles. Was in the Commission Merchants business in Richmond
   from 1854 to 1858, in partnership with

William M. Sutton under the style of
"E. T. Winston & Company." From 1858 to
circa 1860 he conducted the business
independently. During this period he
handled practically all the business of
Mrs. Jane D. Winston, whom he stated he
had known intimately since early child-
hood, some thirty odd years, her business running from three to five thousand
dollars annually. His books were burned
in Richmond.
6. BARBARA J., wife in 1853, of Dr. John
   Lewis.
7. JOSEPH P. WINSTON.
8. OCTAVIUS M. WINSTON.

He married secondly circa 1834, Jane D., a
daughter of Captain Thomas Price of Hanover.
After the death of Mr. Winston she operated
"Popular Springs." Charles T. Dyson was her
farm manager in 1855, '56, '57 and '58 when he
apparently was succeeded by her son Richard M.
Winston who served as such until he entered
the Confederate States Army. Mr. Dyson returned
in 1863 and continued until August 1864 when
he likewise entered the Army. In a deposition
taken during the progress of this suit Mrs.
Jane D. Winston deposed:
"Estate by no means as large and profitable
during the years of 1860, '61, '62, and '63
as previously. We had to replace everything.
We were robbed of teams, crops, etc. by the
Yankees. They came on the second day of harvest in the year 1863. Every man in the field
laid down his cradle and went to the Yankees.
They took two wagons, gear, horse cart, all
the bacon, all the liquor. I had two fields
of wheat, only one was saved. They took my
horses, mules, colts, leaving only my carriage horses and the Doctor's riding horses.
After Mr. Wickham and Mr. Bickerton Winston
had finished their harvest I hired hands to
save one field of wheat. The other was lost
entirely - hogs got the benefit of that.
Three years, I think, they took all my bacon
with the exception of a few pieces I put
away in my closet. The fourth year nearly
4000 lbs. was sent to Richmond and burnt up
when Richmond was evacuated. These different
raids, all the servants left except five.
Of course things had to be replaced to carry
on the farm, of course to a very small extent
as we had't the means of replacing what we
had lost." She was born in January 1803.
Issue of Philip B. Winston and Jane D., his
wife:
9. RICHARD MORRIS WINSTON, born in 1835, died
   16 February 1862. His will was dated 22
   April 1861. Bickerton L. Winston, Admr.
   He married on 10 November 1857 at the
   home of her father, the late Dr. William
   Bankhead of Orange County, Miss Rosalie
   L., a sister of Mrs. Bickerton L. Winston and Miss Nora D. Bankhead. After

their marriage they made their home at "Popular Springs" of which he was some-time manager at the salary of $300 to $350 per annum. After his father's death he attended the school of Mr. Franklin Minor in Charlottesville for one year at the cost of $200.00, afterward attended the law school of the University of Virginia at the cost of $700.00 per session, using the total of $1,400. At the outbreak of the War Between the States he joined the troops at Ashland. Whilst on a furlough for a few days in April 1861 he made his will, and less than a year died in Richmond, Va. The appraisement of his Estate was made on 1 March 1863, Charles T. Dyson, P. H. Winston (since dec'd) and N. B. Priddy were the appraisers. It is said that his family "was numerous."

10. SALLIE P., born in May 1839. Attended the school at Dr. L. B. Price's for six months. Later attended school in Richmond. Visited White Sulphur Springs in Summers of 1854 and 1856 for eight weeks each. Also took trips to Old Point. She married, as his second wife, Dr. Thomas L. Gregory on 22 April 1863, and since have made their home at "Popular Springs."

Others Mentioned: "Hanover Records destroyed at Richmond 3 April 1865; Mrs. Ellen M. Price, a niece of Mrs. Jane D. Winston, had a daughter, Lizzie W. Price who married on 20 January 1863, Dr. John B. Fontaine; Dr. Lucien B. Price "a relative, friend and business advisor of Mrs. Jane D. Winston; Miss Nannie Price; Thomas R. Price; Rev. John Cook "owned a large number of slaves, also two tracts of land which he got by his wife." Considered wealthy, but lacked ready money, and was a constant borrower. Mr. Patrick H. Price "a rich man" was Security on one of his bonds, which Rev. Cook's son proposed paying in negroes. Rev. Cook or Cooke died in November or December after the beginning of the War Between the States; Mr. Bullock, overseer for William Carter at Broadneck; Robert O. Doswell, "friend of the Winston family" Clerk of Hanover, March Court 1862; Roger Gregory and Col. William R. Winn, Attorneys; C. G. Griswold, Attorney; James Lyons, had been counsel for Philip B. Winston, dec'd; John M. Meredith, Judge in 1869, Circuit Ct. of City of Richmond; Joseph T. Priddy, Master Commissioner of Chancery, County Court of Hanover; Nathaniel B. Priddy, was manager for Wm. F. Wickham for 30 years; Dr. Logan Robinson; James G. Sutton; John R. Taylor, Clerk of Hanover County 1869; John B. Young, Attorney; and Douglas & Gregory, Attorneys. S. C. Redd, Notary Public 1869.

It was stated that Guano cost $55.00 to $60.00 per ton for the period from the year 1854 to 1860.

BOWLES & OTHERS VS. BOWLES & OTHERS, 1836 (2)

WILLIAMSOM, JOHN, of Henrico County, died with a will probated in that County 1 December 1806. He was survived by, perhaps among others, a daughter:
1. REBECCA, dec'd, survived by her husband Thomas Bowles, 1836, and issue:
    1. JOHN WILLIAMSON BOWLES.
    2. MARIA P., wife of John Pate
    3. BETSEY, wife of William Davis of Orange County, Va.
    4. LYDDALL BOWLES, a minor in 1836.
    5. MARY ANN BOWLES, a minor in 1836.

GLAZEBROOK VS. GLAZEBROOK, 1866 (15)

WOOD, DR. WILLIAM L., of Hanover County, deceased. Survived by his widow, S. E. Wood, who in this cause is the next friend of her infant children:
1. ETHEL J. WOOD.
2. BETTY E. WOOD.
3. CHARLES B. WOOD.
4. WILLIAM L. WOOD, JR.

WOODSON VS. WOODSON, 1836 (51)

WOODSON, JOHN, of Hanover County, died possessed of a tract of land in the upper end of Hanover, on South Anna River, adjoining Thomas W. Pulliam and others. This land in 1835 was leased by Captain William R. Irby. Issue, probably among others:
1. RICHARD A. WOODSON, who "has a large family."
2. CAPTAIN ISHAM R. WOODSON, of Richmond, Va. in 1836.

Archibald P., Josiah L., and Thomas T. Woodson mentioned, but connection not shown.

———

DOSWELL, PAUL T., of Hanover County, deceased survived by seven children. No mention of his wife; Children infants in 1836.
1. JAMES T. DOSWELL.
2. GEORGE DOSWELL.
3. PAULINA DOSWELL.
4. RICHARD DOSWELL.
5. ROBERT DOSWELL.
6. LUCY ANN DOSWELL.
7. FRANCES DOSWELL

Others mentioned: Parties who had rented Woodson's land: Joseph Anderson who was connected with the Royster family, and Royal Farrow; John D. Andrews; Anderson Bowles "who removed from the Woodson neighborhood to Richmond."; Benjamin T. Childress 1836; Garland R. Childress; Christopher H. Holland in Henrico Co.; John Mosby of Henrico; Powhatan Perkins who has a store in Louisa County; Stephen Pulliam, merchant 1838; Francis W. Scott of Caroline Co.

FOUND LOOSE IN ENDED FILE 42

Benjamin F. Doswell's Will

DOSWELL, BENJAMIN F. "In the name of God amen. I, Benjamin F. Doswell of the County of Caroline, being of sound mind and disposing memory do make and ordain this my last will and testament. Item. I give and bequeath unto my dear wife Maria B. Doswell all my estate both real and personal of every description whatsoever to her and her heirs forever, After the payment of my just debts. Item. It is my wish that my estate both real and personal be subject to the payment of my just debts. Item. It is my desire that my brother in law John T. Anderson and my brother H. C. Doswell act as my executors to this my last will and testament. Signed the 26 of Sept 1828."

Benjamin Doswell (Seal)

Teste:
John T. Thornton
Malvin D. Thornton
Courtney C. Thornton

At a court of Quarterly Session held for Caroline County at the Courthouse on the 10th day of December 1828. This last will and testament of Benjamin F. Doswell dec'd was proved by the oaths of John T. Thornton and Courtney C. Thornton, two of the witnesses thereto and is ordered to be recorded:

Teste, John L. Pendleton, C.C.C.

WRIGHT VS. FITZWILSON, 1838 (49)

WRIGHT, JOHN, of Hanover County, "son of William Wright who was a son of Mary Wright," on 24 January 1837, purchased 76 acres of land from Thomas Fitzwilson of the City of Richmond, who in 1819 purchased of Garland Tucker and Elizabeth, his wife, who in 1812 purchased from William Holliday and Ann his wife, "being their fee simple property in 1805." In 1819 the land was described as being on the road leading from New Castle to Bottom Bridge on waters of Madierquin? Creek, adjoining lands of Col. Elisha Meredith, dec'd, Miller Brown and Nathan Burnett (the latter is stated in 1838 to be of unsound mind and the father of Foster Burnett).

Others mentioned: Thomas Tyler; Thomas F. Wilson and Fanny, his wife.

JONES &C. VS. HOOPER'S ADMR., 1854 (21)

YARBROUGH, ELISHA. "Know all men by these presents that I, Elisha Yarbrough, Jr., of the County of Hanover and State of Virginia in consideration of the natural love and affection I have towards my three children, Viz: Thomas J. Yarbrough, Margaret E. Yarbrough, and Unity H. Yarbrough and for the further consideration of $1 to me in hand paid by the said T. J. Yarbrough &c. have granted bargained and sold and by these presents do give grant bargain Sell and convey to the said T. J. Yarbrough &c. and to their heirs and assigns forever all my personal estate of which I am now possessed consisting of three negroes, Viz: Daniel, Jenny, and Martha also one young horse, two cows, six sheep, together with three beds and bedding, together with all and every other species of property with which I am now possessed: as also my reversionary right title and interest in the Estate of Edmund Hooper, dec'd to them and their heirs forever. Given under my hand and seal this first day of October one thousand eight hundred and twenty six.

Elisha Yarbrough (Seal)

Hanover County, to wit: This Deed of Gift was acknowledged before me in my office by Elisha Yarbrough, Jr., a party thereto and is thereupon admitted to record. Witness my hand the 24th day of February 1827.
Philip B. Winston, C.H.C.
A Copy, Teste, R. O. Doswell, D.C.H.C.

ELISHA YARBROUGH, of Hanover County, on 1 October 1826, recorded 24 February 1827, executed a Deed of Trust on all his personal property to his three infant children. Joseph Hooper qualified as their Guardian 23 July 1828. He is deceased in 1856 and Wm. T. H. Pollard is his personal representative. Hooper's securities were William Allen and Harwood Allen (deceased in 1856).
1. THOMAS J. YARBROUGH.
2. MARGARET E., in 1856 wife of Miles Gathright.
3. UNITY H., in 1856, wife of Thomas C. Jones.

(This suit continues for many more years, but is not included further due to its recent ended date).

YARBROUGH VS. BRADLEY &C., 1859 (54)

Jesse G. Yarbrough's Will

YARBROUGH, JESSE G. "I, Jesse G. Yarbrough of the County of Hanover and State of Virginia do hereby make and ordain this my last will and testament in manner and form following. First, I wish my executor hereafter named to sell all my perishable estate except as much corn and meat as shall be sufficient for the use of the family and out of the proceeds to pay all my just debts. But should the proceeds of my perishable Estate be insufficient then I wish the money arising from bonds due me and becoming due be appropriated to the payment of all my debts. Item. I give to my beloved wife Ann Yarbrough all my Negroes during her natural life except my man John who is now hired out and I wish to be hired out annually and that he have the privilege of choosing his master as long as he continues to conduct himself as heretofore and that the said man John receive two and a half per cent. of his net hire annually, and the balance of his hire to be equally divided between my son William N. Yarbrough and John F. Cross Trustee for use and benefit of my daughter Mary C. Bradley. I give to my wife Ann Yarbrough all my land lying on both sides of the Mechanicsville Road during her natural life (Item 3rd) after the death of my said wife I give to my son Wm. N. Yarbrough the tract of land on which I now live laying on the west side of Mechanicsville Road to him and his heirs forever. Item 4 . I give to John T. Cross Trustee for my daughter Mary C. Bradley all my land laying on the east side of the Mechanicsville road for the use and benefit of my said daughter Mary C. Bradley provided she live upon and occupy it, but should it be the desire of my said daughter to sell the land then the said John F. Cross is hereby authorized to make sale of the same and vest the proceeds of the sale of the same to - used to the purchase of some other place for the use and benefit of my said daughter Mary C. Bradley when she may wish. But in case she prefer to sell the said land it is my will that my son Wm. N. Yarbrough shall have one-half of the purchase money over and above the sum of five hundred dollars. But if the land be no sold and my said daughter Mary C. Bradley shall have a child or children then living at the time of her death then it is my will that suchchild or children shall have the land to them and their heirs forever, but in case there shall be no heir of her body at the death of my daughter Mary C. Bradley, then it is my will that it pass to my son William N. Yarbroughto him and his heirs forever but should a sale be made by the said Trustee at the request of my said daughter Mary C. Bradley and another place purchased with the proceeds of such sale it is my will that the land so purchased at the death of said daughter return to my son Wm. N. Yarbrough to him and his heirs forever, but should my said daughter leave a child or children then to such child or children and to heirs forever. Item 5th. I give to my wife Ann Yarbrough my Bay Mare called Bet, and to my daughter in law Harriet J. Yarbrough my blazed face filly called Martha Bell. I also give to my Grandson Jesse G. Yarbrough, Jr., my negro boy Reuben to be controlled and managed

by my son William N. Yarbrough until my said Grandson shall arrive at the age of twenty one years when he is to have possession of the said boy, but shall not be at liberty to sell him without consent and approbation of his father the said Wm. N. Yarbrough, but if my said Grandson Jesse G. Yarbrough shall die before he arrives at the age of twenty one years and the said boy Reuben living at the time he is to revert to my estate subject to be divided between my son William N. Yarbrough and my daughter Mary C. Bradley upon the same conditions of trust hereinbefore made and after the death of my said wife my will is that all my negroes herein given to her with their future increase if any be divided equally between my two children Mary C. Bradley and my son William N. Yarbrough according to their estimated value at that time and that my man Nelson be one of them assigned to my son Wm. N. Yarbrough if he is living at the time the lot assigned to my daughter Mary C. Bradley to John T. Cross to be managed by him for the use and benefit of my said daughter Mary C. Bradley. I hereby appoint my friend John T. Cross trustee for my daughter Mary C. Yarbrough with full power to carry out the provisions of this my will. Lastly I appoint my wife Ann Yarbrough and my son Wm. N. Yarbrough my Executrix and Executor without being bound in security therefor. Witness the signature and seal of the said Jesse G. Yarbrough the 17th day of Feb. 1858."

                         Jesse G. Yarbrough
Signed and acknowledged
in the presence of
  Hudson M. Wingfield
  Wm. M. Wingfield
  Benj. C. Norment.

At a Court of Monthly Session held for Hanover County at the Courthouse on Tuesday 23 of March 1858. This last will and testament of Jesse G. Yarbrough, deceased was proved by the Oaths of Hudson M. Wingfield, Wm. M. Wingfield and Benjamin C. Norment, the witnesses thereto and is ordered to be recorded.
    Teste, Wm. O. Winston, C.H.C.
    A Copy, Teste, R. O. Doswell, D.C.H.C.

JESSE G. YARBROUGH, of Hanover. Will dated 17 February 1858, probated 23 March 1858. Owned land on both sides of Mechanicsville Turnpike. Survived by his widow Ann, and by two children:
    1. WILLIAM N. YARBROUGH.
    2. MARY C., wife of Robert A. Bradley.

MISCELLANEOUS NOTES
_____

SOME JUSTICES OF THE PEACE

OF HANOVER

Anderson, H. J. 1830.
Anderson, William M, 1856.
Berkeley, Dr. Carter, 1820-1823.
Blunt, Francis, 1820-1839.
Bowe, Frederick, 1833.
Bowles, A. K., 1834.
Bowles, Andrew, 1836.
Brown, John D. G., 1838.
Brown, M. M., 1830.
Burch, Benjamin, 1814-1820.
Burnley, Hardin, 1832.
Cochran, William, 1805.
Coles, Walter, 1811.
Craig, Edward C., 1857.
Crenshaw, Edward B., 1820-1835.
Curtis, Henry, 1839-1846.
Duke, Alfred, 1844-1860.
Ellis, John W., 1814.
Fleming, George, 1844.
Fontaine, Edmund, 1838-1845.
Goodall, Charles P., 1814-1837.
Goodall, Park, 1805-1812
Jones, Bathurst, 1808.
Kilby, John, 1812.
Kilby, T. S., 1856.
Lewis, Lilburne, 1805.
Mason, George B., 1844-1852.
McKenzie, J. M., 1846-1858.
Meredith, Reuben, 1834-1836.
Macon, Miles, 1832-1837.
Minor, W., 1814.
Minor, Warner W., 1820.
Nelson, Philip, 1838-1855.
Nelson, William R., 1835-1837.
Oliver, Benjamin, Jr., 1808.
Page, Francis, 1828-1835.
Pate, John, 1820-1837.
Price, Patrick H., 1832-1856.
Pulliam, Samuel T., 1839.
Shelton, Edwin, 1834-1845.
Shepherd, Philip, 1811.
Smith, J. Alonzo, 1861-1868.
Smith, Richard G., 1848.
Snead, Jesse, 1836.
Snead, Edwin, 1841-1843.
Stanley, John, 1856.
Starke, Joseph, 1836.
Starke, William, 1822.
Street, George, 1808.
Street, Park, 1811-1832.
Sutton, James T., 1835-1845.
Swann, John L., 1820.
Sydnor, W. B., 1859 .
Taliaferro, John H., 1863-1866.
Talley, Ezekiel A., 1838.
Talley, Joseph, 1856.

Taylor, Col. John J., 1822-1834.
Taylor, Lewis W., 1820.
Thompson, Charles, 1836-1838.
Thompson, C. E., 1857.
Tinsley, Charles C., 1838-1839.
Tinsley, Thomas, 1805.
Tyler, Watt H., 1844-1849.
Underwood, James, 1811-1836.
White, Thomas, 1805.
White, Thomas M., 1869.
Wickham, William C., 1856.
Wickham, William F., 1835.
Wingfield, Benjamin, 1848-1852.
Wingfield, Benjamin, Jr., 1842.
Wingfield, Hudson M., 1835-1845.
Wingfield, William, 1838-1839.
Winn, Jesse, 1812-1822.
Winston, Philip B., 1820.
Winston, Edmund, 1838.
Winston, William O., 1808-1812.
Woodson, Tarleton, 1856.

OF ADJOINING COUNTIES

Anderson, Herbert, of Caroline, 1852.
Bird, Phil, of King and Queen, 1858.
Sutton, Stephen, of King William, 1833.
Tompkins, Christopher, of King William, 1833.
Garlick, Braxton, of New Kent, 1851.

SOME CONSTABLES OF HANOVER

Curtis, William H., 1846.
Leadbetter, Isaac, 1836.
Mallory, William W., 1833-1835.
McDowell, James, circa 1840.
Parsley, William, 1855.
Pearson, John, 1822.
Pendleton, James L., 1845.

NOTE: These names were taken from the various
papers in the Chancery Causes treated in this
volume, and are not presented as a complete list.
The years given are the earliest and latest
appearances of the various individuals in the
capacity of a Justice, or Constable, respectively.

_____

Rogers, Thomas, Deputy Clerk of Hanover, 1782.

_____

INDEX OF WILLS

[a] abstract

GENERAL INDEX

OMISSIONS